booksonline

Read this book online today:

With SAP PRESS BooksOnline we offer you online access to knowledge from the leading SAP experts. Whether you use it as a beneficial supplement or as an alternative to the printed book, with SAP PRESS BooksOnline you can:

- Access your book anywhere, at any time. All you need is an Internet connection.
- Perform full text searches on your book and on the entire SAP PRESS library.
- Build your own personalized SAP library.

The SAP PRESS customer advantage:

Register this book today at *www.sap-press.com* and obtain exclusive free trial access to its online version. If you like it (and we think you will), you can choose to purchase permanent, unrestricted access to the online edition at a very special price!

Here's how to get started:

1. Visit *www.sap-press.com*.
2. Click on the link for SAP PRESS BooksOnline and login (or create an account).
3. Enter your free trial license key, shown below in the corner of the page.
4. Try out your online book with full, unrestricted access for a limited time!

Your personal free trial **license key**
for this online book is:

ufg2-ajmr-btvd-siw5

Practical Guide to SAP NetWeaver® PI – Development

SAP PRESS

Mandy Krimmel, Joachim Orb
SAP NetWeaver Process Integration
2010, app. 400 pp.
978-1-59229-344-5

Marcus Banner, Heinzpeter Klein, Christian Riesener
Mastering SAP NetWeaver PI — Administration, 2nd Ed.
2010, app. 225 pp.
978-1-59229-321-6

Olaf Klostermann, Milco Österholm
SAP NetWeaver Business Warehouse: Administration and Monitoring
2010, app. 600 pp.
978-1-59229-330-8

Michal Krawczyk, Michal Kowalczewski
Mastering IDoc Business Scenarios with SAP NetWeaver PI, 2nd Ed.
2009, app. 250 pp.
978-1-59229-288-2

Valentin Nicolescu, Burkhardt Funk, Peter Niemeyer,
Matthias Heiler, Holger Wittges, Thomas Morandell,
Florian Visintin, Benedikt Kleine Stegemann, and
Harald Kienegger

Practical Guide to SAP NetWeaver® PI – Development

Galileo Press

Bonn • Boston

Galileo Press is named after the Italian physicist, mathematician and philosopher Galileo Galilei (1564–1642). He is known as one of the founders of modern science and an advocate of our contemporary, heliocentric worldview. His words *Eppur se muove* (And yet it moves) have become legendary. The Galileo Press logo depicts Jupiter orbited by the four Galilean moons, which were discovered by Galileo in 1610.

Editor Stefan Proksch
English Edition Editor Kelly Grace Harris
Translation Valentin Nicolescu
Copyeditor Mike Beady
Cover Design Jill Winitzer
Photo Credit Fotolia
Layout Design Vera Brauner
Production Editor Kelly O'Callaghan
Assistant Production Editor Graham Geary
Typesetting Publishers' Design and Production Services, Inc.
Printed and bound in Canada

ISBN 978-1-59229-334-6

© 2010 by Galileo Press Inc., Boston (MA)
2nd Edition 2010
2nd German edition published 2009 by Galileo Press, Bonn, Germany

Library of Congress Cataloging-in-Publication Data
Praxisleitfaden SAP NetWeaver PI--Entwicklung. English
    Practical guide to SAP Netweaver PI--development / Valentin Nicolescu, et al.—1st ed.
       p.   cm.
    Includes bibliographical references.
    ISBN-13: 978-1-59229-334-6 (alk. paper)
    ISBN-10: 1-59229-334-4 (alk. paper)
     1. Information technology--Management.   2. Computer network architectures.   3. SAP
NetWeaver.   4. Computer software—Development.   I. Nicolescu, Valentin.   II. Title.

    HD30.2.P735 2010
    005.74—dc22

                                                            2010007129

Contents at a Glance

Contents

PART II Basic System Configuration

Foreword

Even today, there are many companies that still need to integrate their business processes with heterogeneous system landscapes. Therefore, it is important to quickly adapt departmental business processes to new market requirements by standardizing as many processes as possible.

At the same time, there are also a number of individual business processes that distinguish a company from its competitors. In both cases, companies must integrate legacy systems that have been used for many years, but do not support open standards. These systems make it difficult to create a seamless information flow between applications. In addition to pure application-to-application (A2A) communication, companies must also conduct business-to-business (B2B) communication with their business partners.

The challenge of supporting business processes is, on the one hand, the short-term deployment of new processes. On the other hand, companies often differentiate themselves from their competitors by collaborating in networks with business partners to provide their customers with complementary products and services. Innovative solutions that cross corporate, industry, and geographic boundaries are the results of these collaborating organization networks. This has resulted in the evolution of the requirements about how companies work together, provide solutions, and interact with customers. From an integration point of view, standards-based communications, and semantic integration, have become more important.

Companies must often meet these challenges with reduced IT budgets, and economically justify them in the context of business cases. SAP helps companies use appropriate information technology (IT) strategies, especially with regard to the following:

- Service-oriented architecture (SOA) as a basic architecture to ensure interoperability and reusability of existing functionality and flexibility.

- Service-based business applications, which allow the standardization of business processes and reuse of services.

- Model-driven composition of applications for the development of differentiating business processes, to stand out from competitors.

- A platform — the SAP Business Process Platform — for standardized and differentiating business processes to reduce overall costs and simplify management.

SAP NetWeaver Process Integration (PI) 7.1 is, in addition to the SAP NetWeaver Composition Environment, a cornerstone of SOA infrastructure from SAP. The new release of SAP NetWeaver PI represents a natural evolution of previous versions. SAP NetWeaver PI 7.1 is already used by many customers as part of their SOA strategy, thus offering functionalities that are stored in legacy systems in a standardized format via the PI system. In addition, more and more customers are consolidating their heterogeneous middleware environment and using SAP NetWeaver PI as a strategic integration platform.

To ensure compatibility in SAP NetWeaver PI 7.1, no major architectural changes were made. The new SAP NetWeaver PI release provides innovations — especially in the following four areas: flexibility and innovation through SOA, improved performance, increased user productivity, and lower overall operating costs.

- Some of the fundamentals include the Enterprise Services Repository and Services Registry. The Enterprise Services Repository, which is a natural evolution of the former integration repository, serves as a central repository for storing all SOA artifacts, including semantic meaning. The Enterprise Services Repository allows a model-driven development of services, ranging from model- to proxy-based implementation of the associated business functionality in the application. The Enterprise Services Repository is open for both services that are delivered by SAP, and for services that were developed by customers or partners. The implementation of these services can be located in SAP and non-SAP systems.

▶ The Universal Description, Discovery, and Integration (UDDI) 3.0–based service registry serves as a central directory in which the descriptions of all of the service definitions of a customer landscape can be centrally stored, found, and downloaded. A semantic meaning can be attached to services using classifications in the Enterprise Services Repository and the Services Registry. Classifications are delivered by SAP and can also be created by customers and partners.

▶ Another important innovation in SAP NetWeaver PI 7.1 is the increase in performance. This is because of the move from the former Adapter Engine to the Advanced Adapter Engine (AAE). The AAE allows local message processing on the Java stack for certain scenarios, without processing messages on the ABAP stack. This makes message processing up to 10 times faster.

▶ In addition, SAP NetWeaver PI 7.1 provides better user efficiency compared to the previous version. For example, self-developed, Java-based mapping functions can be reused several times without having to copy them. Furthermore, the Enterprise Services Repository supports wizard-based service interface creation from external Web Service Description Language (WSDL) files; multiple WSDL files can be imported simultaneously. The resulting service definitions can be modified and used to generate proxies.

▶ The Integration Directory allows automatic creation of configuration objects based on Process Component Interaction Models, a particular type of model in the Enterprise Services Repository. In addition, validating messages based on XML Schema definitions is offered; this can be used, for example, to prevent payload processing of messages that do not satisfy a pre-defined XML schema definition, thus avoiding unnecessary processor load.

▶ There are also improvements in overall operating costs. For example, SAP NetWeaver PI 7.1 can be installed much faster, now making it possible to install a complete PI system and configure a simple integration scenario in three to four hours. There are also significant improvements regarding sizing, particularly given by the support of a Java EE 5–compatible Application Server (AS) Java that uses less memory. Also, the local processing on the AAE leads to smaller sizing.

▶ Finally, there is enhanced support for standards, such as Web Services Reliable Messaging 1.1 (WS RM), Security Assertion Markup Language 1.1 (SAML), UDDI 3.0, and Business Process Execution Language (WS-BPEL) 2.0. The increased support for standards is specifically aimed at improving interoperability with the integration of non-SAP systems or business partners.

Because SAP NetWeaver PI 7.1 has been generally available since July 2008, has been applied by numerous companies, and offers numerous advantages as described previously, it is only natural to offer another edition of this practical guide for developers. Just as in the first edition, this book helps you learn the features and concepts of SAP NetWeaver PI 7.1 through the use of extensive examples.

We are very pleased to help you familiarize yourself with the new features and benefits of SAP NetWeaver PI 7.1 with this second edition. We again wish you an exciting and informative read.

Dr. Udo Paltzer
Senior Product Manager,
SAP NetWeaver Solution Management
SMR SOA & Platform/SOA Middleware, SAP AG

Prof. Dr. Helmut Krcmar
Chair of Information Management,
Technische Universität München

Preface

This book uses practical examples to provide you with an introduction to process-oriented integration using *SAP NetWeaver Process Integration (PI) 7.1*. Integrating business processes within and across enterprise boundaries has played a central role in system landscape design for many years. While the focus was initially on the internal enterprise level, it has shifted, and is now on the implementation of process chains with external business partners. The increasing complexity of implementing these kinds of scenarios makes for ever-higher demands of consultants and IT staff. "Group thinking" and "thinking outside the box" are just two approaches to overcome this challenge. An important factor in keeping up with this fast pace is engaging on a practical level with the latest state-of-the-art products in the field.

With release 3.0 of SAP NetWeaver Exchange Infrastructure (XI), SAP has created a product that, thanks to its extensive range of functions and easy-to-understand usability design, is particularly suitable for representing and implementing integration processes. In the current release, PI 7.1, many new features have been added, taking the thoughts of business-driven modeling and simplified technical implementation of business processes more into account. The practical exercises in this book are intended to make you familiar with the functional processes, using this application and how it fits into SAP system landscapes as a basis.

Before focusing on the SAP product, **Chapter 1**, Integrating Enterprise Information Systems, takes a look at the approaches, architectures, and standards in the area of integration; this lays the groundwork for the exercises in Chapters 4 and 5. It also explains the significance of *enterprise application integration* (EAI) platforms and takes an initial look at *business process management* (BPM).

Chapter 2, SAP NetWeaver PI, describes how SAP NetWeaver PI fits into the SAP product family and, in particular, clarifies its role within SAP NetWeaver. In doing so, the chapter uses simple examples to meaning-

Content

Structure of the book

17

fully describe the individual components of SAP NetWeaver PI and how they work on a fundamental level. These descriptions also introduce you to the concepts used by the components. One focus of this chapter is the variety of new concepts and features that are new in the current release.

At this point, you are equipped for the second, practical part of the book. To ensure that you can complete all of the exercises in your SAP (training) landscape, **Chapter 3**, Basic System Configuration, takes you through all of the necessary preparations step by step. It explains all of the settings in detail, so you can gain a better understanding of the technical processes in the practical exercises. In addition to purely technical administration, the application of training documents to practical exercises with several participants is addressed.

In **Chapter 4**, Technical Exercises, you carry out the first individual exercises using the prepared training landscape. This chapter focuses on how to use SAP NetWeaver PI components and how to implement the processes. It also teaches you about the most important adapters and monitoring methods in this context. In the exercises, we have placed particular emphasis on making it easy for you to recreate and trace the origins of all objects. In doing so, none of the objects "come out of nowhere." You will also examine the basics of BPM and process modeling in SAP NetWeaver PI, subjects that are dealt with in greater detail in the case study.

Once you have become familiar with the underlying technologies of SAP NetWeaver PI in independent exercises, **Chapter 5**, SARIDIS Case Study in Sales and Distribution, takes you through the process of implementing a complete sales process, from customer inquiry to invoice creation. This scenario is based on the SARIDIS case study used in SAP training courses. As part of the case study, the application of business processes and the associated innovations will be addressed, among other things.

Chapter 6, Enhancements and Outlook, provides you with ideas for expanding the case study you worked on in Chapter 5. It introduces you to the "beer distribution game," which can also be used as the basis of a case study. Finally, the chapter examines the significance of

SAP NetWeaver PI in the context of *Enterprise Service-Oriented Architecture* (SOA), and gives you helpful hints on the future development of SAP NetWeaver PI. In addition, the development of a Common Process Layer (CPL), new and enhanced functions, and the change to a single-stack architecture are also discussed.

Although both the integration solution and the authors of this book have matured, it hasn't altered the basic character of this book. Because we, the authors of this book, are active in the pedagogy and practice fields, this book is suitable for a wider target readership than it may at first appear. With several years' experience of SAP training in collegiate-level education contexts, we know about the practical demands made of consultants and graduates. At the same time, we are faced with the daily challenge of explaining complex issues in a clear, comprehensible manner. As such, the target audience of this book is consultants, IT staff, and decision-makers who want an introduction to SAP NetWeaver PI. With this audience in mind, we have painstakingly chosen highly relevant and practical problems when describing concepts and selecting exercises, and have provided support and advice on how to implement SAP NetWeaver PI in your enterprise.

Audience of this book

This book will also appeal to students who are preparing for "the real world" in various educational institutions. With these information management and information technology students in mind, we have tried to describe the fundamental concepts in a meaningful and memorable way, so they can understand the significance of the individual components and steps.

This wide target readership also means that this book is suitable for the self-taught SAP student, and for use in classroom settings. The source code and examples were designed with a class size of 20 students and one instructor in mind.

To carry out the practical tasks in this book, you should already have some initial experience with SAP products and a basic understanding of how to use them. To better comprehend the exercises, you should also have some basic knowledge of ABAP programming. However, these are not absolute prerequisites, as all ABAP development work is described in detail and available for use as a template. Knowledge of traditional SAP

Prerequisites

integration mechanisms, such as intermediate documents (IDocs), will also help you get the most from this book.

The goal of this practical guide is to enable you to quickly and easily delve into SAP NetWeaver PI and its functions. Our hope is that the information you find in this book is easy to understand, and that the examples can be quickly adapted to your work in the real world. Unfortunately, the complexity of the material doesn't always make it possible for us to present "finished" components and settings. Nonetheless, we have done so wherever possible. The book's companion Web sites — *http://www. sap-press.com* and *http://www. sap-press.de/2159* — contain templates for files, transports, sample code, and everything else to make it easier for you to work on the exercises. In addition to the exercises and the case study, you'll also find many other ideas at the end of the book, which you can use to further develop the practical exercises and apply to other case studies and scenarios.

This book represents the first step in this area for many readers, so we have kept the content as simple and as relevant to everyday practice as possible. This balancing act has meant that in many places we have not described the problems in as much depth as we otherwise could have. We are aware of the fact that many issues in the practical application should be considered in a greater depth. However, this depth is difficult to teach on one hand, and not necessary to gain an overview of functional variety on the other.

There is no doubt that this book would not exist if many people had not at first encouraged us to work on this project, and then actually done what they promised to do — that is, take an active part in creating this work.

We would first like to thank our families and friends, who supported and encouraged us right through the conception and writing phases.

We also want to thank all of the others who provided us with help and advice:

- ▶ Heino Schrader as a representative of the SAP University Alliances Program; without this program, the cooperation over university boundaries would never have been achieved.

- ▶ The staff of the SAP University Competence Center at Technischen Universität München, which provided the basis for the system landscape with servers and expertise.

- ▶ Matthias Mohr and Astrid Hoffmann for allowing us to use the SARIDIS case study. We also thank Mark Lehmann and Marcel Severith for their support in the revision of the case study.

Dr. Valentin Nicolescu
Prof. Dr. Burkhardt Funk
Prof. Dr. Peter Niemeyer
Matthias Heiler
Dr. Holger Wittges
Thomas Morandell
Florian Visintin
Benedikt Kleine Stegemann
Harald Kienegger

PART I
Basic Principles

This chapter explains why it is necessary to integrate information systems, and the basic issues involved in this process. It also discusses the main difficulties of integration and presents concepts for solving these problems.

1 Integrating Enterprise Information Systems

Driven by new business requirements, information technology (IT) departments must quickly adapt systems to the needs of new products and services, and change (internal) administrative processes. The heterogeneity of today's application landscapes makes integrating business information systems one of the main tasks of IT departments. Integration is one way IT can successfully support companies in quickly bringing new products to market.

This chapter outlines the development of enterprise application integration (EAI), and explains why it is so important. A practical example provides an overview of the problems that can arise in the integration process, and the concepts and technologies used to solve these problems. The chapter ends with a review of the components found in a typical integration platform, such as SAP NetWeaver.

1.1 Basic Principles

We begin by taking a look at the basics of integrating business information systems: their historical development, the reasons and goals of integration, and the characteristics of this integration.

1.1.1   Historical Development

Starting-point: monolithic application systems

In the 1950s and 1960s, enterprise IT landscapes were dominated by mainframe computers and the monolithic application systems that ran on them. At the time, very few business processes were supported by IT, so, there was no clear need to integrate these individual solutions. However, as enterprise IT support became more common at the start of the 1970s, there was an increasing need to integrate enterprise applications, such as those used for materials management, human resources, and financial accounting. In the same period, the "Cologne" integration model of Grochla, and the reference models of Scheer and Mertens, led to the first concepts of integrated information processing.

Computer integrated manufacturing and enterprise resource planning

The subject of integration took on a more practical approach with the development of computer-integrated manufacturing (CIM). The main benefit of CIM is that it automates data flow between different applications. For example, in the automobile industry, *bills of materials* (BOMs) can be generated in a *computer-aided design* (CAD) system and then automatically transferred to and used in MM and *production planning and control systems* (PPS).

Since the mid-1980s, *Enterprise Resource Planning* (ERP) providers have been working toward providing preintegrated applications. These applications work very well, provided that only applications of one "software generation" from a single provider are used. However, although they use ERP systems, most companies still have outdated, standalone applications in use, which, because of their complexity and importance to the business, are simply too expensive to replace with standard software. What's more, enterprises often take the best-of-breed approach; in other words, they simply choose the best product on the market in the case of each individual application. Both of these issues highlight the need to integrate IT systems.

Cross-enterprise integration becomes more important

While the initial focus was on integrating internal enterprise application systems (EAI), cross-enterprise integration came onto the scene by the end of the 1970s (see Figure 1.1). Initially, the focus was on bilateral data exchange based on data carriers and proprietary formats. Semantic and industry-specific standards, such as SWIFT (banking),[1] ODETTE

---

1   Society for Worldwide Interbank Financial Telecommunication (SWIFT)

(automotive), and RosettaNet (high-tech), were later added to these formats within the framework of *Electronic Data Interchange* (EDI). While these standards are still in use today, XML-based message formats have increased in importance. Using standards such as the *Resource Description Framework* (RDF),[2] these formats can support the naming conventions of individual industries and, at the same time, be adapted to each individual case.

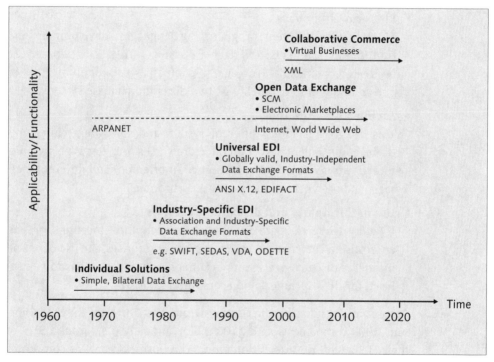

Figure 1.1 Historical Development of Cross-Enterprise Integration (Source: Scheckenbach, 1997)

Today's electronic marketplaces and e-procurement platforms place emphasis on specialist applications that enable process-oriented integration across enterprise boundaries. Widely used standards, such as message formats and protocols, and infrastructure services, such as security, process engines, and monitoring, make implementing this kind of inte-

---

2 The RDF (*http://www.w3.org/RDF*) provides a lightweight ontology system using metadata.

gration cost-efficient, fast, and flexible. Integration platforms — commercial or free — are increasingly used for this purpose. SAP NetWeaver Process Integration (PI) is an example of such a commercial platform.

1.1.2 Reasons for and Goals of Integrating IT Systems

The technical reasons for integrating IT systems can be divided into the following three categories:

▶ **Platform differences**
This includes different programming languages, development and runtime environments, and database systems. These components can be free or commercial. In general, companies use different types of one component in parallel (e.g., two different database systems).

▶ **Architectural differences**
This category includes different system and software architectures (for example, client/server architecture versus four-tier Web architecture, or service-oriented versus function-oriented) and different message modes (synchronous versus asynchronous).

▶ **Use of third-party and distributed services**
If enterprise services are distributed across multiple locations, or if an enterprise wants to use services of other enterprises, the use of online interfaces or batch processing for integration purposes has to be analyzed for their technical and economical aspects.

Technical integration pursues various goals

According to studies by the Gartner Group and Forrester Research, Fortune 1000 companies spend $100 billion annually (i.e., around 35% of their IT budget) on integration work. The business goals of companies that make such high-level investments are:

▶ To develop new products, reach new target customer groups, and incorporate more suppliers

▶ To achieve greater flexibility in the organization of processes and comprehensive process automation

▶ To reduce latency times in information delivery and information processing

▶ To reduce development and operational costs

One technical goal of any integration process is to reduce complexity and to reuse existing software components and systems, and to make internal and external business processes transparent.

1.1.3 Characteristics of Integration

According to Mertens, integration has four main characteristics: object, direction, scope, and degree of automation.

Data, programs, functions, processes, and services are all *integration objects*. Data and programs refer to the technical elements that are to be integrated, while functions, processes, and services represent the business elements. For example, a service could be a credit-check of a potential customer. This service could itself be integrated into an order processing process that is linked to other services.

Consideration of different integration objects

Integration direction differentiates between vertical and horizontal integration (as shown in Figure 1.2):

Differentiation of integration directions

- *Horizontal integration* connects the different stages of the value chain. For example, when the sales department receives a sales order, a staff member in that department forwards the order to the procurement department, then to the production department before the ordered goods are finally delivered.

- *Vertical integration* supports decision-making within the framework of planning and control systems. The main goal is to integrate data from different applications and data storage locations in the operational application systems. The various sales systems in a large mail order company (such as an online store, mail order, or call center) are good examples of vertical integration. Data from the individual sales systems is identified and aggregated to create sales statistics on the company level. Sections 1.2, Practical Integration Example, and 1.3, Integration Concepts and Technologies, discuss the problems that can occur in this context, and their solutions.

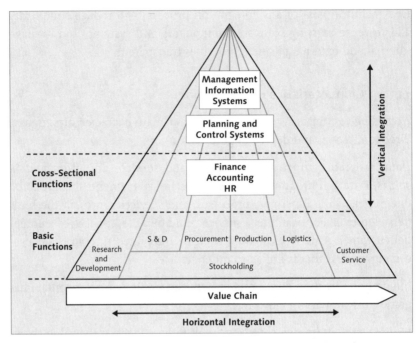

Figure 1.2 Horizontal and Vertical Integration within an Enterprise (Based on Mertens)

Integration scope *Integration scope* differentiates between cross-enterprise and intra-enterprise integration. Based on Mertens, the latter is divided into intradepartment and cross-department integration. An example of cross-department integration is a customer relationship management (CRM) system that accesses data and functions from the marketing, sales, product management, and customer service departments.

Degree of automation and latency periods Depending on the need of human-machine interaction in the integration of IT systems, a distinction is made between fully automated and partially automated integration. Partially automated integration requires functions to initiate and coordinate communication between human and machine. This can be done by components that are developed in-house, components of an integration platform, or a specific *workflow management system* (WMS). Aside from the *degree of automation*, the processing type and its associated *latency period* are also important integration characteristics. There is a distinction between integration that takes place in real time (such as credit card processing in an online store), and integration that only takes place at specific points in time (such as identifying duplicates in address data).

1.2   Practical Integration Example

Now that we've discussed the reasons for, and characteristics of, integration, this section uses a core operational process — invoice verification — to illustrate the challenges that arise when integrating business processes.

Example: SOX-compliant invoice verification process

An invoice verification process checks a number of things. For example, the customer should only pay for goods and services he has ordered and received, and he should only pay for them once. Also, in this age of the *Sarbanes-Oxley Act* (SOX), companies listed on the New York Stock Exchange (NYSE) are required by law to provide evidence of the goods and services they purchase. Therefore, the invoice verification and processing need to be auditable, which means that, starting from an archived invoice, the previously mentioned aspects have to be traceable at a later date.

The invoice itself contains important information for auditing purposes. For example, it usually lists who issued the invoice for which products or services, who ordered them, when they were ordered, plus the material numbers of the goods or services. The purchasing company must also maintain details of purchase orders, goods receipt confirmations, and previously paid invoices for future reference.

Process and application integration

This process usually involves multiple IT systems and applications. For example, orders and goods receipts are often executed in multiple, non-centralized ordering and goods receipt systems. Meanwhile, payments are processed in a centralized accounting system. Therefore, it isn't always obvious which system has to be searched for order information. Also, the payment process may be handled by a *shared service center* for different regions, or the entire process may be outsourced to a *business process outsourcing* (BPO) provider. Both scenarios add another layer of complexity to the integration.

In the case of services, there usually isn't an application that fulfills a role similar to goods receipt. Instead, a workflow is triggered when the invoice is received, which causes the invoice to be released, rejected, or modified by the ordering party. In this case, a workflow can consist of multiple individual tasks (for example, if two employees need to approve an invoice before it can be paid, regardless of the amount).

Specific problems and tasks that occur in integration are discussed in the following text, based on selected process steps from the perspective of the receiving company (see Figure 1.3).

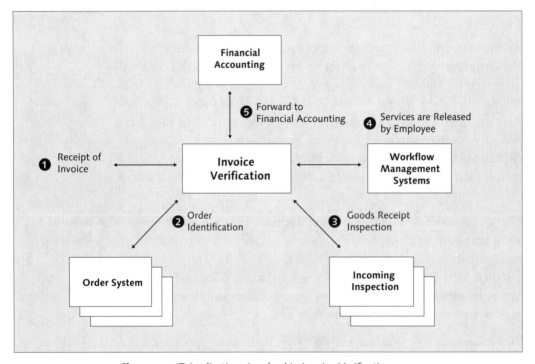

Figure 1.3 IT Applications Involved in Invoice Verification

Invoices can be received (see step ❶) in either paper or electronic form. To comply with statutory and legal requirements, electronic invoices must be digitally signed, and the digital signature must be checked at the invoice receipt stage (business and process complexity).

The actual invoice documents can contain either unstructured data (for example, a PDF document) or structured data (for example, EDIFACT, XML, or CSV). If they contain structured data, it is possible — and indeed, preferable — to automatically import the data into the ordering company's IT system.

Except in cases where the ordering party has the market strength to specify binding requirements regarding invoice content and format to its suppliers (for example, to use a particular standard, such as EDIFACT), schema and data conflicts can arise between internal and external data displays.

▶ A structural *schema conflict* exists if, for example, a supplier uses separate attributes to display the house number and street name, while the ordering party uses a single attribute that combines them both. Similarly, the supplier may represent individual invoice items hierarchically, while the ordering company may combine these in a single order item.

    Aside from structural schema conflicts, various *description conflicts* can occur in integration. These can include scaling conflicts — due to different quantity and currency units — and data-type conflicts. For example, a postal or zip code may be displayed as a number in one system and as a character string in another.

▶ Unlike schema conflicts, *data conflicts* are content based. In the context of integration, they can result from incorrect data and differing representations. A manual transfer error that occurs in the order processing process on the supplier's side can result in an incorrect order number, which then cannot be correctly assigned by the automatic invoice verification process.

    In this case, a workflow is triggered that uses a similarity analysis to provide suggestions for which order is most likely the one in question on the invoice. Individual attributes can also be represented in different ways. For example, a contact person's gender can be coded as *male* or *female* on the supplier's side, while the ordering company may use a salutation, such as Mr. or Ms. The goal when solving these conflicts is to standardize incoming data in an internal format that can be interpreted by downstream applications.

The next step in invoice verification (see step ❷) is to identify the purchase order that belongs to the incoming invoice. For this, you must first identify the originating order system, as there are multiple order sys-

Schema conflicts

Data conflicts

Location transparency

33

tems at various locations. This is accomplished by using system-specific number ranges (such as 123 – 4711 for system 123). Because the actual invoice verification process doesn't contain information about the order systems and their technical location (a condition known as *location transparency*), a service is called that combines all of the information about the landscape of the underlying order system; this service then calls the correct system. This functionality, known as *routing,* is described in detail in Chapter 4, Technical Exercises.

Use of different interface technologies

The incoming inspection (see step ❸) is also executed in different applications at different locations. As before, a suitable encapsulation concept is used to establish location transparency from the viewpoint of the invoice verification process. If the incoming goods inspection systems were developed or purchased at different points in time, the interface technologies being used are also often different. For example, one system may process HTTP and Web service requests, while another may only process CORBA requests. As with location transparency, components that "hide" the technical complexity of the interfaces from the central process are required here. Also, for the incoming inspection to run smoothly, there are often communications restrictions on the network level (for example, firewalls or network address translation [NAT]) that must be considered for errorfree processing.

Communications types: synchronous and asynchronous

As described earlier, services rendered are verified (see step ❹) by creating a workflow. Workflow management systems usually use *asynchronous communication*, which means that requests to the system (in this case, the request to initiate the workflow) won't wait for a response (after all, the ordering party first has to manually release the invoice). Instead, the called system notifies the calling party after the workflow task is completed. This requires an available network and a corresponding callback interface on the part of the caller, who uses the called system to actively respond at any point in time.

In particular, the necessity of a callback system often causes problems because changes need to be made to the IT applications, and to the processes themselves. For example, if the IT application that supports the invoice verification process requires synchronous communication (this is sufficient for steps ❷ and ❹), an adapter is needed to receive incoming requests from the invoice verification process. This process formally responds synchronously to these events and forwards them asynchronously to the WMS. For the response from the WMS, the adapter makes the appropriate callback interface available. When the invoice is finally released, it is forwarded from the WMS to the FI department (see step ❺).

Integrating the various IT systems in an enterprise is a prerequisite for an automated invoice verification process. The integration problems described in this section can also occur in other integration scenarios, and integration platforms such as SAP NetWeaver PI provide corresponding functions (mapping) to solve these problems. This is discussed in greater detail in Section 1.4, EAI Platforms and Their Significance in Enterprises.

1.3 Integration Concepts and Technologies

Several concepts and technologies have been developed to solve the integration problems described in Section 1.2. However, they aren't discussed in detail in this chapter; Appendix B provides a list for additional reading on this topic. Instead, in this section we describe the architectures, integration approaches, and technologies that are most important for using the SAP NetWeaver PI.

1.3.1 Architectures

In the past, due to the lack of suitable concepts and technologies, integrating individual applications involved developing proprietary interfaces and directly connecting IT systems to each other. In practice, this still happens today when integrating a small number of applications. The primary benefit of this kind of *point-to-point integration* is that its implementation requires less time and effort than the introduction of a centralized integration solution. Furthermore, the implementation can be optimized for specific point-to-point data exchange; for example, for processing mass data.

Point-to-point integration

However, because the number of required connections increases exponentially with the number of applications to be integrated, the level of complexity and the time and effort required for maintenance also quickly increases. Moreover, individual applications require information about the formats, interface technologies, and physical availability (for example, location and security mechanisms) of the other applications. If these properties change for one application, the other applications linked to it have to be adapted accordingly.

These disadvantages can be overcome by introducing a centralized component, such as the following:

Concept of hub and spoke architecture

▸ In a *hub-and-spoke architecture* (see Figure 1.4), the hub — named after the main airport of an airline — is the central integration platform. The applications to be integrated — the "spokes" — are connected to the hub either directly or via standardized, and thus lightweight, connectors.

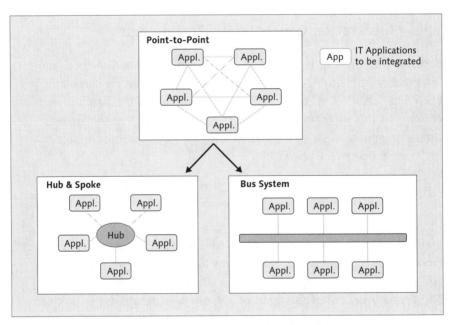

Figure 1.4 Integration Architectures — Hub-and-Spoke and Bus Systems

The goal here is to make as few adaptations to the applications as possible during the integration process. Because the integration platform in hub-and-spoke architectures performs tasks such as routing and mapping, the applications only need limited information about the other applications with which they want to exchange information.

The disadvantage of this architecture is that the central integration platform represents a *single point of failure* (SPOF) and a bottleneck in terms of message throughput. The next system, the bus system, avoids this issue through an access concept without a central coordinator.

The purpose of the *enterprise service bus* (ESB) is to avoid both the "spaghetti" configuration of point-to-point integration and the single central component of the hub-and-spoke architecture. The ESB itself is not a self-contained component; rather, it consists of individual ESB services that are linked to each other in a message-oriented manner on the basis of Web services (see Figure 1.5).

Tasks of the enterprise service bus

Applications integrated with an ESB either already have a Web service interface, or they use an appropriate wrapper. This approach has better scalability and availability than the hub-and-spoke architecture; however, it is more difficult to monitor and administer. In this context, SAP NetWeaver PI can be regarded as an ESB service used to create an ESB.

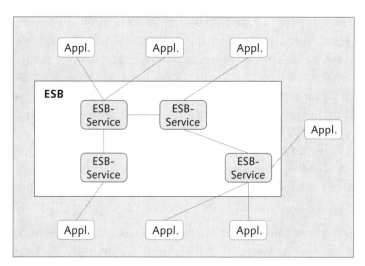

Figure 1.5 ESB

1.3.2 Integration Approaches

There are two kinds of integration approaches: data- and process-oriented. *Data-oriented approaches* focus on the technical viewpoint, while *process-oriented approaches* focus on the business viewpoint.

Data-oriented integration

Data-oriented integration is based on the various layers of a software system. In practice, integration is often based on *data storage*. With data storage, either the systems to be integrated jointly access a relational database, or the datasets are replicated or federated. Database federation is done either physically or virtually. Physical federation involves bringing the data together, while virtual federation keeps the datasets physically separate and virtually combines them using multidatabase languages such as SQL and MED.

Complex business applications typically don't have direct access to the datasets, as data integrity is ensured mainly by the connected application systems, and by the database. Also, required business information, such as the goods receipt confirmation in the invoice verification process described earlier, is not that easy to obtain by means of a simple database query. For this reason, application systems provide interfaces for *functional-level* integration (for example, business application programming interface (BAPI) and remote function call (RFC)).

Integration via presentation layer

For completeness, it's important to mention integration on the presentation layer level. In companies, this approach is used for older applications that do not have direct access to data storage (because of a proprietary database, for example) or its functions, but the company wants to integrate the functionality (e.g., in a portal). To do this, there are several tools that encapsulate a terminal application and make it available via modern interface technologies (such as Web services and *Simple Object Access Protocol* (SOAP)). Another application area of this integration approach is competition monitoring. Airlines, for example, can use this to monitor the booking levels of their competitors' flights to adjust their own prices.

Process-oriented integration

Process-oriented integration uses the previously mentioned functions on the technical level to link systems together, but concentrates on the business process. Integration platforms that support this approach (such as SAP NetWeaver PI) make it possible to model business processes, while also providing a suitable runtime environment. In the spirit of "separation of responsibilities," these tools keep the process logic separate from the individual applications. Configuration is independent of the business process design, so it is possible to exchange individual applications and flexibly use internal and external services (see Section 1.5, Basics of BPM).

This concept is at the forefront of the current discussion about *service-oriented architectures* (SOA). The term "services" here refers to business-relevant, self-contained applications that can be used in various business processes. The literature (see Erl, *Service-Oriented Architecture*, 2006) describes numerous properties to such services, including:

Service-oriented
architectures

▶ **Self-describing**
The service can be fully described on a formal level; that is, what operations are available and which data types can be exchanged. Formal self-description is the basis for the automatic generation of proxies. Here, the word "description" doesn't refer to the semantic description.

▶ **Locatable**
Potential consumers can locate and contact the service. There is a registry that functions as the "Yellow Pages" of services, and allows users to search for services.

▶ **Roughly structured**
Services are roughly structured when they return comprehensive data (for example, a sales order) in response to a service call, instead of delivering individual attributes (such as an order quantity).

▶ **Loosely linked**
Services are said to be loosely linked when possible functional changes within the services have no effect on the available operations.

▶ **Independent**
Services are considered independent if they have no dependencies on other services; in other words, if the availability of a service is not dependent on the availability and proper functioning of another service.

▶ **Reusable**
Reusability is one of the most important and longest-standing requirements in software technology. Its aim is to ensure that components are reused as often as possible without modification to the functional core and interfaces.

There are three basic roles in SOAs:

▶ **Service consumer**
The service consumer first searches for suitable services, manually or automatically implements the interfaces on the basis of the formal self-description, and then uses the service.

▶ **Service provider**
The service provider develops a service, makes it available as a Web service, and processes queries from service consumers on an ongoing basis.

▶ **Service registrar**
The service registrar provides registration services to service providers, and provides corresponding directory services to service consumers (such as service searches based on specific criteria).

The connection between these roles is shown in Figure 1.6. Chapter 2, SAP NetWeaver PI, explains the SAP view of an SOA in greater detail, and the significance of SAP NetWeaver PI in this context.

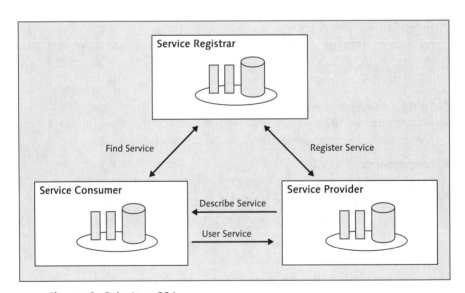

Figure 1.6 Roles in an SOA

1.3.3   Technologies

Several integration technologies have been developed and used, and it is beyond the scope of this book to describe them all in detail. Instead, the important technologies are reviewed in the context of SAP NetWeaver PI. Recommendations for further, more detailed reading on this topic are also presented.

Integration technologies can be generally divided into transport-oriented, object-oriented, message-oriented, and semantic standards.

▶ Transport-oriented standards are closely related to network protocols. SAP NetWeaver PI allows developers to build adapters that provide interfaces to the various standards. The current version of SAP NetWeaver PI enables external services and data to be integrated by means of HTTP, FTP, and SMTP.

Transport-oriented standards

▶ There is a wide variety of object-oriented integration technologies. The most important are CORBA (see Aleksy, et al., *Implementing Distributed Systems with Java and CORBA,* 2005), RMI (see Grosso, *Java RMI,* 2001), and COM/DCOM. SAP NetWeaver PI currently does not provide adapters for these technologies, but it does enable commercial third-party products to be used and in-house adapters to be developed using the *Java Connector Architecture* (see Sharma, et al., *J2EE Connector Architecture and Enterprise Application Integration,* 2002).

Object-oriented standards

▶ Message-oriented technologies have always been very important for integrating business applications. The reason for this is the necessity to use message communication in asynchronous use cases. There are various technologies and products (for example, WebSphere MQ by IBM), and general standards (such as Sun's Java Messaging Service); however, these are not described in this book.

Message-oriented standards

Aside from technologies and standards, which are used to make the required infrastructure available for message exchange, the description and format of messages are also important; which are known as *semantic standards*. SAP NetWeaver PI uses *Web services* (see Alonso, et al., 2004) for this purpose, in particular the *Web Service Description Language* (WSDL) and SOAP.

Semantic standards

SOAP SOAP is independent of transport protocol and communication mode (remote procedure call (RPC) vs. message-oriented), and uses XML for data display. Listing 1.1 shows an example of the structure of a SOAP message.

```
<?xml version='1.0' ?>
<env:Envelope
  xmlns:env="http://www.w3.org/2003/05/soap-envelope">
  <env:Header>
    <n:transaction xmlns:n="http://a.url.com/ns"
      env:mustUnderstand="true">
      <n:id>4711xyz</n:id>
    </n:transaction>
  </env:Header>
  <env:Body>
    <p:payment xmlns:p="http://bank.com/ns">
      <p:ccholder>Sandra Miller</p:ccholder>
      <p:ccnumber>4200000000000000</p:ccnumber>
      <p:valid>11.08</p:valid>
    </p:payment>
  </env:Body>
</env:Envelope>
```

Listing 1.1 Example of a SOAP Message

Every SOAP message consists of an envelope, an optional header inside the envelope, and the content, known as the body. The header contains meta-information about the message. It can contain session IDs and control the routing and encryption. The body contains application-specific data (payload).

SOAP is a World Wide Web Consortium (W3C) (*http://www.w3.org/TR/ soap*) specification and is currently at version 1.2 second edition (April 27, 2007).

WSDL Syntactically, SOAP messages are described using WSDL. A WSDL document provides information about the more sophisticated data types used within a message, and the operations (functions) provided by a Web service. It also describes the formal properties of this service (for example, request-response vs. one-way) and the data types used. A WSDL document also specifies the link between (SOAP) messages and the transport protocol, and states the location of the service (URL). Proxy classes can be automatically generated using WSDL documents; these classes are then used as a basis for the server and for the client.

SAP NetWeaver PI uses a SAP-specific SOAP format[3] (*SOAP with attachments*) for internal message communication. Chapter 4, Section 4.3, Exercise 3: ABAP-Proxy-to-SOAP, demonstrates how external Web services can be integrated in SAP NetWeaver PI. Conversely, interfaces defined in SAP Exchange infrastructure (XI) can be provided externally as a Web service, including an automatically generated WSDL document.

Various — mainly XML-based — approaches have been developed, including Web services in business processes. The *Business Process Execution Language (BPEL) for Web Services* (WS-BPEL is a standard of the OASIS Group (*http://www.oasis-open.org*)). WS-BPEL is supported by several large software providers and is the basis of the SAP NetWeaver PI Business Process Engine (BPE). The executable processes can be displayed in graphical form, and then stored as a WS-BPEL document. The current WS-BPEL version is 2.0 from 2007 (*http://www.oasis-open.org/committees/tc_home.php?wg_abbrev=wsbpel*).

WS-BPEL

In SAP NetWeaver, tools for the creation of WS-BPEL processes are included in SAP NetWeaver Business Process Management (BPM), which was also known under SAPs internal project name, "Galaxy," and is now available as SAP NetWeaver Composition Environment. In 2005, BPEL-4People[4] was introduced as an extension of WS-BPEL, with the aim of modeling manual activities more simply. Although these asynchronous activities could also be modeled in WS-BPEL, BPEL4People provides more complex constructs that simplify the modeling.

WS-BPEL documents specify which Web services can be called in a business process, in what order they can be called, whether these calls are synchronous or asynchronous, and which prerequisites have to be met

---

3   This SAP-specific SOAP format is the reason why SAP NetWeaver PI provides an additional standard SOAP adapter. The SAP-specific extension contains the necessary extensions, such as ensuring the quality of service to guarantee message delivery.

4   For the WS-BPEL extension BPEL4People see: *http://www.sdn.sap.com/irj/scn/go/portal/prtroot/docs/library/uuid/cfab6fdd-0501-0010-bc82-f5c2414080ed*.

before they can be called. The Web services can be system-centered, or services with the purpose of integrating end users (user-centered).

BPEL also provides variable declarations to store the status of business processes. The basic structured activities for specifying process logic that you are familiar with from programming languages are also available in WS-BPEL: loops, conditions, sequences, and exceptions. WS-BPEL processes can be called directly from within SAP NetWeaver PI, and can also be made available externally as a Web service. Chapter 4, Section 4.4, Exercise 4: Business Process Management, describes how to use the BPE and WS-BPEL.

1.4   EAI Platforms and Their Significance in Enterprises

Types of integration platforms

When IT systems are integrated in practice, comprehensive integration platforms are often used instead of in-house software. These platforms provide solutions to the problems discussed in Section 1.2, and are based on the concepts and technologies described in Section 1.3.

Open source and commercial platforms are available. Open source solutions such as jBPM (*http://www.jboss.com/products/jbpm*) and ServiceMix (*http://servicemix.org*) concentrate on individual subareas of integration; for example, business process modeling and execution. Commercial providers include world-leading software providers such as SAP (SAP NetWeaver PI), Microsoft (Microsoft BizTalk), and IBM (IBM WebSphere Business Integration), and providers that specialize in integration, such as TIBCO (TIBCO BusinessWorks) and Vitria Technology (BusinessWare).

Components of integration platforms

Some of the integration platform components used in business-oriented integration processes that you will get to know as part of SAP NetWeaver PI include the following:

▸ **Mapper**
Mappers are used to transform data to avoid data and schema conflicts between the sender and a message recipient.

▸ **Router**

Routers are used to set routing rules, which specify which intermediate points are used to send a message to the intended recipient. Routers are oriented around the metadata and content of a message, and as such are responsible for location transparency.

▸ **Repository**

Repositories contain reusable interface specifications and message mappings, and have information about the individual external systems to be integrated. SAP NetWeaver PI contains the *enterprise services repository* (mappings and interfaces) and the *system landscape directory* (an overview of IT systems and software components).

▸ **Services registry**

The Services Registry supports publication, classification, searching, and testing of Enterprise Services (SAP, partner, or customer services) across the entire IT landscape. The Universal Description, Discovery, and Integration (UDDI)–compliant registry also enables the management and governance of Enterprise Services.

▸ **Queuing mechanism**

The queuing mechanism is used for asynchronous message exchange. It can be used to define different queues for different purposes; for example, to prioritize messages, process bundled messages together, or channel large messages for separate processing. Queues can be defined for both the input and the output, and are discussed in more detail in Chapter 2, Section 2.5.6, Message Queues, and Chapter 3, Section 3.4.2, Defining and Activating Message Queues.

▸ **Adapter**

Integration platforms provide various adapters for the interface technologies described in Section 1.3.3, Technologies, and general interfaces that extend the functionality of these adapters. Adapters are also offered for the most common business applications (and their various versions).

▸ **Business process modeling**

Business process modeling makes it possible to model business processes (mainly graphically), and in many cases to translate the model into WS-BPEL.

▶ **Runtime environment**
This is the runtime environment for mappers, routers, and adapters. As with SAP NetWeaver PI, the process engine is often another component of the runtime environment that makes it possible to execute the previously modeled business processes.

▶ **Configuration**
The configuration is used to administer and configure real-world integration scenarios and business processes.

▶ **Monitoring**
The monitoring function provides tools for monitoring the runtime environment, and makes it possible to analyze individual messages.

It almost always makes sense to use integration platforms[5] in complex integration projects, because it increases flexibility in terms of BPM and makes it possible to reuse interfaces, mappings, and sub-processes in a variety of integration scenarios. If business standard software is used, the integration platform takes care of version-based translations in the adapters and lightens the workload of the developers.

Also, despite the time it takes employees to get used to the individual characteristics of a product, the implementation period of integrating the project is reduced, as the main components already exist and therefore only have to be adapted or configured. This book will help you get used to SAP NetWeaver PI in this regard.

1.5 Basics of BPM

Business process modeling as a facilitator

In BPM, the focus is on a holistic view of business processes with the aim of improving them on an ongoing basis. The reasons for using BPM are as follows:

▶ Model-based planning and adaptation of innovative business processes

---

5 Deciding which integration platform is appropriate for a project depends on the respective requirements (e.g., scope of adapters, infrastructure requirements, and expected message throughput). You can find a comprehensive checklist that supports this selection in *Enterprise Application Integration* (Keller 2002).

- Holistic view of business processes

- Standardization of business processes

Business process modeling is a central task in this context. It involves extracting and representing information required for the identification, optimization, and controlled execution of processes. Informal and semi-formal graphical description languages with textual extensions are usually used for this purpose. These languages serve as a common ground for consultants, employees in the departments, and management, and facilitate communication between each.

The main focus of process modeling is on business work processes. These range from manual processes that are executed without technical support (such as storing goods in the inventory) to partially automated processes (such as software system–supported order receipt) to fully automated processes (such as an automatic posting procedure or a database transaction). The task of business process modeling is to create a consolidated understanding of the business process from the business process viewpoint.

Business process modeling and consolidated processes

The product family of *SAP Enterprise Modeling Applications* was formerly known as ARIS for SAP NetWeaver, and consists of software products, which are classified into four areas according to their principal function:

ARIS product family

- The tools of the strategy platform ensure a wide-ranging business plan.

- On the design platform, the processes for synchronizing IT are planned. Both the order of operations — that is, what is made by whom at a given time, and the necessary software systems of the process — are defined.

- The goal of the ARIS implementation platform is limited to the synchronization of business processes in IT systems; thus, it acts as a connector between business and IT. This is made possible by the tools of the ARIS implementation platform and the SAP Solution Manager, which are discussed later in this chapter.

- The controlling platform is used for continuous monitoring, and to check the performance of the business processes.

Figure 1.7 shows the content and context of the business process modeling tool, ARIS for SAP NetWeaver, and the BPM tools in the SAP NetWeaver stack. ARIS is used for process analysis and process design. As its basis, ARIS uses the SAP reference processes that are available with the ARIS toolset for SAP NetWeaver. The SAP Solution Manager, as a component of SAP NetWeaver, supports the technical implementation and monitoring of business processes in the SAP system. To do this, it uses the SAP NetWeaver PI component that allows processes to be modeled and executed within an application, and across applications. The lower part of Figure 1.7 shows how applications are connected. The tools of the design and implementation platform of the ARIS solutions are used here.

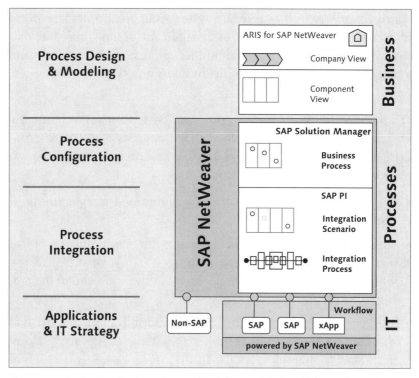

Figure 1.7 Connecting Business Process Modeling and Business Process Execution

Forced integration of ARIS and SAP NetWeaver

It should now be clear how the integration of business process models, technical process configuration, and process execution can be done. The integration of SAP NetWeaver PI with different applications using proprietary and standardized interfaces is very advanced, and is already in use in more than 2500 cases. Integration of ARIS and SAP NetWeaver is available in a second version, and its further development is currently a focal point of the cooperation between IDS Scheer AG and SAP. You will find considerations for the practical use of this interface in Section 1.6.2, Bidirectional Integration.

Figure 1.8 shows how the four tools for collecting process flows (ARIS, SAP Guided Procedures, SAP NetWeaver PI (WS-BPEL), and SAP Workflows) jointly specify the content of BPM runtime. Access can then be implemented independent of the technology using the portal (this is transparent to the user). You can find an overview of Guided Procedures at the SAP Developer Network (SDN) (*https://www.sdn.sap.com/irj/bpx/bpm?rid=/webcontent/uuid/eda 17f0c-0b01-0010-2eac-911c005da65e*).

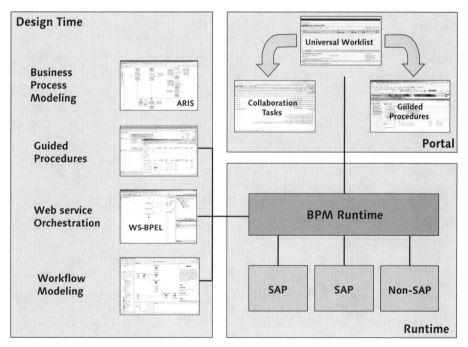

Figure 1.8 BPM Runtime Environment as a PI Platform

Vision: design complex solutions on the basis of standardized services

The ultimate vision — which has already been partly realized, as evidenced by the availability of initial services — is to use SOAs to bridge the gap between business modeling and technical implementation. SAP NetWeaver PI (an SOA) plays a crucial role as an integration platform and therefore a link between processes and services.

In summary, albeit in simplified form, we can visualize the business components or services as components with standardized interfaces (as shown in Figure 1.9), which are integrated by means of the business process via an integration platform (such as SAP NetWeaver PI), in accordance with the business requirements.

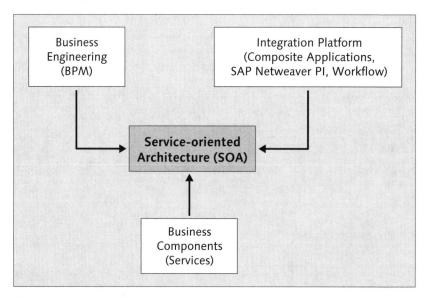

Figure 1.9 Enterprise SOA Brings Together Business Processes and Their Technical Implementation

1.6   Use of ARIS Business Architect and SAP Solution Manager

In the past, it has often been said that the exchange between the process models on the professional and technical level would be useful to avoid problems such as inconsistencies and double-counting, and thus improve the quality of process models with fewer resources. As explained in this section, with ARIS Business Architect and the SAP Solution Manager, there are now tools available that support the integration of professional and technical process models with software tools.

1.6.1 Concept

Information models on a business requirements level are used to document business processes, and represent the basis for communication between the business specialist and IT experts. The process-based implementation of SAP system (re)design activities should therefore define a common database. This base serves to align communication between developers and operational departments to achieve common goals faster, with less effort, and with fewer errors caused by ambiguity. By using ARIS Business Architect in combination with SAP Solution Manager, the appropriate interface with the corresponding functionality is provided for each of these two groups of persons involved.

Bidirectional data exchange between ARIS and SAP

Depending on the particular project role, project members have different tasks and goals, which results in different requirements for the tools deployed for the fulfillment of these tasks. Professionals running the process need tools to design business requirements, which allow a detailed description of business processes to be implemented and their underlying information model. Technology experts are involved in the creation of a process model that takes the technical configuration into account. Using this process model, the design specification of the SAP system implementation is specified and formalized based on the business requirements. To do this, users need tools that also allow the representation of technical system characteristics.

Figure 1.10 shows the schema of the coupling and distinguishes between the ARIS models on model levels 0-5, and the SAP Solution Manager on model levels 2-5. While ARIS puts the focus on business modeling for documentation purposes, SAP Solution Manager focuses on the model-based adjustment (customizing) of the SAP system.

Data synchronization on defined model levels

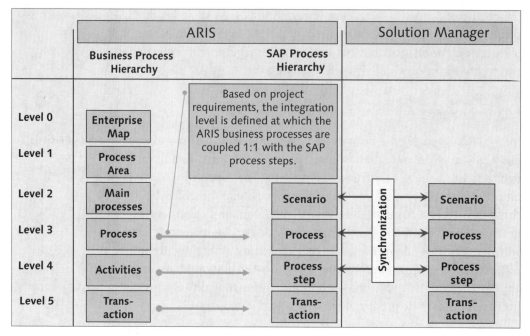

Figure 1.10 Coupling of ARIS and SAP

Focus on integrity, timeliness, and clarity

For both tools, the following general principles apply:

- **Integrity**
  This principle contains the requirements for accuracy and completeness (i.e., all relevant content is fully and realistically displayed in both systems). A full set of appropriate objects and model types is necessary as part of the modeling methodology.

- **Timeliness**
  All project members should use the same data. The data should always be up to date in all systems, or the ability to synchronize data should be given.

- **Clarity**
  Data and processes should be modeled in a way that they are clearly understandable for all persons involved. This is achieved by reducing complexity in the representation and standardization of the model.

The following demands on the modeling and business processes tools are given for documenting business requirements:

► Ability to represent all levels of the process architecture to be implemented (main processes, partial processes, processes, functions, subprocesses)

► Holism of representation (process logic, organizational structure, IT systems)

► Option to synchronize with the technological process model in SAP Solution Manager

► Method for versioning models and change tracking

► Ability to control the access permissions by a role concept

► Easy access to the fully modeled business processes for all project members

From an SAP implementation project perspective, there are additional requirements for the business process functionalities in SAP Solution Manager:

► Capability to represent all levels of the process architecture to be implemented (scenarios, processes, process steps, subprocesses)

► Ability to represent all SAP-relevant objects (organizational units, systems, documentation, transactions, links, master data)

► Rules for access permissions to the process models for everyone involved, or only to certain groups of people

► Recording of changes to the structure and documentation during the implementation

► Full use of standard functionality, thereby reducing the effort of in-house developments

Now that the tools for a technical link between ARIS models and Solution Manager models are available, practice has shown that they can also be operationally implemented. Results are automatically exchanged between the tools, which reduces duplicate data entries and inconsistencies.

1.6.2   Bidirectional Integration

The integration of ARIS Business Architect with SAP Solution Manager can be done in two ways, where either can be the starting point of integration; models that have been designed in a SAP Solution Manager project can be imported into ARIS Business Architect and vice versa. The direction of integration can therefore be a bottom-up approach, from technical to business model, or a top-down approach. However, for both cases, the takeover of model information is not applicable to all model types.

The key steps of integration are as follows:

▸ **Process-based SOA with direct connection to the enterprise service repository**
In the functional model, real services from the enterprise services repository can be accessed directly. These can be completed by additional data; for example, responsibilities, processes, etc. As part of the assignment of existing technical processes to technical services, implementation gaps will also become obvious.

▸ **Use of SAP reference content during the blueprint phase**
Reference content — for example, from SAP systems with industry-specific solutions — can be used to create the business blueprint. The structured provision of reference content in the form of business scenarios, applications maps, and processes can significantly accelerate the blueprint creation. Furthermore, the preparation can be supported through the use of a software wizard that is provided in the ARIS environment.

▸ **Definition of the target process**
Analogous to the blueprint phase, the modeler also benefits in the modeling of target processes from provided reference content. The design of target processes can also be geared with the Best Practices provided by SAP in the SAP Solution Manager or SAP Solution Composer. ARIS offers a special treatment for blueprint models and target processes used as training materials.

► **Connection/synchronization between ARIS Business Architect and SAP Solution Manager**
Process models from a project in SAP Solution Manager can be imported into an ARIS modeling environment, where they can be supplemented with additional information. These supplements can consist of a company-specific explanation of a process, a manual task, or information on the process flow. This information is only kept in the ARIS environment, and is not transferred to the SAP Solution Manager during the next synchronization. Changes to technical objects that originate from SAP Solution Manager can be executed in both systems, and are synchronized via the ARIS-SAP interface, which significantly reduces manual reconciliation between ARIS and SAP models.

The result of integrating ARIS business process modeling with the SAP process implementation is a shared, distributed database for the business processes and enterprise services, which is kept consistent with the aforementioned synchronization mechanisms. Following the idea of SOA, every tool saves, in addition to common data, data specific to the particular model level (operational/ technical).

The first step of the integration is made — an extension is likely

Due to this, the principle of loose coupling was introduced, because the tools don't share *one* common (data) repository. This makes it easier for both manufacturers to develop their products, because they only have to ensure that defined synchronization interfaces continue to be served. For new functionality, extended services must be implemented and used where appropriate.

This chapter describes how you can include SAP NetWeaver Process Integration (PI) in an overall integration concept, and the functionality and interactions of SAP NetWeaver PI components.

2 SAP NetWeaver PI

In this chapter, we introduce you to SAP NetWeaver PI (release 7.1). Since the last edition of this book, which was written for release 3.0 of SAP Exchange Infrastructure (XI), numerous extensions and improvements have been made to the SAP NetWeaver PI system — not only in terminology, but also in available functionality.

Enhancements and new features

However, before we go into the details of the SAP NetWeaver PI system and its components, we'll classify SAP NetWeaver PI as a component of SAP NetWeaver, in Section 2.1, SAP NetWeaver PI as Part of SAP NetWeaver. In Section 2.2, Functionality of SAP NetWeaver PI, the functionality of SAP NetWeaver PI is presented based on a small example, before we then go into the individual components in Section 2.3, Components. This section gives you an overview of the entire architecture, while also explaining some of the essential components of SAP NetWeaver PI to help you better understand what is happening where.

In Section 2.4, Objects, we introduce the individual objects that are required for processing messages. This should increase your general understanding of the system, and help you deal with concepts that have changed from previous releases. In Section 2.5, Advanced Concepts, we discuss additional concepts that are part and parcel of SAP NetWeaver PI, and, finally, in Section 2.6, New Concepts in SAP NetWeaver PI 7.1, we explain the latest ideas since release 7.1.

2.1 SAP NetWeaver PI as Part of SAP NetWeaver

If you examine a company's processes today, you'll find that these processes are always business related and that they run across different internal and external applications. They also involve the interaction of people (employees, customers, interested persons, suppliers, and so on) who must be integrated into the process. Along with these processes, a large amount of data (master data and transaction data) is created and stored, either in databases or as unstructured documents, such as PDF or Word files.

Data to information

Both data types must be made available to the user in a consolidated and aggregated form. After all, an employee does not want to look at several different lists to determine the aggregated revenues of his customers in a specific region, or to identify changes compared to the previous year. Instead, the employee wants to use a tool that provides all of this information right away, and presents it in an appealing manner; for example, as a bar chart. This is what turns pure data into real information. And finally, the individual process steps carried out in different applications must be integrated via an integration platform to become consistent processes — for example, via SAP NetWeaver PI.

2.1.1 Challenges of PI

Challenges of process integration

In general, there are four main challenges related to the integration process (see Figure 2.1):

- **Application-to-application (A2A) processes**
  A2A processes enable companies to seamlessly integrate their SAP and third-party applications. The process flow should be represented in a comprehensive way, based on sending and receiving messages. SAP NetWeaver PI serves as a central platform (middleware), allowing the design, configuration, and execution of business processes in a heterogeneous system landscape.

- **Business-to-business (B2B) processes**
  Companies can seamlessly link their own processes with those of their partners, based on the ability to send and receive messages and the use of uniform standards. SAP NetWeaver PI supports various communication channels, and the coordination and control of processes.

▸ **Business Process Management (BPM)**

BPM, using SAP NetWeaver PI, enables the modeling, configuring, executing, and monitoring of processes, although they run on business applications or on the central Integration Server (IS). Companies can use preconfigured content to implement their business processes or embed application-specific details.

▸ **Enterprise services**

With SAP NetWeaver PI, companies have a single infrastructure with which they can define, implement, and use uniform services. SAP NetWeaver PI supports the use of Web services and their standards. Both enterprise services for user interaction, and A2A and B2B interactions, are supported by SAP NetWeaver PI.

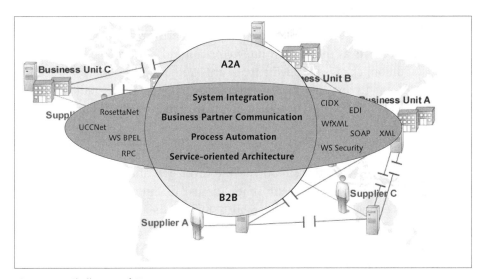

Figure 2.1 Challenges of PI

Integrating People

In Chapter 1, Section 1.2, Practical Integration Example, the challenges of integrating business processes was described on the basis of invoice verification. If you recall, the invoice verification process checks whether the goods and services that have been ordered and delivered correspond to each other, and determines whether or not the invoices have been paid.

Man as a process integrator

At the same time, it must be possible to audit the invoice verification process. This includes the following problems:

▶ Different schemas, formats, and goods receipt types must be processed. The different systems involved employ different interface technologies and communication types.

▶ The process is not automated. The auditor often manually interferes with the process, making the process inconsistent, because the auditor has to use several different systems.

▶ The process is prone to errors, because the auditor can simply forget an invoice that's included in the list of invoices to be verified.

▶ The process is time-consuming and cumbersome, as it tends to reduce the user's productivity and motivation.

The reason for this time-consuming and error-prone process is that a person acts as the process integrator, and not the software solution. In addition, changes of media types are another source of errors, because documents and information is forwarded automatically; rather, the person acting as a process integrator has influence on the processing of the data.

To attain process efficiency, the procedure — and above all, the information technology (IT) support of the invoice verification process — has changed significantly over time. The use of Internet technologies and new end-devices has considerably optimized the invoice verification process. For example, you can now use *optical character recognition* (OCR) software to scan invoices and display them in a portal, along with the data from the purchasing application and the goods receipt system. This way, different user interfaces (UIs) are merged into a uniform browser display. Thus, users no longer need to familiarize themselves with different application UIs, and can work more efficiently.

Similarly, you can integrate office applications in the portal solution; for example, to create a document for the supplier stating that an invoice has been rejected. This means that a person acting as the integration layer is required to improve the invoice verification process.

Integrating Information

The integration of a search engine in the portal enables fast searches through structured and unstructured documents; for example, to find additional invoices from the same supplier. In addition to providing extensive search options, the necessary components for integrating information must be able to merge different types of supplier master data, such as the supplier number maintained in different systems, into a cross-reference table. Moreover, the component should provide relevant information on the supplier in the way of analysis and reports. Sometimes, orders are not completely fulfilled, or the delivery occurs after the agreed upon date. To analyze such deviations at an aggregate level (for example, deviations of a supplier in New England within the last few months), you need an appropriate application.

Search through structured and unstructured data

These are typically the functions provided by a Business Intelligence (BI) solution. The source systems, such as the warehouse, the ordering system, or the accounting system, provide separate documents, such as purchase orders, goods receipt documents, and invoices that all pertain to the same purchase order. These documents are then imported into a data warehouse; for example, using an *Enterprise Application Infrastructure* (EAI) platform. The data warehouse allows you to consolidate the data and run certain analyses; furthermore, it lets you navigate the details of purchase orders to identify the cause of the deviation, a functionality that is made possible by InfoCubes and *operational data stores* (ODS).

Business intelligence

If an integration layer exists that combines consolidated and aggregated information with the business process, you can enhance the invoice verification process with an analysis function. Otherwise, the information can be displayed along with the operational data as embedded analysis for the user.

Integrating Processes

A third integration layer is necessary in the invoice verification process. In addition to integrating data from different systems, you'll need to determine when and under what circumstances individual systems and applications need to be integrated. As discussed in Chapter 1, Integrating Enterprise Information Systems, this is the central task of the PI layer.

What, when, and under what circumstances

Business process management

To continuously improve the process, you can use BPM functions. For example, BPM functions let you combine the individual steps of the invoice verification process to automate it or to reduce the lead times of individual processes. BPM functionality is another element within a PI layer, and represents an essential part of modern integration platforms.

Business process management and integration broker

SAP NetWeaver PI provides both functions — that of integration broker and BPM — into one integrated platform. Figure 2.2 shows how new technologies can be used to meet the specific integration requirements. As such, the relevant information (regardless of where it originates) is displayed in a standardized portal interface. Invoices have been digitalized upfront via OCR, and distributed through an EAI layer. PDF forms are interactively integrated for further processing, information can be forwarded via email whenever necessary, and you can launch the appropriate analyses and reports for specific data.

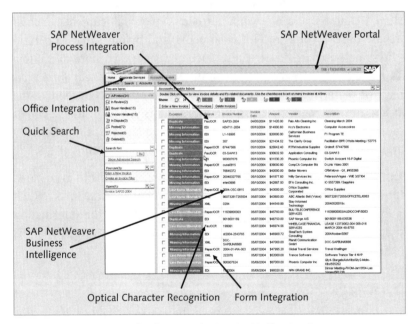

Figure 2.2 Using New Technologies in the Invoice Verification Process

Application Platform

Application server

Last but not least, different integration layers must run on one application platform. In this case, an application server is used. SAP NetWeaver

Application Server (AS) combines two traits: In addition to an infrastructure for program development and execution of SAP's own programming language, ABAP, it also allows you to develop Java 2 Enterprise Edition (J2EE) applications.

Lifecycle management plays an essential role for each of the components described here, as it ensures that the components are kept in a valid, up-to-date, viable, and usable state. This is accomplished with implementation tools, change management processes, software logistics, upgrade options, and installation aides.

2.1.2   SAP NetWeaver

The example of the invoice verification process has shown that real business processes are carried out across several applications that require different kinds of integration. SAP NetWeaver contains all of these integration layers, as shown in Figure 2.3.

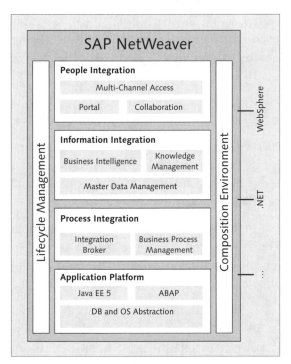

Figure 2.3 Integration Layers of SAP NetWeaver

Integration layers
As such, SAP NetWeaver represents the integration and application platform of SAP. In addition to SAP NetWeaver PI, you should also take into account all other SAP NetWeaver components when implementing integration projects.

As you can also see in Figure 2.3, SAP NetWeaver contains the *SAP NetWeaver Composition Environment* (CE), which provides design tools and methods, and services and processes that allow you to implement and operate *composite applications*. Composite applications are described in greater detail in Chapter 6, Section 6.4, Further Development of SAP NetWeaver PI.

The composition environment uses all components of SAP NetWeaver, and enables the integration of heterogeneous environments and *legacy applications*, particularly in strongly user-focused application environments.

SOA
SAP NetWeaver PI is used to enable a loose coupling of applications. The composition environment plays a major role in conjunction with service-oriented architectures (SOA). Chapter 6, Section 6.4, describes the role of SAP NetWeaver as a composite platform, how SAP NetWeaver evolves into the *business process platform* (BPP), and the central role of SAP NetWeaver PI.

2.1.3   SAP NetWeaver PI as a Central Infrastructure of SOAs

The architecture of SAP NetWeaver PI 7.1 is based on an established architecture for implementing cross-system business, and plays a central role in supporting an SOA for business applications. The focus is placed on the service-based integration of applications.

SOA
Functions of the individual applications are not "included" in the application anymore, but offered by the application as a callable service. In doing so, the design, creation, classification, and the use of standardized services is supported by an SOA. For this, SAP offers the following tools:

▶ The compilation of services — for example, the ARIS Business Designer or the Enterprise Services Repository — can be used, as can functions of the SOA management that enable creation and maintenance of services.

▸ For storing metadata and managing enterprise services, SAP provides the Enterprise Services Repository and Services Registry, which also has a central role for SAP NetWeaver PI.

▸ The service bus and the PI runtime provide the infrastructure for distributing messages, and is also part of SAP NetWeaver PI.

▸ The consumption of services is realized using the aforementioned Services Registry. The registry contains metadata about the services, and is comparable to Universal Description, Discovery, and Integration (UDDI).

▸ In addition, SAP offers executable enterprise services that are delivered standard with the product.

Thus, not only is an architecture (environment) available, but a "ready-to-run" SOA.

Software components from SAP applications are provided as a service. An enterprise service (for example, the check of material stock, retrieval of customer data, etc.) provides context-oriented business logic.

2.1.4   IT Practices

Whereas the previous sections of this chapter described the components of SAP NetWeaver, the following sections introduce you to a new SAP concept, offering you a new perspective on SAP NetWeaver: IT practices. The concept is presented here, because the technical capabilities of SAP NetWeaver components, such as SAP NetWeaver PI, are (intentionally) moved to the background when talking about IT practices and scenarios.

IT practices make it easier for developers to present the added value of technological components to the user department. Thus, the role of IT can change from a passive one that acts only upon request, to an active one that participates in the decision-making process by suggesting easier, and often more efficient, processes.

New perspective on IT

In the past, the SAP NetWeaver diagram shown in Figure 2.3 has often been referred to as the "refrigerator." One way to think of SAP NetWeaver is as a fridge, from which you take individual components from "compartments" to create an application. In essence, you "help yourself" by taking out of SAP NetWeaver what you need to "create your meal."

However, this analogy isn't very useful if you want to create a link between the perspective of various user departments and the IT department to the application landscape and business processes; the user departments often don't have any insight into the technical architecture on which the applications are based, while the IT department usually isn't familiar with the business processes. In other words, the IT department may know what is in the fridge, but it may not know which meals it can prepare with the ingredients.

IT practices allow companies to effectively combine the requirements of user departments with IT solutions. Therefore, IT practices provide specific solutions for implementing business requirements by means of IT.

End-to-end process integration

For this reason, SAP has closed the "fridge," and cut it into slices that represent 10 essential IT practices. Figure 2.4 illustrates these 10 IT practices, with specific emphasis on end-to-end process integration in which the technical components of SAP NetWeaver PI are largely used.

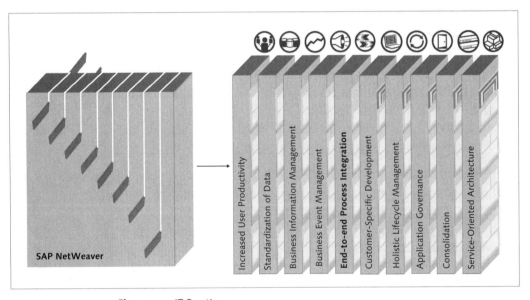

Figure 2.4 IT Practices

IT practices illustrate how IT can create business applications and processes. For example, a process containing data from the business warehouse can begin in the portal and send a message to SAP NetWeaver PI, eventually integrating suppliers in the business process. IT practices contain integrated and predefined IT scenarios, based on SAP NetWeaver components, and geared toward core enterprise business tasks. For example, IT practices allow a higher degree of information transparency (business information management) or solve problems inherent in implementations across different platforms (holistic lifecycle management).

In the next step, the IT scenarios lead toward the perspective of the user departments. Table 2.1 shows the IT scenarios of IT end-to-end PI.

IT scenarios

Enabling A2A Processes	Enabling B2B Processes	BPM	Enabling Platform Interoperability	Business Task Management
▸ A2A Integration	▸ Business Partner Integration Using Industry Standards ▸ Small Business Partner and Subsidiary Integration	▸ Usage and Adaptation of Predefined Content ▸ Process Automation ▸ Combining Embedded and Unbounded Processes	▸ Enabling Co-Existence of Several Portals ▸ Ensuring A2A and B2B Integration ▸ Providing Web Services Interoperability ▸ Managing Heterogeneous System Landscapes ▸ Development of SAP NetWeaver-compliant applications	▸ Central Access to Tasks ▸ Support for Offline Processes

Table 2.1 IT Scenarios and Scenario Variants of End-to-End PI

Within the IT scenarios, business departments address their requests to the IT department; for example, how industry standards such as RosettaNet or CIDX are mapped in a B2B scenario, or how small partners or subsidiaries are integrated. Both examples are variants of the IT scenario Enabling B2B Processes. A variant of an IT scenario consists of a set of IT processes that let you accomplish specific business goals.

B2B integration   For example, in a B2B integration (according to the RosettaNet standard), you must configure the system landscape, install the RosettaNet Business Package that contains the necessary RosettaNet processes (PIP), and configure and monitor the connection to the RosettaNet partner.

SAP customers can implement IT practices step-by-step with corresponding projects. In this context, you must decide which SAP NetWeaver components are needed to implement a specific IT scenario (or IT scenario variant), because you won't always need to install the entire SAP NetWeaver stack.

2.2   Functionality of SAP NetWeaver PI

In this section, we discuss the operation mode of release 7.1, and then focus on the individual components and objects of SAP NetWeaver PI. A simplified integration scenario is used to illustrate how communication between two systems takes place and what tasks are addressed.

The main purpose of SAP NetWeaver PI is to forward inbound messages to the appropriate receivers. At first glance, this task may not seem very demanding: For each inbound message, the appropriate receiver determines who receives the message.

However, if you consider that messages are often sent in different protocols, and that even within a specific protocol there are numerous ways to map a message, the message distribution process becomes more complex. Therefore, to properly distribute messages, SAP NetWeaver PI must also act as a data converter. Messages must be converted from one protocol to another and from one type of presentation to another.

According to the *shared collaboration knowledge* principle, all of the information handled in this process should be managed centrally. An inbound message does not contain any information on the target system. This information is instead derived with a complex set of rules consisting of the message format, the sender, and the message content.

Shared collaboration knowledge

Figure 2.5 illustrates the communication between two software components via an IS.

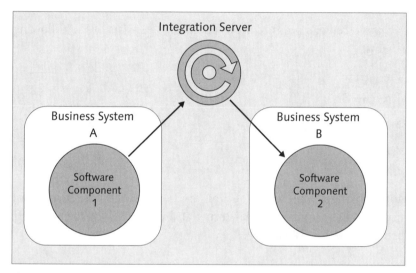

Figure 2.5 Sender and Receiver Communicate via an IS

Using a specific example, the following sections trace the path of a message and distribution process as carried out by SAP NetWeaver PI.

2.2.1 Address Example

Let's suppose that a sending system distributes address data to different receiving systems, and for each zip code there is only one responsible receiving system. The sending system sends the addresses exclusively as Simple Object Access Protocol (SOAP) documents; the receiving systems processes different formats. The system that's responsible for zip code area *1xxxx* is an internal SAP system that only communicates via intermediate documents (IDocs).

Introductory example

From the sender's point of view, an address consists of the following elements:

► Name (first and last name)

► Title (Mr., Ms., etc.)

► Street

► City

► Zip code

From the receiver's point of view, an address consists of the following elements:

► First name

► Last name

► Street

► Zip code

► City

Before looking at the details of how the IS handles the addresses, we must introduce some essential terms and concepts you'll encounter when using SAP NetWeaver PI.

2.2.2 Classification of Messages

Data converter

Messages can be sent and received in different protocols: as email, as a file, as a SOAP document, as an IDoc, as a Java Message Service (JMS) or Common Object Request Broker Architecture (CORBA) document, and so on. As a data converter, an IS must be able to convert such formats into each other. For this, the SAP IS first translates all inbound messages into a SAP NetWeaver PI–internal format, which we'll refer to as the *SAP NetWeaver PI format* from now on. This is a special XML format for SAP NetWeaver PI. Only when the document leaves the IS will it be translated into the format that's expected by the receiver. This procedure ensures that all messages exist in a uniform format within the IS (the SAP NetWeaver PI format).

As such, adapters must be available for each supported format. The adapters are responsible for translating messages into the SAP NetWeaver PI format (and vice versa). From the IS's point of view, the protocols only differ by the adapters used for the translation to the SAP NetWeaver PI format. The *adapter types* of a message are discussed in the following sections.

In the SAP NetWeaver PI format, each message has a concrete data type, which describes the elements and attributes of which the related messages consist. From a technical viewpoint, the data types are described as XSD documents. They define simple or complex XML data structures that can be built using an editor or imported. The structure of the data type is determined by its classification.

There are several types of data types, such as:

Data types

▶ The definition of Core Data Types (CDT) and aggregated data types complies with the UN/CEFACT Core Component Technical Specification (see ISO 15000-5), which provides a methodology for semantic data modeling to achieve a common understanding of data structures and message types on a syntax-independent level. SAP supports these standards; for example, to define global data types (GDT) as the basis for business objects and enterprise services. Thus, the implementation of cross-company processes can be greatly facilitated. The GDTs that are created as core data types or aggregated data types in the Enterprise Services Repository are designed to be reused in many application scenarios. Thus, the CDTs can be described as context-free.

▶ In free-modeled data types, there are basic data types that define the properties of elementary fields. Several of these fields can be summarized in a complex data type. They describe the structure of a node in an XML document. Thus, it is possible to build nested data types. When defining the data type, the user specifies how many instances of a node may occur (cardinalities) at runtime. The free-modeled data types only support the XML schema language elements (such as strings or integers). Built-in data types are included in the language range of XML schema and use the prefix *xsd*.

The address example uses the data types displayed in Figures 2.6 and 2.7.

Name	Category	Type	Occurrence	Details
▼ DT_Address1	Complex Type			
Name	Element	xsd:string	1	maxLength="50"
Title	Element	xsd:string	1	
Street	Element	xsd:string	1	maxLength="50"
City	Element	xsd:string	1	maxLength="50"
PostalCode	Element	xsd:integer	1	totalDigits="5"

Figure 2.6 Data Type of Address1 Presented by the Enterprise Services Repository

Name	Category	Type	Occurrence	Details
▼ DT_Address2	Complex Type			
LastName	Element	xsd:string	1	maxLength="40"
FirstName	Element	xsd:string	1..unbounded	maxLength="40"
Street	Element	xsd:string	1	maxLength="40"
PostalCode	Element	xsd:integer	1	totalDigits="5"
City	Element	xsd:string	1	maxLength="40"

Figure 2.7 Data Type of Address2 Presented by the Enterprise Services Repository

To describe a concrete message in SAP NetWeaver PI, the data type's information must indicate whether the message was inbound or outbound. This *communication category* is always described from the viewpoint of the connected system, not of the IS. Messages sent to the IS are referred to as *outbound messages*, while those sent by the IS are referred to as *inbound messages*. From SAP NetWeaver PI's point of view, inbound messages are referred to as *inbound interfaces*, whereas outbound messages are called *outbound interfaces*.

Synchronous and asynchronous communication

Finally, the *communication mode* must contain information as to whether the message sender expects an immediate response (*synchronous* communication mode) or whether the sender keeps on working regardless of any response by the receiver (*asynchronous* communication mode).

As you may have noticed, the address example uses the asynchronous communication mode. Thus, addresses that arrive in the IS as SOAP documents are asynchronous outbound messages of the SOAP adapter type and Address1 data type. Messages sent by the IS, on the other hand, are asynchronous inbound messages of the IDoc adapter type and Address2 data type, as illustrated in Figure 2.8.

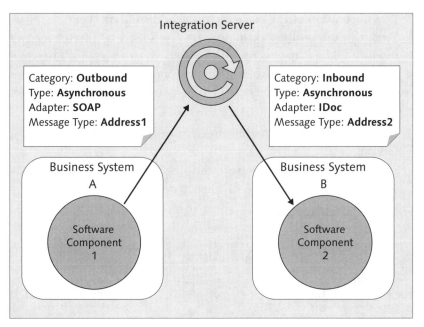

Figure 2.8 Address Example

The following subtasks must be carried out to distribute an inbound message:

Distributing a message

1. **Translation of the inbound message to the internal SAP NetWeaver PI format**
   Basically, two adapters are available for each format processed by SAP NetWeaver PI. These adapters are responsible for translating between the SAP NetWeaver PI format and the external format. The adapters are integrated in SAP NetWeaver PI via an Adapter Framework that can also be used to integrate project-specific adapters. The adapter sends the message in SAP NetWeaver PI format to the IS.

2. **Receiver determination/interface determination**
   The IS uses a complex set of rules to determine the receiver and the interface being used. The rules are based on the following elements:

   ▶ Sender details (if known)

   ▶ Message type

   ▶ Message content

3. **Transformation of the message in the derived data types**
   Similar to our address example, data types used by the sender and receiver seldom match. For this reason, you can store transformation rules (mappings) when defining data types. These transformation rules are then used by the IS to translate messages into the target format.

4. **Translation of the outbound message into the outbound message format**
   The appropriate adapter converts the message from the SAP NetWeaver PI format into the receiver format and sends the message.

Figure 2.9 illustrates this process.

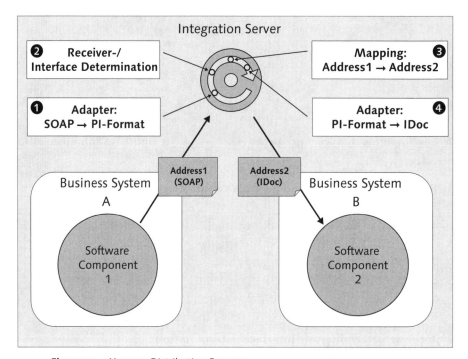

Figure 2.9 Message Distribution Process

2.2.3   Steps for Implementing a Message Flow

If you want to implement a new message path in SAP NetWeaver PI, it is useful to divide the preliminary and actual implementation work in two different task areas. However, before the actual message flows can be implemented, some preparatory work must be carried out:

▶ **Technical configuration**
The technical configuration is responsible for setting up the SAP NetWeaver PI system and integrating it with the existing SAP landscape. In particular, different technical remote function call (RFC) connections must be set up and assigned to each other in the SAP NetWeaver PI system and connected SAP systems so the following processes can be implemented:

  ▶ Generation of proxies from the SAP NetWeaver PI system in the connected SAP systems

  ▶ Exchange of RFC messages between the SAP NetWeaver PI system and connected systems

  ▶ Central monitoring

▶ **Design**
In the next step, different design objects in the System Landscape Directory (SLD) are created. These are, for example, the required software components or products. In addition, the necessary data types, message types, service interfaces, and mappings between these objects are described.

Design time

Entry of this information does not depend on any concrete implementation; in other words, it doesn't depend on the involved systems. The previously mentioned objects can be developed in SAP NetWeaver PI or imported from external systems, and they are managed in the *Enterprise Services repository*. In the address example, the two address formats and the transformations between the formats are entered in this step.

Another part of the implementation after the creation of abstract messages flows is the configuration of specific message flows.

▶ **Configuration**

To dispatch concrete messages, you must configure the abstract message flow for concrete systems. For this you'll need to enter the concrete integration partners and store the rules for the receiver determination. If necessary, you must complement adapter data (such as Web services). All configuration data is stored in the integration directory.

In our address example, detailed information on the sending system and the receiving systems are stored in this step. Moreover, you must enter rules that enable the sending system to derive the appropriate receiver, the message type, and the communication channel from an address' zip code that has been received.

▶ **Runtime**

Now that all configuration objects have been maintained for the message flows, the different integration scenarios can be executed. This phase is referred to as the runtime.

It is now possible to send messages to the SAP NetWeaver PI system; these messages are then forwarded to the appropriate receiver(s). A comprehensive monitoring concept is necessary to control these processes as you need to identify errors in the message flow. Inbound and outbound messages must be monitored for all involved components (adapters, IS, and so on). The Runtime Workbench and the SAP NetWeaver Administrator, who will cover all monitoring tasks, are available for this purpose.

In the address example, it is important to analyze inbound SOAP documents, inbound and outbound internal SAP NetWeaver PI documents, and the IDocs sent by the IDoc adapter.

2.3 Components

The SAP NetWeaver XI consists of several components. The individual components are shown in Figure 2.10. They are explained in detail in the following sections. Particular attention is paid to the functionalities of each component and an overview of their application is given.

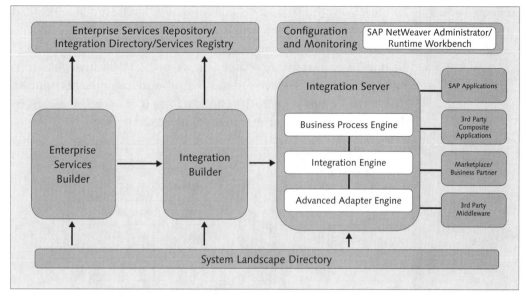

Figure 2.10 Architecture of SAP NetWeaver PI (Release 7.1)

2.3.1 SLD

The SLD maps the internal system landscape. This includes the involved systems and their interrelationships (for instance, which system acts as the IS), and the software products installed in the system landscape.

Maintenance of the system landscape

When recording systems, you need to distinguish between technical systems and business systems. In the case of SAP systems, the SAP installation is mapped as a technical system, while the associated clients (logical systems) are mapped as business systems. For ABAP systems, there can be a business system for each client. In addition to SAP systems, you can also record any other system in the SLD.

The separation between technical and business systems holds a significant advantage: Because business systems, instead of technical systems, are referenced, changes to the IT infrastructure (for example, the migration of a system on a new hardware) have no effect on integration scenarios in SAP NetWeaver PI. Thus, changes in the system environment can be performed without causing significant maintenance work on the SAP NetWeaver PI system.

Software products
and software
components The software products active in the system landscape are recorded regardless of the system on which they are installed. In this context, you can record different components for each software product, and different versions for each software component. Figure 2.11 illustrates the relationship between software products and software components using an ERP Central Component (ECC) system (release 6.0) with SAP ERP HCM (also release 6.0) as its corresponding software component.

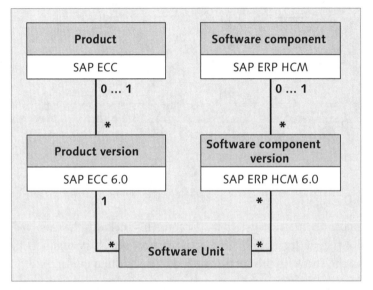

Figure 2.11 Software Product (Versions) and Software Component (Versions)

Unlike the software products and software components (versions) that are visible in the SLD, the software feature (software unit) has no visible object. In a second step, software components installed on the system are assigned to each business system.

All business systems can be referenced later as message senders or receivers while configuring message flows. If you think of the communication with external systems, it becomes evident that not every possible message receiver must be recorded in the SLD.

Table 2.2 provides a brief overview of the properties of the SLD.

SLD Profile	
Tasks	Mapping of application systems and software products used in the company
Data	Internal systems Software products and software product versions Software components (versions)
Affected Processes	Design phase: import of SAP objects Configuration: sender/receiver of messages Runtime
Required Maintenance	During the installation of the SAP NetWeaver PI system Future extensions of the system landscape Installation of new software products/releases

Table 2.2 SLD

2.3.2 Enterprise Services Repository and Services Registry

The Enterprise Services Repository stores formal descriptions of all messages that can be processed by SAP NetWeaver PI. These include, among others, the data types and the required transformations between data types. As such, the Enterprise Services Repository provides all metadata available at design time, and represents the central data basis for the IS for its role as a data converter.

Enterprise services repository

The integration processes are also defined in the Enterprise Services Repository. Once all of the necessary objects (for example, service interfaces) are defined, integration processes can be created using the process editor. It is a cross-system process for processing messages.

Starting with release 7.1, the Enterprise Services Repository in SAP NetWeaver PI is not only a tool for storing metadata, but also contains a registry. The Services Registry is a registry similar to the Yellow Pages for Web services. It is a central component of the SOA landscape, and includes — in addition to the services and service definitions — references to the Web Service Description Language (WSDL) metadata, the callable service endpoints, and the service provider.

Services registry

The services stored therein can be arranged by classification. This is especially useful when looking for registered services. In addition to searching for services, the registry also supports the implementation of new services. Administrators can find available service endpoints and manage the connections between consumer and provider systems. The Services Registry is UDDI 3.0 compliant and thus supports not only solutions from SAP, but also non-SAP services.

As shown in Figure 2.12, both components, the Enterprise Services Repository and the Services Registry, interact; only a portion of a service description data (for example, the WSDL document) is stored in the Services Registry. Associated objects, such as XSD documents, are located in the Enterprise Services Repository.

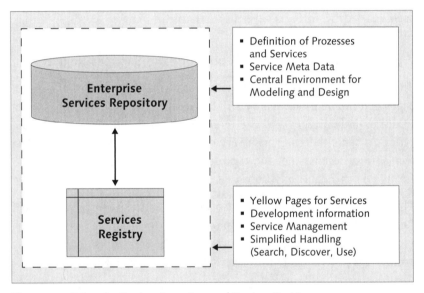

Figure 2.12 Enterprise Services Repository and Services Registry

The Services Registry, in contrast to the Enterprise Services Repository, is an optional component of SAP NetWeaver PI.

Table 2.3 contains the profile of the Enterprise Services Repository; Table 2.4 provides a brief overview of the Services Registry.

Enterprise Services Repository Profile	
Tasks	Provision of definitions and metadata of enterprise services and an integrated modeling environment for enterprise services, data types, mappings, and other design objects, such as integration processes
Data	Integration processes
	Interfaces
	Data types
	Message types
	Workspace
	Transformations (mappings)
Affected Processes	IS
	Adapter Framework
	Service registry
Required Maintenance	During message and object design for communication

Table 2.3 Enterprise Services Repository

Services Registry Profile	
Tasks	Registry to make Web services available
Data	Services
	Service definitions
	WSDL Documents
Affected Processes	IS
	Publishing of services
	Enterprise services repository
Required Maintenance	Define service endpoints
	Services

Table 2.4 Services Registry

2.3.3 Integration Directory

In the integration directory, configuration data is stored for runtime. Design objects stored in the Enterprise Services Repository are enriched

Configuration data in the integration directory

with data from the actual system landscape, to enable both A2A and B2B processes at runtime.

The necessary communication components (business system, business component, and integration) are stored here, and can act as a sender or receiver of messages. Integration processes, which run on the *Business Process Engine* (BPE) of the IS, know at design time where a message comes from and where it goes. Unlike these processes, business systems and business components have to be enriched with additional information in the integration directory. The business systems in the integration directory refer to business systems in the SLD, and can be imported from there.

Communication channel
To define how a sender or receiver communication component is reached, the *communication channel* has to be maintained. In addition, the integration directory provides the set of rules based on which the system can derive the appropriate receiver(s) and message formats for an inbound message.

Another part of the integration directory is to configure the communication between Web service providers and Web service consumers. All of the information that was collected in the integration directory at configuration time is available in the caches of the Integration Engine (IE) (or the *Advanced Adapter Engine* (AAE)), and can be used at runtime.

Table 2.5 contains the profile of the integration directory.

Integration Directory Profile	
Tasks	Storage of communication components
	Storage of a set of rules to derive receivers and message formats from inbound messages
Data	Derivation rules
	Sender and receiver descriptions
	Direct connections
Affected Processes	IS
	Adapter Framework

Table 2.5 Integration Directory

Integration Directory Profile	
Required Maintenance	Configuration of message flows
	Configuration of direct connections
	Entry of communication components

Table 2.5 Integration Directory (Cont.)

2.3.4 Runtime Workbench

The Runtime Workbench provides numerous tools that support the troubleshooting process:

▶ A component monitoring function allows you to check the connections to all systems involved. This also includes locally installed AAEs and decentralized IEs (on backend systems).

Monitoring in the Runtime Workbench

▶ A message monitoring function provides you with access to all messages processed by SAP NetWeaver PI. It lets you check the status of messages and analyze errors that occur. By default, this is only possible for asynchronous scenarios; for synchronous scenarios, you must configure it separately.

▶ The end-to-end monitoring function allows you to monitor the path of a concrete message through SAP NetWeaver PI. The end-to-end monitoring offers two views on data. First, the process overview, which displays the total number of processed or erroneous messages for each component involved. And second, the instance point of view, which shows you the path of a message through the components involved. In the latter, you can display detailed information for each processing step.

▶ The alert configuration informs you about errors during message processing. The alert inbox lists the faulty processing operations. It is also possible that administrators can be notified via email, fax, or short message service (SMS). However, you should be careful; during the installation of SAP NetWeaver PI and message flows, numerous problems occur that could lead to a flood of messages.

The Runtime Workbench profile can be found in Table 2.6.

Runtime Workbench Profile	
Tasks	Tool to monitor the SAP NetWeaver PI and its components, processes and messages Tools for performance analysis
Data	SLD BPE Adapter engines (central and noncentral) IEs (central and local) Enterprise Services Repository Integration Directory
Affected Processes	Component monitoring Message monitoring End-to-end monitoring Computing Center Management System (CCMS)
Required Maintenance	Alert configuration Error handling

Table 2.6 Runtime Workbench

2.3.5 SAP NetWeaver Administrator (NWA)

The SAP NWA serves as a central monitoring tool, enabling users to monitor the entire system landscape beyond the functions of the runtime workbench. The NWA is supposed to be the future of overall monitoring for all SAP solutions (based on SAP NetWeaver). It will succeed the Visual Administrator and include all of its relevant functions. Because the SAP NWA is a Web-based tool, you'll save yourself the local software installation that was required for the Visual Administrator.

The following workspaces are available in SAP NWA:

Components of the NWA

- *Operation Management* enables the general administration of components and users.

- *Configuration Management* enables configuration, management of virtual servers, Web services, and UDDI servers.

- *Availability & Performance Management* enables monitoring of runtime parameters.

- *Problem Management* provides different administration tools (log viewer, etc.).

- *SOA Management* provides services for configuring, administrating, and monitoring message distribution.

The SAP NWA profile can be found in Table 2.7.

SAP NWA Profile	
Tasks	Tool for administration, monitoring, and problem analysis
Data	SAP NetWeaver system landscape
Affected Processes	Component monitoring
	Message monitoring
	Performance monitoring
	End-to-end monitoring
Required Maintenance	Check and set configuration settings
	Administration of instances
	Analysis of log files and traces
	Alert configuration

Table 2.7 SAP NWA

The SAP NWA and its functions will not be discussed in more detail at this point; this subject is discussed in more detail in Chapter 3, Basic System Configuration.

2.3.6 IS

The IS is within SAP NetWeaver PI, and is the central location for processing incoming messages and forwarding them to the appropriate target systems. It represents the central component of the SAP NetWeaver PI system for runtime.

Components of the ISs

This section deals with the setup of the IS, its components, and the various steps of message processing. Moreover, the concept and operation of the AAE are illustrated, and the difference between a centralized and decentralized IE is explained. In addition, the IE and the processing of SAP NetWeaver PI messages, and the different steps of message processing, are covered. Finally, we'll explain the BPE, another part of the IS, which manages correlations and the processing of messages in the context of BPM.

Advanced Adapter Engine (AAE)

The AAE is necessary to connect SAP systems and applications, or third-party applications, to the SAP NetWeaver PI system. The AAE is, as its name suggests, an extension of the previous versions of the adapter engine; "advanced" refers to the functionalities added since SAP NetWeaver PI 7.1 (see Section 2.6).

The IE is responsible for processing the messages on the IS. You have the option of directly addressing the AAE using proxy technology[1] from systems that support this connection type. Should this not be the case, you need adapters to convert the messages from an external format into the SAP NetWeaver PI format.

(Advanced) Adapter Engine

The AAE is a standard software component of the central IS. However, additional noncentral AAEs can be installed. This is usually done for performance reasons (e.g., load balancing), or existing network constraints (e.g., firewalls, etc.).

The AAE on the Java connector architecture (JCo), runs on SAP NetWeaver AS Java (Java-Stack), and provides the runtime environment for most adapters. Figure 2.13 shows an overview of the aforementioned scenarios.

Adapter Framework

The Adapter Framework provides the foundation of the adapter engine. The framework, and the AAE, is based on the AS Java and the JCo. It provides interfaces to configure, manage, and monitor the adapter, and allows for the connection of both SAP and non-SAP systems. The AAE provides a comprehensive set of adapters that are supplied by SAP. However, many other third-party adapters can also be implemented.

---

1 The proxy technology is part of the SAP NetWeaver PI connectivity and enables communication between the systems and the central IE.

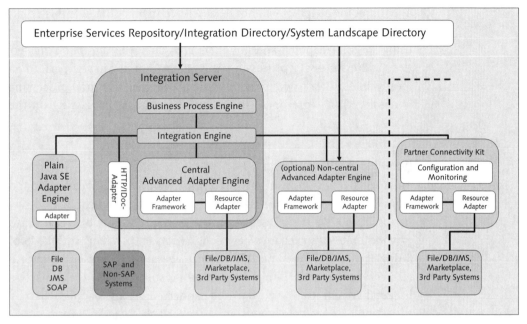

Figure 2.13 SAP NetWeaver PI Connectivity

The following adapters are already delivered by SAP:

▶ The RFC adapter is used to communicate with SAP systems.

▶ The File/FTP adapter enables the exchange of data and files with external systems.

▶ The Java Database Connectivity (JDBC) adapter provides access to databases.

▶ The Business Connector (BC) adapter enables communication with the SAP BC.

▶ The SOAP adapter is used for integrating Web services.

▶ The JMS adapter enables communication with the JMS application programming interface (API).

▶ The Marketplace adapter connects marketplaces to the IE.

▶ The Mail adapter ensures access to email servers.

▶ The CIDX adapter supports the Chem eStandard.

▶ The RNIF adapter enables communication via RosettaNet standard.

The preceding adapters will not be described in more detail at this point; in Chapter 4, Technical Exercises, we discuss how systems are connected using specific adapters, and how data is exchanged. The following sections address message processing. With the AAE, this can also performed locally, in contrast to the previous adapter engine. This local processing is described in more detail in Section 2.6.1, Local Processing on the AAE.

Integration Engine (IE)

Central and noncentral

The IE is part of the runtime environment of SAP NetWeaver PI, and is used for message processing in accordance with the configured scenarios. There is a basic distinction between a central and a local IE; to provide a message exchange between the backend systems and the IS of SAP NetWeaver PI (central IE), the message must be presented in SAP NetWeaver PI format. Either this protocol is supported by the respective backend system itself, or it must be connected via an adapter, whereby the adapter makes the conversion to the SAP NetWeaver PI format.

Application systems that have a local IE can directly exchange messages with the IS (central IE) of SAP NetWeaver PI, and do not need an adapter for converting the messages into SAP NetWeaver PI format. These systems can act as both a transmitter and receiver of messages in the SAP NetWeaver PI format, but they have no integration logic. Neither routing nor mapping functions can be performed locally. This continues to be done by the (central) IS of the SAP NetWeaver PI system, which is called by the application system. The local IE is available since release 6.20 of SAP Web Application Server (WAS) (via add-ons), for ABAP and for the Java stack, and can be used to exchange data using proxy technology.

Messages that are already in the internal SAP NetWeaver PI format are passed by the respective adapters or by using proxy technology via HTTP(S) to the IE,[2] processed there, and forwarded.

Pipeline processing

Message processing takes place in the pipeline, which is a defined sequence of steps (*pipeline elements*) a message runs through. During processing, these elements call services that provide functionalities, such as reading or processing messages. The type, number, and sequence of

---

2 From now on, we use the term "IE" to refer to the central IE.

these services are fixed for each pipeline and cannot be changed. Figure 2.14 shows some pipeline steps (some elements are left out for clarity).

The following list briefly highlights the individual processing steps; not every single step is explained explicitly at this point. A detailed look at some of these processing steps can be found in Section 2.5 and Section 2.6.

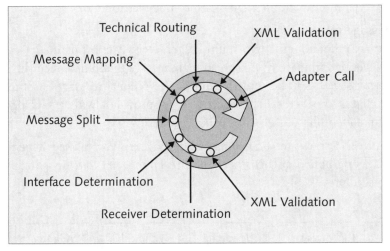

Figure 2.14 Pipeline Processing in the IE

▶ **XML validation**
Since SAP NetWeaver PI 7.1, the system validates the message payload; by means of stored XML schema files, messages can be tested for their syntactic correctness. Detailed information can be found in Section 2.6.4, XML Validation.

Validation of the message payload

▶ **Logical routing**
Logical routing includes both the receiver and the interface determination. During the receiver determination step, all of the valid receivers of a message are identified. This is done using configuration objects stored in the cache. The SAP NetWeaver PI message is enriched with the appropriate receivers (communication components), and the choice of the receiver can be determined depending on the contents of the message, where you can enter as many recipients as you want.

Receiver and interface determination

The settings are stored in the configuration object in the Integration Directory.

In the pipeline service of the interface determination, the valid receiver interfaces are determined. The service interfaces (formerly message interfaces) determine in which format the incoming message will be forwarded to the recipient, and which mappings have to be used for the transformation. For one incoming message, several messages (with different message types) can be distributed.

▶ **Message split**

Multiple receiver

For an inbound message, multiple receivers can be defined (see receiver determination). To spread that message to multiple receivers, the message has to be copied *n* times. The original message is set to the status `completed`, and each copy is provided with a globally unique identifier (GUID) for further processing.

Figure 2.15 shows the branching of a message. As you can see, in general, an outbound queue is opened for each receiver to allow parallel message processing.

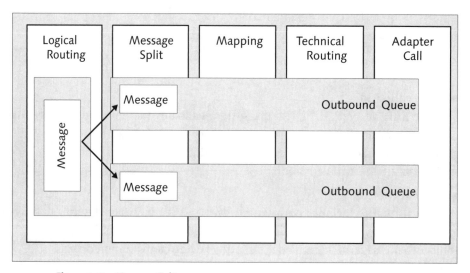

Figure 2.15 Message Split

90

▶ **Message mapping**

In most cases, the structure of the incoming message does not match the message structure expected by the receiver. In these cases, a mapping is needed to map the two different structures to each other. SAP NetWeaver PI offers several possibilities for how this mapping can be realized. For more information about mapping, see Section 2.5.7, Mappings.

Different structures

▶ **Technical routing**

Technical routing determines the technical receiver of a message, and stores how the generated message should be sent. A technical routing contains both the *receiver agreement* and the *communication channel*. The receiver agreement determines how a message is transformed so it can be processed by the receiver. The communication channel contains the technical parameters for sending the message to the receiver system. Because the receiver can receive a message in a variety of ways (for example, the message could be saved as a file on the file system of the receiver, or data could be written directly into the local database), for each of these scenarios, a corresponding communication channel must be defined.

Technical receiver of a message

▶ **Adapter call**

In the last step of the pipeline processing, the target system is called via the appropriate adapter.

Target system call

Business Process Engine (BPE)

In complex system processes, stateless message processing on the IS is not always sufficient. At design time, developers implement *integration processes* in the Enterprise Services Repository to correlate messages and handle more complex processes using loops. At configuration time, the modeled processes are imported into the Integration Directory and adapted to the specific system landscape. At runtime, the IS executes these processes on the BPE, and stores information about already-started and ongoing processes.

A central part of the runtime environment of cross-component Business Process Management (ccBPM) is the BPE. Figure 2.16 shows an overview of the architecture of SAP NetWeaver PI 7.1 in relation to ccBPM.

Architecture

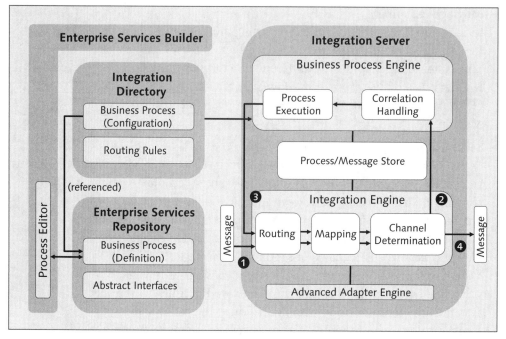

Figure 2.16 Architecture of SAP NetWeaver PI in Relation to ccBPM

The implemented processes are usually based on the message processing of the different applications in the system landscape. The four steps in Figure 2.16 show the close relationship between the IE and the BPE:

▸ The messages are sent from any sender to the IE (❶).

▸ There the message is processed and passed to the BPE (❷). The correlation handling checks whether there is already a process instance for that message, and if it can be assigned to this instance.

▸ After the message is processed on the BPE, it is passed back to the IE (❸).

▸ There it is reprocessed and sent to a corresponding receiver (❹).

Workflows The BPE only communicates with the applications of backend systems through messages. It has no access to processes, the user, or organizational management within the application systems. However, the BPE is closely linked to the workflow engine of SAP systems. At runtime, workflows are automatically generated from integration processes that are running on the affected application systems (for example, in SAP ECC 6.0). An integration process may send messages to the workflow engine; it can also process messages from the workflow engine.

2.4   Objects

Now that you've had a brief overview of the SAP NetWeaver PI components, let's look at the objects you'll use to map a message distribution process.

The organizational unit that groups all design objects is the *software component*. Software components are recorded in the SLD and contain a component name, a component version, and a reference to a software product that consists of a vendor, product name, and product version.

Each software component must be assigned to the technical systems on which it is installed. Typical examples of software components include the components of an R/3 system; SAP delivers the components of its products with the corresponding definitions.

Software components in the Enterprise Services Repository

2.4.1   Software Products in the Enterprise Services Repository

In the address example, the first task is to create the software product PI Book and the software component Addressallocation, both of which have version number 1. From a technical viewpoint, the software component corresponds to the development class of previous ECC systems, or to the packages in Java development. Software components can then be assigned to technical systems in the SLD, and activated for the business systems on which they're installed.

To define integration scenarios within a software component, you must first import the relevant software component into the integration repository. There you can assign it one or more namespaces, which can contain the development objects described in the following sections. Apart from that, you can specify the SAP system you can import interfaces from, such as RFC modules or IDocs, if necessary.

Integration scenario

Create the namespace http://www.sap-press.com/PI/Adressallocation in the address example. Figure 2.17 displays the resulting software product. Because the practical part of this book details how the individual objects are created, this section just provides a quick overview of the process.

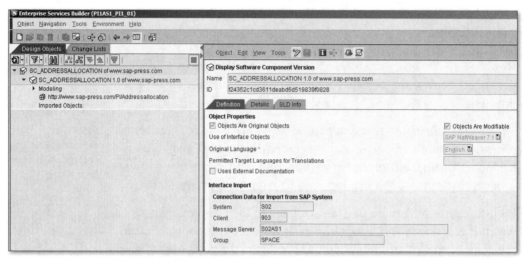

Figure 2.17 Software Component and Corresponding Namespace in the Enterprise Services Repository

2.4.2 Service Interfaces and Mapping Objects in the Enterprise Services Repository

Service interface This section describes the required interfaces. In the address example, a system sends an address in `Address1` format, which will be distributed in `Address2` format. From the external systems point of view, there is an outbound interface in the `Address1` format, and an inbound interface in the `Address2` format. These are created as service interfaces (formerly message interfaces) in SAP NetWeaver PI. A service interface consists of the following elements:

▸ A name

▸ A description

▸ A category (inbound/outbound/abstract)

▸ A mode (synchronous/asynchronous)

- An interface pattern (stateless XI 3.0–compatible, stateless, stateful, Tentative Update & Confirm/Compensate (TU&C/C))

- One or more roles (request, response, fault)

The category specifies whether messages are sent through the interface to (outbound) or from (inbound) SAP NetWeaver PI. If a format is used for both inbound and outbound messages, it must be recorded in the system twice. The mode indicates whether or not a response to a message is expected (synchronous or asynchronous mode).

Message types describe the exact data format of the interface. Depending on the communication type (inbound/outbound) and communication mode (synchronous/asynchronous), one or more of the following roles must be specified:

Message type

- **Request**
  Data format of the message received by the SAP NetWeaver PI system (this information is required for outbound messages and all synchronous messages).

- **Response**
  Data format of the message sent from the SAP NetWeaver PI system (this information is required for inbound messages and all synchronous messages).

- **Fault**
  Data format in which processing information (for example, in the case of erroneous processing) is sent from the SAP NetWeaver PI system (this information is possible for inbound messages and all synchronous messages).

For technical reasons, the service interface is not directly assigned to the used data types. Instead, the message types simply contain a description and the data type. With the exception of data types used to define hierarchical data types, each data type is referenced by at least one message type.

The address example contains two different data types: The first address format (Address1) contains a name field that includes both the first and last name, whereas the second address format (Address2) contains separate fields for the first and last name. Corresponding data types are internally stored as XSD documents; they can either be imported or recorded via a data type editor. For each field, you must enter the following information:

▶ A denominator

▶ A category (complex type or element)

▶ A type (XSD type or a previously defined data type)

▶ A cardinality (1 or n)

▶ If necessary, type-specific details; for example, the length of strings

Mapping objects At design time, you must also enter the conversion rules for the interfaces. As shown in Figure 2.18, two different mapping objects exist:

▶ **Message mapping**
Message mapping specifies how to transform a message from one data type into another. Technically speaking, message mappings are XSLT documents that can either be imported or entered via the mapping editor contained in SAP NetWeaver PI.

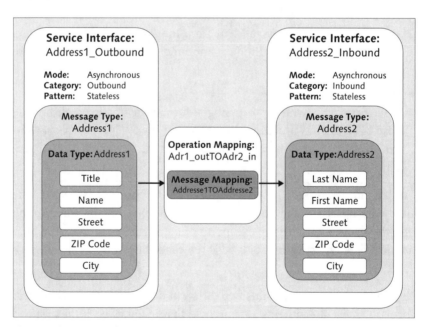

Figure 2.18 Design Objects in Enterprise Services Repository

▶ **Operation mapping**

Interface mapping defines the message mappings you can use to transform one message interface into another. Because a service interface can contain up to three different message types (input/output/fault), you must specify the associated mappings for each relevant message type. In other words, interface mapping is basically a collection of message mappings.

Figure 2.18 also illustrates that the following design objects are used in the address example:

Design objects

▶ Address1, a data type for addresses with one name field

▶ Address2, a data type for addresses with separate first and last names

▶ A message type for the Address1 data type

▶ A message type for the Address2 data type

▶ An outbound interface for dispatching an asynchronous message in the Address1 format

▶ An inbound interface for receiving an asynchronous message in the Address2 format

▶ A message mapping from Address1 to Address2

▶ An operation mapping from the outbound interface in the Address1 format to the inbound interface in the Address2 format

2.4.3 Configuration Objects in the Integration Directory

All objects described up to this point can be entered at design time, which means they are not related in any way to the actual senders and receivers of messages. In the following sections, you will configure the concrete message path: the sender sends a SOAP document to the SAP NetWeaver PI system, which forwards an IDoc to the appropriate (internal) receiver. To do this, a wizard is available in the integration directory that generates all of the required configuration objects on the basis of the actual sender and receiver descriptions.

Configuration objects

A detailed description of the wizard and the configuration of objects is an essential part of Chapter 4. In this section, we'll make a first classification of the objects. Unlike design time, where all generated objects are assigned to a software component, this job is done at configuration time by the configuration scenario. For the address example, we'll create a configuration scenario called "Address allocation."

SOAP message In the example, a SOAP document is received from an external system. Because external systems are not stored in the SLD, you must first create a *business component* that represents the sender of addresses. Here, the name of the sender and a communication channel is stored for the SOAP adapter type. The communication channel contains detailed information on how the sender's SOAP documents are transferred to SAP NetWeaver PI and how they will be processed by SAP NetWeaver PI. Because each sender can use different protocols to communicate with SAP NetWeaver PI, you can store numerous communication channels for each business component.

Now you can configure the following message path. Whenever the SAP NetWeaver PI system receives, from the Address allocator sender, a SOAP document that contains an Address1 (outbound) type message, and whose address is located in zip code area 1, the message must be transformed into the Address2 (inbound) type and sent as an IDoc to SAP system ZIP1.

The message path is configured using the Configuration Wizard, located in the integration directory. It requires the following information:

▸ The message's sender and format, and the adapter through which it was sent.

▸ To whom the message will be sent, the format to be received, and the adapter to be used.

▸ The mappings used to transform the involved formats.

The Configuration Wizard uses this information to generate the following objects:

▸ **Sender agreement**
The *sender agreement* defines the communication channel used to send messages into the SAP NetWeaver PI system for a given sender and message interface. In the example, Address1 (outbound) messages

from the `Address allocator` sender are sent as SOAP documents to the SOAP adapter of SAP NetWeaver PI.

▶ **Receiver agreement**
The *receiver agreement* determines the communication channel used to distribute messages to a receiver. In the example, the `ZIP1` receiver receives messages as IDocs via the IDoc adapter.

▶ **Receiver determination**
The *receiver determination* defines to whom an inbound message must be distributed. Receiver selection can be determined by the message's content, and any number of receivers can be specified here. In the example, we have stored one receiver for each zip code area, and the receiver is selected by using a corresponding rule.

▶ **Interface determination**
The *interface determination* defines the format the inbound message must be in when forwarded to the receiver, and which mappings must be used for the transformation. In this context, you can send several messages (with different message types) that refer to one inbound message. In the example, the message interface `Address2` (inbound) is assigned.

2.5 Advanced Concepts

This section describes additional details and functions of SAP NetWeaver PI. It discusses development models and adapter concepts, and describes mappings, monitoring, and the special features of the different message senders and receivers.

2.5.1 Outside-In vs. Inside-Out

Numerous methods are available for integrating applications with an SAP NetWeaver PI system. These methods are generally divided into two development models: the *inside-out model* and the *outside-in model*.

Differences in
development and
management *Interfaces* allow applications to communicate with SAP NetWeaver PI. The differences between the inside-out and outside-in models can be found in development (the definition) and management (the way integration knowledge is saved).

- ▶ **Outside-in approach**
  With the outside-in model, the communication interface used by an application is defined in a platform-independent format (such as XML) and is centrally stored. The integrated application imports the interface first before it is implemented.

  An example of the outside-in model in SAP NetWeaver PI is integration via ABAP proxies. In SAP NetWeaver PI, the interface is mapped in the service enterprises repository in the form of service interfaces, which are XML schemas. A connected ECC system imports this interface information and uses it to generate an ABAP object that contains a method whose definition matches the definition of the message interface.

  Once the object has been generated, it can be used in the ABAP Workbench. Proxy generation is possible as of release 6.40. Systems with release 6.20 can be enhanced with the APPINT 2.0 add-on, which allows proxy generation. For a further explanation of this scenario, see Section 2.5.2, Communication Components.

- ▶ **Inside-out model**
  In the inside-out model, the communication interface is developed within the connected application and imported during integration with SAP NetWeaver PI. In this context, it is essential that further development of the interface occurs in the application and not in SAP NetWeaver PI. Every change to the interface requires a new import of the interface definition in SAP NetWeaver PI.

  Examples of the inside-out model are integration via the RFC or IDoc adapters. In this case, an existing RFC-enabled function module or IDoc is imported in the Enterprise Services Repository and connected using the relevant mappings.

2.5.2 Communication Components

In SAP NetWeaver PI, communication components represent the senders and receivers of messages. SAP NetWeaver PI contains three different types of communication components:

▶ **Business systems**
Business systems are components located within your own system landscape. Typically, these are systems that you physically control. They are entered in the SLD. Moreover, the systems are assigned products in the SLD, which allow you to determine which messages can be sent and received by a business system.

▶ **Business components**
In SAP NetWeaver PI, *business components* (formerly business services) represent communication components of external providers; for example, a hotel reservation service that can be addressed via a SOAP interface. Business components are provided by systems that cannot be controlled by you. Because the business components are not entered in the SLD, you cannot use the SLD to determine which messages can be sent or received by a specific business component. For this reason, the senders and receivers of the service interfaces from the Enterprise Services Repository are directly assigned to the business component in the enterprise services directory.

▶ **Integration processes**
Integration processes in the integration directory represent configurable instances of integration processes in the Enterprise Services Repository. These are defined in the Business Process Execution Language (BPEL) process designer in the Enterprise Services Repository. From a component's point of view, the configuration instance is treated like all other components; it can send and receive messages. It is not necessary to explicitly specify which messages of a service can send and receive, as this implicitly results from the design of the process in the Enterprise Services Repository.

Correspondingly, the major difference between the partners in the SAP NetWeaver PI configuration is represented by the location that stores information on the "capabilities" of the partner. In this context, the term "capability" describes the ability to send and receive messages.

2.5.3 SAP NetWeaver PI Connectivity

Connection to the IS

The term SAP NetWeaver PI Connectivity covers the various ways to link systems to the central IS (SAP NetWeaver PI) and to exchange messages. However, the messages have to be available in SAP NetWeaver PI format to be processed by the IS. In Section 2.3 we introduced the AAE, which can convert messages in SAP NetWeaver PI–internal format. Next, we will look at other ways that data between the SAP NetWeaver PI system and the backend systems and business partners is exchanged.

Proxy Technology

We already mentioned proxy technology in connection with the IE. Application systems that have a local IE can exchange messages directly with the central IE. Since release 6.20 of SAP WAS, application systems have been capable of using a local IE to exchange messages in SAP NetWeaver PI format.

Exchange messages in SAP NetWeaver PI format

Figure 2.19 shows the data using proxy technology. By communicating this way, the AAE is not used, because the message already exists in the SAP NetWeaver PI protocol, and the proxies are generated from centrally stored service interfaces (in the Enterprise Services Repository).

A distinction is made between client proxies and server proxies. The client proxy is provided at runtime with data from the outbound service interfaces, and then forwarded to the IS. The server proxy is addressed by the corresponding inbound service interfaces and trigger functions on the receiving end. From SAP NetWeaver PI's point of view, generating proxies represents the transition from design time to runtime.

Partner Connectivity Kit (PCK)

For small businesses

Besides the AAE, the PCK is also part of the adapter technology. Small businesses and subsidiaries are often not in a position to operate their own SAP NetWeaver PI system; to allow a data exchange with partners or headquarters, they can use the PCK. The PCK is a Java Enterprise edition (EE)–based application and is based on the Adapter Framework, which is also used for the AAE.

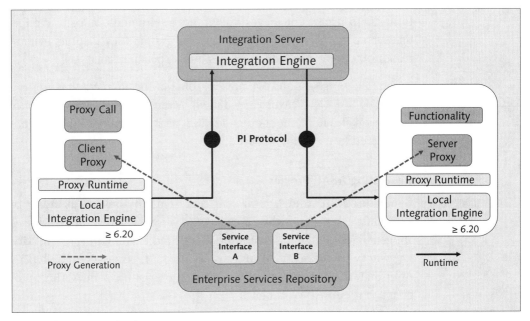

Figure 2.19 Proxy Technology

The PCK provides the following functionalities:

▶ Exchange of messages (between senders and receivers) using the definition of communication profiles (services, communication channels, and communication partners)

▶ The transformation of information into the SAP NetWeaver PI format using an adapter

▶ The conversion of unstructured, semistructured, and structured data using the SAP Conversion Agent by Informatica

▶ The mapping between source and target structure using a graphical mapping editor

▶ Monitoring capabilities to monitor the adapter and the messages

▶ Providing information about the adapter development

2.5.4 Adapter

Adapter technology is a key component of SAP NetWeaver PI, and enables communication between systems that communicate in different formats. To process messages, they must be provided in a specific format for a particular system. To do this, the system uses adapters that are responsible for converting messages into a specific format.

In the following sections, we present some of the adapters that are supported by SAP NetWeaver PI by default. Moreover, there is opportunity to develop and implement other adapters as well; however, this will not be covered in the following sections.

Generating ABAP Proxies

Transaction
SPROXY

Generating ABAP and Java proxies represents the outside-in model of SAP NetWeaver PI. In the case of ABAP proxies, ABAP proxy classes are generated on the basis of interfaces stored in the Enterprise Service Repository by means of ABAP proxy generation (Transaction SPROXY). After that, the classes can be integrated into existing or new ABAP programs in the ABAP Workbench.

ABAP proxy generation includes the software components and the associated namespaces. The structure more or less corresponds to the structure used in the Enterprise Services Repository. According to the outside-in model, the namespaces include all object types that are mapped in ABAP in the context of proxy generation. These include the service interfaces (with the exception of abstract interfaces), and the message and data types. Previously generated ABAP objects are displayed for each of these types.

To create an ABAP proxy, you must first create a package in the ABAP Workbench.[3] Once the package is created, you must call the ABAP proxy to generate ABAP objects from the required objects in the Enterprise Services Repository. ABAP proxy generation also allows you to change existing ABAP proxy objects; for example, if you need to change the interface in the Enterprise Services Repository.

---

3   If you use SAP WAS 6.40, you must also create an SAI_TOOLS usage declaration for the package to generate ABAP proxies.

An `EXECUTE` method is created for each generated outbound proxy, which can then be used to send a message via the proxy. Outbound proxies can only be integrated within the application that uses the proxy.

The generated inbound proxies process messages received from external sources. To accomplish this, a proxy interface and an implementing class are generated. After the proxy is created, the logic that processes the inbound message must be implemented in the implementing class. Inbound proxies are implemented in both the application and proxy objects.

RFC Adapter

The RFC adapter contained in the Adapter Framework represents one of the inside-out implementations of SAP NetWeaver PI. The RFC technology is widely used in the SAP ECC environment to integrate applications in the SAP system. However, the RFC adapter in SAP NetWeaver PI can only be used with certain restrictions. For example, the context (session) in a called system is not kept over several RFC calls. Transactional contexts with several RFC calls also currently aren't possible.

Inside-out implementation

The adapter engine uses the SAP JCo in the background. If you are familiar with JCo, you shouldn't have any problem setting up and configuring the RFC adapter.

As with most other adapters, the RFC adapter basically consists of two components: the sender adapter and the receiver adapter. One sender and one receiver communication channel is needed for each connected system; however, it is possible to set up several communication channels for each system. For example, you might need to set up several communication channels for the receiver adapter if you are using different BAPI configurations.

When configuring the sender adapter, it is important to note that each activated communication channel virtually represents a separate RFC destination through the JCo. For each of these active sender channels, you must maintain a separate RFC destination in the connected ECC system in Transaction SM59. At a minimum, the receiver adapter requires the logon data for the system to be integrated.

RFC destination

The implementation of the inside-out method for the RFC adapter can best be described as the integration of concrete function modules. The metadata of function modules, such as Business Application Programming Interfaces (BAPIs), must be imported into the Enterprise Services Repository before they can be used in SAP NetWeaver PI. *Importing*, in this case, means providing knowledge about the interface of a function module in the Integration Builder.

In contrast to the outside-in method, the function module (in this example, a BAPI) is not maintained in the Enterprise Services Repository, but in the connected RFC system. Another important point for the import of interfaces is that importing an interface from an ECC system has nothing to do with the configuration of the message flow for this system.

Other Adapters

This section describes some additional important adapters from the Adapter Framework, including their functionality. Integration with different adapters represents an essential feature of SAP NetWeaver PI, as it allows you to communicate with many different platforms.

▶ **File adapter**

Messages via file exchange

The *file adapter* lets SAP NetWeaver PI exchange messages by file transfer. The transport protocols supported by the file adapter are a network file system (NFS), FTP, and FTPS. You can use one of these protocols for each configured communication channel.

The file adapter sends or receives the payload of a SAP NetWeaver PI message through the Adapter Framework. There's a special characteristic regarding the sending of messages, which also occurs in other adapters: only the payload of a message is sent through the adapter. However, the payload isn't enough to use the logical routing from the integration directory. The additional information needed to do this — the sender and the service interface — are added in the Adapter Framework on the basis of the sender agreement assigned to the sender channel. Only messages of a specific service interface can be sent through a specific communication channel.

On the other hand, a receiver adapter can be used to receive messages with different service interfaces. However, you cannot configure different file storage locations for a service interface. If you want to do that, you must create several communication channels.

▶ **SOAP adapter**

The *SOAP adapter* allows you to send and receive XML messages that comply with the SOAP standard. The supported transport protocols are HTTP and HTTPS.

As is the case with the FTP adapter, the problem with the SOAP adapter is that a standard SOAP message does not contain any information on the sending service or the service interface that's used. If you use the SOAP adapter, the sending service can be derived from the parameters of the sender's URL, while the service interface must be directly specified in the communication channel.

▶ **JDBC adapter**

The *JDBC adapter* represents a special case in SAP NetWeaver PI in many respects. The central task here is to generate a SQL statement for a relational database from PI-XML messages, and to create an XML message from the result sets of a database operation. To do this, the JDBC adapter uses specific message formats, which must be defined as data types in the Enterprise Services Repository.

For database access

The JDBC adapter's receiver uses different message protocols to send an SAP NetWeaver PI message to a database. The simplest way is the use of a native SQL string. If this message protocol is used, the system expects any SQL statement as the message content that can be processed by the connected database. The XML-SQL format represents another message protocol. This message type must meet the requirements of a specific, previously defined format so the adapter can send it to the database. Possible formats are available for INSERT, UPDATE, DELETE, or stored procedures. The respective message format must be defined in the Enterprise Services Repository.

The sender of the JDBC adapter processes a SELECT and an UPDATE statement for each send operation. These statements must be specified in the adapter configuration. The result of a send operation is represented by the result set of the SELECT statement. This result set is transferred into an XML structure that must be defined in the Enterprise Services Repository, similar to the receiver adapter. You can, for example, use the UPDATE statement in the sender adapter to check a flag that marks the previously read result set as transferred.

2.5.5 Quality of Service (QoS)

With the message attribute of QoS, the transmitter determines how a message should be delivered. A distinction is made whether the sender of the message is waiting for a direct response (synchronous communication mode) or continues to work independent of the recipient's reactions (asynchronous mode of communication).

▶ **Synchronous processing**

Best Effort
The QoS in SAP NetWeaver PI for synchronous messages is known as Best Effort (BE). The associated RFC variant is sRFC (synchronous RFC). Here, the sender system sends a request and waits for a response (for example, the query of customer data). The sender process is blocked until the receiving system sends a response or an error occurs. In such a scenario, the responsibility of dealing with errors lies with the sender and not with the SAP NetWeaver PI system. The service interface contains at least two message types, one for the request and one for the response. In addition, a fault message type can also be used.

Synchronous scenarios are implemented when a direct response of the receiver system is necessary (for example, for user interactions such as the direct decision of a call center agent).

▶ **Asynchronous processing**

Exactly once and exactly once in order
The QoS for asynchronous processing in SAP NetWeaver PI is *exactly once* (EO) or *exactly once in order* (EOIO). In asynchronous scenarios, a sender system sends a data record, and doesn't wait for a direct response of the receiver system. In asynchronous scenarios, the sender can continue work even without the receipt of a response, and is thus decoupled from the processing of the receiver.

If the SAP NetWeaver PI system is used as a data broker, it is not necessary for the recipient to be available at the moment of sending. The message is marked as persistent with a GUID on the SAP NetWeaver PI system, and sent at a later date to the receiving system. The GUID ensures that a message is only processed once, and thus prevents inconsistencies that might arise from multiple processing.

The difference between EO and EOIO is in the order the messages are processed. Messages with the quality of service EOIO must be processed in a certain order according to the process logic.

2.5.6 Message Queues

To process a large number of messages in SAP NetWeaver PI, *queues* are used. These queues allow the parking and subsequent processing of messages that arrive at a time when they cannot be processed directly.

The pipeline runs on the ABAP stack of the SAP NetWeaver PI system, which means that the messages processed there are treated by work processes. An administrator sets a maximum number of work processes that are available for this task.

Waiting queues for messages

It's possible that several messages passed for processing to the IE can be defined as work processes. For this reason, the IS (and the sender and receiver systems) works with queues. Depending on the QoS, the messages can be persisted on the IS and processed one after another. The messages are written in database tables and reread for processing.

Asynchronous messages (EO, EOIO) are stored on the central IE (on the IS) in inbound and outbound queues.

> **Note: Changing the Meaning of Inbound and Outbound**
>
> The terms *outbound* (message from the sender system) and *inbound* (message to the receiving system) are already known. The message flow is considered from the perspective of the sending or receiving system.
>
> In the context of the queue concept, inbound and outbound queues are considered from the perspective of the central IE. The incoming messages are held, therefore, in the inbound queue, and the outbound messages in the outbound queue. These different meanings of terminology cause confusion in some cases.

Inbound processing includes the receiver determination, interface determination, and message split steps, while outbound processing covers the mapping and technical routing steps. Depending on where the message

Inbound and outbound processing

is processed (in the pipeline), it is either written to the inbound or outbound queue.

As shown in Figure 2.20, the local IE (on the sender or receiver system) also has queues. These are known as sender or receiver queues, and store messages in their respective backend systems.

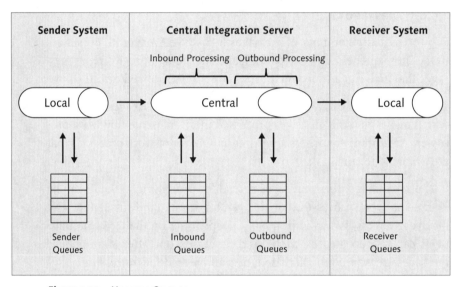

Figure 2.20 Message Queues

Different queues are defined for the respective QoS. There are separate queues for EO, EOIO, and BE, which are used for message processing. The idea behind this separation is simple; imagine, for example, a synchronous communication that uses the IE. In this case, the queue is occupied until the response from the receiver system is sent back to the sender system. During this time, processing other messages on the queue is not possible.

The QoS is not the only crucial element for the setup of special queues; the size of the message and its priority are also important in structuring queues. For example, you can define special queues for very large messages or for prioritized messages (either high or low priority). Thus, efficient utilization and effective processing of messages is guaranteed, because queues are not unnecessarily blocked and important messages arrive promptly at the receiver.

2.5.7 Mappings

Because the structure of the incoming and outgoing messages often do not match, they are adjusted during the mapping step. In SAP NetWeaver PI, mappings can be used in both business processes and between a sender and receiver.

At design time, the mappings in the Enterprise Services Repository are stored in the form of operation mappings (formerly interface mappings). The operation mapping connects two service interfaces to each other, and indicates which service interfaces are used for input or output of the mapping. Multiple service interfaces can be specified on both the input and the output side.

Operation mapping

The real logic of how data is transferred from one format to another is not in the operation mapping itself, but in the mapping objects (*mapping programs*). The following mapping programs are available:

Mapping programs

▶ Message mappings are created by means of the graphical mapping editors in the Enterprise Services Builder.

▶ Java mappings are created externally and imported.

▶ XSLT mappings are created externally and imported.

▶ ABAP-XSLT mappings are created on the IS (ABAP-Stack) and referenced.

▶ ABAP mapping classes are created on the IS and referenced.

In principle, you can distinguish between two types of mappings: structure mapping and value mapping. Structure mapping maps semantically related fields of the outbound and inbound interfaces (and their corresponding message types) to each other. Both structure and value mapping use conversion rules to transfer the field contents into the target format.

Mapping programs can be mapped in different ways. The easiest way to create a mapping program is with *message mapping,* which is created in the graphical editor of the Enterprise Services Builder, the central modeling interface of the Enterprise Services Repository.

Standard functions

This editor lets you assign individual components of the source and target messages to each other, as shown in Figure 2.21. If you cannot assign all messages to each other, you can also use predefined functions such as SUBSTRING, CONCAT, or SUBTRACT. You can also use conditions using the IF function, or you can use Java to build your own custom functions.

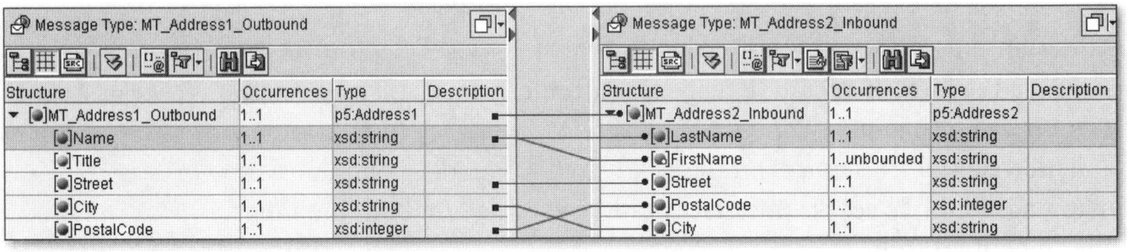

Figure 2.21 Message Mapping Using the Graphical Mapping Editor

XSLT mapping

Another very powerful feature is the XSLT mappings. These mappings can be defined outside of SAP NetWeaver PI and be imported as archives with the Enterprise Services Repository. XSLT mappings can be written as ABAP XSLT transformations, or directly in XSLT. Although the mapping programs were created externally, you still have the option of editing the XSLT file afterward.

A drawback of XSLT mapping is the fact that the XSLT mapping is processed from the start at each mapping step. This has an impact both on performance and on the throughput of messages.

ABAP Mapping

In addition, the option of mapping programs in the form of an ABAP class is given. The ABAP mappings are mapping programs that are developed in the ABAP Workbench of the IS, and executed at runtime on the SAP NetWeaver AS ABAP. During pipeline processing, the ABAP mappings are only processed on the ABAP stack of the IS process, and there is no access to the Java stack.

So far there is no way to deliver ABAP mappings with SAP applications and to deploy them on the IS. Therefore, these mapping programs are exclusively custom development.

Finally, you still have the option to use Java classes on the Java EE engine; in these classes, the mapping can be freely programmed. The mapping programs are written directly in Java programming language, and can then be imported into the Enterprise Services Repository. However, you cannot make any subsequent changes therein. If you want to change the Java mapping, you need to do this outside of the Enterprise Services Repository and then import the mapping program again.

Java Mapping

2.6   New Concepts in SAP NetWeaver PI 7.1

In release 7.1 of SAP NetWeaver PI, there are some changes that relate not only to the terminology. Along with name changes, such as service interface (formerly Message Interface) or Enterprise Services Repository (formerly Integration Repository), many new features were also added.

New features in release 7.1

Some of these new features have been already addressed in previous sections, but not explained in detail, so we'll look at some here. However, it is not possible to go into detail on all of the extensions. For more information, see the SAP Developer Network (SDN) (*http://sdn.sap.com*) or the SAP Help Portal (*http://help.sap.com*).

2.6.1   Local Processing on the AAE

As of SAP NetWeaver PI 7.1, you can use certain functions that were previously implemented by the IE on the AAE. The messages are fully processed on the AAE, without using the IE. Here, a significant gain in performance can be realized, which is partly due to the elimination of the step to store persistent messages and partly to direct adapter-to-adapter communication (without using the IE).

Performance improvement

More flexibility in terms of the system landscape can be achieved by using local processing. Security measures — for example, the use of firewalls — can prevent communication with the central IS. Complete scenarios can then be fully outsourced to a noncentral AAE (see Figure 2.22). The local processing, as shown in Figure 2.22, supports both synchronous and asynchronous scenarios, and can be used for all adapters that run on the AAE (Java EE). Some features are not provided yet; which can include:

- ▶ Routing to multiple receivers
- ▶ Integration processes (ccBPM)
- ▶ Scenarios with the following adapters:
  - ▶ IDoc
  - ▶ Plain HTTP
  - ▶ Industry standards
  - ▶ Web service adapter
  - ▶ XI (PI) adapter
- ▶ Multi mappings
- ▶ ABAP mappings

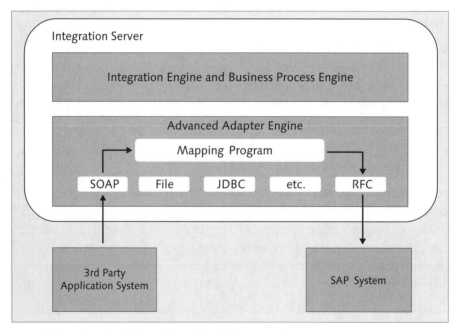

Figure 2.22 Local Processing on the AAE

However, SAP plans to extend the local processing for IDoc scenarios in subsequent enhancement packages. [4]

---

4 The IDoc adapter will be based on Java EE in future releases, and therefore run on the AAE.

2.6.2   Integrated Configuration

In addition to the gain in performance due to local processing on the AAE, there are other advantages, particularly in the configuration of these scenarios. With integrated configuration, you specify settings for these scenarios in which the message processing is done by the AAE. Thus, the integrated configuration replaces conventional configuration objects that are needed for communication via the IS (IE).

Instead of classical configuration objects

These objects include both the above-mentioned sender or receiver agreements, and the receiver and interface determination. All configuration settings for exchanging messages are made clearly in a single object, the integrated configuration. An integrated configuration in the Integration Builder is shown in Figure 2.23.

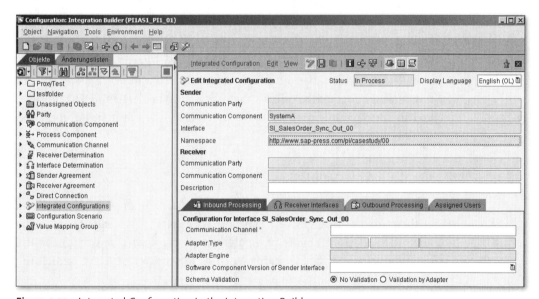

Figure 2.23   Integrated Configuration in the Integration Builder

During design time, the Enterprise Services Repository is still needed. Here, you define simple mappings (1:1) and the required design objects that you want to use in the integrated configuration at configuration time. Because the integrated configuration is designed for scenarios using the AAE, the same restrictions as described in Section 2.6.1 apply.

These include, for example, scenarios that require a message split or a payload-based routing.

2.6.3 Enhanced (Dynamic) Receiver Determination

Name of receiver
unknown

In some situations, you may not know the receiver at configuration time; in this case, you can specify that the recipient of a message is determined dynamically at runtime. Instead of defining the receiver in the receiver determination, which is how you would do it in a classic scenario, you can designate the receiver using a mapping program by assigning a mapping to the receiver determination. During the mapping, you can then determine the receiver by means of a list (for example, a table) or from the payload of a message. During the dynamic receiver determination, you don't have to specify an explicit name in contrast to the classic version.

As a prerequisite for a dynamic receiver determination, you must define an operation mapping and assign the service interface `ReceiverDetermination` as the target interface. You also need a message mapping or a mapping program that allows the recipient to be determined at runtime. This message mapping must be assigned to the appropriate operation mapping.

2.6.4 XML Validation

Since release 7.1, SAP NetWeaver PI provides the opportunity to check the structure of the SAP NetWeaver PI message payloads through the XML validation. This is particularly important with regard to the use of industry-specific standards, such as RosettaNet or CIDX, which use explicitly described structures.

Check message
syntax

The structure check takes place on the basis of data types stored in the Enterprise Services Repository. The scheme that is used for the validation is stored in the file system of the SAP NetWeaver PI system. Both inbound and outbound messages can be considered in the context of the validation. As shown in Figure 2.24, examining the XML payload can be performed on the AAE and on the IE.

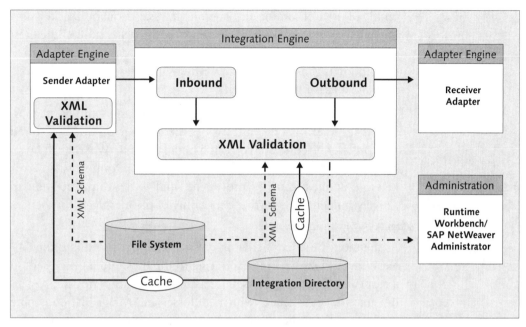

Figure 2.24 XML Validation

Where to place the validation process is determined in the Integration Builder, in the sender and receiver agreements. Figure 2.25 shows the selection option for the sender agreement.

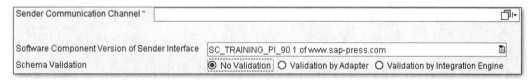

Figure 2.25 Maintaining the XML Validation in the Integration Builder

Here, you can specify whether the validation is performed by the adapter, the IE, or not at all, as desired:

▶ **Validation on the IE**

For validating a messages payload, the data types to be checked are provided by the Enterprise Services Repository during the validation

Validation by means of the IE

on the IE. Both incoming and outgoing messages can be checked during message processing. When errors occur (the structure of the message does not match the structure of stored data types) an error description is generated. This description includes a status of the message and a list of inconsistencies.

The message processing is then interrupted, and the status of the message is set to Erroneous. In this case, the message on the IE is stored and can later be edited or corrected in the Runtime Workbench by an administrator. The responsible administrator is informed via an error message about the faulty processing, and is now in a position to actively influence the further processing of the message.

▶ **Validation on the AAE**

Validation by means of the AAE

As mentioned earlier, incoming messages are translated into the SAP NetWeaver PI internal format during runtime, before they are sent to a particular target adapter (sender adapter). As part of this step, a central component is called, which addresses an XML validation engine to compare the payload with a configured schema. If validation errors are detected during this step, the AAE triggers an exception that terminates further processing of the message and informs the sender. This is done using a synchronous response call.

All adapters, including those of third parties, can support an XML validation. However, in the case of industry-specific adapters, the sender is informed about structural defects via an asynchronous message.

The AAE doesn't store the messages, as opposed to the validation on the IE. This structure check only triggers an alarm and notifies the sender about the faulty processing. Therefore, there is no way to retroactively correct the message and to start the process again.

Another difference in the validation on the IE is the validation of inbound messages (to the receiver). This step is only possible when processing messages using the IE. The AAE is therefore only able to validate incoming (outbound) messages.

2.6.5 Interface Pattern: Communication Patterns between Sender and Receiver

Since release 7.1 of SAP NetWeaver PI, in addition to the processing mode (synchronous or asynchronous), interface patterns (processing modes) can also be defined as a property of the service interfaces (formerly message interfaces), which is attributed to the use of Web services and SOAs. In the following sections, a distinction between stateless and stateful communication is made.

Use of Web services and SOAs

A service is described as *stateless*, if, between two consecutive calls, no state has been saved. After the first call is completed, all temporary variables and objects are deleted, whereas a stateful service can keep a state which is held across calls. An example might be a shopping cart application; it is necessary to load all of the items ordered in the same shopping cart to ensure a purchase order for all of the selected goods at the end. The information from the first call is therefore made available to the following messages.

The terms *stateless* and *stateful* refer to the receiving end of a message, and not to the SAP NetWeaver PI system. The Interface pattern determines the communication in the receiving system.

The following is a list of interface patterns that can be used starting with SAP NetWeaver PI 7.1:

▶ **Stateless (XI 3.0–compatible)**
The stateless (XI 3.0-compatible) interface pattern supports the proxy runtime and the SAP NetWeaver PI adapter, and can only be used in connection with SAP NetWeaver PI. If you use an older SAP NetWeaver PI system (for example, XI release 3.0), you can migrate your message interfaces from the Integration Repository as service interfaces to the Enterprise Services Repository from SAP NetWeaver PI. With this migration, the STATELESS (XI 3.0-compatible) interface pattern is assigned to the newly created service interfaces.

Stateless communication

Service interfaces with the STATELESS (XI 3.0-compatible) interface pattern can only contain one operation, which must have the same name as the service interface.

▶ **Stateless**
Although the STATELESS interface pattern can also be used in connection with Web services technology, you still have the option of using it in scenarios implemented with SAP NetWeaver PI. The difference between the STATELESS (XI 3.0-compatible) and STATELESS interface patterns is the use of Web services technology, which also allows point-to-point connections, enabling communication scenarios without the use of a SAP NetWeaver PI system. In addition, you can define multiple operations in service interfaces with the STATELESS interface pattern.

▶ **Stateful**

Stateful communication

The STATEFUL interface pattern is available for both communication scenarios that use SAP NetWeaver PI, and point-to-point connections. The successively performed calls can be based on a state with the provider. This interface pattern only supports synchronous communication scenarios, and is typically used only for some specific technical scenarios.

▶ **Tentative Update & Confirm/Compensate (TU&C/C)**
The TU & C/C interface pattern makes sure that data can be consistently recorded at the receiver, despite a synchronous communication scenario. TU & C/C lets you process multiple synchronous calls (for example, database changes) in a transactional context (logical unit of work). Here, the update calls are collected (tentative update), until a confirmation (confirm) or an adjustment (composite) is sent by the sender. Only then can the change or the discarding of changes be performed on the receiving end. However, this scenario is applicable only in A2A scenarios, not in B2B scenarios (i.e., within a system landscape).

In Figure 2.26, the recently listed interface patterns and their use in different communication scenarios (via the process integration and point-to-point connections) are presented again.

2.6.6   Direct Communication

Without central instance

Throughout this chapter, direct communication has been mentioned again and again. So, in this section we will briefly describe this communication scenario and discuss some details relevant to release 7.1.

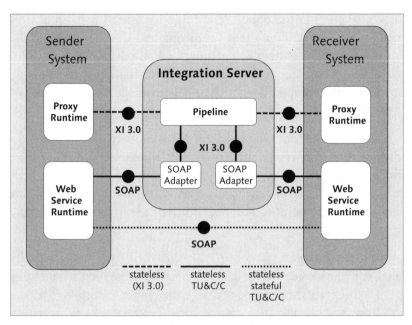

Figure 2.26 Interface Patterns in SAP NetWeaver PI

In direct communication, two systems using Web services communicate with each other without a central instance being integrated (IS). A comparison of the two scenarios is shown in Figure 2.27.

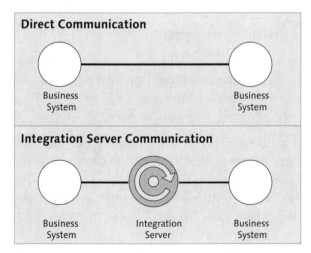

Figure 2.27 Direct Communication Compared to IS Communication

Therefore, you have the option of sending a request (for example, for customer data) directly to a receiver system and to directly obtain the desired information. However, you must renounce the functionality during message processing, due to the lack of a central IS. As an example, let's explore the mapping between messages, which is a central task of the IS.

Point-to-point connection

With direct connections, you have the opportunity to improve the performance of your message processing; this is because you don't have central middleware and you don't have to perform any message processing on the IS. However, in this context, the administration effort increases, because point-to-point connections are usually not centrally administered.

Central maintenance of direct connections

However, since release 7.1 of SAP NetWeaver PI, you can centrally model, configure, and manage direct connections. The required message types and interfaces are created at design time in the Enterprise Services Repository, and configuration data is stored centrally in the Integration Directory.

You can implement the Web service for direct communication with both Java services and ABAP services. These forms differ in the establishment of the connection, in the generation of the proxy (in ABAP), and in the setup of Java provider programs.

2.6.7 Web Service Reliable Messaging

One goal of SOAs is the modularization of large applications in well-defined units (services). So, for mission-critical applications, communication services must be reliably implemented. In the context of the Web service standard, a variety of specifications can be used.

Web service communication

For example, to ensure a reliable exchange of messages, the *Organization for Advancement of Structured Information Standards* (OASIS) developed a standard to ensure a reliable exchange of messages via Web services. This standard is supported as of SAP NetWeaver PI 7.1 using the *Web Services Reliable Messaging Protocol*) (WS RM).[5] As you can see in Figure 2.28,

---

5   You can find additional information about the setup of direct communication on the SAP Help portal at *http://help.sap.com*.

this input type was realized on the IE (ABAP), and ensures the message exchange using Web services.

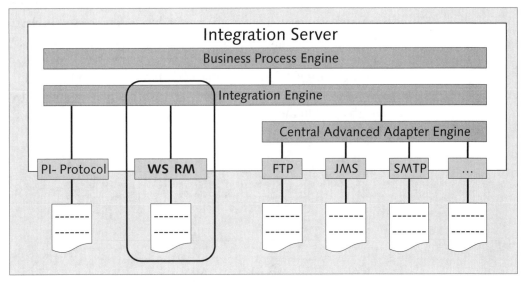

Figure 2.28 WS RM Input

The WS RM protocol ensures that the messages are reliably transmitted. To ensure the correct order of incoming messages, one or more messages can be grouped into sequences. These sequences are provided with a unique identification, and the messages within a sequence are numbered sequentially. This ensures that messages are processed completely and correctly (i.e., in the correct order).

2.6.8 Message Packaging

As a central middleware and integration interface in the midst of a complex system landscape, SAP NetWeaver PI faces numerous challenges. One of these challenges is high-performance message processing.

SAP NetWeaver PI 7.1 provides a variety of ways to improve performance to ensure an efficient distribution of messages. One such possibility is *message packaging*, where you can combine asynchronous mes-

Performance gain through message packaging

123

sages into packages and process them together in a logical unit of work (LUW).

As described in Section 2.5.6, Message Queues, messages are saved during processing in queues and then processed by work processes. In classical processing, this happens for each individual message. In Figure 2.29, this scenario is shown schematically. An incoming message is written to the queue, processed by each pipeline step, and processed until it is forwarded to the recipient. For every message, work processes are needed that are executed in the form of ABAP programs.

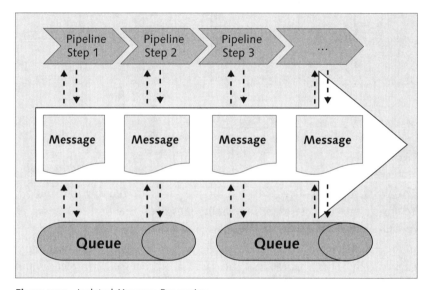

Figure 2.29 Isolated Message Processing

This message processing can be optimized by working with message packages. Using message packaging, you can combine messages that are processed together as a package (see Figure 2.30). Thus, the work processes no longer process each message individually. In this case, only one call to the ABAP program (per package) is performed, which allows effective processing of the message and generates significantly less load on the system (by calling programs).

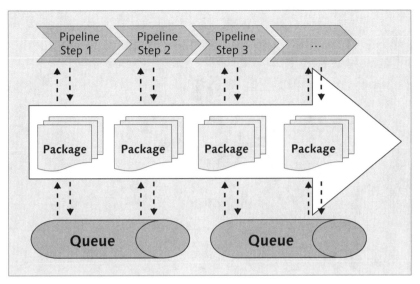

Figure 2.30 Message Packaging

2.6.9 Mapping Lookups

In some mappings, it may be necessary to directly access data in a backend system to enrich the message processing. For example, if you want direct access to a value such as free beds during a hotel reservation, you need this information from the corresponding application system to guarantee the correct processing.

In Figure 2.31, this scenario is presented. System A sends a message (❶) to the central IS. The mapping (❷) requires additional information from another system. In step ❸, a call is performed (for example, using the JDBC adapter) to obtain the desired information. Then, the message can be processed and forwarded to the receiving system (❹).

SAP NetWeaver PI 7.1 lets you access values or value tables during runtime. This capability is called mapping lookup. At runtime, an application system can be called during the mapping to obtain values for the mapping. This measure is implemented by using lookup APIs, which provide methods for connecting to systems.

Mapping lookups

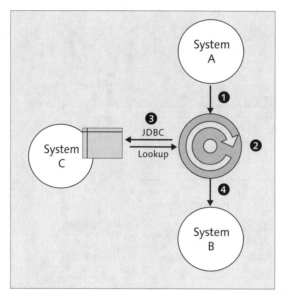

Figure 2.31 Mapping Lookup

In SAP NetWeaver PI, you can rely on this feature using message, Java, and XSLT mapping. The lookup APIs are always called from a Java coding, and are therefore the only mappings available, as they are based on the Java EE engine. They cannot be used with all adapters. SAP NetWeaver PI supports lookups by using the RFC, JDBC, and SOAP adapters. These are adapters that run on the AAE, and therefore are also based on Java.

In addition, the adapters must support synchronous calls because a request to an application system is sent during the lookups, and the called system directly returns the answer (value) for the mapping.

RFC and JDBC lookup

To use an RFC lookup, the relevant RFCs must be stored in the Enterprise Services Repository. Only then can you access values in a backend system at runtime using an RFC lookup. In the case of the JDBC adapter, the table structure of the table to be accessed must be known. Here, the corresponding information must have been stored in the Enterprise Services Repository, too.

PART II
Basic System Configuration

Before you can begin with the exercises and the case study discussed in this book, you must prepare your systems for the examples. This chapter guides you through the necessary steps to prepare for the exercises and the case study.

3 Basic System Configuration

In this chapter, you will first examine the technical conditions for processing the upcoming exercises. Afterward, you will make various setting adjustments that are necessary to complete the exercises. For this, you'll need to have administrator privileges.

The following sections walk you through the necessary preparations for working on the individual exercises; they also pave the way for the case study. However, in some cases further configurations have to be done for specific exercises beyond the preparations discussed here.

3.1 Prerequisites

To work on the exercises, you need SAP NetWeaver Process Integration (PI) 7.1, which should contain the highest available *support package* (SP) stack, if possible. The exercises described here have been carried out on SAP NetWeaver PI 7.1 SP7.

Tested under SAP NetWeaver PI 7.1 SP7

Apart from the SAP NetWeaver PI system, you need two more systems, or at least two different clients. In the following sections, we assume that you have successfully completed the installation of SAP NetWeaver PI 7.1 and have customized the systems as described in the installation and configuration guides provided by SAP. Furthermore, it is assumed that the System Landscape Directory (SLD) you will use for the exercises is located in the SAP NetWeaver PI system.

You also need a user within the SAP NetWeaver PI system for the preparatory steps. This user must have comprehensive rights. For example, you can use the `pisuper` user or a copy of it. Like the former user, `xisuper` in SAP XI 3.0 has been renamed to `pisuper` in SAP NetWeaver PI; all of the technical users who had "xi" in their names have been changed in the system. Whenever the name change from XI to PI has technical implications, we will mention it at the appropriate point.

SAP GUI, Java Web Start, and SAP NetWeaver Developer Studio for the frontend

You will use different applications in the frontend. For example, you will need the latest version of the SAP GUI (currently version 7.10), including the latest patches (currently patch 13). You'll need the SAP GUI to access the SAP NetWeaver PI functions in the ABAP part of the system. For the screenshots in the practical parts, the SAP Signature resp. Nova design of the SAP GUI was used, which has been available since patch 11. You can set it on the control panel of the SAP GUI or via TWEAK SAP GUI from the start menu.

You can access the relevant Java components using Java applications, which are automatically downloaded via *Java Web Start* when used for the first time. For this, you need a Java software development kit (SDK) installation that contains Java Web Start, which is available for several platforms at *http://java.sun.com*. We recommend that you use the most current version of Java for Java Web Start applications.

Access to the SAP NetWeaver PI system via the Java Web Start application occurs through port 5*XX*04, *XX* being the instance number of the SAP system. Most test systems use 00 as the instance number. You can determine the port number within the SAP NetWeaver PI system via Transaction SMICM. To do that, follow the menu path GOTO • SERVICES and check the value of P4. To implement the optional Java mapping example, you will also use SAP NetWeaver Developer Studio, which should also be installed in the frontend.

Source code of the examples available online and in Appendix A

You will use specific programs for different exercises. By importing ABAP code, you can simplify your preparation for some exercises. These programs can be downloaded from the website that accompanies this book (*http://www.sap-press.com*), and you can also find the source code in Appendix A, Exercise Materials. You will be told which programs you should use in the exercises.

The development of SAP Exchange Infrastructure (XI) 3.0 to SAP NetWeaver PI 7.1 had some technical impact. Thus, the parallel installation of Application Server (AS) ABAP with AS Java in one step enables some simplifications in the SAP NetWeaver PI system. During the installation, client 001 is automatically configured as the central Integration Engine (IE). This can make manually switching connections after a client copy necessary (see SAP Note 940309).

Changes from SAP XI 3.0 to SAP NetWeaver PI 7.1

A significant simplification is the use of the Configuration Wizard, which automatically creates all of the required remote function call (RFC) connections between the ABAP and the Java part of the system, and also adjusts the exchange profile settings. In doing so, a master password for all technical users in the SAP NetWeaver PI system can be set. The ex post change of the master password for SAP NetWeaver PI service users that you specified during installation is described in SAP Note 999962. The Configuration Wizard is started in the SAP NetWeaver Administrator (NWA) (see the installation guide of SAP NetWeaver PI at *http://service. sap.com/instguides*).

Although the advanced integration of ABAP and Java in the SAP NetWeaver PI system simplifies the general setup significantly,[1] this development has no impact on the connection of business systems to the SAP NetWeaver PI system. Thus, various activities are performed manually in the business systems for the connection. These activities are considered in detail in the following sections.

3.2   Defining the Connected Systems in the SLD

SAP systems that have not been previously included in an integration scenario require various setting adjustments so that they can be used to send or receive messages. The following sections describe the necessary steps to integrate a business system with the SAP NetWeaver PI system.

---

[1]   One effect of this integration, which also manifests itself in the following configuration, is access to ABAP services such as Business Server Pages (BSPs) on Java port 5 # # 00. The current ABAP port 80 # # is not explicitly used anymore.

3.2.1 Creating the Systems: Technical Systems

System Landscape Directory as a central system directory

The system definition in the SLD represents the basis for communication. When defining the systems, you must specify how the new system can be accessed and what software products (including their versions) are available in it. These details are particularly useful for systems within the company's internal information technology (IT) landscape.

Transaction SXMB_ IFR calls SAP NetWeaver PI tools

Open the SAP GUI and log in as the superuser of your SAP NetWeaver PI system in the client of the Integration Server (IS) (001 by default).[2] Start Transaction SXMB_IFR to navigate to the SAP NetWeaver PI tools. Select the SLD and log on to it as the pisuper superuser. Later, you can also access the SAP NetWeaver PI tools directly via the following URL: *http://<Host>:<J2EE-Port>/dir/start/index.jsp*. However, before you can do that, you must log on to the SAP GUI and change the superuser's default password.

In contrast to SAP XI 3.0, SAP NetWeaver PI 7.1 lets you display the SAP NetWeaver Composition Environment tools with the link *http://<Host>:<J2EE-Port>/rep/start/index.jsp*. These tools consist only of the Enterprise Services Repository and the SLD; however, the PI tools link, below the SLD, brings you to the complete list of SAP NetWeaver PI tools.

Management of computer systems

Although SAP Web Application Server (WAS) ABAP and SAP WAS Java automatically log in to the SLD as technical systems during installation, we want to carry out this step manually for the Enterprise Central Component (ECC) 6.0 system[3] with system ID S02. In later exercises, and in the case study with its client 903 as system A, analogous steps must also be performed for system B (in this case, an SAP ECC 5.0 system).

---

2 Through the integrated installation of the ABAP and Java stacks in the PI system, client 001 is configured as the central IS. If you use this client in a test system, create a client copy of 001 as a backup. Otherwise, SAP Note 940309 gives a summary of all of the activities necessary to switch the client of the central IS.

3 Among other things, this component contains the functions of R/3 systems and represents the center of the SAP Business Suite within an enterprise system landscape.

To do this, you must click on the TECHNICAL SYSTEMS link in the LAND-SCAPE section (see Figure 3.1). You can select the different types of technical systems to view the systems that have already been registered.

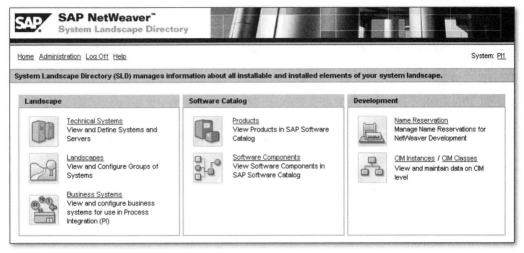

Figure 3.1 SLD

To create an ABAP-based system, such as SAP ECC 6.0, select New Technical System. The creation of the new system is done in six separate steps. If the screens should differ because of another support package from the screens shown, or if you are uncertain, you can always click on the information icon on the right of an input field for more information about that field.

The new system is based on an SAP WAS ABAP. Select the corresponding option and navigate to the next step. The system now prompts you to specify details about the system to be integrated (see Figure 3.2). You must first enter the AS ABAP NAME (SID); you can find the three-digit alphanumeric ID in the relevant SAP system by following the SYSTEM • STATUS menu path. In addition to the SID, you will also find the required DATABASE HOST NAME in the Database data section in the lower right-hand area. The INSTALLATION NUMBER is displayed in the SAP System data section above the Database Host Name. Once you have entered all of the values, continue with the next step.

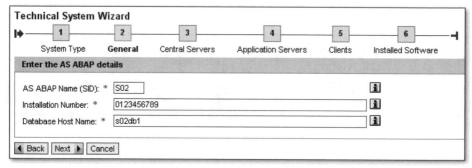

Figure 3.2 Technical System Wizard, Step 2 – General information

The third step of the wizard asks you for details about the central AS and the message server (see Figure 3.3). In most cases, these two servers are identical; however, you should verify this with the landscape administrator.

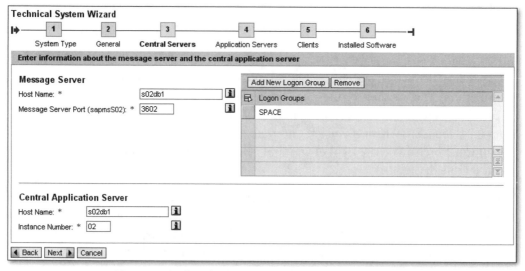

Figure 3.3 Technical System Wizard, Step 3 – Central Servers

Transactions SM51 and SMLG contain important system data

You can find the required data, for instance, in Transaction SM51. This transaction contains a list of all servers that belong to the system. Search for the Enqueue entry in the Message Types column; this is typically the central AS. The first column in this row contains an entry of the following type: *<host>_<SID>_<Instance number>*. In Figure 3.3, the INSTANCE NUM-

BER is 02. Copy the values into the relevant input fields of the wizard. The message port's number has the following structure: *36<Instance number>*. You can determine the available logon groups in your SAP system by using Transaction SMLG; the logon groups available in the system should be listed automatically in the wizard. Continue with the next step.

In the next screen, you can specify additional ASs that belong to the SAP system in question. To do that, enter the relevant host name and add it to the lower list. If your SAP system only consists of the central AS, you can continue here without specifying anything.

ABAP-based SAP systems are divided into different clients. The following step shows you how to assign clients to your logical systems (see Figure 3.4).

Each client is assigned a logical system

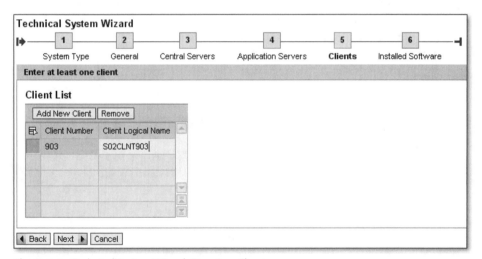

Figure 3.4 Technical System Wizard, Step 4 — Clients

You can view the clients and their logical systems with Transaction SCC4. If you discover that the clients you want to use haven't been assigned any logical systems yet, you can use Transaction BD54 to create new logical systems, and then assign those new systems using Transaction SCC4. Before you do that, however, you should consult with your landscape administrator, as this step can be critical.

The names of logical systems usually have the following structure: *<SID>CLNT<Client>*. In our example, the name is S02CLNT903. The logical system is used for application link enabling (ALE) scenarios and in various SAP modules, such as finance;[4] communication with intermediate documents (IDocs), for example, represents such a scenario.

It is sufficient to specify one client of the system. After successfully establishing the automated data update of the technical system, the SLD will be automatically notified about other clients. Now continue with the selection of installed software products in the next step.

Installed software components can be viewed in the SAP system

Now you can choose which SAP product is installed on the new technical system to specify installed software products and components, and their versions (see Figure 3.5). In this case, it is an SAP ECC 6.0 system. You can limit the selection of software products displayed using the FILTER ON/OFF button in the top right corner to show suitable input fields for the filter. Then type "ECC" in the left input field of the filter for software products, and confirm entry with the Enter button. Now only software products with the term "ECC" in their names will appear.

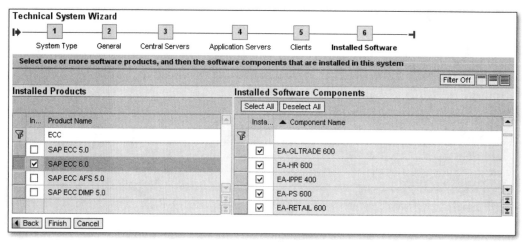

Figure 3.5 Technical System Wizard, Step 6 — Installed Software

For system S02, select the entry from SAP ECC 6.0 by placing a checkmark next to the name. Through the selection of the software product, all software component versions that may belong to this software product

---

4 Due to the critical importance of finance in a company, changes to logical systems during operation should be only made on training or sandbox systems.

appear on the right. In this list, you can use the white box to filter the software component versions, too. You can use the three buttons next to the FILTER ON/OFF button to change the table length of the displayed messages to avoid unnecessary scrolling.

Take your time in deselecting the components not installed in your system by unchecking the checkbox next to them. To see the list of components you can access in your SAP system, follow the SYSTEM • STATUS menu path and click on the looking glass icon in the SAP System Data section.

Once you have deselected noninstalled components, exit the Wizard by clicking the FINISH button. The list of all WAS ABAP systems now contains the newly created system (see Figure 3.6). Unlike the SLD in XI release 3.0, a computer system entry is created for each technical host of the system (in addition to the AS ABAP technical system). If a system is distributed across multiple hosts — for example, if database and ASs are running on different hosts — multiple entries are automatically created for a system.

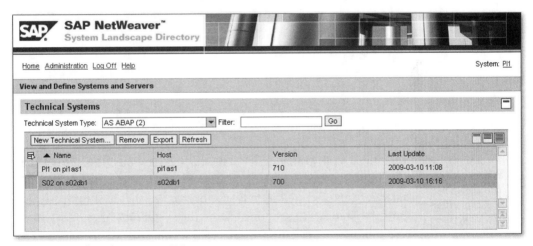

Figure 3.6 Technical Systems in SLD

3.2.2 Creating the Systems: Business Systems

Now that you have published the new technical system in the SLD, you must define which business systems can be accessed in the technical

Maintenance of business systems

137

system. For this, you must once again go to the initial screen of the SLD and select Business Systems in the Landscape section. The system will then display a list of all existing business systems. Click on New Business System to call the appropriate wizard.

R/3 and ECC systems use SAP Web AS ABAP

In the first step, you must select the type of technical system. Because you want to set up the new business system on the technical system you have just created, you must select AS ABAP. Continue to the next step.

You can now select your system from a list of all technical systems of the corresponding type. Once you have done that, the system displays all existing clients of this system (see Figure 3.7). The URL of the associated technical system can be specified optionally; in this book it's not used, so you can leave it as OTHER. The URL can be used to distribute the central Web service configuration data. Select the relevant client in this list if you have specified several clients before, and if they are shown.

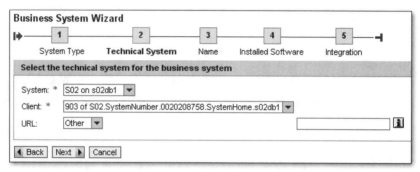

Figure 3.7 Business System Wizard, Step 2 — Technical System

Clients of the business systems are maintained as application systems

In the third step, you assign a name for the new business system. This must be unique within the system landscape, and can be up to 256 characters long. Name the first system that will be used primarily as a sender "SystemA." In the fourth step, the system displays a list of software products installed in the selected technical system. You can usually skip this step.[5] The fifth and final step of the wizard prompts you

---

5   You do not need any additional software products for the practical exercises in this book. However, in other scenarios, you must use more than one software product. In such a case, you should check the products listed here.

to define the role of the business system (see Figure 3.8). Here, you can choose between INTEGRATION SERVER and APPLICATION SYSTEM.

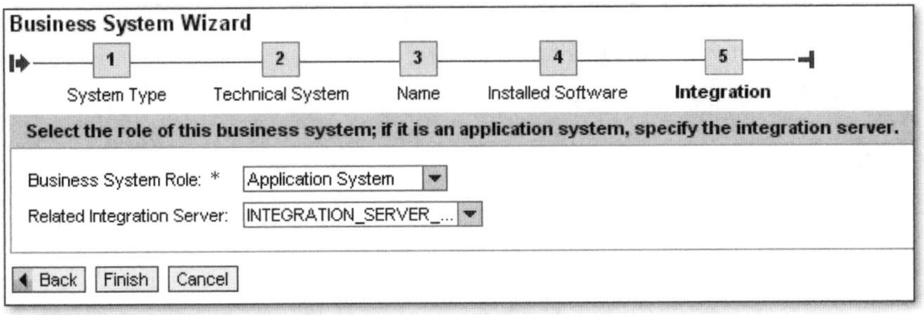

Figure 3.8 Business System Wizard, Step 5 — Integration

Because we don't want the new business system to act as an information broker, you should select the APPLICATION SYSTEM role. You must also select the IS. The system displays a list of all business systems that have been created as ISs. Select the system you want to use for this course from the list and exit the wizard by clicking the FINISH button.

The list of all business systems now contains the newly created business system, SYSTEMA (see Figure 3.9). Now repeat the steps to create a business system named SystemB. If necessary, you must repeat the steps for defining other technical systems.

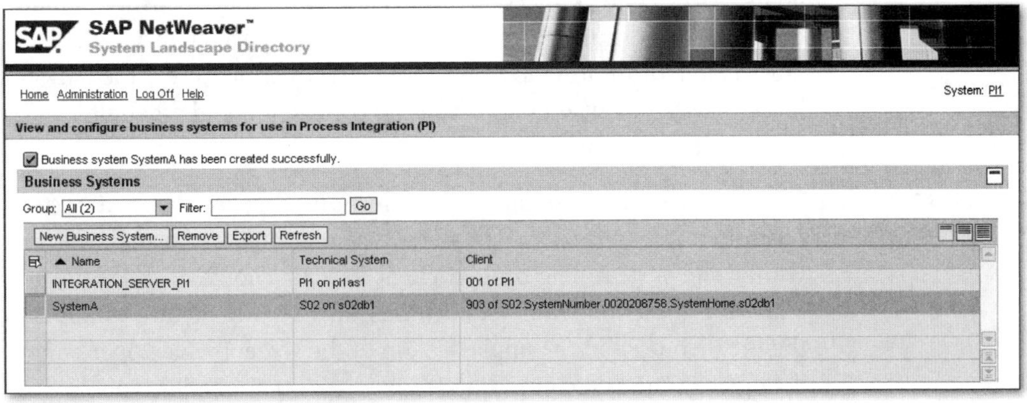

Both SystemA and SystemB must be configured

Figure 3.9 Business System Landscape

3.3   Integrating the SAP Systems with the SLD

Regular update of
SLD data

As a technical system in the SLD, the SAP systems you want to use are now familiar with different business systems. However, the job of the SLD is to provide up-to-date data about the connected systems at any time. For this reason, you must establish a connection between the SLD and the SAP systems to enable automatic updates of the available data. This can be done, for example, by querying the clients or release statuses of the software components being used. Moreover, integration with the SLD is also necessary for using ABAP proxies.

Note
APPINT 2.0 add-on for SAP Web AS 6.20

APPINT 2.0 add-on
for SAP Web AS
6.20

If you want to integrate an SAP system based on SAP WAS 6.20, you must ensure that the APPINT 2.0 add-on is installed. This add-on contains the basic functions of SAP XI 2.0 that enable an SAP system to act as a local IS. This makes using proxies based on AS ABAP 6:20 possible.

3.3.1   Creating the RFC Connections

First, create two RFC connections of the TCP/IP type. The LCRSAPRFC connection is used to import the exchange profile of SAP NetWeaver PI. The exchange profile contains parameters used to define basic settings such as the host names and ports used by the SAP NetWeaver PI components. The second connection, SAPSLDAPI, is used by the ABAP application programming interface (API) to connect to the SLD. In addition, you must maintain information on how and with which users the SLD can be accessed. Finally, you must test the connection and schedule regular data synchronizations.

LCRSAPRFC is a
TCP/IP connection

You only need to create the RFC connections once for each SAP system, regardless of how many clients you have declared as business systems within one system. Log on to a client of your choice in system A or B and call Transaction SM59. Follow the EDIT • CREATE menu path, or click the Create button in the upper section of the screen, which opens a new dialog box. The first connection is called LCRSAPRFC and is type T – TCP/IP CONNECTION. Enter a description for the connection and confirm your entries by pressing the Enter key.

If you use an Internet Demonstration and Evaluation System (IDES) system, the system displays an error message saying that the connection already exists. In this case, you must exit the current transaction, search the relevant destination in the TCP/IP Connections category, and open it for editing.

This destination already exists in IDES systems

If the system does not return an error message, the layout of the lower part of the screen changes so that you can enter additional parameters. For this, you must select the REGISTERED SERVER PROGRAM activation type. For the PROGRAM ID, enter a name with structure LCRSAPRFC_<PISID>, where <PISID> represents the SID of your SAP NetWeaver PI system. You can determine the SID by logging on to your SAP NetWeaver PI system using the SAP GUI and following the SYSTEM • STATUS menu path. In our case, the SID is PI1. Due to the registration you are carrying out with this step, a connection to the program of the same name can be established on the gateway server (in this case, the SAP NetWeaver PI system). The server program with the same program ID has been created during the installation of SAP NetWeaver PI.

ABAP and Java components find each other through a registered program ID

Although the program ID is not the cleanest of all solutions, it lets you increase the speed of your work. By default, the program ID to be used is installed during the installation of SAP NetWeaver PI. However, depending on the type of SAP system you want to integrate, we recommend that you use program IDs of the structure LCRSAPRFC_UNICODE for Unicode systems or LCRSAPRFC_NONUNICODE for non-Unicode systems. A more precise differentiation of the connections can be achieved by complementing the SID of the connected backend system, so that, for example, schema LCRSAPRFC_<SID>_UNICODE results. This distinction helps in troubleshooting if necessary.

The use of new program IDs makes a previous registration on the Java side of SAP NetWeaver PI necessary, which you can only do if you have the relevant administrator privileges. If you do, you can create separate entries for the LCRSAPRFC and SAPSLDAPI connections in compliance with the SAP installation guide. Here you have to make sure that you create a program ID for Unicode and one for non-Unicode systems, where such systems are still present in your landscape and should be connected to SAP NetWeaver PI.

Connection data is
stored in
Transaction
SMICM

The remaining values to be entered in this screen are the GATEWAY
OPTIONS. The GATEWAY HOST is the host name of your SAP NetWeaver PI
system, which you have seen in the URL of the SLD call in the previous
section. The GATEWAY SERVICE is created according to structure sapgw##,
with ## being the instance number of the SAP NetWeaver PI system. You
can determine the instance number from the Java 2 Enterprise Edition
(J2EE) port when calling the SLD, as the port is structured according to
pattern 5##00.

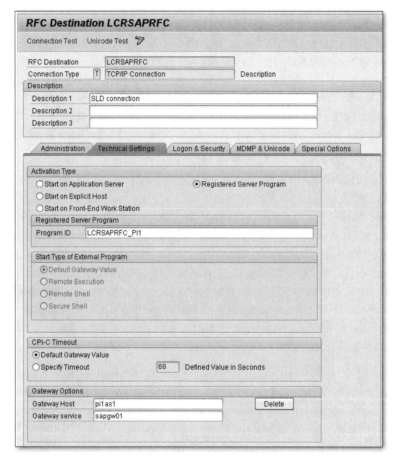

Figure 3.10 Creating the RFC Destination LCRSAPRFC on the ABAP Side

The host of SAP NetWeaver PI, where the system with the instance number 01 runs, is pilas1, which results in the gateway service sapgw01. Figure 3.10 displays the necessary settings in the TCP/IP connection, LCRSAPRFC. For systems with an AS ABAP from 7.00 (for example, SAP ECC 6.0), you must also make sure that the Unicode flag is set on the MDMP & Unicode tab.

Save your settings and run both the connection and the Unicode test via the corresponding buttons. Both tests should run successfully. If you are not sure about the exact data of the RFC connection, starting with SAP NetWeaver PI 7.1, you can have a look in the destination LCRSAPRFC in the SAP NetWeaver PI system and copy the values. This connection is created by the Configuration Wizard in the SAP NetWeaver PI system and contains the correct data.

Similar to the first RFC connection, you can now create SAPSLDAPI. The Program ID for this destination is SAPSLDAPI_<PISID>, or, if you have already registered other programs on the Java side, the corresponding program ID. Both the Gateway Host and Gateway service remain unchanged. Once you have saved the settings, you must also run the connection and Unicode tests.

SAPSLDAPI is created like LCRSAPRFC

3.3.2 Configuring the SLD Integration

Next, you'll need to configure the data exchange process with the SLD, based on those two connections. For this, call Transaction SLDAPICUST and click the Display <-> Change icon to go to the change mode. If there is an existing entry, you should consult with your landscape administrator to find out whether or not the entry is needed.

Maintaining the SLD access data in Transaction SLDAPICUST

If so, you can create an additional row by clicking the Insert Row icon. Mark this row as Primary by clicking the corresponding checkbox, and specify the host name of the SAP NetWeaver PI system. Depending on the release of the backend system and support packages of the SAP NetWeaver PI system, the host name must be specified in the short format or as the fully qualified host name (see SAP Note 608322). In most cases, however, the fully qualified host name is required. From AS ABAP 7.10 on, you can use this transaction to test the specified data, using a separate Test button.

Properties of the specified user

Regardless of the host name, enter the J2EE resp. HTTP port number of your SAP NetWeaver PI system in accordance with the Scheme 5##00 in the corresponding column. Unlike XI 3.0, the user for this connection may not be XIAPPLUSER or PIAPPLUSER, because in SAP NetWeaver PI 7.1, this user does not have the necessary role SAP_SLD_CONFIGURATOR. You can instead specify user SLD_CL_<PISID>, which is created by the Configuration Wizard, or an appropriate copy.

The password (SLD_CL_<PISID>) was specified when starting the Configuration Wizard in the SAP NWA. Because it can be expected that your landscape administrator has already changed the password, you should check with him. The password can be specified after clicking the button in the PASSWORD column. Save these settings and exit the transaction. Figure 3.11 shows an overview of the settings described so far.

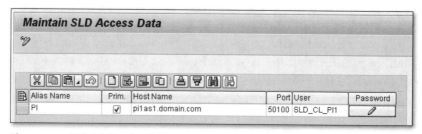

Figure 3.11 Maintaining the SLD Access Data

Checking the SLD integration using Transaction SLDCHECK

Due to the many configuration steps that need to be performed, this process is prone to errors. For this reason, you should use a separate transaction to test integration with the SLD. Transaction SLDCHECK checks all of the settings made so far. If the check is successful, the transaction should call the SLD in a separate browser window, and should not display any error messages in red.

In addition, two dark green summaries should confirm the correct connection: "Summary: Connection to SLD works correctly" and "Summary: Connection to the XI Profile works correctly." If an error is displayed, you should double-check the settings you have made up to this point, or refer to the decision tree provided by SAP, which you can find in SAP Note 768452.

The final step in setting up the SLD integration consists of scheduling the automatic data transfer to the SLD. Transaction RZ70 allows you to check and configure the data transfer.

You can keep almost all of the default settings. On the left side of the screen, you can see that a batch job is scheduled, which transfers data about the system to the SLD every 720 minutes (12 hours). Enter the host and gateway services of the SAP NetWeaver PI system on the right in the SLD BRIDGE: GATEWAY INFORMATION section. These values correspond to those used in the RFC connections to the SLD.

In addition, the lower part of the screen lets you define the data collection programs to be used. At this point, it is helpful to have the system generate a proposal, which you can do by clicking the PROPOSAL icon in the bottom-right of the screen. Next, click the START DATA COLLECTION AND JOB SCHEDULING icon in the upper part of the screen to start the corresponding process. The system displays a detailed message telling you that all selected collection programs have been executed and that the data has been successfully transferred. In addition, a background job was scheduled, which automatically sends the data to the specified intervals to the SLD.

If you didn't explicitly specify an RFC destination the first time the data collector is called, two new TCP/IP RFC connections, SLD_UC and SLD_NUC, are automatically created within the SAP system. If, during the start of the data collector, an error message tells you that the new RFC destinations could not be called, you must make sure that the program IDs, SLD_UC and SLD_NUC, are registered in the SLD.[6] This behavior can occur if the destinations already existed, such as in an IDES system.

Figure 3.12 shows an overview of the settings. Now exit the results display and activate your configuration by clicking the MATCH icon in the top left-hand area of the screen.

---

6 You can find additional information on configuring the SLD integration in SAP Notes 700127 and 584654.

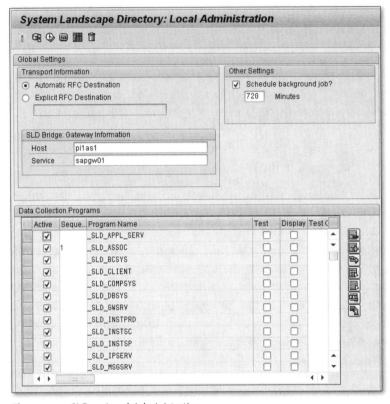

Figure 3.12 SLD — Local Administration

3.4 Configuring the Local IE

Direct data exchange with SAP NetWeaver PI

Now that you have configured a regular data exchange between the SAP system and the SLD, you must configure the local IE of the SAP system. If you use an SAP system with an SAP WAS 6.20 or higher, the direct communication function between the central and the local IE can be used. This connection is a prerequisite for implementing ABAP proxy scenarios.

In the following sections, you will define the role of the local IE and establish the technical settings required for processing XML messages in the business systems. In addition, you will establish a connection to the Integration Builder. Finally, you will set up a user that allows you to monitor the local IE from the Runtime Workbench.

Note

We occasionally use the term "XI" in the following sections; this is because SAP re-used many technical elements of release XI 3.0 without updating the terminology.

3.4.1 Defining the Role of the Business System

The client of the SAP system that you want to use has already been assigned the role of a business system in the SLD, but you must also make a corresponding local setting. In addition to defining the role, specify the connection to SAP NetWeaver PI. Although connection data already exists in the SLD, local maintenance allows you to add authentication data as well. This logon data is needed to use ABAP proxies. You must specify the logon data in a separate RFC destination.

Defining the client role in Transaction SXMB_ADM

Open Transaction SM59 in business system A to maintain the RFC destinations. Then follow the EDIT • CREATE menu path to create the new connection, XI_INTEGRATIONSERVER. In IDES systems, this connection may already exist. If so, you can customize the existing destination.

Creation of RFC destination XI_INTEGRATION SERVER

Select connection type H – CONNECTION TO ABAP SYSTEM and enter a description. When you confirm your entries by pressing the [Enter] key, the lower part of the screen is adjusted accordingly. Go to the TECHNICAL SETTINGS tab and enter the host name of your SAP NetWeaver PI system as the target host. Select the service number of the Java port of SAP NetWeaver PI, which is usually structured according to pattern 5##00. In contrast to XI 3.0, at this point the ABAP port is not explicitly used anymore. The PATH PREFIX is */sap/xi/engine/?type=entry*. Figure 3.13 displays an overview of the data of the first tab.

Go to the LOGON & SECURITY tab and select the SAP STANDARD logon procedure. In the LOGON section, enter the data of USER PIAPPLUSER in the IS client in the SAP NetWeaver PI system. This data is used later for authentication with the SAP NetWeaver PI service when SAP NetWeaver PI is called by the ABAP proxy. Figure 3.14 displays the settings of this tab.

Figure 3.13   Technical Settings of RFC Destination XI_INTEGRATIONSERVER

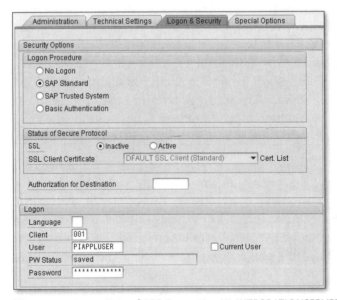

Figure 3.14   Logon Data of RFC Connection XI_INTEGRATIONSERVER

Save the destination and run a connection test by clicking on the corresponding button. If necessary, you must confirm that you will accept all additional cookies. The results display should show status code 500, which means that the SAP NetWeaver PI service was called without data. If the system displays a different status code, you must check the logon data and, if necessary, whether the corresponding sap/xi/engine service has been released in Transaction SICF in SAP NetWeaver PI; the activation should happen automatically during the setup using the Configuration Wizard.[7]

To define the role of the business system now, and to integrate the stored destination, you must call Transaction SXMB_ADM in your business system. Follow the INTEGRATION ENGINE • CONFIGURATION • INTEGRATION ENGINE CONFIGURATION menu path from the directory structure and execute this action by double-clicking the menu item at the end of the path, or via the corresponding Execute Function [F8] icon. This takes you to the configuration data of the IE.

In this screen, follow the EDIT • CHANGE GLOBAL CONFIGURATION DATA menu path, which integrates the screen and causes some new icons to display. Next, select the LOC APPLICATION SYSTEM role for this business system and specify the IS by entering DEST://XI_INTEGRATIONSERVER. The keyword DEST:// ensures that the newly created RFC destination XI_INTEGRATIONSERVER will be used (see Figure 3.15).

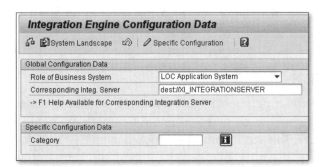

Figure 3.15 Configuration Data of the IE

---

7   Section 3.4.3, Activating the XI Service, contains detailed instructions on how to
    proceed in Transaction SICF.

Save the settings and go one step back until you reach the tree structure of Transaction SXMB_ADM.

3.4.2 Defining and Activating Message Queues

Defining and activating queues to process asynchronous messages

Asynchronous messages are processed in such a way that all messages are first arranged in *queues* that ensure the dispatch or reception of individual messages in the correct sequence based on the type of delivery. Because local IEs can also receive such messages, the queues must be defined and activated.

Follow the path INTEGRATION ENGINE • ADMINISTRATION • MANAGE QUEUES menu path from the directory structure of Transaction SXMB_ADM and execute this step by double-clicking the path entry. The system then displays a list of queues that must be created. The queues are distinguished by the type of processing (inbound vs. outbound), by the delivery options (exactly once (EO) and exactly once in order (EOIO)), and by the priority of the message.

Furthermore, a queue for particularly large messages must be created (see Figure 3.16). Make sure that all queues are marked, and click on the REGISTER QUEUES button to register the queues. Upon successful completion, you will receive feedback on the status bar. Then click on the ACTIVATE QUEUES button to activate the registered queues. After an appropriate success message you can follow the GOTO • QRFC MONITOR menu path or click the appropriate button to check the status of the queues. Leave the transaction afterward.

3.4.3 Activating the XI Service

You must activate the XI service on each IE

As already described during the configuration of the SLD integration, the IEs communicate with each other using the Internet Communication Framework (ICF). This service must be activated in each system that contains a separate IE, regardless of whether it is local or central. Unlike the connected business systems, the following steps have already been performed in SAP NetWeaver PI during the execution of the Configuration Wizard.

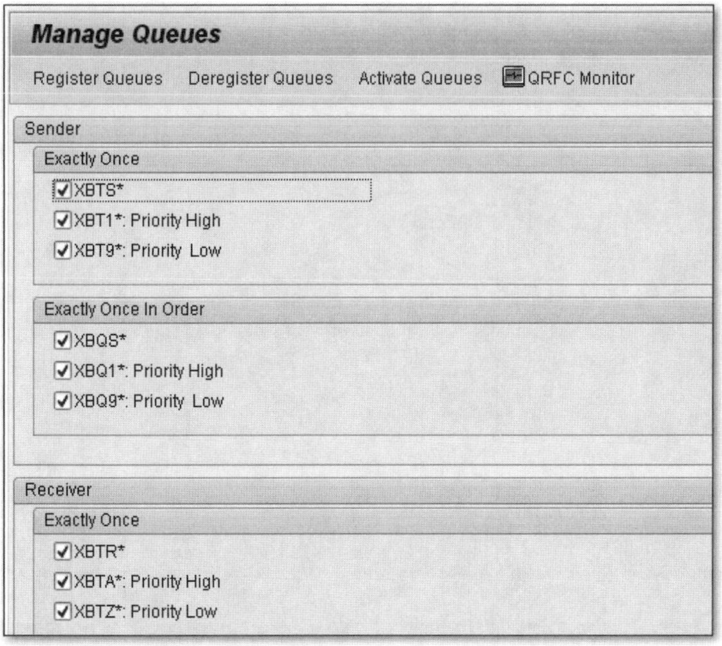

Manage Queues

Register Queues   Deregister Queues   Activate Queues   QRFC Monitor

Sender

Exactly Once

☑ XBTS*

☑ XBT1*: Priority High

☑ XBT9*: Priority Low

Exactly Once In Order

☑ XBQS*

☑ XBQ1*: Priority High

☑ XBQ9*: Priority Low

Receiver

Exactly Once

☑ XBTR*

☑ XBTA*: Priority High

☑ XBTZ*: Priority Low

Figure 3.16 Managing Queues

Call Transaction SICF in your business system to access the directory structure of the existing services. Make sure that the SERVICE hierarchy type is selected in the selection screen, and start the selection by following the PROGRAM • EXECUTE menu path, or the corresponding icon. Within the directory structure, navigate along the DEFAULT_HOST • SAP • XL menu path and consider the services located in this directory (see Figure 3.17).

Check to see if the ENGINE service has already been activated (i.e., if it is colored black). If it hasn't been activated, select this service and click on SERVICE/VIRT.HOST • ACTIVATE in the menu bar. Confirm the security question that appears with the first Yes OPTION. The second Yes option activates all subdirectories and services for a directory, which is not necessary at this point. Exit the transaction as soon as the activation is complete.

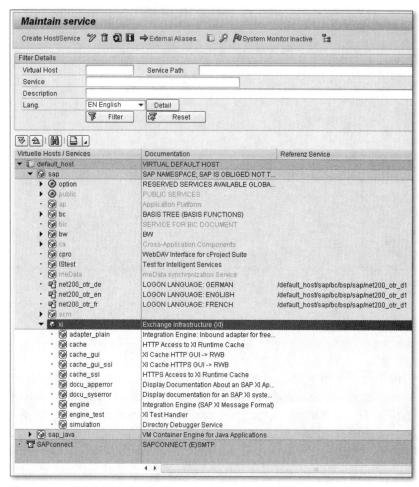

Figure 3.17 Maintaining the Services

3.4.4 Establishing the Connection to the Integration Builder and the Runtime Workbench

The last step in configuring the IE involves creating a connection to the contents of the Integration Builder. Like the central IE, local ISs also require information on the objects that have been created in the Integration Builder. This is a particularly important prerequisite for configuring ABAP proxy scenarios. The connection is established by using an RFC connection with the fixed name INTEGRATION_DIRECTORY_HMI, where HMI stands for HTTP Method Invocation.

Start Transaction SM59 to create a new connection. The destination should be assigned the name INTEGRATION_DIRECTORY_HMI and be a Type H – CONNECTION TO ABAP SYSTEM connection. In addition, enter a description of your choice and confirm your entries by pressing the ⌈Enter⌋ key.

Creating the RFC connection INTEGRATION_ DIRECTORY_HMI

If a security message displays, you can skip it. The lower part of the screen will change, and then you can specify the TARGET HOST by entering the SAP NetWeaver PI system's host name. The service number describes the SAP NetWeaver PI server's J2EE port and is structured according to the 5XX00 schema. The PATH PREFIX to the target host is firmly defined for SAP NetWeaver PI 7.1: */dir/CacheRefresh*. Keep in mind that the prefix is case sensitive (see Figure 3.18).

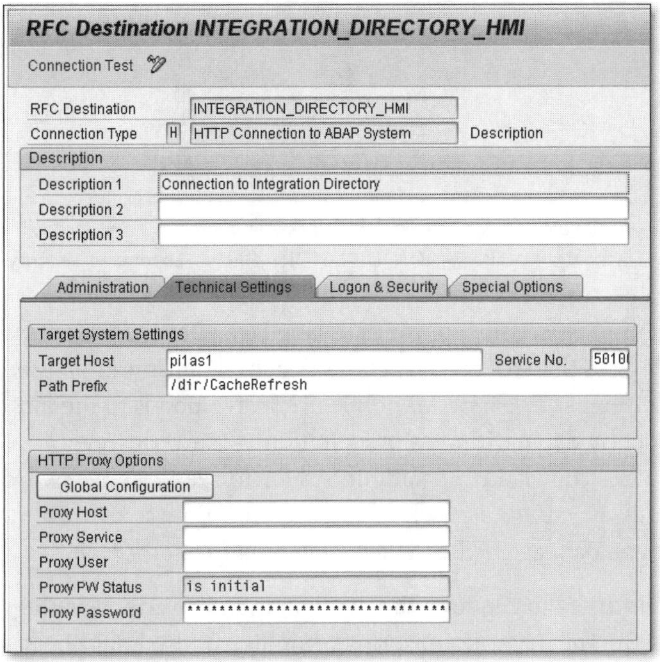

Figure 3.18 RFC Destination INTEGRATION_DIRECTORY_HMI — Technical Settings

Connection uses
the user PIISUSER

Now go to the LOGON & SECURITY tab and make sure that the BASIC AUTHENTICATION logon procedure is selected (see Figure 3.19). In addition, you must check to see if the Secure Sockets Layer (SSL) setting corresponds to your landscape. To log on, you must use the user PIISUSER in the client of the central IS within your SAP NetWeaver PI system (001 by default).

Figure 3.19 RFC Destination INTEGRATION_DIRECTORY_HMI — Logon and Security

In addition, you must set the appropriate language. Depending on the language settings of the SAP NetWeaver PI system, English can be used in most cases. The master password of this user corresponds to the master password set by default in the Configuration Wizard. However, you should check with your landscape administrator to see if the password has been changed. Save the newly created connection at this point, because the logon data can be lost when switching to another tab.

The SPECIAL OPTIONS tab requires the configuration of various settings (see Figure 3.20). The TIMEOUT in terms of milliseconds should be set to 30000. In the HTTP SETTING section, make sure that the compression option is set to INACTIVE and that no compressed response is expected. Regarding HTTP COOKIES, all cookies should be accepted.

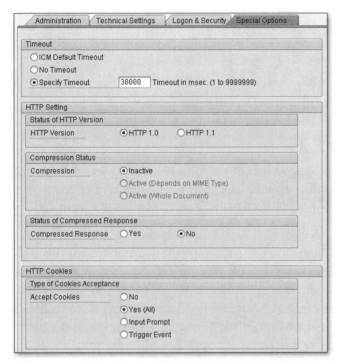

Figure 3.20 RFC Destination INTEGRATION_DIRECTORY_HMI — Special Options

Save the connection and follow the UTILITIES • CONNECTION TEXT menu path, or click on the Connection Text icon. Select the Accept All Further Cookies option in the security prompt that appears, and click on Yes. If, instead of the security prompt, an input field pops up where you must enter a user name and password, either the logon data was incorrect or there was a mistake when entering it.

Return code 200 in case of successful connection test

The next screen displays the result of the connection test. With a successful test, status 500 of the HTTP response will appear; this represents an internal server error due to a lack of data transmission (see Figure 3.21). Exit the test and Transaction SM59.

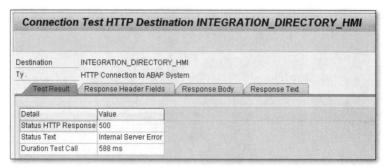

Figure 3.21 RFC-Destination INTEGRATION_DIRECTORY_HMI —
Connection Test

User PIRWBUSER
to log on to the
business system

To monitor the configuration of the local IE, the Runtime Workbench
tries to log on with a specific user, which we now have to create. You
must create the user PIRWBUSER in every client of the SAP system that has
been set up as a local IE.

To do this, call Transaction SU01 and enter the name of the new user. Follow the USERS • CREATE menu path, or click on the corresponding icon.
The system now displays the Address tab, in which you only need to
maintain the last name of the user. Enter the password that corresponds
to the master password set in the Configuration Wizard in the Logon
data tab, and repeat this entry. Depending on the password, a warning
message may appear saying that the password is not backward compatible. In releases up to and including 6.40, passwords are not case sensitive in the ABAP part of the AS; all passwords are treated as capitalized.

Keep this in mind later when creating RFC connections between systems
with AS ABAP 6.40 and earlier. Make sure that the type of the user is B
Service. Go to the Roles tab and select the SAP_XI_RWB_SERV_USER_MAIN
composite role; all contained single roles are listed. Save the user with
the USERS • SAVE menu path or the Floppy disk icon.

Mass generation of
the roles SAP_XI*
and SAP_SLD*

Sometimes the SAP NetWeaver PI authorization roles and the associated profiles have not been used in the business systems, and therefore
haven't been generated yet. If that's the case, you must call Transaction
PFCG in the business systems. Then follow the UTILITIES • MASS GEN-

ERATION menu path and enter SAP_XI* to specify all roles whose names begin with "SAP_XI" (see Figure 3.22).

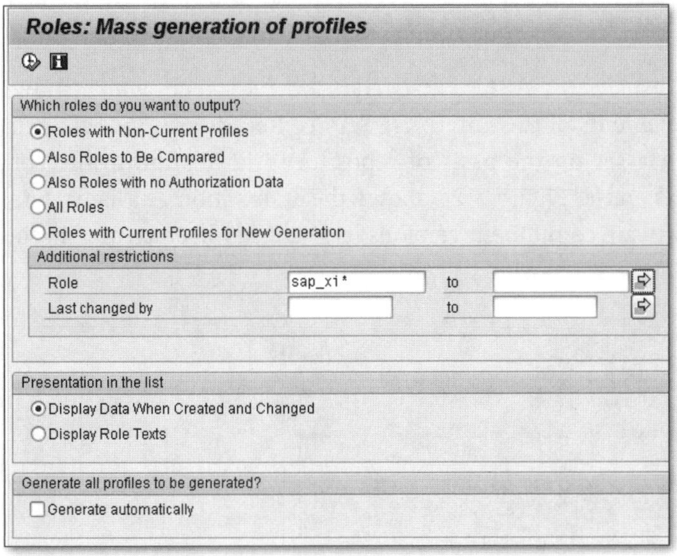

Figure 3.22 Mass Generation

If you select the PROGRAM • EXECUTE menu path, or click on the corresponding icon, the system displays a list of profiles it has found, including their generation statuses. Next, select the ROLES • GENERATE PROFILE menu path and generate the profiles. Repeat these steps for the SAP_SLD* profiles. If users exist that already use these roles, you must also carry out a mass comparison according to the same schema by following the UTILITIES • MASS COMPARISON menu path in Transaction PFCG.

The previously presented activities must be carried out similarly for the system or the client, which will later serve as system B.

3.5 Adapter-Specific System Settings

Although you have to configure more settings in the following exercises, you will primarily deal with content-related aspects. The settings made in this section, however, involve the system administration level and are therefore described separately.

General configuration of different adapter types

157

3.5.1 Checking the ABAP-Proxy Integration

Testing via
Transaction
SPROXY
The local IE, which requires the same information on existing repository objects as the central IE, is used by ABAP proxies to integrate the SAP system. To verify this on your system, start Transaction SPROXY.

The system displays the ABAP PROXY GENERATION screen, which shows all existing elements of the Enterprise Service Repository. You will generate proxy classes on the basis of repository information in the corresponding exercise. Figure 3.23 shows the transaction at a later date, when the software component versions have already been created in the Enterprise Services Repository.

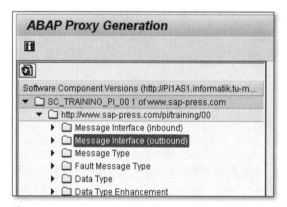

Figure 3.23 Transaction SPROXY with the Objects of a Software Component Version

3.5.2 Settings for Using the RFC Adapter

Connection of RFC
adapters to an RFC
destination
Using the RFC adapter on the sender's side requires an RFC connection that — similar to the destinations already created — bridges the gap between the ABAP world of the SAP system and the Java world of the Adapter Framework in SAP NetWeaver PI. Depending on whether you carry out the exercise scenario on your own or in a team, you must perform this step once or more times with the relevant variation.

To create a new RFC destination in your system, call Transaction SM59. Create a new T – TCP/IP type connection whose name should be structured according to the schema SystemA_Sender-<Participant number>.

This differentiation of participants is necessary so each group participant can create a separate communication channel. If you want to use the same communication channel for all participants in the RFC exercises, you do not need to add the participant number. The name of the connection for the trainer is SystemA_Sender-00. If you work through the exercises in parallel on multiple clients of a system, it's advantageous to incorporate the client number into the destination's name to avoid overlapping.

> **Note**
>
> The participant number is preceded by a hyphen (-). If you use an underscore here, the system may return an error message, depending on the release. While creating the destination works smoothly, saving can cause seemingly nonsensical errors.

Next, you'll need to enter a description for the destination. Go to the TECHNICAL SETTINGS tab and select the REGISTERED SERVER PROGRAM activation type. Enter a PROGRAM ID that corresponds to the name of the RFC connection. Technically speaking, the differentiation of multiple instances of an RFC communication channel occurs at this point; however, it is useful to use a meaningful name for the RFC connection here for reasons of clarity. Set the CPI-C TIMEOUT to the DEFAULT GATEWAY VALUE.

As you did before with other RFC destinations, you must enter the host name and the gateway service of the SAP NetWeaver PI system in the GATEWAY OPTIONS section. Save the settings without testing the connection. At this stage, a test would fail because the corresponding communication channel hasn't been registered. Check that the Unicode flag in the MDMP & UNICODE tab is activated.

Figure 3.24 shows an overview of the settings described here.

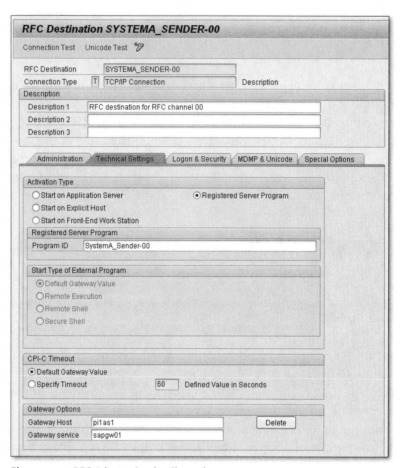

Figure 3.24 RFC Adapter Sender Channel

3.5.3 Settings for Using the IDoc Adapter

Settings required in all involved systems

Delivering messages with the IDoc adapter requires you to configure a lot of elements on both the business system and the SAP NetWeaver PI system. RFC connections are used to deliver the messages to the receiving system. This holds true for delivering IDocs to SAP NetWeaver PI, and for the delivery from SAP NetWeaver PI to the business system. In addition, the SAP NetWeaver PI system requires the metadata of the defined IDocs, which is queried through an RFC destination. This second RFC connection is defined as a port.

Because the system that stores the metadata in the IDoc exercise is also the receiving system, you don't need to maintain the second RFC connection in the SAP NetWeaver PI system. A simplification of the configuration for sending IDocs from SAP NetWeaver PI is available in SAP NetWeaver PI 7.1 insofar as no separate sending communication channel must be created. Necessary settings for automatic processing of inbound IDocs are carried out in the corresponding exercise and case study later in this book.

You must first create a new user, RFC-COMM, in systems A and B, and in the SAP NetWeaver PI system via Transaction SU01. The user should have the same last name. Define a password in the Logon data tab and enter it a second time. In addition, you must make sure that the user type B system is selected.

RFC-COMM allows logon via RFC

Go to the Profiles tab and select authorizations that are as comprehensive as possible. Save your entries. The newly created user enables the connection between the SAP NetWeaver PI system and the business systems for IDoc communication via the RFC destination.

Start Transaction BD54 in system A to make the logical name of the client of system B known to system A. Confirm the warning that the table of logical systems is a client-independent object.

Business system and logical name of the sending business system

Follow the EDIT • NEW ENTRIES menu path, or click the New Entries button. Enter the logical system of the client of system B and a description. You can find the logical system by calling Transaction SCC4 in system B. In most cases, the name has the structure <SID>CLNT<Client> (see Figure 3.25). Save your entries.

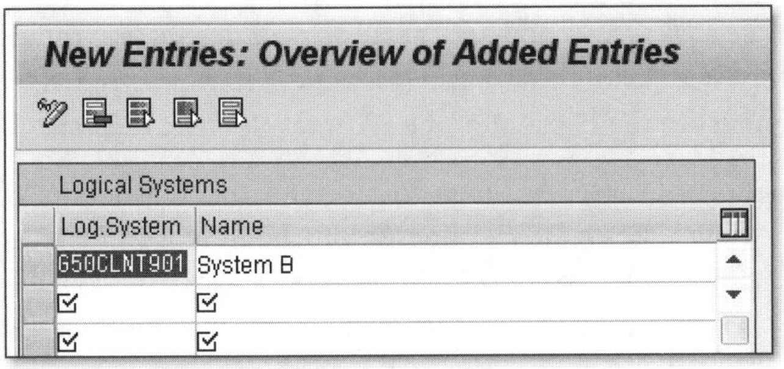

Figure 3.25 Declaration of Sending Logical Systems

Depending on the settings in each client, the changes may have to be stored in a transport request. In this case, select an existing transport request, or create a new one with the appropriate icon and save it. System A now knows the name of the logical system of system B. Repeat this step in system B to make system A known so it can be used later in the case study.

Delivery of IDocs occurs via RFC connections between SAP systems. This holds true for deliveries from business systems to SAP NetWeaver PI and vice versa. This means that, in each business system, you must create a destination to SAP NetWeaver PI and a connection from SAP NetWeaver PI to each business system.

Go to the SAP NetWeaver PI system and call Transaction SM59 to maintain the RFC connections. Create a new 3 – ABAP CONNECTION RFC connection, and call it `SystemA_IDoc`. Repeat these steps for system B.

> **Note**
>
> The name of the RFC connection does not contain any participant number, because the system only recognizes the logical system of the sender. Multiple creations wouldn't make any sense in this case.

Enter the host name of system A in the TARGET HOST field and add the SYSTEM NUMBER in the field to the right (see Figure 3.26). Go to the LOGON & SECURITY tab and maintain the data of the RFC-COMM user you have previously created in the SAP systems and carry out a connection test, which should now be successful.

The test of the remote login will fail, however, because the RFC-KOMM user was created as a communication user and therefore cannot be used to log on. Save the RFC connection and create an RFC destination called `PI_System` in the two business systems. This destination uses the RFC-KOMM user to connect to the IS client of the SAP NetWeaver PI system.

For the port that establishes the connection to the IDoc metadata, you must "wrap" the newly created RFC connection in a different way. To do this, call Transaction IDX1 in your SAP NetWeaver PI system and create a new port by clicking on the blank sheet icon. Assign a name with the structure SAP<SID> to the port; in our case, the port for system A is called SAPS02 and the client is 903. Perform this step for system B, also.

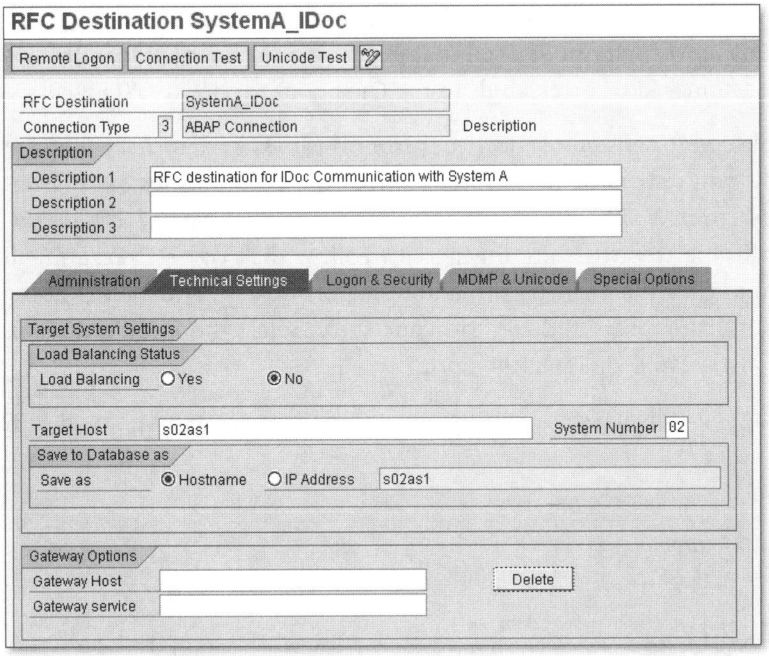

RFC Destination SystemA_IDoc

Remote Logon | Connection Test | Unicode Test

RFC Destination	SystemA_IDoc	
Connection Type	3 ABAP Connection	Description

Description

Description 1	RFC destination for IDoc Communication with System A
Description 2	
Description 3	

Administration | **Technical Settings** | Logon & Security | MDMP & Unicode | Special Options

Target System Settings

Load Balancing Status

Load Balancing ○ Yes ⊙ No

Target Host	s02as1	System Number 02

Save to Database as

Save as	⊙ Hostname ○ IP Address	s02as1

Gateway Options

Gateway Host		Delete
Gateway service		

Figure 3.26 RFC Connection for the IDoc Adapter — Technical Settings

Add a meaningful description and select the newly created RFC destination `SystemA_IDoc` or `SystemB_IDoc`. Save the settings and take a look at the saved entry in the directory structure on the left. Figure 3.27 shows that the client has been attached to the name of the port. However, when used later, the name of the port is SAPS02.

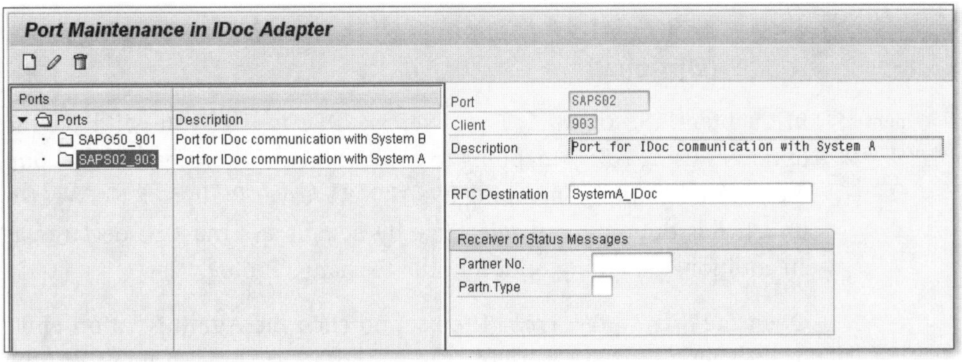

Port Maintenance in IDoc Adapter

Ports			Port	SAPS02
▼ 🗁 Ports	**Description**		Client	903
· 🗀 SAPG50_901	Port for IDoc communication with System B		Description	Port for IDoc communication with System A
· 🗀 SAPS02_903	Port for IDoc communication with System A			
			RFC Destination	SystemA_IDoc

Receiver of Status Messages

Partner No.	
Partn.Type	

Figure 3.27 Port Maintenance in IDoc Adapter

Case study uses
transactional ports

The automatic dispatch of IDocs in the case study requires defining transactional ports that can be used to transfer data via transactional RFCs. A transactional RFC corresponds to the Quality of Service (QoS) EOIO.

Because you will only send IDocs from business system A in the case study, you only need to perform the following steps in system A. Start Transaction WE21 in system A and highlight the TRANSACTIONAL RFC item in the tree structure on the left. Follow the PORT • CREATE menu path, or click the CREATE icon. Enter the port name "PI_SYSTEM" in the screen that appears and confirm your entry. Select the RFC destination you just created and save the port.

Figure 3.28 displays the settings for the port of the transactional RFC call.

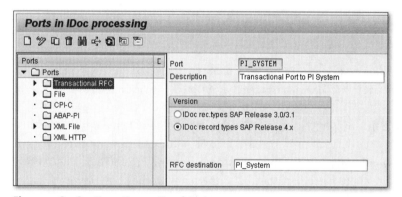

Figure 3.28 Creating a Transactional Port

3.5.4 Adding ABAP Mappings to the Available Mappings (Optional)

Enhancement of
the Exchange
Profile

In Chapter 4, Section 4.1, First Exercise: RFC-to-File, you will have the option of using ABAP mapping to convert messages instead of the commonly used graphical mapping in SAP NetWeaver PI. In SAP NetWeaver PI 7.1, this option is not selectable by default and must be declared as an additional mapping option in the Exchange Profile.

Open the SAP NetWeaver PI tools, and click the Administration entry in the menu on the top right. Then choose Exchange Profile from the menu on the left side, under the entry Property administration option.

Navigate in the left directory structure of the new window to the menu path: INTEGRATION BUILDER • INTEGRATIONBUILDER.REPOSITORY • COM.SAP. AII.REPOSITORY.MAPPING.ADDITIONALTYPES. Once there, type a new value: R3_ABAP | Abap-class (see Figure 3.29).

If this parameter already contains another entry, append the new value using a semicolon (;) to separate the values from each other. ABAP mapping can now be selected in the operation mapping.

You can test the change of the parameter in the Enterprise Services Repository. Should you already be logged in to the Enterprise Services Repository, quit the program, and start it again so that the change can be displayed. Create a new operation mapping, or open an existing one, and look at the possibilities for mapping the messages at the bottom. The new entry, Abap-class, should now appear in the dropdown list (see Figure 3.30).

Test the new mapping option

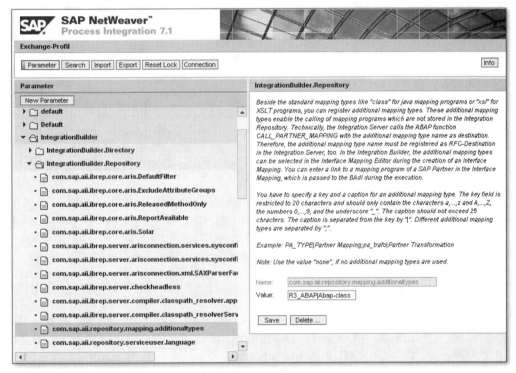

Figure 3.29 Adding ABAP Mapping to the Exchange Profile

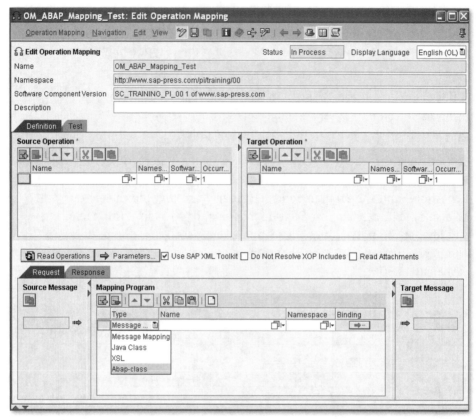

Figure 3.30 ABAP Mapping Option in an Operation Mapping

3.5.5 Preparations for Using Alert Monitoring (Optional)

Activation of the Alert Monitoring Services

Alert monitoring allows dispatching and monitoring of messages that are sent — for example, during an integration process — and contain technical information. The alert monitoring can be found in the Runtime Workbench under the terms *alert configuration* and *alert inbox*. Some activities of the alert configuration can also be carried out in the traditional SAP GUI in SAP NetWeaver PI.

The alert inbox, however, is the only place where an alert is always available (as opposed to the optional configuration of email, short message service (SMS), and fax). To receive certain category alerts, either a user name must be hardcoded, or the user can define specific alert categories (depending on the roles assigned to him).

Depending on the support package level of SAP NetWeaver PI, it is possible that both the subscription and the setting of various sending methods cannot be called. These two functions are provided by services of the SAP NetWeaver PI system, and may not be accessible due to their long names. The exact description of these types of errors can be found in SAP Note 1080668. To fix this error, you have to apply a correction from SAP Note 1038797, which provides an ABAP program to correct the name issue for certain services.

Program `BSP_UNLOCK_LONG_APP` can be started via Transaction SE38, and has to be called for the services `ALERTPERSONALIZE_RULES` and `ALERTSUB-SCRIPTION` (see Figure 3.31). Then the two functions can be activated in the alert inbox.

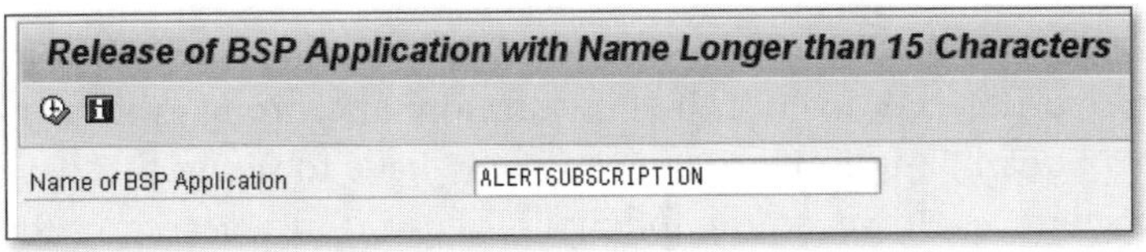

Figure 3.31 Call of Program BSP_UNLOCK_LONG_APP for Service ALERTSUBSCRIPTION

Training participants will have the opportunity to send an alert message from an Integration Process in the fourth technical exercise; they will create a separate alert category for this. To group the alert categories of the participants in a classification (equivalent to a folder), you, as the lecturer, must specify an appropriate classification.

Definition of an alert classification

Log on to the SAP NetWeaver PI system and call Transaction ALRTCDEF to create a new classification. Switch to change mode, and open the context menu of the root entry ALL CLASSIFICATIONS. From the context menu, choose the CREATE option (see Figure 3.32). Enter a classification and a description, "`PI_BOOK`". Save the changes and select a customizing transport request. Students can create their alert categories in this classification.

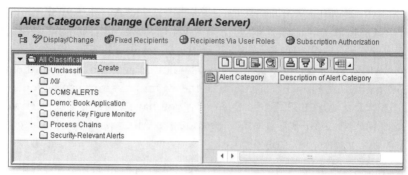

Figure 3.32 Creation of a New Alert Classification

3.6 Course-Specific Preparations

Preparations for exercises that are carried out in a course

The basic system settings made so far are primarily used to integrate SAP systems with SAP NetWeaver PI. If you want to work through the exercises in this book in a training course, you only have to set up this new configuration once. However, the following steps may be necessary for each course, so you can complete the exercises.

In principle, you can have students make these settings by themselves, but depending on the system landscape, it may make sense to keep students who are not experienced with SAP NetWeaver PI from working in the SLD. For this reason, you must familiarize yourself with the authorization objects required for the creation of the participant users.

In addition, you will create a software product with a software component for each student, and import them into the Enterprise Service Repository. These steps must be performed so that each student gets a separate software product with which they can work independently. Thus, the following steps will increase the level of clarity, and are intended to prevent individual students from interrupting each other when processing various objects.

Creating users in all involved clients

Depending on the experience of your students with regard to using enterprise software, you should define the authorizations assigned to users of the system. You can use Transaction SU01 to create a new user in the SAP NetWeaver PI system by entering the name of the new user and following the USERS • CREATE menu path, or by clicking the corresponding icon.

In the Address tab, you must enter a last name for the user. If necessary, users can complete the remaining details later on. In the Logon data tab, it is mandatory to enter the initial password. Finally, the Profiles tab contains a list of user profiles that have been assigned. Assign names to the users in the client of system A according to the schema, SYS_A-##, and in system B according to the schema, SYS_B-##, so you can tell with which system you are currently working. You should use schema PI-## for the users in the SAP NetWeaver PI system.

Table 3.1 lists the most important profiles for the exercises in this book. Each student should be assigned the first three profiles to be able to implement an entire integration scenario. There are some inherent risks in authorizing access to the SLD. Therefore, you should only assign it to experienced users. The authorization is primarily important for creating software products and software components. If you are planning to use role-based subscription of alert messages in addition to the technical exercise in Chapter 4, Section 4.4, Fourth Exercise: Business Process Management, you should assign all of the trainees the SAP_XI_DEVELOPER profile.

Depending on how you implement the exercises, the users need different roles

The last profile for the administration of the SAP NetWeaver PI system should only be assigned to the instructor.

User profile	Description
SAP_XI_DISPLAY_USER	Read-only access to Enterprise Services Builder and Integration Directory
SAP_XI_SUPPORT	Read-only access to Enterprise Services Builder and Integration Directory, and to certain administration sites on AS Java
SAP_XI_DEVELOPER	Design and development of Integration Processes
SAP_XI_CONFIGURATOR	Configuration of business integration content
SAP_XI_CONTENT_ ORGANIZER	Maintenance of content in the SLD

Table 3.1 Important SAP NetWeaver PI User Profiles for Dialogue Users

User profile	Description
SAP_XI_MONITOR	Monitoring of SAP NetWeaver PI components and messages
SAP_XI_MONITOR_ENHANCED	Monitoring of SAP NetWeaver PI components and messages and changing messages
SAP_XI_ADMINISTRATOR	Technical configuration and administration

Table 3.1 Important SAP NetWeaver PI User Profiles for Dialogue Users (Cont.)

Once you have assigned the relevant profiles, you must save the user; you can also use it as a template for creating other users. Depending on the type of SAP system you want to integrate with the SAP NetWeaver PI system, you should consult with your landscape administrator regarding the profiles to be used. If you use an IDES system, you can also use the IDES_USER and IDES_DEVELOP profiles. In addition, you may need to assign privileges for using RFC connections, depending on how you implement certain exercises.

3.6.1 Creating and Assigning the Software Product

Create software products in the SLD

Start Transaction SXMB_IFR to access the SAP NetWeaver PI tools, and log on to the SLD. In the SLD overview, you can find the Software Components item in the Software Catalog menu.

In the software catalog, click on the New... button. In the first step of the wizard, select the option to CREATE A NEW SOFTWARE COMPONENT AND VERSION (see Figure 3.33).

Version number required for software products

In the second step, you create a new software component and a corresponding version. However, because this component must first be assigned to a product, a product must first be created. Click on the Create New Version button, to the right of the version number field. Enter the name of the product according to the scheme *SP_Training_PI_##*. SP indicates a software product and ## stands for the participant's number.

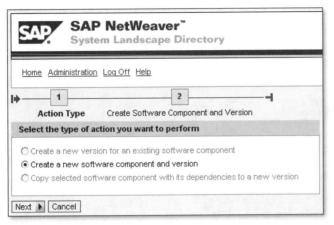

Figure 3.33 Definition of a Software Product — Step 1

You can enter any name as a PRODUCT VENDOR, but you should use a URL to ensure that the name is unique. Although you can use any version number, you should first enter version 1 (see Figure 3.34). Then click the CREATE button to create the new version.

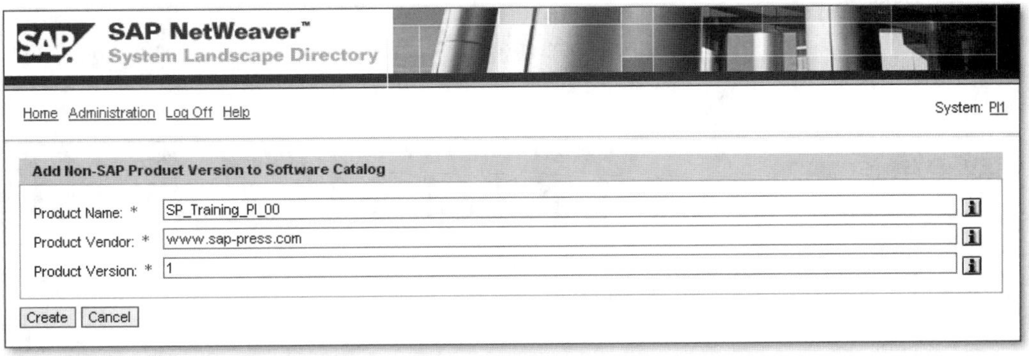

Figure 3.34 Creation of a New Software Product Version

After creating the product and its version, return to the second step of the wizard. Assigning a software component to a product requires a software unit. Software units are used mainly for assigning software products to usage types, and thus allow assigning ABAP and Java developments, which provide the same function.

Creation of a new software unit

Click on the CREATE NEW UNIT button to the right of the corresponding input box. Enter a name according to schema *SU_Training_PI_##*, where SU stands for the software unit and ## for the participant's number (see Figure 3.35). Click CREATE to go back to the second step of the wizard.

Figure 3.35 Creation of a New Software Unit

Creating the software component and version number

Because the product doesn't need more than one component in the exercise scenarios, it is assigned the name SC_Training_PI_##, and is set to version 1. Enter the appropriate values in the two fields, and check that the new software component has the status RELEASED (see Figure 3.36).

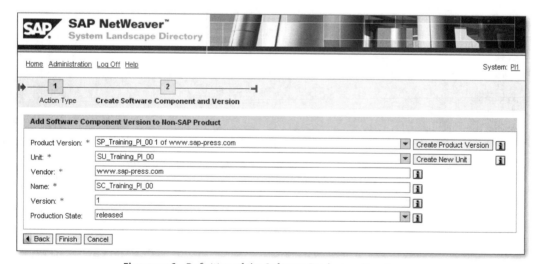

Figure 3.36 Definition of the Software Product — Step 2

Complete the wizard by clicking on the FINISH button. If you have forgotten an item or want to change something, you can always do this in the software catalog. Either look for the appropriate software product or a component, and change the values in the lower details area. This lets you, for example, create software units or software components for a specific product. If you want to use a separate software component for the case study, you can create it the same way.

You can now see your new software component in the components list. Return to the initial SLD screen via the HOME link in the upper left, and select Technical Systems in the Landscape; this is done to declare that you will run your software product on the machines that also run the SAP systems. Select the SYSTEMA that you created previously from the list of technical systems.

Assigning the software product to a technical system

The bottom part of the screen contains detailed data about the technical system, which is divided into several tabs. Navigate to the INSTALLED SOFTWARE tab, where you can see the already-installed software; in this case, it is only SAP ECC 6.0. Click on the ADD NEW PRODUCT button above the listing to assign the software product you just created to this technical system.

On the left side, you can see a list of software products; on the right side, you can see a list of all software components. Both tables have a filter box that you can use to search for the created software product or software component. Enter the products "SP" into the filter box, and confirm the entry by pressing the Enter key.

In the resulting list, your software product will appear. By clicking on it, the components contained in your product software components are displayed in the list on the right side. Mark you component(s) with a checkmark (see Figure 3.37) and save your selections. This returns you to the installed software of the technical system, where you can now see your new software product.

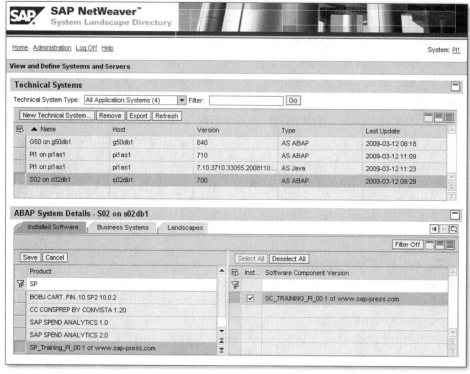

Figure 3.37 Adding a Software Product

Assigning the
software product
to a business
system

Now that the new software product has been assigned to the technical system and is available to all business systems running on the appropriate technical system, it must also be assigned to business systems that intend to use it. Once again, return to the initial SLD screen and click on the Business Systems link in the Landscape section to define that your business system uses this software product.

To do this, click on SYSTEMA in the list of business systems. The bottom part of the screen shows detailed data about the technical system, which is also divided into several tabs. Navigate to the INSTALLED SOFTWARE tab, AND YOU CAN see that your software product appears on the left list, as it is available on the technical system. However, it is not marked, which means it is not used by this business system. Change this by marking your product with a checkmark, and then save the change (see Figure 3.38).

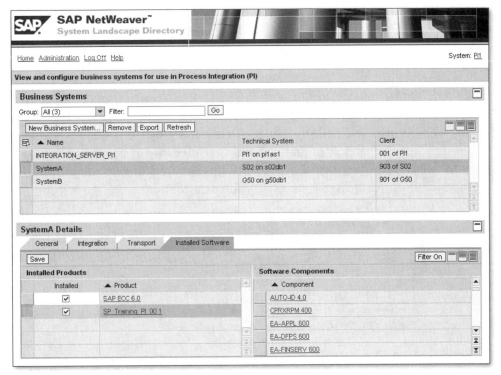

Figure 3.38 Assigning the Software Product to the Business System

3.6.2 Importing the Software Product in the Enterprise Services Repository and Setting it Up

In addition to displaying the installed applications and components of a business system, the newly created software product is also used to organize the development of integration scenarios in the Integration Builder. Before doing so, however, you must import the information on the new product and the software components into the enterprise services repository.

Starting the Enterprise Services Builder

First, return to the SAP NetWeaver PI tools website (for example, by using Transaction SXMB_IFR) and select the Enterprise Services Builder in the Enterprise Services Repositories section. This starts the associated Java Web Start application. Log on using your user ID from the IS client of the SAP NetWeaver PI system. Please note that, prior to logging in, you must have changed the initial password of that user.

After entering the login data, you will be prompted to select an application profile. The application profile determines your rights within the Enterprise Services Builder. The Process Integration and Unrestricted profiles allow all Integration Repository activities that you may know from XI 3.0, while the Service Definition profile only allows the definition of services (it does not allow maintenance of integration scenarios or mappings). For all exercises in this book, select the Process Integration profile (see Figure 3.39), and then continue.

Figure 3.39 Selection of an Application Profile

In the left tree, right-click Local Software Component Versions to open the context menu, and select New. This opens a wizard that lets you create a new software component version. To import the created software component version from the SLD, select Import from SLD in the top pane. Then click on the Display button; all software component versions will be loaded from the SLD.

Select your software component, SC_Training_PI_##, in version 1 and import it (see Figure 3.40). You can use the search box above the list, where you must explicitly specify wildcards with an asterisk (*). The data of the selected software component version are copied into the wizard, and you can trigger the actual creation by clicking the Create button. Depending on the quantity of software components, both the compilation of the list and the import can take a while.

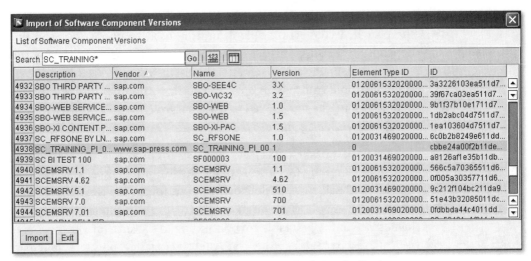

Figure 3.40 Importing Software Component Versions into the Enterprise Services Builder

Expand this branch so you can see the versions of this software component. Double-click on the software component version to open the corresponding datasheet and follow the OBJECT • DISPLAY/EDIT menu path within the datasheet. The color of some fields now changes from gray to white.

Setting up the software component in the Enterprise Services Builder

You must now enter two changes within the datasheet:

▶ On the one hand, you will maintain the data for a connection to an SAP system so that you can later import RFC and IDoc interface information.

▶ On the other hand, you will create a namespace for each participant in which you can create all additional objects within the Enterprise Services Builder.

To import interface data, such as function module interfaces or IDocs from ABAP-based SAP systems, you must enter the appropriate connection data. Maintain the data of an SAP system, such as system A. As you will see, information about the user and password are still missing to initiate a data import. Critical authorization details are only requested during the import itself.

Setup for import of SAP objects

Despite the declaration of the system data at this point, it's possible that the provided connection data cannot be used to import objects; this depends on the support package being used. If this is the case, you can enter the hostname and system number in the Import Wizard, and override the stored information. When you first import external interface definitions in Chapter 4, Section 4.1, First Exercise: RFC-to-File, we will address this issue again.

Creating namespaces for the course participants The lower part of the datasheet contains a list of namespaces that is still empty. Click on the Open icon above the list of namespaces at the bottom of the detail view. In the new window, follow the NAMESPACE DEFINITION • DISPLAY/EDIT menu path to switch to edit mode. Enter a new namespace in the first table row, according to the structure `http://www.sap-press.com/pi/training/##`, where ## again represents your participant number.

When specifying the namespace, it isn't important whether or not the URL actually exists. Your company's Internet domain eliminates any possible namespace collision. You can create additional rows with the green Plus icon at the top of the table.

Save your settings. The color of the object in the lower tab will change from red to white. Go through the tabs below the details view, then back to the software component version, and save it (see Figure 3.41). This will create branches for each namespace under the software component version in the tree.

Unlike earlier SAP NetWeaver PI releases, the system does not automatically create a directory for each type of object under a namespace; the paths are only created if objects have been created in the namespace. Due to the omission of the automatic creation of directories and data types, the software component version doesn't have to be activated separately using the change list.

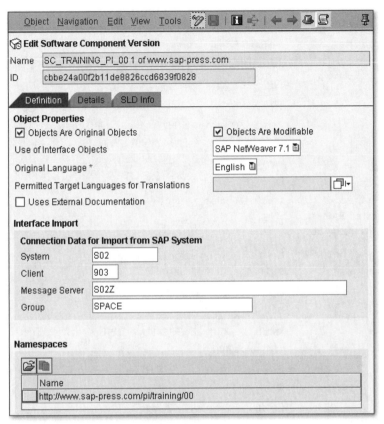

Figure 3.41 Editing the Software Component Version

To ensure that all of the preparatory steps have been done correctly, use the checklist provided in Table 3.2. If you encounter any errors or problems during the course of the exercises that you cannot solve with the help of this book, you can also refer to the Troubleshooting Guide for SAP NetWeaver PI. You can find the Troubleshooting Guide in the SAP Support Portal (*http://service.sap.com*) by following the menu path: SAP NETWEAVER • SAP NETWEAVER PI 7.1 • OPERATIONS • PROCESS INTEGRATION.

Checklist and
SAP NetWeaver PI
Troubleshooting
Guide

Area	Configuration	OK
Prerequisites	Systems A and B run on SAP WAS 6.20+	
	SAP GUI version 7.10+ is installed in the frontend	
	Java Web Start is installed in the frontend	
	Port 5XX00 of the J2EE Engine is released in the SAP NetWeaver PI system	
	ABAP Port 80XX is released in all business systems	
Define the connected SAP systems in the SLD	Create technical systems A and B in the SLD	
	Create business systems A and B in the SLD	
Integrate the SAP systems with the SLD	Create RFC connection `LCRSAPRFC` in business systems A and B	
	Create RFC connection `SAPSLDAPI` in business systems A and B	
	Settings in Transaction SLDAPICUST in systems A and B	
	Execute Transaction SLDCHECK in systems A and B successful	
	Configure the data exchange in Transaction RZ70 in systems A and B	
Configure the local IE	Create the RFC destination `XI_INTEGRATIONSERVER` and definition of the role of the business system in Transaction SXMB_ADM in systems A and B	
	Define and activate message queues in systems A and B	
	Activate the XI service in systems A and B	
	Create the RFC connection `INTEGRATION_DIRECTORY_HMI` in systems A and B	
	Create user PIRWBUSER in systems A and B (if necessary, mass generation and mass comparison)	

Table 3.2 Checklist for Basic System Settings

Area	Configuration	OK
Adapter-specific system settings	Start of Transaction SPROXY in both business systems	
	Create RFC connections `SystemA_Sender-<Participant number>` in business system A	
	Create `RFC-COMM` users in both business systems and the SAP NetWeaver PI system	
	Mutual publishing of the logical systems in systems A and B	
	Create RFC connections `SystemA_IDoc` and `SystemB_IDoc` in the SAP NetWeaver PI system	
	Create RFC connections `PI_System` in both business systems A and B	
	Create ports for business systems A and B in the SAP NetWeaver PI system	
	Create the transactional port `PI_System` in business system A	
Course-specific preparations	Create system users in the business systems and in SAP NetWeaver PI	
	Create and assign software products in the SLD	
	Import and set up the software product in the Enterprise Services Builder	
	Mappings enhanced by option `Abap-class` (optional)	
	Alter monitoring has been prepared (optional)	

Table 3.2 Checklist for Basic System Settings (Cont.)

The exercises in this chapter show you how to use SAP NetWeaver Process Integration (PI) components by presenting scenarios that are linked in content, but technically independent, to prepare you for the case study in the following chapter.

4   Technical Exercises

Using the available concepts and adapters of SAP NetWeaver PI is the basis for implementing complex integration scenarios. This chapter shows you how to configure adapters, create mappings, and monitor scenarios. The individual exercises build on each other and get more complex to help you gain the knowledge necessary to implement the case study presented in Chapter 5, SARDIS Case Study in Sales and Distribution.

Although the individual exercises depend on each other, you can use the lists of every exercise to track which objects are reused so you can start with a more advanced lesson. Predefined objects aren't used in the exercises, so you can reproduce all of the steps for completing the integration scenario at any time.

All of the exercises are designed in such a way that they can be performed by members of a class at the same time. Still, some steps can only be carried out once. Any steps that must be performed by the instructor either prior to or during the course will be noted.

Appropriate for several participants

> **Note**
>
> Although the exercises are appropriate for workgroups, you can also complete them on your own. If you do, you should also perform the steps that would be implemented by the instructor.
>
> Even if you are going to complete the exercises alone, we recommend using a user number, as this simplifies comparisons between your work and the described procedure. In this case, you should use the instructor's number — 00.

Most exercises are completed as a development consultant, and, particularly in the beginning of the exercise block, you will assume the role of the system administrator or lead developer. In some places, you will have the opportunity to develop your own small applications in ABAP or Java. You hardly need any prerequisites for this, because the sample listings can be found in Appendix A, Exercise Materials, and in digital form on the website for this book (*http://www.sap-press.com*).

The exercises deal with selected adapters and aspects of the PI environment. Various elements played a role in selecting the integration scenarios. On one hand, we present adapters that enable the presentation of reproducible exercises. On the other, we identify aspects that are necessary to implement the case study.

Even though the individual exercises do not have to be completed in the given order, we did choose their order for a reason. In this chapter, you will implement integration scenarios that will prepare you for the case study in Chapter 5. Using PI messages, you will create material in another system and verify its success. In the final step, the creation of material master data is reported to the person responsible for all materials. A business process ensures that these reports are delivered in bundles per agent.

To begin, you will use an ABAP program in system A, which records the data of a material to be created and transfers this data to the PI system using the remote function call (RFC) adapter (see Section 4.1, Exercise 1: RFC-to-File). There, the material master record is converted to a file in PI format via the file adapter. In the next exercise, this file is read by the file adapter and converted into an intermediate document (IDoc), which is transferred to and directly processed on system B (see Section 4.2, Exercise 2: File-to-IDoc).

In the third example, you will check to ensure that the material has been created successfully. Based on an ABAP proxy, you will send a call to the PI system. This request is converted to a Web service call provided by system B. The response of this control is synchronously returned to calling system A (see Section 4.3, Exercise 3: ABAP-Proxy-to-SOAP). The agent uses an ABAP program to report the successful creation of the material master records using a business process (see Section 4.4, Exercise 4: Business Process Management). As an alternative to the design of the second exercise, the example from the second scenario will be read-dressed in a fifth scenario, replacing the receiving IDoc adapter through a Java database connectivity (JDBC) database (see Section 4.5, Exercise 5: File-to-JDBC).

Even though the contents of the individual exercises are based on one another, you can start with any of the exercises by using the appropriate templates.

4.1 Exercise 1: RFC-to-File

In the first exercise, you will use your own ABAP program to call a remote-enabled function module that transfers material master data via the RFC adapter to the PI system. Once there, the data is converted to PI XML format and stored as a file. To keep things simple, the file is created directly on the PI server's file system.

Course of the first exercise

Although the file technically remains on the PI system, from a logical viewpoint you will configure the receiving file adapter for system B. The communication in this integration scenario is asynchronous, because no business response is returned after sending the material data. The roles of systems A and B, and the adapters used in this exercise, are illustrated in Figure 4.1.

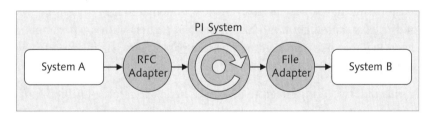

Figure 4.1 Scheme of Exercise 1: RFC-to-File

4.1.1 Basic Principles

Because this book does not focus on the development of ABAP programs and remote-enabled function modules, we will only give you a basic explanation of the program and function module used. You can get an

New ABAP components

185

appropriate transport with the function module and the program for 20 participants and 1 instructor from the book's web page (*http://www. sap-press.com*) and implement it in your system A. For implementing the transport, consult your landscape administrator, if necessary.

If you want to create the program and the function module yourself, you will find the corresponding sample source code in Appendix A.

Structure of the function module

First, log on to the client of system A as the user SYS_A-##. There, you can view the remote-enabled function module using the Function Builder in Transaction SE37. Select the function module Z_RFM_MATERIALINPUT_##, where ## is your participant number.

You will see that from the function module's point of view the parameters are only imported and no value is returned. This is one of the two prerequisites for asynchronous communication from a sending RFC adapter.

Except for the interface definition, the function module does not contain any ABAP code. This means that the function module is used as a kind of dummy that forwards the transferred data to SAP NetWeaver PI and serves as an interface. The information about where to forward the data transferred to the function module is contained in the calling program.

Function of the ABAP program

The program Z_PROG_MATERIALINPUT_##, which you can find with the function module in the same transport request, and that you can view in Transaction SE38, has two functions: First, it accepts the basic material master data that will be used to create a new material in system B. Second, it calls the function module (described earlier) with the parameters listed in Table 4.1. The naming of these parameters is explained in the second exercise, in Section 4.2.

In this call, two things need to be mentioned: The remote-enabled function module is called to a specific destination (i.e., in the system behind this RFC connection). In the case of destination SystemA_Sender-##, this is the PI system, so the values transferred to the function module are forwarded to the PI system. The second aspect is the call in the background that makes the communication asynchronous.

Transferred Data	Description
MATNR	Material number
MAKTX	Material description
ERSDA	Creation Date (will be added automatically)
ERNAM	User name of creator (will be added automatically)
MTART	Material type
MBRSH	Industry sector
MATKL	Material group
MEINS	Quantity unit
BRGEW	Gross weight
GEWEI	Weight unit
MTPOS_MARA	General item category group

Table 4.1 Data Transferred to the Function Module Z_RFM_MATERIALINPUT_##

4.1.2 Design

At first, you need to create the various data and message types, and the service interfaces, with the required mappings in the Enterprise Services Repository. In a later phase of the configuration, these elements will be linked to the connected business systems (system A and system B).

Creating the design objects in the Enterprise Services Repository

First, call Transaction SXMB_IFR from one of the connected systems or from the PI system itself. This opens the PI tools menu in your web browser, which should look familiar to you if you prepared for the exercises (see Chapter 3, Basic System Configuration). At the top-left, select the entry to the Enterprise Services Repository.

First steps

After the Java Web Start application has been updated and you have logged into the PI system as the appropriate user, the user interface of the Enterprise Services Repository is displayed. Make sure that you do not log on using the initial password; instead, change it during the logon to the SAP GUI.

On the left side, you will find the software components that have already been declared. This includes the software component SC_Training_PI_## with the namespace http://www.sap-press.com/pi/training/##, which is where you will store your elements in the Enterprise Services Repository.

For a better overview, restrict the view to your software component. In the tree structure, click on your software component, and, above the tree, click the ONLY DISPLAY SELECTED SUBTREE icon. The Enterprise Services Repository should then look like Figure 4.2.

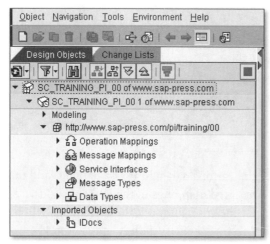

Figure 4.2 Entry to the Enterprise Services Repository

Folders have been introduced with SAP NetWeaver PI 7.1. Their use is optional, and serves the organizational division of design and configuration elements. Folders can be used in both the Enterprise Services Repository and the Integration Builder; the Enterprise Services Repository folder is created via the context menu of a namespace. It is possible to assign design elements directly to a folder when they are created. Folders are logically associated with a namespace. Figure 4.3 shows the namespace http://www.sap-press.com/pi/training/00 in the selection window and the folder TESTFOLDER directly underneath. This folder is in turn associated with the sub SUBFOLDER. In the selection window, you can choose either the superordinate or the subordinate folder.

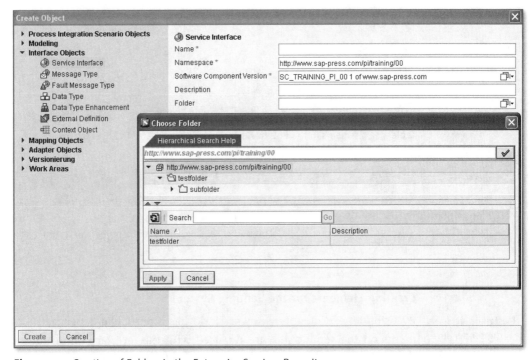

Figure 4.3 Creation of Folders in the Enterprise Services Repository

If you decide to detail the development structure beyond the presented structure, you can assign already-existing elements to a folder via drag and drop. For each of the folders, you can create a substructure in the form of subfolders. These are not limited by their number.

Another advantage of this concept is the authorization administration. You can assign authorizations to the folders on the group, role, and user levels. However, because authorization management is not the focus of this book, we won't discuss it here in detail.

An overview of the elements required for this exercise is given in Table 4.2. The roles of individual elements and their connections have already been explained in Chapter 2, SAP NetWeaver PI.

Object Type	Sender Side	Receiver Side
Service interface	Z_RFM_ MATERIALINPUT_##	SI_Material_Asnyc_ In
Message type		MT_Material
Data type		DT_Material
Operation mapping	OM_Z_RFM_MATERIALINPUT_##_to_SI_Material_ Async_Out	
Message mapping	MM_Z_RFM_MATERIALINPUT_##_to_MT_Material	

Table 4.2 Elements in the Enterprise Services Repository for the First Exercise

Note
If the connection to the Enterprise Services Repository is interrupted while an object is being edited, you can click on the Administration option in the Process Infrastructure (PI) tools and release the locked object for editing in the Lock Overview area.

Solutions to interrupted connections

Creating Elements for the Sending System

Design objects on the sender side

By using an RFC adapter, this scenario has a particular aspect: all elements on the sender side are replaced with the interface definition of the RFC module. The interface is imported from system A and not created in the Enterprise Services Repository to accelerate work and reduce the error rate.

To import the RFC interface, expand the bottom directory, Imported Objects, right-click to open the context menu, and find the Import of SAP Objects function. In the following window, select the ACCORDING TO SOFTWARE COMPONENT VERSION option in the CONNECTION DATA area, because the system data has already been stored (see Figure 4.4). If this option is not available, enter the host name and the system number (system A). Next, enter your user SYS_A-## and the appropriate password before continuing.

Import the RFC interface

The next step lets you choose between RFC and IDoc interfaces. Expand the RFC option, and all remote-enabled function modules in system A are determined and displayed. Because this data collection can take a while, when you perform these steps in a group you can import all of the interfaces before starting the exercise. From the list, select function module Z_RFM_MATERIALINPUT_## (see Figure 4.5) and continue with the import.

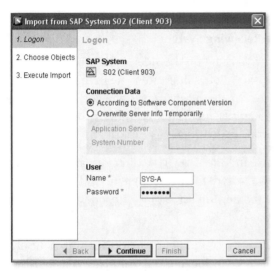

Figure 4.4 Import of RFC Interfaces — Login

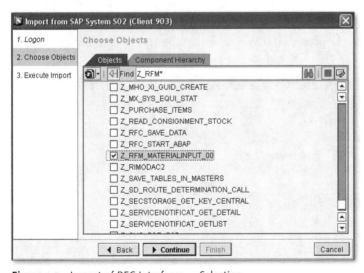

Figure 4.5 Import of RFC Interfaces — Selection

In the final step of the import process, check your selection and finish the import. After the import has completed, you can see your newly imported interface for your software component version in the IMPORTED OBJECTS • RFC directory. It is marked with a separate icon that indicates that this element has not been activated yet.

Creating Elements for the Receiving System

Design objects on the receiver side

While all of the elements are created on the side of the sending system by importing the RFC interface, you will create a data type, a message type, and a service interface for the receiving system. We recommend beginning with the independent elements (i.e., with those on the lowest hierarchy level), which, in this case, is the data type.

Creating a data type

Within your namespace, expand the DATA TYPE directory and open the creation dialog via the New entry of the context menu. In this window, you can enter the name of the new object, along with a description (see Figure 4.6).

The namespace and the software component version are automatically completed because you called the dialog in the appropriate context. Also, it is important to note the left area of this screen, which lists the elements that can be created within the Enterprise Services Repository. You can change what kind of element you want to create at any time. You will see a similar structure later when working in the Integration Directory.

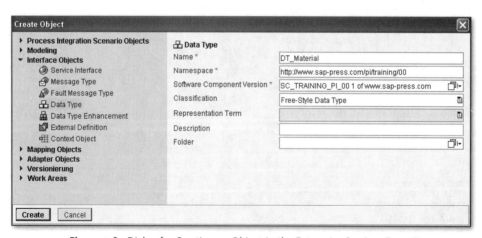

Figure 4.6 Dialog for Creating an Object in the Enterprise Services Repository

Name the new data type `DT_Material` and click on CREATE. The details window of a new data type is displayed on the right side. Because the structure of this window is typical of all detail views in the Integration Builder, it is used to explain some functions.

Next to the menu line of the Enterprise Services Repository is a separate details menu; the most important functions of which are also displayed as icons to its right. In addition to the icons for switching between the display and changing mode, and for creating a copy, you will also find an icon for the where-used list of this element (for example). The icon group to the right allows you to control the view; for example, you can hide header data or detach the details window as an independent element.

In the case of your data type, the lower area of the details window contains a list of all data type elements. Using the relevant icons, you can add new rows to the top of the table and enter the elements from Figure 4.7. Please note that this is the type `xsd:string`. Only the `BRGEW` element has the type `xsd:decimal`; you will perform a calculation using this value later. In addition, add the missing element `NTGEW` of the type `xsd:decimal`. You will use this element to calculate the net weight of the material (based on the gross weight) in the message mapping. Save the data type after all of the elements have been inserted.

Structure of the DT_Material data type

Name	Category	Type	Occurrence	Default
▼ DT_Material	Complex Type			
MATNR	Element	xsd:string	1	
MAKTX	Element	xsd:string	1	
ERSDA	Element	xsd:string	1	
ERNAM	Element	xsd:string	1	
MTART	Element	xsd:string	1	
MBRSH	Element	xsd:string	1	
MATKL	Element	xsd:string	1	
MEINS	Element	xsd:string	1	
BRGEW	Element	xsd:decimal	1	
NTGEW	Element	xsd:decimal	1	
GEWEI	Element	xsd:string	1	
MTPOS_MARA	Element	xsd:string	1	

Figure 4.7 Editing a Data Type

Creating a
message type

Because data types in the PI environment are used exclusively for modularizing data formats, and cannot appear in a mapping or interface themselves, they are embedded in message types. While data types can only be assigned to message types in a 1:1 ratio, data types can be combined in any ratio.

To create a message type, open the appropriate context menu by right-clicking on the Message Types directory. Select the New option. The familiar creation dialog box is displayed, this time for a message type. Name the new object MT_Material and enter a description. Continue with the detail view by clicking Create. Pay attention to the Data Type Used area in the middle; this is where you should insert the data type you just created. You have three ways of doing so:

Methods for
selecting the
data type

▶ The most obvious method is typing the name and the namespace; however, this involves the risk of typos.

▶ The second option is to select the object in an ABAP-based SAP system, such as in the input help. To do this, click on the hand and question mark icon to the right of the namespace field. A window opens, containing all of the data types created in your software component version for selection. The NAME and NAMESPACE fields are then populated.

▶ The third option is to drag and drop the selection. This is particularly suitable if your software component version contains a lot of data types, but there are only a few in your namespace. You can also pick the data type from the directory structure to the left and drop it on the hand next to the namespace field. Only by dropping it over the hand can you ensure a correct data transfer.

As you can see, all three ways work, even without activating the data type.

After selecting the appropriate data type, the lower area of the details window shows the structure of the used data type (see Figure 4.8). Check the structure and save the message type.

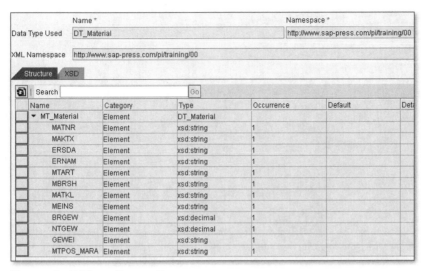

Figure 4.8 Editing a Message Type

The last object on the receiver side is the service interface, which determines if a message can be received or sent, and whether the message is sent synchronously or asynchronously.

Creating a service interface

To create this service interface, open the context menu of the corresponding directory. Enter the name SI_Material_Async_In and an appropriate description, and then click Create to get to the details window. You can choose from the Inbound, Outbound, and Abstract options for the interface category; the individual categories were discussed in Chapter 2.

Because we are dealing with the interface on the receiver side, select INBOUND. The communication mode determines whether a response regarding the contents is expected or not. Because this is a one-way scenario, select the ASYNCHRONOUS mode.

You probably noticed that the input options for message types change every time the attributes are modified. You should now see the fields for the REQUEST MESSAGE TYPE and the FAULT MESSAGE TYPE. However, you will only use the former (see Figure 4.9). Using one of the three methods discussed earlier, select the message type MT_Material as the input message, and then save your service interface.

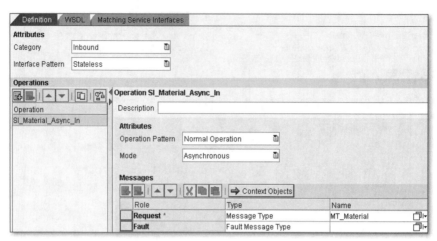

Figure 4.9 Editing a Service Interface

Creating the Mapping Objects

The connection between the elements of the sending and the receiving side is established via mapping. The contents conversion of the data formats in the form of message mapping is embedded in the operation mapping that connects a pair of inbound and outbound interfaces.

Creating the message mapping
To begin, create the message mapping. In your namespace, open the context menu of the Message Mappings directory. In the creation dialog, enter the name MM_Z_RFM_MATERIALINPUT_##_to_MT_Material, where ## represents your participant number. Choose a description and create the object.

Selecting the outbound and the target message
The center area of the details window is divided into two parts, allowing you to select the sending message type on the left side and the receiving message type on the right side. First, start with the message type on the sending side: You can either use the input help, or drag the appropriate message type to the Enter a source message label. In this exercise, there is no explicit message type on the sender side, so use the RFC interface.

Regardless of the selection method, you must choose which RFC message you would like to use. This is because synchronous communication is expected for an RFC interface. Therefore, you can choose between

Z_RFM_MATERIALINPUT_## and Z_RFM_MATERIALINPUT_##.Response. Select the former because no response is expected.

The left part of the center area now lists the elements of the RFC interface. For the receiving part, select your MT_Material message type.

If you look at the elements on the right side, you'll find a red mark next to every entry. This indicates an incomplete mapping for the respective target element. Because we didn't change anything in the OCCURRENCE column when creating a data type, the default value of **1..1** is applied. This means that this element is mandatory. If one of the target fields does not receive a value from the mapping, an error occurs. The connection between the elements of the two message types can also be established via three different methods:

▸ The most obvious method is connecting via drag and drop, where it isn't important which side is dragged to the other. The two elements are displayed in the lower screen area and connected automatically.

▸ The second option is to double-click on the source and target element to move them to the lower screen area, where they are displayed as rectangles. There you can connect the two rectangles by dragging the white area of the sending element to the corresponding area of the receiving element. This method should be used if the mapping is extended by predefined functions.

▸ The third method is suitable for connecting a large number of elements of the same name. To do this, parent elements must be selected on both sides. In this mapping, these are Z_RFM_MATERIALINPUT_## on the sender side, and MT_Material on the receiver side. Then, above the sending message type, select the MAP SELECTED FIELDS AND SUB-STRUCTURES IF NAMES ARE IDENTICAL icon. An alert dialog box appears, asking you to confirm the action. After dismissing the dialog, all of the elements on the sender side are connected to those on the receiver side. It's important to note that mapping of element names is case sensitive.

Perform a mapping using the third method, and have the result displayed in the overview by clicking on the DEPENDENCIES icon. The two message types then move apart and give way to the display of connection lines.

Methods for mapping elements

Graphical function for calculating the net weight

You will also notice that the marks next to the receiver elements have now turned green. Only the NTGEW element is still red, because it was not automatically provided with a value.

For demonstrating the integrated mapping functions, we assume that the net weight of the material is 90% of the gross weight. To map this, first select the NTGEW element on the receiver side, and then the BRGEW element on the sender side, by double-clicking on these items so both are displayed in the bottom area. To make this calculation, you first need a multiplication function that calculates the net weight from the gross weight with a constant of 0.9.

In the toolbar at the bottom of the screen, select the functions for Constants and click on the Constant function to the right, which is then displayed as a rectangle in the work area of the mapping. The cog wheel means that you can maintain parameters within this function. Double-click on the constant rectangle and change its value to 0.9 for the 90% of the net weight.

Now change to the Arithmetic area in the toolbar to insert the multiply function in the work area. Connect the BRGEW and Constant 0.9 elements to the MULTIPLY function by dragging the white subareas. In fact, these functions would be sufficient for calculating the correct net weight. However, the three decimal places permitted for the xsd:decimal type might be exceeded. If this message mapping were tested, it would result in an error.

Before the result of the calculation can be mapped to the NTGEW element, it must be formatted using the FORMATNUMBER function from the Arithmetic functional area. Configure the internal parameter NUMBER FORMAT of the function so that the result matches the scheme 000.000. Insert the FORMATNUMBER function between the MULTIPLY function and the target element NTGEW (see Figure 4.10). All rectangles and the mark next to the NTGEW target element should now be colored green. Save the message mapping.

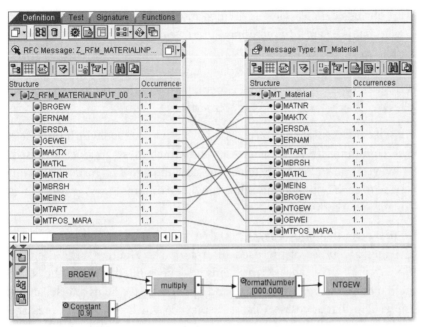

Figure 4.10 *Message Mapping of the RFC-to-File Exercise*

To ensure that the new mapping works, a test function is added to the Enterprise Services Repository, which you can select via the TEST tab in the top area of the details window. The left side of the test area displays the structure of the sending message type whose elements are populated with test values. Be sure to use a decimal point as the decimal character for the BRGEW element.

Testing the mapping

The test itself is started with the START THE TRANSFORMATION icon (indicated by a vise) at the bottom-left of the test area. If the test program does not find any errors, the structure of the receiving message type with its respective values is displayed on the right. In particular, you should verify whether the NTGEW element has been populated correctly.

The operation mapping is the last object of the integration scenario you are creating in the Enterprise Services Repository. Start the creation dialog by opening the context menu of the Operation Mappings directory in your namespace. Name the operation mapping OM_Z_RFM_MATERIALIN-PUT_##_to_SI_Material_Async_In, and then enter a description for the object. Create it by clicking the Create button.

Creating the operation mapping

This object's detailed view is divided into an upper interface area and a lower mapping area. In the upper interface area, select the sender interface; this is the RFC interface Z_RFM_MATERIALINPUT_## . Note that the RFC interface is not stored in your namespace; instead, you will find it via the IMPORTED OBJECTS • RFC menu path. Perform the same steps for the SI_Material_Async_In target interface.

By selecting the two interfaces, you have now specified which interfaces will communicate with each other and which message types are used. However, you still need to determine how the two data formats are converted to each other, because there might be different message mappings for the same message pair.

In the lower mapping area, click the READ OPERATIONS button to display the message types of the used interfaces (see Figure 4.11). After the SOURCE and TARGET OPERATION fields have been filled, click on the NAME field located between the source and target message fields and select the input help that appears. A list is displayed, which contains all message mappings that exist between the interfaces in this sender and receiver scenario; you should only see mappings of the scheme MM_Z_RFM_MATE-RIALINPUT_##_to_MT_Material . Select the mapping with your member number.

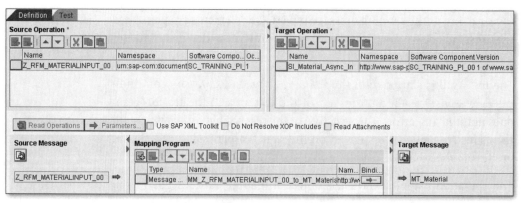

Figure 4.11 Operation Mapping of the RFC-to-File Exercise

If you take a closer look at the MAPPING PROGRAM area, you will notice that the tabular structure allows you to select several mappings. All selected message mappings are processed sequentially according to their order in the table. When creating the message mapping, for example, you can use the TEST tab to perform a test which, in addition to the message mapping, also checks interface compatibility. Save your operation mapping after it has been successfully tested.

As you can see, all newly created objects were usable throughout the entire Enterprise Services Repository, even though they were not activated. However, you can't access all of these objects in the Integration Directory in this state, so the next step is to activate your change.

Activating the new design objects

To do this, go to the directory structure on the left and select the Change Lists tab. The tree structure is hidden, and your software component version is displayed, which you should fully expand. Beneath that list, you will find a Standard Change List containing all newly created objects. Verify that all elements presented in Table 4.2 are included in the change list.

Select the Activate option from the change list's context menu. A window containing all of the objects of the list is displayed. You have the option of excluding specific objects from the activation, but activate the entire list and return to the Objects tab. Notice that the icons indicating that the new objects are not yet activated have disappeared.

> **Note**
>
> You can also activate individual items via their context menu.

4.1.3 Configuration

Based on the objects created in the Enterprise Services Repository, you can now set up communication between systems A and B in the Integration Directory. The Integration Directory can be called by Transaction SXMB_IFR, by a direct link in the web browser, or by following the ENVIRONMENT • INTEGRATION BUILDER menu path in the Enterprise Services Repository.

First steps in the Integration Directory

As with the Enterprise Services Repository, the interface is divided into two parts; however, the objects are no longer arranged according to software component versions. Instead, they are arranged according to object types. Above the directory structure, you'll see three tabs: Change Lists,

Objects, and Scenarios. The Change Lists tab serves the same function as in the Repository. The Objects tab lists all objects of the Directory by their type. Except for the scenario, which you will create for all of your objects in the Integration Directory; this exercise uses all of the elements listed in Table 4.3.

Object Type	Sender Side: System A	Receiver Side: System B
Communication channel 1	RFC_ Senderchannel_##	File_ Receiverchannel_##
Sender agreement	| SystemA | Z_RFM_ MATERIALINPUT_## | |	
Receiver agreement		| SystemA | | SystemB | MI_ Material_Async_In
Receiver determination	| SystemA | Z_RFM_MATERIALINPUT_##	
Interface determination	| SystemA | Z_RFM_MATERIALINPUT_## | | SystemB	

Table 4.3 Elements in the Integration Directory for the RFC-to-File Exercise

Setting Up the Business Systems and Their Communication Channels

Creating a configuration scenario

To create the PI_Training_## scenario, use the context menu of an existing scenario, or click the Create Object icon on the bottom left of the menu bar. Save the object so the scenario is displayed in the listing on the left side, select the new scenario, and then restrict the view by clicking on the Only Display Selected Subtree icon above the list. Creating a configuration scenario serves the organizational division of configuration objects.

Follow the COMMUNICATION COMPONENT • BUSINESS SYSTEM menu path. Below the branch, you will see at least two business systems, SystemA and SystemB, which were declared in the System Landscape Directory (SLD) during the preparations for the exercises. Click the Assign Configuration Scenarios option in the context menu of system A, and select the scenario you just created.

Due to this mapping, this business system and its communication channels are displayed in your scenario. Repeat this step for business system B. You need to configure a sending RFC adapter for system A and a receiving file adapter for system B.

Using the context menu from the Communication Channel path, open the creation dialog and enter system A as the Communication Component, the name RFC_Senderchannel_##, and an appropriate description. In the details window, use the input help to set the adapter type to RFC. Select the SENDER direction for this adapter. In the TRANSPORT PROTOCOL field, choose the RFC entry. For the MESSAGE PROTOCOL and ADAPTER ENGINE fields in the upper area, just use the default values.

Creating an RFC sender channel

The RFC SERVER PARAMETER area establishes a TCP/IP connection to the RFC destination on the side of system A. During the preparation of the exercises (in Chapter 3, Section 3.5.2, Settings for the Use of the RFC Adapter), you created an RFC connection named SystemA_Sender-##. This RFC connection is registered on the gateway server of the PI system and is waiting for a corresponding counterpart.

Connection to the existing RFC connection

In the APPLICATION SERVER field, enter the host name of the PI system, and in the APPLICATION SERVER SERVICE field, enter the gateway service of the PI system according to the scheme sapgwXX, where *XX* represents the instance number. The PROGRAM ID follows the scheme SystemA_Sender-## and, like the two values mentioned earlier, exactly matches the values entered in the corresponding RFC connection in system A. The SNC option specifies whether communication over an RFC connection takes place via a secure network connection (SNC). The UNICODE checkbox must be enabled if system A is a Unicode system.

The RFC METADATA REPOSITORY PARAMETER section is used to identify and log on to the system that provides metadata about the RFC interfaces used. This integration is required because the metadata is cross-checked by the PI system when calling the sending RFC adapter. In this example, the RFC interface is imported from system A during the design phase. Enter the APPLICATION SERVER and the SYSTEM NUMBER of system A, and your user SYS_A-##, your password, and the corresponding client, before saving the communication channel. If you enable the communication

Access to RFC metadata

channel at a later stage, the connection test for the destination SystemA_Sender-## is carried out successfully from system A.

Figure 4.12 provides an overview of all of the settings for this communication channel.

Creating a file receiver channel

The receiving communication channel for system B is created with the context menu from the Communication Channel path. The name of the new channel should be File_Receiverchannel_##. Select system B as the Communication Component.

In the details window, select the FILE adapter type using the input help and specify the RECEIVER direction. Set the TRANSPORT PROTOCOL to the FILE SYSTEM (NFS) parameter, which means that the PI system can use its own local file system to access the directory the file is created in.

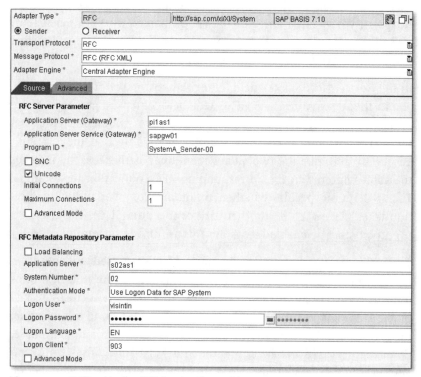

Figure 4.12 Setting Up the RFC Sender Channel for System A

An alternative to the *Network File System* (NFS) is the *File Transfer Protocol* (FTP), which allows access to the file systems of remote computers. If you select FTP, you can specify the server and user data to log on to a remote FTP server. The MESSAGE PROTOCOL field should be set to the FILE value that causes the written file to be stored in PI format. The File Content Conversion characteristic, however, lets you write the file as a list containing several entries.

The FILE ACCESS PARAMETERS determine the directory to which the file is written, and the scheme for its name. After consulting your landscape administrator, we recommend using */tmp* for Unix installations or *C:\ temp* for Windows.

Setting the source file

You can choose the FILE NAME SCHEME. However, you should select the name *xi_output_##.dat* for this exercise, where ## represents your participant number. We will refer to this file during the course of this scenario, so, if you select a different name, you need to take this into account in Section 4.1.4, Process and Monitoring (see Figure 4.13).

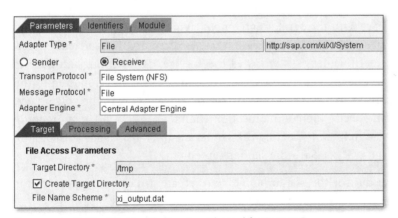

Figure 4.13 Setting Up the File Receiver Channel for System B

The Processing Parameters on the PROCESSING tab specify how to create the file; that is, if the name scheme specified earlier is used as-is, or if, for example, a time stamp, a counter value, or the message ID should be included in the file name. Select the Directly write mode and the Binary file type. The write mode, Directly, causes data to be written out without using a temporary file. The file type, Binary, makes it so not only text can be output.

In addition to the basic settings, you can also dynamically specify the file storage path by using variable replacement or triggering an operating system command before or after the message processing. Save the receiver channel.

Creating the Connection Elements

Connection elements between the sender and the receiver side

Based on the basics we just created, and the objects in the Enterprise Services Repository, the integration scenario can be completed using some connection elements. The first two missing elements you need to create are the sender and the receiver agreement. They determine how a message is converted from or to the interface of a specific business system so the PI system or the receiving system can further process the message. In the case of the incoming RFC communication channel, for example, the message must be converted from the RFC adapter format to the PI XML format.

Creating a sender agreement

Let's start with the sender agreement, which you can create using the context menu of the SENDER AGREEMENT directory. In the creation dialog, select business system A as the service. The sending interface is the RFC interface Z_RFM_MATERIALINPUT_##, which you imported to the Enterprise Services Repository. In the details window of the new object, you can specify the communication channel of the sender by opening the input help and selecting the sender channel RFC_Senderchannel_## (see Figure 4.14). Save the sender agreement.

Creating a receiver agreement

As you did for the sender agreement, create a receiver agreement for business system B and the receiving interface SI_Material_Async_In. Note that you also need to specify the sending business system A. In the details window, select the channel File_Receiverchannel_## as the communication channel of the receiver and save the agreement.

Creating a receiver determination

For logical routing, messages in the PI system first need a receiver determination, which specifies available receiver services for a business system and interface pair. Create a new receiver determination with the corresponding context menu for the sending business system A and the interface Z_RFM_MATERIALINPUT_##.

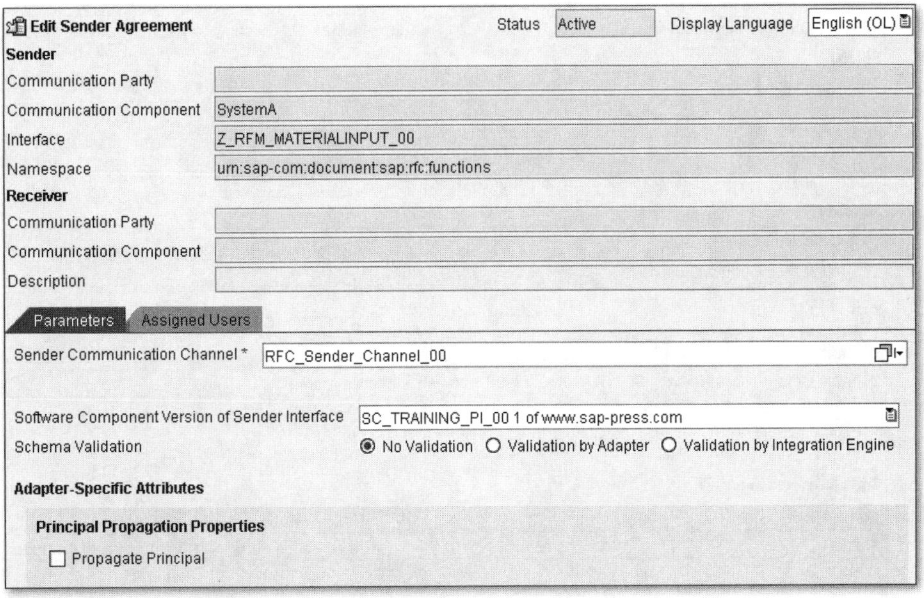

Figure 4.14 Creation of the RFC Sender Agreement

In the details window, the CONFIGURED RECEIVERS area allows you to specify various receivers. If the review result of the relevant condition is true, the message is delivered to this system (see Figure 4.15).

This can also mean that the message is delivered to several systems. For example, the condition can check elements of a message for specific content. If none of the configured systems is specified as the receiver, you can specify a default receiver below the receiver table. In the COMMUNICATION COMPONENT column of the existing row, select business system B as a potential receiver. Because the message in this exercise should always be delivered to this receiver, you don't have to set a condition.

Save the receiver determination and then look at the lower area, CONFIGURATION OVERVIEW, which now includes the SYSTEMB entry. Expand the entry. As you can see, no matching interface determination and no

Creating the interface determination

appropriate operation mapping could be determined. Above this listing, click on the New icon to create a new interface determination.

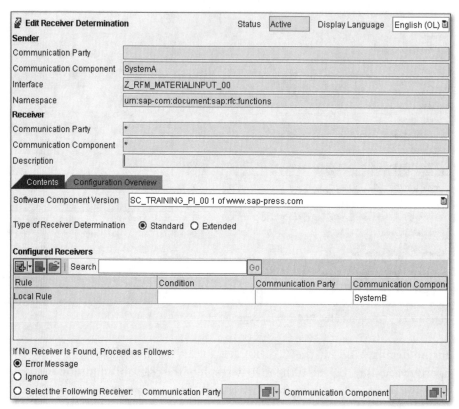

Figure 4.15 Creation of the Receiver Determination

By calling the creation dialog from this context, all mandatory fields can be populated; you only need to enter a description. In the details window of the RECEIVER INTERFACES area, use the input help to select your service interface SI_Material_Async_In from the namespace. To the left of it, specify the only operation mapping available for the combination of the sending and receiving interfaces (see Figure 4.16). Save and close the interface determination and return to the receiver determination.

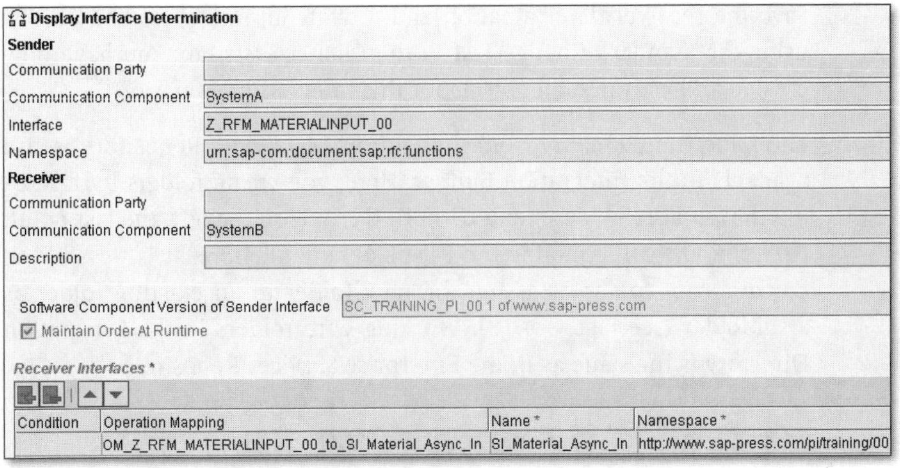

Figure 4.16 Editing the Interface Determination for the RFC-to-File Exercise

In the lower area, click the REFRESH icon so that the receiver agreement for receiving system B is also displayed with the target interface and the matching operation mapping (see Figure 4.17).

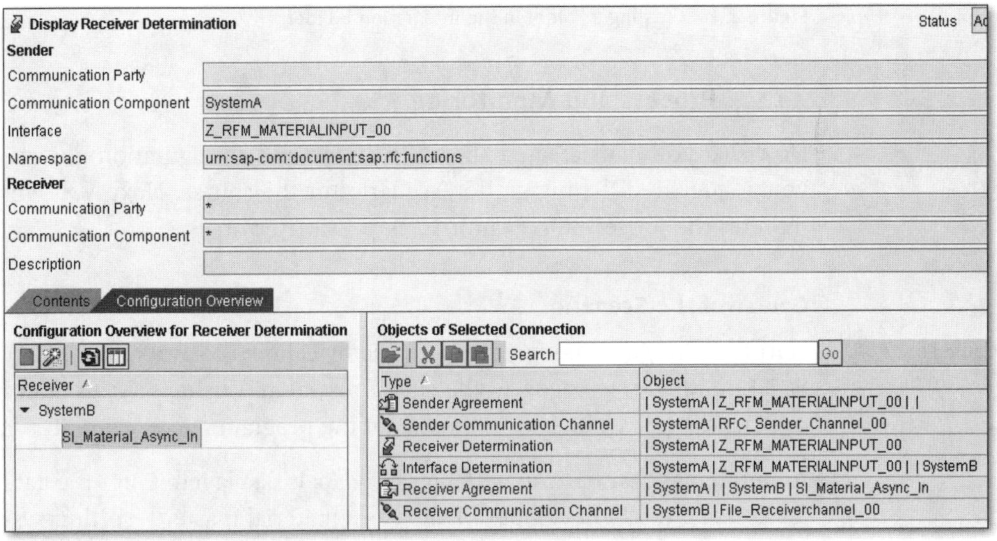

Activating the new configuration objects

Figure 4.17 Editing the Receiver Determination for the RFC-to-File Exercise

Save the receiver determination and activate all newly created objects using the Standard Change List in the Change Lists tab. You have now created and activated all objects for this integration scenario.

The folder functionality from the Enterprise Services Repository is also available in the Integration Builder. Here, you create folders by following the OBJECTS • NEW menu path. In the tree on the left, the last point, ADMINISTRATION, contains the FOLDER element. Here, it is possible to create a root folder or assign the new folder to an existing folder as a subfolder (see Figure 4.18). Working with folders in the Integration Directory is the same as in the Enterprise Services Repository.

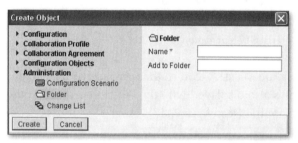

Figure 4.18 Creating a Folder in the Integration Builder

4.1.4 Process and Monitoring

Now that you have created all of the design and configuration objects, you've prepared the integration scenario for the course. Next, you will monitor the process and examine any possible errors.

Course of the Scenario

Calling the ABAP program in system A
Start the configured integration scenario by calling the program Z_PROG_MATERIALINPUT_##. Log in to the client of system A using your user and call Transaction SA38; type the name of the program and execute it.

An input mask for basic material master data is displayed. Enter the data for creating the PI developer manual as a material master record in system B. This material is just used for test purposes; you won't use it to create a production or sales order, for example.

The data corresponds to the mandatory fields of the two views, Basic Data 1 and 2, from Materials Management (MM) in SAP R/3 or SAP ERP Central Component (ECC), respectively. Because this data is used in the second exercise to actually create a material using an IDoc, we recommend using the data from Table 4.4.

Field	Recommended Value
Material	PI_BOOK-##
Material description	arbitrary (for example, »SAP PI developer book ##«)
Material type	FERT (Finished product)
Industry sector	1 (Retail)
Material group	030 (Documentation)
Quantity unit	ST (Piece)
Gross weight	arbitrary (for example, 1.2)
Weight unit	KGM (kilogram)
General item category group	NORM (Normal item)

Table 4.4 Recommended Values for Creating a Test Material

This data works in an Internet Demonstration and Evaluation System (IDES) R/3 or ECC system without further adaptation. For the second exercise, you can use the appropriate template files later.

Entering the recommended values

Enter the data in the individual fields and note that the input help displayed for some fields only returns values of the sending system that might not exist in the receiving system (see Figure 4.19).

After you follow the PROGRAM • EXECUTE menu path, or click the corresponding EXECUTE icon, you will receive a success message. This message only notifies you that the function module belonging to the program has been called successfully. However, it does not confirm that the message has been successfully delivered.

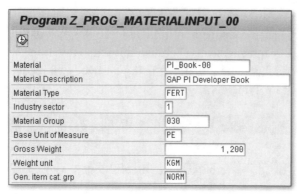

Figure 4.19 Calling the Program Z_PROG_MATERIALINPUT_##

Monitoring
the process Correct delivery and processing of the message can be verified in the PI system. Log on to the appropriate client and call Transaction SXMB_ MONI. Follow the menu path: INTEGRATION ENGINE • MONITORING • MONITOR FOR PROCESSED XML MESSAGES. This opens a selection mask that lets you select all processed messages. If the PI system is used only for training or testing purposes, a restriction is hardly necessary. Otherwise, you could restrict the selection to messages with the sending server SystemA, for example.

Execute the message query via the PROGRAM • EXECUTE menu path or the corresponding EXECUTE icon. If your message was successfully delivered and processed, you should see an entry showing a black-and-white checkered flag in the STATUS column (see Figure 4.20).

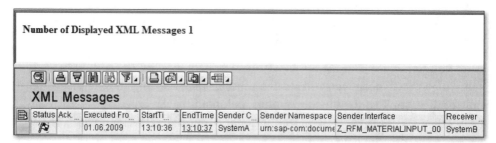

Figure 4.20 Display of the First Message in Transaction SXMB_MONI

A green flag means that the message is currently being processed, while a black-and-white checkered flag means the message processed successfully. Most other icons represent an error in our case. You can display the legend of all possible icons via the GOTO • LEGEND menu path, or the corresponding LEGEND icon.

To get the ultimate proof that the message was successfully processed, look at the created file. You can do this using Transaction AL11 in the PI system, by clicking on the row of the directory alias DIR_TEMP. In the file list, search for a file matching the scheme *pi_output_##.dat*. Double-click on the file to open it. Because the display is limited to a specific width and the lines are not wrapped automatically, we recommend using Transaction ZAPCMD or the file tools provided on the book's website (find it at *http://www.sap-press.com*).

Viewing the created file

Troubleshooting in Monitoring

To find the cause of an error in the message display of Transaction SXMB_ MONI, double-click in any field of the corresponding row. This brings you to the DISPLAY XML MESSAGE VERSIONS view (see Figure 4.21).

Process analysis

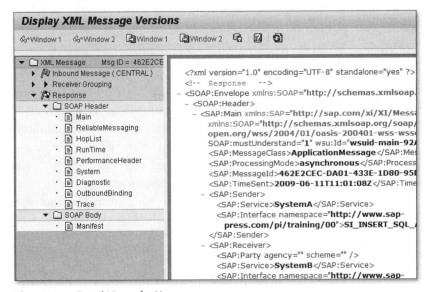

Figure 4.21 Detail View of a Message

In the case of an asynchronous message, you will see the different statuses of the message on its way through the central Integration Engine

(IE). In the directory structure to the left, navigate to the place that has an error icon. In the windows on the right side, look for an error message indicating the cause. In most cases, the error was caused by a mapping or an object that was inadvertently selected from the input help.

Checking the adapters

In some cases, however, the error was caused by incorrectly configured communication channels or adapters. To check this, start Transaction SXMB_IFR, which is used for calling the PI tools. On the bottom right, select the Runtime Workbench and logon using your user PI-##.

You will see the options for the Runtime Workbench, most of which you will become familiar with while working on the following exercises and the case study. Even though you already know a different way of displaying a message overview using Transaction SXMB_MONI, you can use the MESSAGE MONITORING menu option to view the message status in the PI system. First, select COMPONENT MONITORING, and display the components with every possible status.

In the directory structure of the components, follow the menu path: DOMAIN.XX.<PI-HOSTNAME> • INTEGRATION SERVER • ADAPTER ENGINE. A status view opens beneath the directory structure, providing you with information about the general status of the Adapter Engine. On the top-right, click the ADAPTER MONITORING button (see Figure 4.22).

Selecting the adapter type

After expanding the namespace http://sap.com/xi/PI/System, a new browser window opens and displays the selection of all available adapters. A gray diamond next to an adapter type indicates that a communication channel for this type hasn't been created. A green square indicates that all communication channels of this type have been correctly configured and that no error has occurred during processing. A red circle, however, indicates that at least one communication channel of this type is faulty.

You'll need to see if an error occurred for the adapter types RFC or FILE. For a closer analysis, you can click on the relevant type to list all of the communication channels. If the communication channel displays an error, you are presented with a detailed error description to the right, which you can use to correct the error.

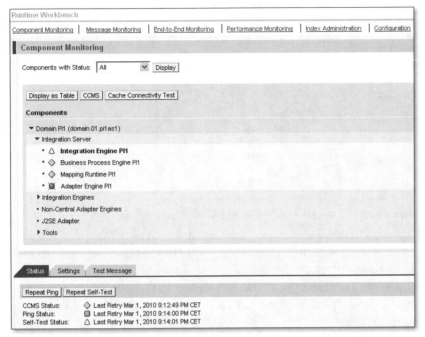

Figure 4.22 Entry Point to Component Monitoring of the Runtime Workbench

4.1.5   Alternative Mapping: ABAP Mapping (Optional)

As an alternative to the graphical mapping that you used in this exercise, you will learn how to implement the same mapping using an ABAP class. To do this, you must perform some preparatory steps, and receive authorization for development in the SAP NetWeaver PI system.

Creating the ABAP Mapping

The ABAP mapping is created as a normal ABAP class in the PI system, and, in operation mapping, is referred to by the class name. As a result, the Execute method is called automatically, and does the mapping. This method must be implemented by you; an ABAP mapping cannot be imported into Enterprise Services Repository when developing the ABAP mapping separately.

Creation of an ABAP class for the mapping

Log on to the PI system and call the class builder with Transaction SE24. Enter the name of the new class following the schema ZCL_PI_ABAP_MAP-PING_##, and click CREATE (see Figure 4.23). In the pop-up window, type in a meaningful description for the new class and click Save. If you haven't yet entered a developer key for your user, you will have to do so now.

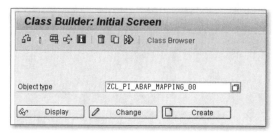

Figure 4.23 Creating the ABAP Mapping Class in Class Builder

Use of the IF_MAPPING interface

Because the ABAP mapping is a normal ABAP class, you must provide the names of transport requests and of a package for this development (unless you are planning a local development). Once you do this, the class builder will open, and you can see your new ABAP class. Click on the INTERFACES tab and choose the ABAP interface IF_MAPPING (see Figure 4.24). This interface contains the Execute method with the corresponding signature, and thus represents the definition of the new method.[1]

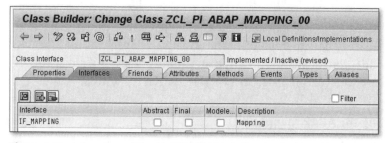

Figure 4.24 Integration of the IF_MAPPING Interface in the New Class

Target message structure

After integrating the interface, the METHODS tab displays the Execute method that you now must implement. To do this, double-click the method name and save the changed class. Before developing the actual coding, let's look at the XML view of the message (see Listing 4.1).

---

1 You can find detailed information about the interface in the SAP Help Portal at: *http://help.sap.com/saphelp_nwpi711/helpdata/de/ba/e18b1a0fc14f1faf884ae-50cece51b/frameset.htm.*

```
<?xml version="1.0" encoding="UTF-8"?>
<ns1:MT_Material
 xmlns:ns1="http://www.sap-press.com/pi/training/##">
    <MATNR>PI_BOOK-##</MATNR>
    <MAKTX>SAP PI Developer Book</MAKTX>
    <ERSDA>01062009</ERSDA>
    <ERNAM>SYS_A-##</ERNAM>
    <MTART>FERT</MTART>
    <MBRSH>1</MBRSH>
    <MATKL>030</MATKL>
    <MEINS>PT</MEINS>
    <BRGEW>1.200</BRGEW>
    <NTGEW>001.080</NTGEW>
    <GEWEI>KGM</GEWEI>
    <MTPOS_MARA>NORM</MTPOS_MARA>
</ns1:MT_Material>
```

Listing 4.1 XML View of a Message Sent after the Mapping

You can access this view in either the file that is created as the result of the first exercise, or by testing the message mapping of the first exercise and displaying the results in the XML view. The only value that is changed in the mapping is the net weight, which is automatically calculated based on the gross weight. The structure and the remaining values are not changed by the mapping, thus keeping the ABAP mapping simple.

You can find the detailed source code of the ABAP mapping in Appendix A. Copy the source code, replace the placeholder ##, and activate the method so it can be used later in the operation mapping.

Structure of the new method

Because a detailed discussion is beyond the scope of this book, we will only briefly discuss the method. First, the iXML library for ABAP Objects is initialized, which allows you to simply parse and reassemble XML documents.[2] Then objects for factories and the input stream are declared. After the definition of the input document, the relevant nodes are declared and extracted from the input document using the `get_elements_by_tag_name` method.

---

2 Detailed information on the iXML Library of SAP can be found on the SAP Help Portal at: *http://help.sap.com/saphelp_nwpi711/helpdata/de/86/8280ba12d511d5 991b00508b6b8b11/frameset.htm.*

After the output document has been declared, it is filled with the values from the input document; most values can be inserted without change. Only the net weight is recreated as a node and calculated on the basis of gross weight. In addition, you must correct the date format from YYYY-MM-DD to DDMMYYYY, so that the file can be transferred into a new material via IDocs (in the next exercise).

After the node assignments to the new document are completed, a custom message is inserted into the trace; this lets you see the details of the execution of the newly-created method in Transaction SXMB_MONI. Finally, the output stream is declared, and a renderer is created that is responsible for compiling the output document.

Integrating ABAP Mapping

Adjustment of the operation mapping

After creating and activating the new mapping, you must insert it in the existing operation mapping OM_Z_RFM_MATERIALINPUT_## to_SI_Material_Async_In, and activate the object again. To do this, simply open the aforementioned operation mapping, and then switch to change mode. In the bottom-center section of the screen, change the entry in the TYPE column from Message Mapping to Abap-class. Then enter the name of the created ABAP class ZCL_PI_ABAP_MAPPING_## (see Figure 4.25). The ABAP mapping cannot be tested in the Enterprise Services Repository. Save and activate the change; other changes, such as changes to the configuration, are not necessary.

Testing the changed process

You can run the scenario once again by calling the program Z_PROG_MATERIALINPUT_##. The behavior results in the same outcome. By tracing your message in the message monitoring of Transaction SXMB_MONI, you'll find the log entry you specified in the ABAP class (see Figure 4.26).

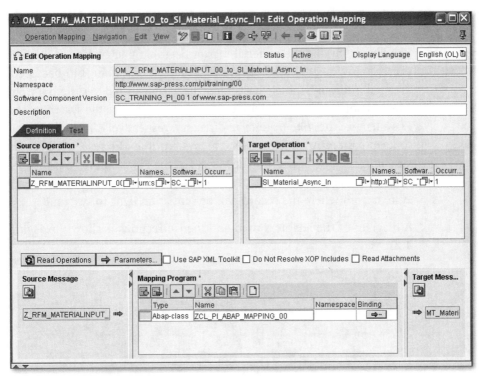

Figure 4.25 Integrating ABAP Mapping in Operation Mapping

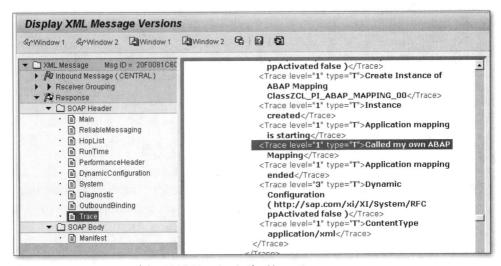

Figure 4.26 Trace Entry of the ABAP Mapping in the Message

4.2 Exercise 2: File-to-IDoc

Course of the
second exercise

The file containing the material master data that you created in the first exercise now needs to be integrated in business system B to become a material. Although the file has already been transferred to system B from a logical point of view, it technically still resides on the file system of the PI system, in the */tmp* or *C:\temp* directory, respectively. This allows you to keep system A as the sender and system B as the receiver, because system A can also access the file system of the PI system to read the file. System A reads the file using the file adapter and transfers it to the PI system from where the record will be sent as an IDoc to system B.

A diagram of the adapters used and their directions is shown in Figure 4.27.

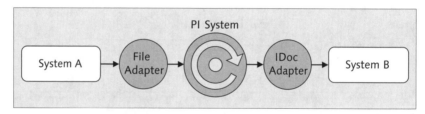

Figure 4.27 Scheme of the Second Exercise File-to-IDoc

> **Note**
>
> Jumping in at
> Exercise 2
>
> If you didn't do the first exercise, you can find the templates for the file in Appendix A. In this exercise, you will reuse several design elements of the receiving side from the first exercise.

4.2.1 Basics

Overview of the
new objects

Now that you have familiarized yourself with the receiver side of the file adapter, it's time to get to know the sender side. The data mapping to an IDoc presents a certain challenge in this exercise, because IDocs contain very sophisticated and complex data structures. Despite the age of this format, it still plays an important role in the SAP environment, partly because of its automatic processing option.

You can take advantage of this in this scenario by creating a partner agreement in system B. This agreement ensures that the incoming material master data is automatically processed in IDoc form (i.e., that the corresponding material is created automatically).

The partner agreement you will create is not a new element for SAP NetWeaver PI, but an element of the traditional application link enabling (ALE) communication. The partner agreement can only be created once for a sending system (i.e., system A) because the differentiation is made according to the logical system of the sending application. The client of the sending system A, however, can only be assigned a single logical system.[3]

Function of the partner agreement

Log on to system B and call Transaction BD54 to verify that the name of the logical system (system A) is known. Every system must know the names of the logical systems of the IDoc partners. The name of the logical system is usually structured according to the scheme `<SID>CLNT<client>` (see Figure 4.28).

Creating the partner agreement

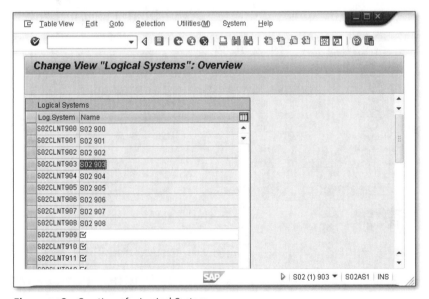

Figure 4.28 Creation of a Logical System

---

3   If you perform this exercise with other class members, we recommend having the instructor perform the following steps.

Leave Transaction BD54 and call Transaction WE20. The left part of the screen shows the existing partner agreements sorted by partner types. The right side contains detailed information about the selected agreement.

From the menu bar, follow the PARTNERS • CREATE menu path, or click the CREATE icon to create a new partner agreement. Enter the name of the logical system of system A (the one you just checked) as the partner number. Take care to select the partner type LS (logical system) in the details window. Make sure that the partner status value in the Classification tab is set to A, for active.

Configuring the inbound parameters Next, specify that incoming IDocs of the MATMAS (Master Material) type are automatically processed according to a specific pattern. To do this, save the partner agreement and, in the lower area, Inbound parameters, click the Create inbound parameter icon. In the new screen template, select the message type MATMAS (see Figure 4.29).

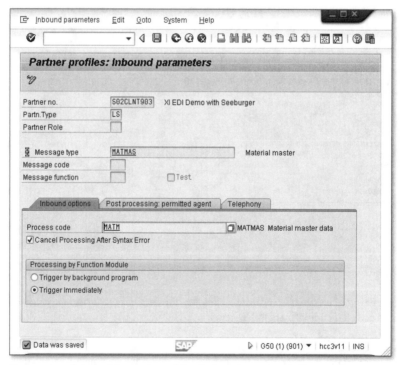

Figure 4.29 Inbound Parameters of the Partner Agreement in System B

Below the INBOUND OPTIONS tab, select the predefined process code, MATM. If a syntax error occurs, don't terminate the process, as this helps you easily identify potential errors later on. However, if you successfully tested your integration scenario, you can enable the CANCEL PROCESSING AFTER SYNTAX ERROR option by selecting its corresponding checkbox. The PROCESSING BY FUNCTION MODULE option should be performed immediately. Save these settings to exit this transaction.

You just created a partner agreement for communicating with system A via an IDoc.

4.2.2 Design

Object creation in the Enterprise Services Repository is much easier after working through the first exercise. If you have already gone through all of the processes, you can reuse some design objects from the first exercise. Reused objects are indicated with an asterisk (*) in Table 4.5.

Overview of the new design objects

Object Type	Sender Side	Receiver Side
Service interface	SI_Material_Async_Out	MATMAS.MATMAS02
Message type	MT_Material *	
Data type	DT_Material *	
Operation mapping	OM_SI_Material_Async_Out_to_MATMAS_MATMAS02	
Message mapping	MM_MT_Material_to_MATMAS_MATMAS02	

Table 4.5 Elements in the Enterprise Services Repository for the File-to-IDoc Exercise

The sender side, which corresponds to the receiver side from Exercise 1, is already complete, except for the outbound service interface. Open the creation dialog in the SERVICE INTERFACES path, and create the service interface SI_Material_Async_Out. This is taken from the OUTBOUND category, and is used in the ASYNCHRONOUS mode. The output message corresponds to the MT_Material message type already created in the last exercise (see Figure 4.30). Save the completed interface.

Creating the outbound service interface

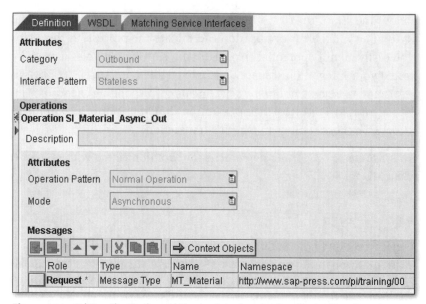

Figure 4.30 Editing the Outbound Service Interface for the File-to-IDoc Exercise

Importing the IDoc metadata
On the receiver side, you first need to import the metadata of the MAT-MAS.MATMAS02 IDoc. You can import the metadata the same way as you imported the RFC interface in Exercise 1. In the Enterprise Services Repository, navigate to your software component version and open the import dialog via the context menu of the Imported Objects directory. If systems A and B run different SAP systems so that the required IDoc type is unknown in system A, you can log on to business system B. Otherwise, you can import from system A.

In the next step, expand the IDocs area, mark the MATMAS.MATMAS02 type, and import it. Like the interface definition of RFC interfaces, the interface definition of IDocs can be used both as a message type and as a service interface, so more objects are not required on the receiver side.

Creating the message mapping
Create a new message mapping named MM_MT_Material_to_MATMAS_MATMAS02, assign the MT_Material message type on the sender's side, and assign the MATMAS.MATMAS02 IDoc type on the receiver's side. Message mapping is a challenge when using IDocs, because the data structure is very complex and can contain several hundred entries. To keep track, Table 4.6 presents the relevant fields of this example.

Data Element of MT_Material/ Constants	Data Element of MATMAS. MATMAS02	Segment of MATMAS. MATMAS02
Constant: 1	BEGIN	None (IDOC)
MT_Material	E1MARAM	None (IDOC)
MT_Material	SEGMENT	E1MARAM
Constant: 005	MSGFN	E1MARAM
MATNR		E1MARAM
Constant: KBG	PSTAT	E1MARAM
Constant: KBG	VPSTA	E1MARAM
Constant: 000	BLANZ	E1MARAM
ERSDA		E1MARAM
ERNAM		E1MARAM
MTART		E1MARAM
MBRSH		E1MARAM
MATKL		E1MARAM
MEINS		E1MARAM
BRGEW		E1MARAM
NTGEW		E1MARAM
GEWEI		E1MARAM
MTPOS_MARA		E1MARAM
MT_Material	E1MAKTM	E1MARAM
MT_Material	SEGMENT	E1MARAM/E1MAKTM
Constant: 005	MSGFN	E1MARAM/E1MAKTM
MAKTX		E1MARAM/E1MAKTM
Constant: D	SPRAS	E1MARAM/E1MAKTM
Constant: DE	SPRAS_ISO	E1MARAM/E1MAKTM

Table 4.6 Assignment of Data Elements in the Message Mapping of the File-to-IDoc Exercise

As you can see, element names in the DT_Material data type were not chosen by chance. Some fields of the IDoc structure are populated with constants that were not queried in the material input mask.

In particular, pay attention to the BEGIN and SEGMENT fields, and to the segments that control the creation of the IDoc or its segments, respectively. While BEGIN must be assigned a specific value, you can assign any field to the SEGMENT fields (and the segments themselves), because this only determines the number of segments in the IDoc. Later in this section, you will work with this more.

In addition, it's worth mentioning the MSGFN fields found in every segment. These fields specify the function to be used by the data in the receiving system. The 005 constant stands for changing or creating.

If you closely examine the structure of the IDoc, you will notice that most segments allow for multiple integrations. Most IDocs are appropriate for mass processing. This IDoc can be used for creating several material master data sets; however, the IDoc in this example is only used to create a single material master record. Documentation of this and all other IDoc types can be found in Transaction WE60.

If you examine the table containing the element assignment, you will see that only two of the segments are provided with data. The unused segments can be disabled to prevent them from generating fields. For such a segment, open the context menu and select the Disable Field function. The icon next to the segment is then crossed out and the segment is no longer checked for data. Disable all segments except E1MARAM and its child segment, E1MAKTM.

Next, create the message mapping (see Figure 4.22) using Table 4.6 and test it. If it runs smoothly, save it. The work area of Figure 4.31 shows how the constant is assigned to the BEGIN element in the message mapping.

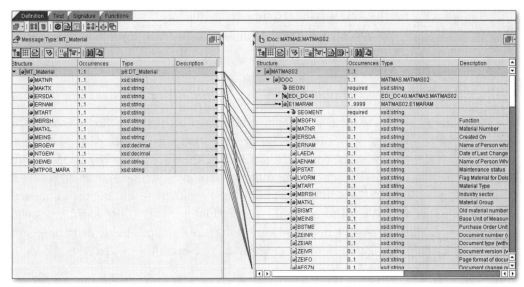

Figure 4.31 Message Mapping of the File-to-IDoc Exercise

Next, create the operation mapping OM_MI_Material_Async_Out_to_MAT-MAS_MATMAS02 based on the message mapping MM_MT_Material_to_MAT-MAS_MATMAS02 via the context menu in the appropriate path. Use the two service interfaces SI_Material_Async_Out and MATMAS.MATMAS02, import the interfaces into the lower area of the details window, and assign the message mapping you just created (see Figure 4.32). In the TEST tab, test the operation mapping and save the object.

Creating the operation mapping

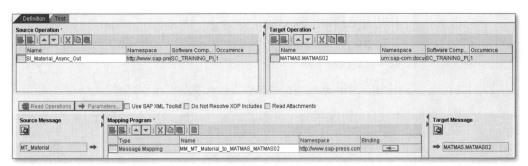

Figure 4.32 Operation Mapping for the File-to-IDoc Exercise

Because this was the last new design object for this exercise, you should now apply all of the changes in the Change Lists tab before switching to the Integration Directory.

4.2.3 Configuration

Now use the PI tools menu or the direct URL to switch to the Integration Directory. In the previous exercise, you already created the basic elements for the configuration. Because there are hardly any overlaps with the first exercise at the configuration level, you will create all required objects — even the communication channels — and use the Configuration Wizard to create the connection elements. This wizard saves you from several steps and contributes to a smooth implementation.[4] An overview of all of the configuration objects in this exercise is shown in Table 4.7.

Object Type	Sender Side: System A	Receiver Side: System B
Communication channel	`File_ SenderChannel_#`	`IDoc_ ReceiverChannel`
Sender agreement	`| SystemA | SI_ Material_Async_Out | |`	
Receiver agreement		`| SystemA | | SystemB | MATMAS. MATMAS02`
Receiver determination	`| SystemA | SI_Material_Async_Out`	
Interface determination	`| SystemA | SI_Material_Async_Out | | SystemB`	

Table 4.7 Elements in the Integration Directory for the File-to-IDoc Exercise

---

4 This exercise was created on the basis of PI release 7.1 SP7. In this version, it may happen that not all objects are created when generating the configuration objects using the Configuration Wizard. Missing objects must then be created, as described in Section 4.1.3, Configuration. In addition, the value help may not display the right entries within the wizard. In such a case, directly enter the data of the object.

Setting Up the Communication Channels

To create the sending communication channel for the file adapter, open the creation dialog using the context menu of the Communication Channel object. The new communication channel should be named File_ SenderChannel_##. Enter system A as the communication component. Enter a description and create the new object.

Creating the file sender channel

In the Details window (see Figure 4.33), select the FILE adapter type and ensure that SENDER is selected. Set the TRANSPORT PROTOCOL to FILE SYSTEM (NFS), because a local directory is accessed. With the MESSAGE PROTOCOL, the FILE setting ensures that the file is read without being converted. The ADAPTER ENGINE is the Integration Server (IS).

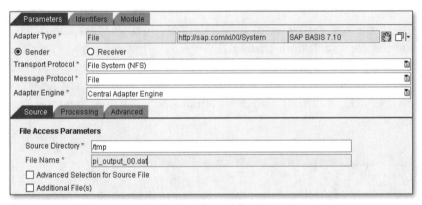

Figure 4.33 Setting up the File Sender Channel for System A

In the SOURCE DIRECTORY field, select the setting you used for the receiver channel in the RFC-to-File exercise (see Section 4.1.3). If you followed the recommendations, this is */tmp* for Unix, or *C:\temp* for Windows. The file name should be *pi_input_##.dat*, where ## represents the participant number.

In the PROCESSING tab, you can keep the Quality of Service as Exactly Once. Set the Poll Interval (Sec) to a value between 3 and 10 minutes; otherwise, the load on the IS can be too high. The Retry Interval field specifies the number of seconds the adapter should wait before retrying after a failed read. (This value is not relevant to this exercise.) The Processing Mode of the communication channel can take various characteristics depending on your permissions at the operating system level.

One option is the Archive, which causes the file to be moved to another folder. Alternatively, the file can be deleted or left unchanged in the test operation, which causes the data record to be sent continuously. Use archiving with a time stamp if an appropriate folder is available. The file cannot be archived in the source directory. If you do not have an appropriate folder, you can just delete the file. The processing order can be freely chosen; however, you should set the File Type to Binary.

Creating the IDoc receiver channel

The receiving communication channel for IDocs is only created once (as described in the basics of this exercise) because you cannot distinguish channels between several participants.[5]

Using the context menu of the Communication Channel object, create the communication channel `IDoc_ReceiverChannel` and enter the description. Set the ADAPTER TYPE to IDOC, and set the direction to RECEIVER. The TRANSPORT PROTOCOL, MESSAGE PROTOCOL, and ADAPTER ENGINE fields don't normally offer options, so just ignore them (see Figure 4.34).

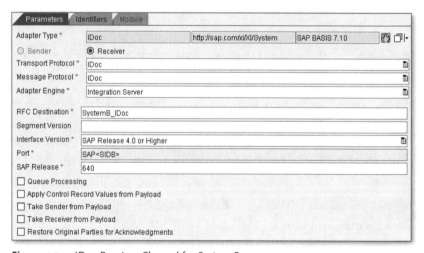

Figure 4.34 IDoc Receiver Channel for System B

---

5 The IDoc communication channel can only be created once by the instructor.

For the RFC DESTINATION, select the `SystemB_IDoc` connection, which you created while preparing for the exercises. The SEGMENT VERSION is used for integrating with legacy SAP systems, and can be used for sending only those segments that already existed in a specific R/3 release. The INTERFACE VERSION field (which is mandatory) serves the same purpose but refers to the entire interface definition. For this field, select the SAP RELEASE 4.0 OR HIGHER option. Enter the PORT for system B, which was created according to the `SAP<SIDB>` scheme during the preparation (the system ID (SID) for system B is SIDB). In the SAP RELEASE field, enter the release of the receiving SAP system. In the case of SAP ECC 6.0, the entry is 700. Save the object and activate the two new communication channels.

To ensure that the file communication channel has been configured correctly, you can view the adapter in Component Monitoring. Open the Runtime Workbench and display all components by clicking on the entry on Component Monitoring. In the list, click on the Adapter Engine. A new area appears below the list, which contains the Adapter Monitoring button on the right side. Select the File adapter type and check its status.

Checking the
file adapter

If no errors occurred, the status should be green. If an error has occurred, you will find a detailed description of the error status. Some errors only occur during data processing, so you should return to the adapter monitoring if you encounter problems at a later stage.

Creating the Connection Elements

In this exercise, the connection between the two communication channels or between the sender and the receiver interface is created using the Configuration Wizard. The wizard is started via the TOOLS • CONFIGURATION WIZARD menu path, or by clicking the corresponding icon in the Integration Directory's toolbar. The wizard collects data for the step-by-step configuration, and creates the appropriate objects. In the progress bar on the left side of the wizard, you can use the orange mark to identify your current position in the configuration process.

Calling the
Configuration
Wizard

In the first step, you can select whether to configure an internal or partner communication. Internal communication takes place entirely within

Determining the
communication
type

the enterprise landscape, while partner communication either entirely or partially involves external business partners. For our scenario, select the Internal Communication option.

Setting the sender parameters

In the next screen (see Figure 4.35), you can specify the values for the sending side. Before you specify other values, however, you should select the sending ADAPTER TYPE; in this exercise, this is the FILE adapter. Next, select business system A as the COMMUNICATION COMPONENT. In the INTERFACE field, specify the interface as SI_Material_Async_Out. When selecting the values using the input help, you may need to delete the search criteria and search once more to find a specific interface. If you used the input help for entering the interface, the namespace is populated automatically. Otherwise, specify your namespace as http://www.sap-press.com/pi/training/##.

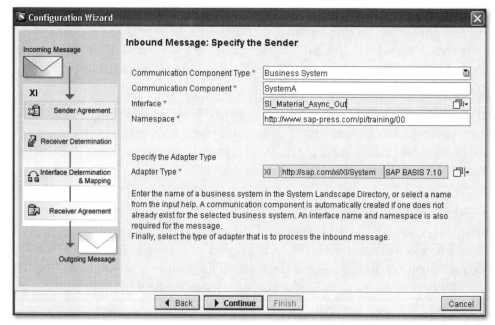

Figure 4.35 Configuration Wizard — Information about the Sender in the File-to-IDoc Exercise

Setting the receiver parameters

When you continue to the next step, you are presented with the same input mask for the receiver side (see Figure 4.36). As before, first select the ADAPTER TYPE IDOC. Set the service to business system B and set the

Interface to `MATMAS.MATMAS02`. By selecting the IDoc adapter type, the namespace is already defined.

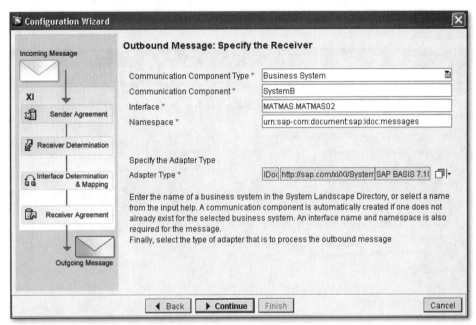

Figure 4.36 Configuration Wizard — Information about the Receiver in the File-to-IDoc Exercise

In the next input mask, the communication channel on the sending side is queried to automatically create the sender agreement `|SystemA|SI_Material_Async_Out||`. Specify your sending file communication channel `File_SenderChannel_##` of system A.

Determining the sender channel

The next step is for creating the receiver determination `|SystemA|SI_Material_Async_Out`. At first, it checks to see if a receiver determination for the sending interface already exists for the relevant system. If the object does exist, it is extended. Otherwise, a new object is created that does not require any input. Because this training scenario shouldn't contain an appropriate receiver determination yet, this step is only for your information.

Creating the receiver determination

The next step for creating the interface determination `|SystemA|SI_Material_Async_Out||SystemB` can either be used for information or for

Creating the interface determination

checking (see Figure 4.37). Ensure that the MATMAS.MATMAS02 interface has been selected and that the operation mapping is displayed. If the mapping isn't displayed, this usually indicates that it has not been created (or at least not activated).

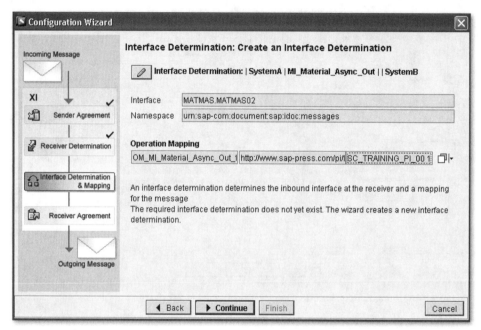

Figure 4.37 Configuration Wizard — Information about the Interface Determination of the File-to-IDoc Exercise

Creating the receiver agreement The last object checked for this scenario is the receiver agreement |SystemA||SystemB|MATMAS.MATMAS02. To create this object, you only need the receiving communication channel IDoc_ReceiverChannel, which should have been entered already. Continue to the last step.

After you have made the necessary changes, you can directly assign the new objects to a specific scenario. Select your scenario (PI_Training_##) and click the FINISH button. The required objects are now created, and reused objects are modified. After the objects have been generated successfully, you will receive a detailed log on the updated and created objects. In release 7.1 SP7, it is possible that not all objects are created. Missing configuration objects must be created manually, as described in

Section 4.1.3. Finally, the changes must be activated in the Change Lists tab.

4.2.4 Process and Monitoring

The process of the integration scenario in this exercise is triggered by creating the file *pi_input_##.dat* in the directory of the sending file adapter. When creating and placing the file, you can use the template from Appendix A. However, the file should already be in the appropriate directory after processing the first exercise. It may be that the file could not be processed directly after saving the File-ReceiverChannel; in this case, call the appropriate program Z_PROG_MATERIALINPUT_## from the first exercise again to create a new file.

Controlling
the process

Depending on the poll interval that has been set in the communication channel, the file is archived or deleted after several minutes. If the process is successful, you can look at your new material, PI_BOOK-##, in Transaction MM03 of business system B shortly after the file disappears. In the first screen, select your material and confirm your input by pressing the Enter key. Select the two views, BASIC DATA 1 and BASIC DATA 2, and check the details. To keep the used IDoc structure small, only these two basic views have been created (see Figure 4.38).

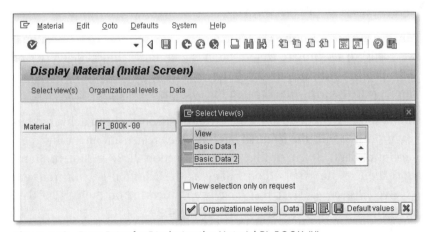

Figure 4.38 Entry Point for Displaying the Material PI_BOOK-##

Extending the
sent data

Using two utilities, you have the option of accessing more views; Transaction WE60 stores the documentation of the entire IDoc type with all of its field names. If you are already familiar with MM in the SAP system, and now want to know which field of the input mask corresponds to a field in the IDoc, you can get this information by pressing F1 . For example, open any material using Transaction MM03 and highlight a field. Press the F1 key and click the Technical Information icon. In most cases, the Field Data area contains the exact field name matching that of the IDoc.

Checking the file
processing

If the material hasn't been created in system B (even after you have waited for a while) you will need to troubleshoot the problem. The first possible source of an error is the file adapter, because it doesn't read and archive the file. In the Component Monitoring of the Runtime Workbench, recheck the status of the corresponding adapter. Some errors are only obvious while a message is being processed.

The next item to troubleshoot would be the message monitoring on the XI system. You can open this via Transaction SXMB_MONI, or the message monitoring in the Runtime Workbench. There you can see if the message has reached the PI system, and analyze whether a content error has occurred for an Integration Builder object. However, if the message shows a black-and-white checkered flag, it has been successfully forwarded to system B.

You can use Transaction SM58 (the monitoring function for transactional RFC calls) to see if there were problems with the technical delivery. For example, one possible error could be a missing or faulty partner agreement created when you prepared the systems for the exercises.

Checking the
incoming of
the IDoc

If you still haven't discovered the error, the IDoc has been delivered but not processed (i.e., the material has not been created automatically upon receipt of data). To check this, start Transaction BD87 in system B and click the Execute icon without changing the selection criteria. You will receive a list of all IDocs that have been processed on the current day, categorized by various statuses (see Figure 4.39).

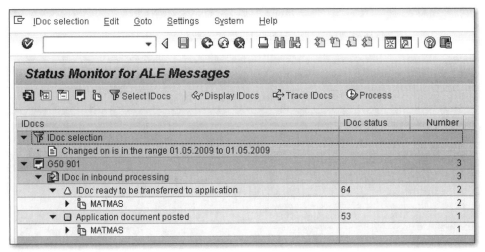

Figure 4.39 Status Monitor for ALE Messages

To determine the exact source of error when processing a message, click on the appropriate category (e.g., APPLICATION DOCUMENT POSTED). The selection is restricted to the messages in this category. Because system B only differentiates IDocs processing by the names of the logical systems, delivered messages cannot be distinguished by participants.

Navigation in the Status Monitor for ALE messages

If you double-click on one of the messages in the list, the corresponding details are displayed. On the left side, expand the Status records directory and the numbers underneath. Every number represents a specific message. In this exercise, you will even find messages for messages that have been successfully processed.

If you double-click on one of these numbers, the status record is displayed. To see a descriptive error message, follow the GOTO • APPLICATION LOG menu path, or click on the appropriate button. You will see warnings and error messages that occurred while the message was processed, and you can see if you have overlooked a field or filled it with the wrong data (see Figure 4.40). IDoc fields are checked, and the input in the relevant transactions.

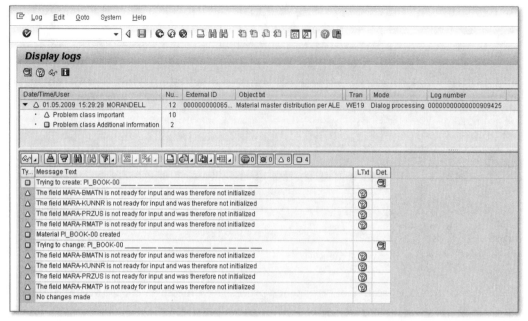

Figure 4.40 Application Log of an IDoc Message

4.3 Exercise 3: ABAP-Proxy-to-Simple Object Access Protocol (SOAP)

Course of the exercise

In the second exercise, you used an IDoc to import the data you created as a file in the first exercise into business system B. In addition, you could verify that the material master record was properly created. However, in real life, you can't always access both the sending and receiving system.

Therefore, we will implement an integration scenario in this third exercise that allows you to control the successful material creation from system A. You will create an ABAP proxy in system A and call it synchronously. The request is forwarded to a Web service on system B, and a response is returned shortly afterward. The PI system serves as the mediator between the different adapter and data formats.

The scheme of this exercise for synchronous communication is illustrated in Figure 4.41.

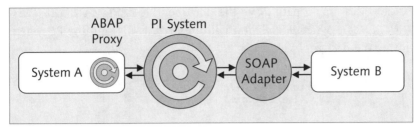

Figure 4.41 Scheme of Exercise 3 ABAP-Proxy-to-SOAP

4.3.1 Basics

The Web service is addressed via the SOAP adapter, and is based on the business application programming interface (BAPI) BAPI_MATERIAL_EXISTENCECHECK, which is provided by system B. As of the technical basis of SAP Web Application Server (WAS) 6.20, remote-enabled function modules can be addressed as Web services without specifying any further settings. As with the import of RFC and IDoc interfaces, these Web services can also export the Web Service Description Language (WSDL) description from the SAP system and use it in the PI system.

Origin of the Web service

To obtain the WSDL description for the appropriate BAPI, use a Service, which you can find via the URL scheme *http://<Host SystemB>:<Port 80XX>/sap/bc/bsp/sap/webservicebrowser/search.html?sap-client=<client>*. The *XX* in the port number represents the instance number of the respective server. The specifications about host and port can be obtained from Transaction SMICM by following the menu path: Goto • Services.

Web Service Repository

Open the appropriate URL in the Web browser and log on as user SYS_B-##. In the search field, enter the name of the BAPI (BAPI_MATERIAL_EXISTENCECHECK), and confirm your selection by pressing the Enter key. The search result shows the BAPI with two links on the right side (see Figure 4.42).

The question mark (?) opens the function module's documentation, if there is any. The WSDL label opens the WSDL description of this function module in a separate window. Because Microsoft Internet Explorer, for example, automatically adds functions for collapsing and expanding individual sections to WSDL descriptions, it is necessary to save the source text of the display. This can be done by following the View •

SOURCECODE menu path. Save the document as *BAPI_MATERIAL_EXIS-TENCECHECK_SystemB.wsdl*. You will import this file into the PI system during the design phase.

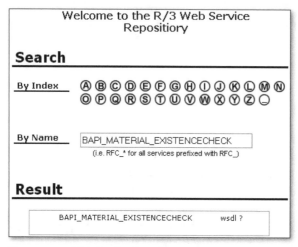

Figure 4.42 Web Service Repository

The calling ABAP proxy class is created based on a service interface existing in the Enterprise Services Repository. Because inbound and outbound data formats match those of the Web service, you will use the imported WSDL definition as the data and message type of the outbound service interface as well.

4.3.2 Design

Overview of the design objects

In contrast to the previous exercises, you are now facing your first synchronous scenario. This means you not only have to create the design objects to access the Web service, but also for the way back. In this respect, this example is easy because you are using the existing WSDL interface, so you don't have to create any data or message types. In other cases, a synchronous scenario can involve creating up to four different data types and the corresponding message types. While the message mapping is created separately for every direction, the same operation mapping is used for both directions. The new objects to be created for this exercise are listed in Table 4.8.

Object Type	Sender Side	Receiver Side
Service interface	SI_ABAP_PROXY_MAT_EXIST_##_Sync_Out	SI_ws_bapi_material_existencecheck_Sync_In
Message type	ws_bapi_material_existencecheck	
Data type		
Operation mapping	OM_ABAP_PROXY_MAT_EXIST_##_to_ws_bapi_material_existencecheck	
Message mapping (request)	MM_ABAP_PROXY_MAT_EXIST_##_to_ws_bapi_material_existencecheck	
Message mapping (response)	MM_ws_bapi_material_existencecheck_to_ABAP_PROXY_MAT_EXIST_##	

Table 4.8 Elements in the Enterprise Services Repository for the ABAP-Proxy-to-SOAP Exercise

Creating the Interface Objects

First, open the context via the INTERFACE OBJECTS • EXTERNAL DEFINITIONS menu path in your namespace. Create the external definition ws_bapi_material_existencecheck, which will contain the WSDL description of the Web service on system B. In the details window, ensure that the CATEGORY WSDL is selected, and, next to the FILE field, click the CLICK HERE TO IMPORT EXTERNAL DEFINITIONS icon. Select the BAPI_MATERIAL_EXISTENCECHECK_SystemB.wsdl file on your local machine, which you just transferred from the Web Service Repository (see Figure 4.43).

Importing the WSDL description

After the import, you can see the contents of the file in the IMPORTED DOCUMENT tab. Select the MESSAGES tab to see both of the message types created by the import. Based on the corresponding function module, the Web service contains the definition for the inbound and outbound message. In addition, you can use the message names to determine the connection to the corresponding BAPI.

The import of the external definition is handled as a message type with integrated data types. As a result, the service interface must be created manually on the receiving side. Open the creation dialog by choosing the context menu from the INTERFACE OBJECTS • SERVICE INTERFACES menu path and create the SI_ws_bapi_material_existencecheck_Sync_In service interface.

Creating the synchronous inbound interface

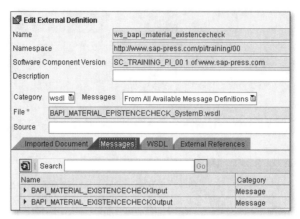

Figure 4.43 Importing the External Definition for the ABAP-Proxy-to-SOAP Exercise

Although the Web service processes both inbound and outbound messages due to its synchronous character, it is primarily used as an inbound interface in this scenario. Accordingly, set the INBOUND category and the SYNCHRONOUS mode. This combination gives you the option of specifying both an input and an output message. When selecting a message type from a Web service, you cannot use the drag-and-drop method. Therefore, the easiest option is to use the input help. Below the newly created external definition, select the message type BAPI_MATERIAL_EXISTENCECHECKInput for the input message and the corresponding counterpart for the output message (see Figure 4.44). Save the service interface.

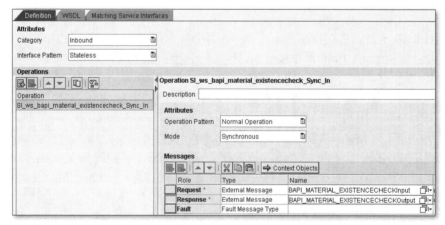

Figure 4.44 Creating the Service Interface for the Web Service of the ABAP-Proxy-to-SOAP Exercise

Now that the receiver's interface objects have been created, a service interface is still needed for the sender side. The data and the message type are based on the imported WSDL description. Open the creation dialog for service interfaces and create the interface SI_ABAP_PROXY_MAT_ EXIST_*##*_Sync_Out. The included participant number is not necessary in the Integration Builder; however, the ABAP classes created later must be distinguishable.

Creating the service interface for the ABAP proxy

The new interface belongs to the OUTBOUND category and the SYN-CHRONOUS mode. For the Request Message, select the BAPI_MATE-RIAL_EXISTENCECHECKInput message type from the external definition, ws_bapi_material_existencecheck. The Response Message is of the BAPI_MATERIAL_EXISTENCECHECKOutput type from the same external definition (see Figure 4.45). Save the interface and activate all interface objects.

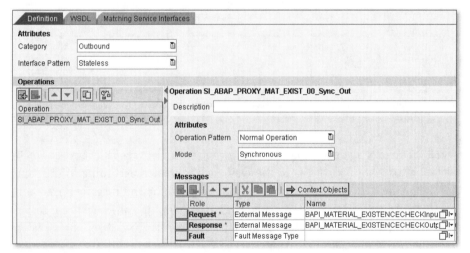

Figure 4.45 Creation of the Service Interface for the ABAP Proxy of the ABAP-Proxy-to-SOAP Exercise

Creating the Mapping Objects

Despite previously naming the mapping objects, we won't strictly name the message mappings according to their message types. The reason is that the same message types are used on both the sending and receiving sides, so a standard name doesn't have to be descriptive.

Creating the message mapping for the way to the Web service

As such, create the message mapping `MM_ABAP_PROXY_MAT_EXIST_##_to_ws_bapi_material_existencecheck` via the MAPPING OBJECTS • MESSAGE MAPPINGS menu path. This serves as the mapping for the way from the ABAP proxy to the Web service. As an outbound message, select the `BAPI_MATERIAL_EXISTENCECHECKInput` type from the external definition `ws_bapi_material_existencecheck`, which can be found in the External Definitions directory. The target message is of the same type. The mapping of the way to the Web service is fairly easy, because only the two `MATERIAL` fields need to be connected (see Figure 4.46). Test and save the message mapping.

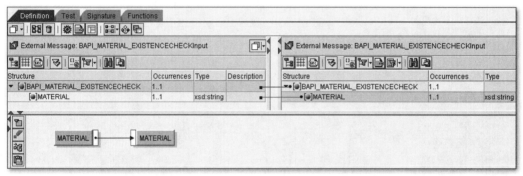

Figure 4.46 Creating the Message Mapping for the Way to the Web Service in the ABAP-Proxy-to-SOAP Exercise

Creating the message mapping for the way back
The message mapping `MM_ws_bapi_material_existencecheck_to_ABAP_PROXY_MAT_EXIST_##` for the way back is created according to the same pattern. However, both the outbound and inbound messages are `BAPI_MATERIAL_EXISTENCECHECKOutput`. The mapping can quickly be implemented by clicking the MAP SELECTED FIELDS AND SUBSTRUCTURES IF NAMES ARE IDENTICAL icon.

Extending the message mapping by a user-defined function
This simple mapping is used to take the first steps in the area of user-defined mapping programs. For this, you create a user-defined function within the graphical mapping. The function's goal is to fill an element with specific content depending on the contents of another element; the function is an `IF` construction that could also be implemented using one of the predefined functions. If the Web service detects that the tested material is available, it provides a return code without a descriptive mes-

sage. If an error occurs, however, a detailed error description is returned. The adaptation of the success and failure responses is achieved using the new function.

One of the affected elements is MESSAGE, which should include a description. The controlling element is NUMBER, which contains a value of 000 in the case of a successful connection.

To create a user-defined function, double-click on the MESSAGE target element and add the outbound field NUMBER to the work area. In the bottom-left of the work area, click the CREATE NEW FUNCTION icon to create a user-defined Java function. Name the function SUCCESSMESSAGE and enter a description (see Figure 4.47).

Creating a user-defined function

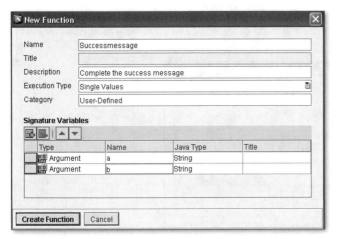

Figure 4.47 Creating the User-Defined Function for the ABAP-Proxy-to-SOAP Exercise

Because it is a simple function it is sufficient to only load the values (SINGLE VALUES) in the cache. In the list of arguments, use the appropriate icon to create another argument, b, that, just like argument a, is of the STRING type. The arguments are the transfer parameters to the function.

You now have the option of creating a Java function that is only valid within this mapping. This procedure should not be confused with the deployment of Java classes, which is referred to as *Java mapping*, and

Structure of the source code

which is described in Section 4.5.5, Alternative Java Mapping (Optional), using an example.

You are still working within the graphical mapping of SAP NetWeaver PI. In the lower part of the work area, the function selection has switched to the USER-DEFINED area, and you can see your new function as a selection option. The newly displayed window represents a small Java editor that already contains a few settings. Insert the source code from Listing 4.2 in the implementation part of the function (see Figure 4.48). You do not have to import any additional classes because the most important classes are imported automatically.

```
if (a.equals ("000"))
   return "The material is available";
else return b;
```

Listing 4.2 Source Code of the User-Defined Function of the Message Mapping

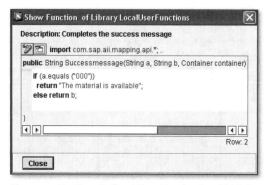

Figure 4.48 User-Defined Function for the ABAP-Proxy-to-SOAP Exercise

Integrating the user-defined function

Save the new function and insert it between the existing NUMBER and MESSAGE (source) and MESSAGE (target) rectangles by clicking on the function name. Drag the connections between the three objects so that NUMBER is connected to the upper white field of the function on the left side. The upper input field of the function is automatically assigned to argument **a.** Connect MESSAGE (source) to the second white field on the left side and assign the function result to the target field (see Figure 4.49).

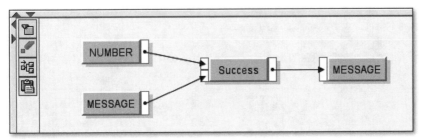

Figure 4.49 Integration of the User-Defined Function for the ABAP-Proxy-to-SOAP Exercise

Save and test the entire mapping. Use the value 000 for NUMBER and another value including any message input for testing. If NUMBER equals 000, the message stored in the function should appear in the MESSAGE field.

The two message mappings for both directions of the exchange must now be embedded in the operation mapping OM_ABAP_PROXY_MAT_ EXIST_##_to_ws_bapi_material_existencecheck. Open the creation dialog for the new operation mapping and enter the name and an appropriate description.

Creating the synchronous operation mapping

The details window does not show any changes yet compared to an asynchronous communication. For the outbound interface, select the interface SI_ABAP_PROXY_MAT_EXIST_##_Sync_Out using the input help. The target interface is the service interface, SI_ws_bapi_material_exis-tencecheck_Sync_In. In the lower area of the details window, click on the Read Interfaces button and pay attention to the Request label underneath. The simple label turns into two tabs that can be used for configuring each direction (see Figure 4.50).

In the REQUEST tab, select the NAME field in the list of mapping programs, and use the input help to select your mapping. Now click on the RESPONSE tab and repeat this step. In both cases, the input help should only display one entry. Save the operation mapping and activate all mapping objects of this exercise.

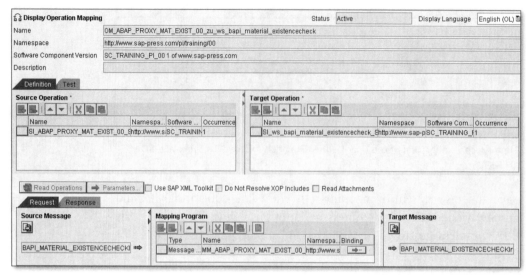

Figure 4.50 Operation Mapping for the ABAP-Proxy-to-SOAP Exercise

Generating the ABAP Proxy

Providing an
ABAP package

The SI_ABAP_PROXY_MAT_EXIST_##_Sync_Out service interface created in the Enterprise Services Repository is the basis of proxy generation. An ABAP class is automatically created to allow communication with this interface from an ABAP program. In contrast to remote-enabled function modules, however, no adapter is used. Data is exchanged in the PI format between the local and central IE.

For the remaining steps, you need developer permission in system A, a package Z_PI_TRAINING, and a corresponding transport request. The package can be created using Transaction SE80. If you already developed the RFC modules yourself during the first exercise (see Section 4.1, Exercise 1: RFC-to-File) or downloaded the appropriate transport from the website for this book (*http://www.sap-press.com*), you can use the corresponding package.

Generating a
proxy class

Log in to system A via the user SYS_A-## and call Transaction SPROXY. The structure of this screen is similar to the Enterprise Services Repository: The created software component versions are displayed on the left, with the namespaces listed beneath them. Within the namespaces, however, only the objects of the Interface Objects branch are displayed.

In your namespace, expand the Message Interface (outbound) branch and double-click the service interface SI_ABAP_PROXY_MAT_EXIST_##_ Sync_Out. You will be asked if a proxy should be created for this interface; answer Yes. You are then asked for specific settings for the proxy class. Enter the package Z_PI_TRAINING and the prefix Z.

After confirming this information, a warning dialog pops up during the generation process, informing you that there have been name collisions or name shortenings. The reason for this is because the names of the generated ABAP objects may contain a maximum of 30 characters, while the Integration Builder accepts longer names.

The details window of the newly generated proxy class contains four tabs. The PROPERTIES tab informs you about the classification of the object and the name ZCO_SI_ABAP_PROXY_MAT_EXIST_##. The NAME PROBLEMS tab lists all elements that caused problems during the generation process. The name of the class has been shortened, but is still descriptive and distinguishes the individual participants.

Properties of the proxy class

In the right column of this list, you can see which object in the Enterprise Services Repository corresponds to the rows and their contents. The second row displays the structure of the message type BAPI_MATERIAL_EXISTENCECHECKOutput. Change the last two letters to OU so the structure is named ZSI_ABAP_PROXY_MAT_EXIST_##_OU (see Figure 4.51). The counterpart to the message type BAPI_MATERIAL_EXISTENCECHECK-Input should also be renamed to ZSI_ABAP_PROXY_MAT_EXIST_##_IN for consistency. The last structure, which corresponds to BAPIRETURN1, should be renamed to ZSI_ABAP_PROXY_MAT_EXIST_00_RE.

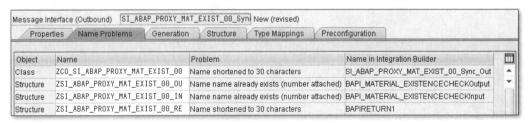

| Message Interface (Outbound) | SI_ABAP_PROXY_MAT_EXIST_00_Syn| New (revised) | | | | |

| | Properties | Name Problems | Generation | Structure | Type Mappings | Preconfiguration | |

Object	Name	Problem	Name in Integration Builder	
Class	ZCO_SI_ABAP_PROXY_MAT_EXIST_00	Name shortened to 30 characters	SI_ABAP_PROXY_MAT_EXIST_00_Sync_Out	
Structure	ZSI_ABAP_PROXY_MAT_EXIST_00_OU	Name name already exists (number attached)	BAPI_MATERIAL_EXISTENCECHECKOutput	
Structure	ZSI_ABAP_PROXY_MAT_EXIST_00_IN	Name name already exists (number attached)	BAPI_MATERIAL_EXISTENCECHECKInput	
Structure	ZSI_ABAP_PROXY_MAT_EXIST_00_RE	Name shortened to 30 characters	BAPIRETURN1	

Figure 4.51 Naming Problems when Generating the ABAP Proxy for the ABAP-Proxy-to-SOAP Exercise

<table>
<tr><td>Activation of
the proxy class</td><td>The GENERATION tab displays a list of all of the created objects, regardless of any naming problems. The STRUCTURE tab displays a hierarchical arrangement of all objects. For example, you can see that the new class ZCO_SI_ABAP_PROXY_MAT_EXIST_## contains a method called EXECUTE_SYNCHRONOUS. Below this method, you can view the parameters from the ABAP program's point of view.</td></tr>
</table>

Save the proxy class and specify the corresponding transport request. Check the objects by following the PROXY • CHECK menu path, or by clicking the Check icon. The list of checking messages should contain four yellow warnings, but no red error messages. Confirm the list and activate the objects via the PROXY • ACTIVATE menu path, or by clicking the Activate icon. After you've activated the objects, the activation log can contain warning messages; however, you can ignore the log in this case, because there shouldn't be any errors.

For checking, you can call the Class Builder using Transaction SE24, and display the class ZCO_SI_ABAP_PROXY_MAT_EXIST_##. Within the Methods tab, you can see that the method EXECUTE_SYNCHRONOUS has been created in addition to the constructor. In addition, the GET_PROTOCOL and GET_TRANSPORT_BINDING methods are displayed, which have been created but not yet implemented. These two optional methods are not required for this exercise.

4.3.3 Configuration

Overview of
configuration
objects

Change to the Integration Directory and log in, if necessary. Before you use the Configuration Wizard to configure the objects, you first need to create a communication channel for the receiver side. On the side of the sending system, no communication channel is used, because communication with a proxy does not require an adapter.

The configuration objects you create for this exercise are listed in Table 4.9.

Creating the SOAP
communication
channel

Open the context menu of the Communication Channel path and create a new communication channel for the communication component SystemB. Name it "SOAP_Receiverchannel_##" and enter a description. Continue with Create, and, in the details window, select the SOAP adapter type. The communication channel is created as a RECEIVER. Ensure that the TRANSPORT PROTOCOL is set to HTTP. The other parameters in the header can be left unchanged.

Object Type	Sender Side: System A	Receiver Side: System B
Communication channel		SOAP_ Receiverchannel_##
Receiver agreement		| SystemA | | SystemB | SI_ws_ bapi_material_ existencecheck_ Sync_In
Receiver determination	SystemA | SI_ABAP_PROXY_MAT_EXIST_##_ Sync_Out	
Interface determination	| SystemA | SI_ABAP_PROXY_MAT_EXIST_##_ Sync_Out | | SystemB	

Table 4.9 Elements in the Integration Directory for the ABAP-Proxy-to-SOAP Exercise

In the CONNECTION PARAMETERS area, enter the URL of the target system according to the following scheme: *http://<host SystemB>:<ABAP-Port>/sap/ bc/soap/rfc/sap/BAPI_MATERIAL_EXISTENCECHECK?sap-client=<client>.*
The client of system B is required to determine against which client user authentication should be performed. To be sure, use Transaction SICF in system B to verify that the corresponding service is active. This service allows you to call remote-enabled function modules as Web services.

In the details window of the communication channel, enable the CONFIGURE USER AUTHENTICATION option. The USER and PASSWORD fields are displayed. Enter the data of your user SYS_B-## (see Figure 4.52), and save the communication channel.

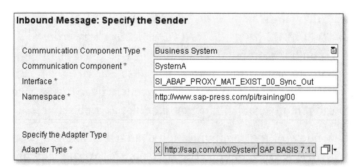

Figure 4.52 Setting Up the SOAP Receiver Channel for System B

Using the Configuration Wizard

After the final piece for the configuration has been created, start the Configuration Wizard via the TOOLS • CONFIGURATION WIZARD menu path, or by clicking the CONFIGURATION WIZARD icon. The integration scenario you are implementing belongs to the Internal Communication category. The sender is business system A, which sends data using the service interface SI_ABAP_PROXY_MAT_EXIST_##_Sync_Out. The adapter is of the XI type and should already be set (see Figure 4.53).

Inbound Message: Specify the Sender

Communication Component Type *	Business System
Communication Component *	SystemA
Interface *	SI_ABAP_PROXY_MAT_EXIST_00_Sync_Out
Namespace *	http://www.sap-press.com/pi/training/00

Specify the Adapter Type

Adapter Type *	X http://sap.com/xi/XI/Systerr SAP BASIS 7.1C

Figure 4.53 Settings of the Sender in the Configuration Wizard of the ABAP-Proxy-to-SOAP Exercise

The receiver is business system B, which receives information via the SOAP adapter type. The service interface used is SI_ws_bapi_material_existencecheck_Sync_In (see Figure 4.54).

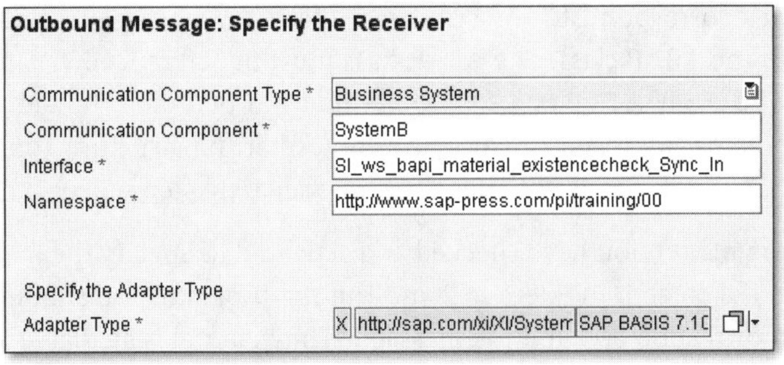

Outbound Message: Specify the Receiver

Communication Component Type *	Business System
Communication Component *	SystemB
Interface *	SI_ws_bapi_material_existencecheck_Sync_In
Namespace *	http://www.sap-press.com/pi/training/00

Specify the Adapter Type

Adapter Type *	X http://sap.com/xi/XI/Systen SAP BASIS 7.1C

Figure 4.54 Settings of the Receiver in the Configuration Wizard of the ABAP-Proxy-to-SOAP Exercise

In the next step, you won't need to create a sender agreement, because no conversion takes place. The next screen informs you that the receiver determination SystemA|SI_ABAP_PROXY_MAT_EXIST_*##*_Sync_Out is created for this scenario. The interface determination shown in the next step should already display the appropriate operation mapping for the target interface SI_ws_bapi_material_existencecheck_Sync_In. Continue with the next step.

The receiver agreement |SystemA||SystemB|SI_ws_bapi_material_exis-tencecheck_Sync_In should refer to the communication channel you just created, SOAP_Receiverchannel_*##*. Make sure that the new objects are added to your PI_Training_## scenario and finish the wizard. Activate all new and changed configuration objects in your change list.

4.3.4 Process and Monitoring

In this scenario, the proxy class with the EXECUTE_SYNCHRONOUS method must be integrated in an ABAP program. Log in to the client of system A as user SYS_A-*##* and call Transaction SE38 or SE80. You can create the program for calling the proxy method yourself or import the corresponding transport from the website for this book (*http://www.sap-press.com*). If you develop the transport yourself, you will find the sample source code of the Z_MATERIAL_EXISTENCECHECK_*##* program in Appendix A of this book. You can partially use the data types of the BAPI_MATERIAL_EXIS-TENCECHECK BAPI, which you can view using the Function Builder in Transaction SE37.

Creating a calling ABAP program

Most variables correspond to the structures that have been generated together with the ABAP class. The ABAP class must be referenced via an object so that the EXECUTE_SYNCHRONOUS method can be called. In addition, for the wa_input response structure, note that the structure contains wa_return, and is therefore detached in a separate step.

Test the program after you have checked and activated it. Specify the PI_ BOOK-## material created in Exercise 2 and run the program. You should receive the return code 000 and the message "The material is available", as shown in Figure 4.55.

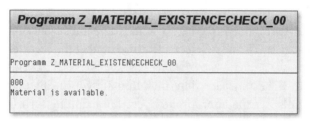

Figure 4.55 Successful Availability Check of a Material

In contrast to asynchronous scenarios, a synchronous scenario usually doesn't leave any marks. Only asynchronous messages are stored in the persistence layer of SAP NetWeaver PI to enable a later analysis.

4.4 Exercise 4: Business Process Management (BPM)

Course of the exercise

The fourth exercise deals with a simple scenario where a department manager or a material manager must be informed about the successful creation of materials. On the sending side, notification is sent using the RFC adapter, while the result is stored as a file in system B.

The important part of this process is that notifications are collected and sorted by creating users. If three messages have been created by one user, those three messages are merged into one and transferred to the material manager. This is controlled using an integration process.

As such, the focus of this exercise does not lie on using new adapters, but on the introduction of SAP NetWeaver PI *cross-component Business Process Management* (ccBPM). You will deal with the corresponding tools in the

Enterprise Services Repository, and the representation in the Integration Directory. Figure 4.56 contains a rough overview of this scenario.

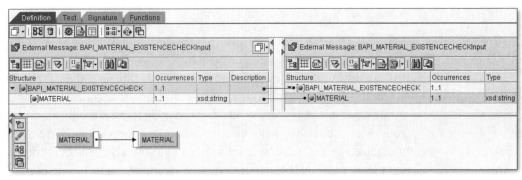

Figure 4.56 Scheme of Exercise 4 BPM

4.4.1 Basics

ccBPM is mainly about integrating processes that can be implemented within one company or across several different companies. For that purpose, a *Business Process Engine* (BPE) is used to merge individual transformations that were implemented using the Adapter Engine and the IE to a business process.

Basics of cross-component Business Process Management

The *Business Process Execution Language* (BPEL) is used to describe the business processes. Process models are created via a graphical editor that is introduced in the following section. In contrast to the SAP Business Workflow, the BPE communicates with applications on backend systems exclusively using messages.[6] It cannot access processes within applications, the user, or organization management on backend systems. Therefore, the following applies:

▸ The BPE doesn't control processes within applications. However, you can use messages to integrate applications in cross-system processes.

▸ The BPE doesn't control user interactions; they can only be controlled on the backend systems.

---

6 More information about this topic can be found in the SAP Help Portal at: *http://help.sap.com/saphelp_nwpi71/helpdata/EN/3c/831620a4f1044dba38b370f77835cc/frameset.htm*.

The BPM itself does not provide any cross-system monitoring for business documents processed within an integration process. Within the technical monitoring, however, you can display the log of an integration process and the corresponding messages.

Before you start working on this exercise, it's important to look at the steps taking place within the business process. At first, the business process records all messages of a specific interface and sorts them by their creators. A loop is opened for each creator name that collects messages of this type, until three are reached. As soon as three identical messages from the same creator have been collected, the loop ends. These three individual messages are merged into a single message in a new format and then sent. How these considerations are implemented in the BPM of SAP NetWeaver PI is explained in the course of the design phase.

As in Exercise 1, the RFC call starting the integration process is made using the program Z_PROG_MATERIALINFO_##, which calls the remote-enabled function module Z_RFM_MATERIALINFO_##. The module only works with the material number, the creator name, and the creation date parameters. Again, the source code can be found in Appendix A, and the corresponding transport can be downloaded from this book's web page (*http://www.sap-press.com*).

4.4.2 Design

Before you put the individual objects together to form an integration process, let's first deal with the design objects in this exercise.

Creating the Design Objects

In the context of using business processes, you will get to know a new category of service interfaces: *abstract interfaces*. The important thing to know about abstract interfaces is that they don't have a direction. This means they aren't assigned to the Inbound or Outbound category, and can be used in both directions. The only restriction is that abstract interfaces can only be used in integration processes.

This property requires them to be declared separately as interfaces of the Abstract category, even for imported objects. However, if the abstract interfaces are used for receiving or sending messages within a process, you need a counterpart in the defined direction.

Communication between an abstract and a direction-related interface does not require a mapping, as long as the same message type is used. The mapping objects in this exercise are solely used for generating a single message from the three collected messages; you will deal with the particular aspect of mappings that can have several messages on one side. Because the target format of the integration process needs to be created, the required design objects are listed in Table 4.10.

Object Type	Sender Side	Integration Process/Receiver
Service interface	`SI_RFM_MATINFO_##_Async_Abstract`	▶ `SI_MatInfo_List_Async_Abstract` ▶ `SI_MatInfo_List_Async_In`
Message type	`Z_RFM_MATERIALINFO_##`	▶ `MT_MatInfo_List`
Data type		▶ `DT_MatInfo_List` ▶ `DT_MatInfo`
Operation mapping	`OM_RFM_MATINFO_##_Async_Abstract_to_MT_MatInfo_List_Async_Abstract`	
Message mapping	`MM_RFM_MATINFO_##_to_MT_MatInfo_List`	
Integration process	`IP_MatInfo_##`	

Table 4.10 Elements in the Enterprise Services Repository for the ccBPM Exercise

First, import the definition of the RFC function module `Z_RFM_MATERIALINFO_##` from business system A.[7] In the Imported Objects directory, use the context menu and log in as user `SYS_A-##`. Based on the `Z_RFM_MATERIALINFO_##` message of this imported interface, create the service interface `SI_RFM_MATINFO_##_Async_Abstract`. Make sure that you set the CATEGORY to ABSTRACT.

Creating the objects for the sender side

---

7 Importing the interface definition requires that the function module `Z_RFM_MATERIALINFO_##` exists on system A and that it is remote enabled. This can be done by importing the corresponding transport request, or by manually creating the function module. The source code can be found in Appendix A.

This interface is asynchronous. Choose the STATELESS option for the INTERFACE PATTERN. For OPERATION PATTERN, select the only possible value, NORMAL OPERATION (see Figure 4.57). Save the interface. In doing this, you have created all objects on the sender side.

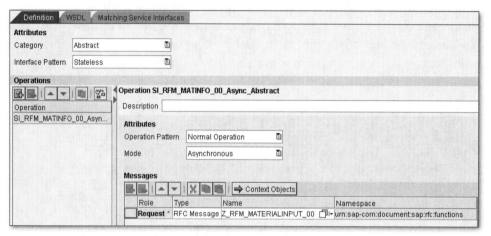

Figure 4.57 Definition of the Abstract Interface SI_RFM_MATINFO_##_Async_ Abstract

Creating the data types
The message type containing the collected notifications at the end of the process is based on a multilevel data type. This means that there is an atomic data type, DT_MatInfo, which can contain the contents of one message. To merge several messages into one, the atomic data type must be integrated in a parent type. For this example, the parent data type is DT_MatInfo_List.

Start by creating the DT_MatInfo data type, and add three elements containing the material number (material_number), the creator (created_ by), and the creation date (creation_date). The first two values are of the xsd:string type, while the creation date is of the xsd:date type (see Figure 4.58). Save this data type.

	Name	Category	Type	Occurr...	Default	Deta...	Busi...	De...	UI ..
	▼ DT_MatInfo	Complex Type							
	material_number	Element	xsd:string	1					
	created_by	Element	xsd:string	1					
	creation_date	Element	xsd:date	1					

Figure 4.58 Structure of the DT_MatInfo Data Type

Next, create the `DT_MatInfo_List` data type so it only contains a single element. This element, `MatInfo`, is of the `DT_MatInfo` type, which you can select using the search help. Once you have created a nested structure, you can record a notification.

To convert the data type into a list, though, you need to change the occurrence of this element. When you double-click in the OCCURRENCE column of the element, a new window opens. Click on Properties; from the input help of the MaxOccurs field, select the unbounded entry so an unlimited number of notifications can be recorded. Confirm your selection and save the data type. The data type should now be structured as shown in Figure 4.59.

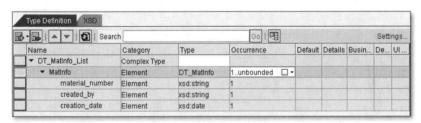

	Name	Category	Type	Occurrence	Default	Details	Busin...	De...	UI ...
	▼ DT_MatInfo_List	Complex Type							
	▼ MatInfo	Element	DT_MatInfo	1..unbounded					
	material_number	Element	xsd:string	1					
	created_by	Element	xsd:string	1					
	creation_date	Element	xsd:date	1					

Figure 4.59 Structure of the DT_MatInfo_List Data Type

Create the message type `MT_MatInfo_List` and base it on the `DT_MatInfo_List` data type. Integrate this new message type in the service interface `SI_MatInfo_List_Async_Abstract`, which you will use later in the integration process. The service interface belongs to the `Abstract` category and the `Asynchronous` mode. You can leave both pattern fields unchanged (see Figure 4.60). Save the abstract interface.

Creating the remaining objects on the receiver side

Sending a message via this interface requires a counterpart in the form of an interface belonging to the Inbound category. Therefore, create a service interface SI_MatInfo_List_Async_In that also uses the MT_Mat-Info_List message type (however, this interface is used as an Inbound interface for asynchronous communication). Save this interface object. You have now created all objects for the receiver side.

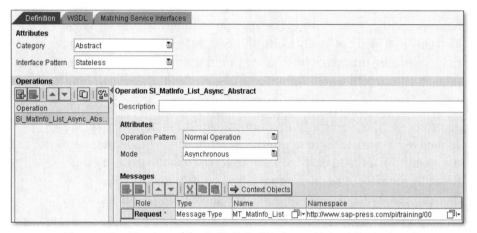

Figure 4.60 Structure of the SI_MatInfo_List_Async_Abstract Service Interface

Creating the mapping objects

Mapping isn't required for connecting abstract and direction-related interfaces of the same message type. However, for converting the three notifications into a single message, a mapping is required at the message and interface level.

Start by creating the message mapping MM_RFM_MATINFO_##_to_MT_Mat-Info_List. The outbound message is Z_RFM_MATERIALINFO_## of the RFC interface of the same name. The target message is the MT_MatInfo_List type you just created.

As you can see, the mapping does not present much of a challenge with regard to its contents. However, its characteristics show that several outbound messages are transformed into a target message. To see this, navigate to the SIGNATURE tab, where the two used messages can be found, including their occurrences. For the outbound message, set an occurrence of 0..UNBOUNDED, and then return to the DEFINITION tab (see Figure 4.61).

Now map the three fields to one another and connect the node Z_RFC_
MATERIALINFO_## on the outbound side to the target node MatInfo, as
shown in Figure 4.62. Save the mapping and test it by duplicating the
subtree Z_RFM_MATERIALINFO_## on the outbound side, using the menu
and populating it with data.

Figure 4.61 Setting the Occurrence in the Message Mapping

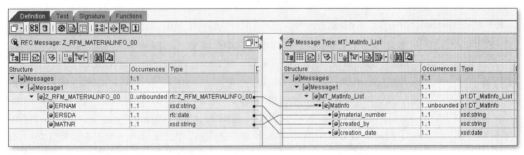

Figure 4.62 Message Mapping of the ccBPM Exercise

This message mapping still needs to be integrated in an appropriate operation mapping. The special thing about this mapping is that both the
sending and the receiving interface belong to the Abstract type. Still, you
can handle and map these interfaces as usual.

*Creating the
operation mapping*

Create the operation mapping OM_RFM_MATINFO_##_Async_Abstract_to_
MT_MatInfo_List_Async_Abstract and use SI_RFM_MATINFO_##_Async_
Abstract as the outbound interface. The target interface is of the SI_
MatInfo_List_Async_Abstract type. The occurrence setting you just
specified for the message mapping also needs to be specified for the
operation mapping. You can set the OCCURRENCE of the outbound interface directly in the DEFINITION tab to a value of 0...UNBOUNDED. In the
lower area, import the interfaces and select the message mapping you
just created (see Figure 4.63).

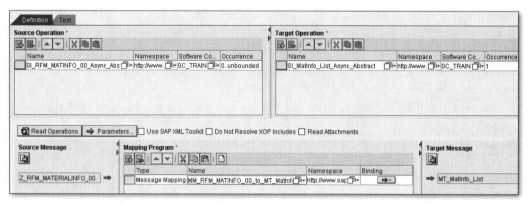

Figure 4.63 Setting the Occurrence in the Operation Mapping

Creating the Integration Process

Creating the integration process

You have now created all of the objects you will use during the integration process. Open the context menu of your namespace and choose the New option, or follow the OBJECT • NEW menu path, to get to the General Creation Wizard. In the wizard, navigate to the menu path: PROCESS INTEGRATION SCENARIO OBJECTS • INTEGRATION PROCESS. Make sure that your namespace and software component version are displayed. Name the new integration process IP_MatInfo_##, and enter a description (see Figure 4.64). For this object, it is necessary to assign the participant number, because your process will later be visible in the entire SAP NetWeaver PI.

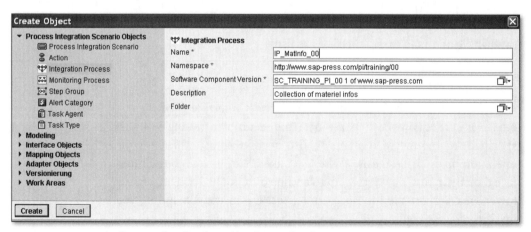

Figure 4.64 Creating a New Integration Process

creating the object brings you to the Details window, which is a graphical process editor. Detach the window using the Fixing pin icon, and hide the header to have as much space as possible (see Figure 4.65).

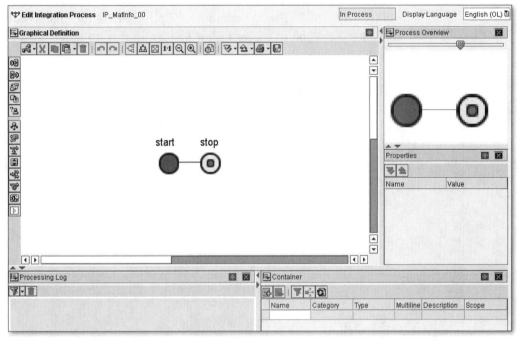

Figure 4.65 Structure of the Graphical Process Editor

The editor itself is divided into several areas. The most obvious element is the graphical work area, where you can add objects by dragging and dropping them from the list on the left side. You will find functions for controlling the view at the top of the work area.

Structure of the process editor

The space to the right of the work area is divided into two parts: The upper area contains an overview for particularly large integration processes. (The slider lets you set the zoom.) Below the Process Overview section, the Properties section shows the elements selected in the work area. In the bottom-left section of the editor is the Processing Log, which displays error messages and annotations. To the right of the log is a list of the Container elements. These containers are the process-internal representation of interfaces or variables you can create for internal use.

Alternative functions of the panes

All of the panes provide additional alternative functions, which you can select using the list icon next to the name of the pane. If you have already worked with SAP business workflows, the principles of the process editor will remind you of the workflow builder. In this exercise, you will only get to know the work area and container panes; you will create a correlation in another function. An overview of all of the possible views in the various panes is shown in Figure 4.66.

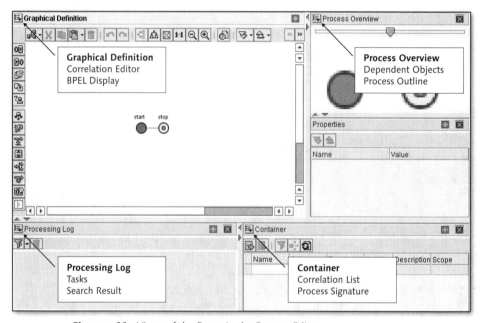

Figure 4.66 Views of the Panes in the Process Editor

Creating the container elements

Let's start by creating the container elements. As mentioned earlier, the container elements contain objects that are only used within the process. In the case of messages, however, these internal objects equal an abstract interface. A particular aspect of these message container elements is that they can also exist in a multiline format; this means that a list of messages can be addressed with a single element. However, these multiline containers can only exist within the process; they can't be sent in their original format.

For this integration process, you will need three message container elements. The first container element, MatInfo, receives the incoming messages with the material information. This element is instantiated up to three times over the course of the integration process. The individual material information will be appended after receipt to the second element, MatInfoContainer. It functions as a collecting list of material information because of its multiline property. However, this list can only be used within the integration process.

A conversion into the third message element, MatInfo_List, has to take place to allow the data to leave the process. This element is based on a service interface that can contain information about multiple materials, and thus does not require the multiline property in the integration process. The messages, and the containers used as their interrelationships, are shown schematically in Figure 4.67.

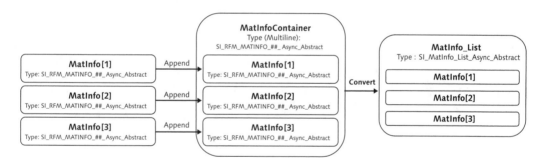

Figure 4.67 Use of the Container Elements in the Integrations Process

The first container, called MatInfo, belongs to the ABSTRACT INTERFACE category and uses the interface SI_RFM_MATINFO_##_Async_Abstract. You can find this entry in the input help of the TYPE column, which only lists abstract interfaces of your software component version. This container always contains the message currently sent to the process by the RFC sender.

Note that the MULTILINE column can be used to make this container a multiline container (this is not used for the first container object). The DESCRIPTION column allows you to give the object a description to reflect its function. The SCOPE column displays the validity area of the element. Usually, the entire process is the validity area. You can only restrict the validity of these blocks if you insert the blocks in the work area.

Using the same pattern, create the `MatInfoContainer` element, which belongs to the same category and type, but is a multiline element. This element stores `MatInfo` messages until they are sent in a single message. Before being sent, however, this element must be converted, due to its multiline character. The target element of this conversion is `MatInfo_List`, which also belongs to the ABSTRACT INTERFACE category, but references the `SI_MatInfo_List_Async_Abstract` type.

Last but not least, you need a variable that counts how many times the loop runs. This variable should be named COUNTER, and should be of the simple `xsd:integer` type. The list of your container elements should now correspond to the one shown in Figure 4.68.

Name	Category	Type	Multiline	Description	Scope
MatInfo	Abstract Interface	SI_RFM_MATINFO_00_Async_Abstract	☐	Received data set of one mat info	Process
MatInfoContainer	Abstract Interface	SI_RFM_MATINFO_00_Async_Abstract	☑	Collection of mat info for internal proces...	Process
MatInfo_List	Abstract Interface	SI_MatInfo_List_Async_Abstract	☐	Collection of mat info to send	Process
Counter	Simple Type	xsd:integer	☐	How many mat infos have been received	Process

Figure 4.68 Container Elements of the Integration Process

Creating the correlation

Before you get to the graphical modeling, you need to create a correlation. Using this correlation, the process can identify related messages by their content. In this exercise, the process must map and collect messages from the same creator; thus, the correlation consists of the `created_by` field contents of the incoming messages.

To create a correlation, click the SWITCH EDITOR icon, and select the alternative function Correlation List of the CONTAINER pane. Enter the name `MatInfo` for the correlation. Highlight the new entry and click on the

DETAILS icon above the list. The graphical work area changes into the Correlation Editor view.

In the upper area of this view, the newly created correlation is already selected. The area below it is divided into three parts: On the left, you can see the correlation containers of the correlation fields. The center part lets you select involved messages. The right area lets you specify the actual fields.

In the left area, specify the name `created_by` and maintain the `xsd:string` type. The message to which the correlation should apply is the `SI_RFM_MATINFO_##_Async_Abstract` type, which can be specified in the center area. By selecting the interface, it is also displayed in the right area, which up to now wasn't available for input. Open the input help next to the Created_by field, thus opening the EXPRESSION EDITOR. Select the ERNAM element from the displayed message. For this, you must first activate the CONTAINER ELEMENT option and make sure that the INTERFACE entry is shown in the selection menu (see Figure 4.69).

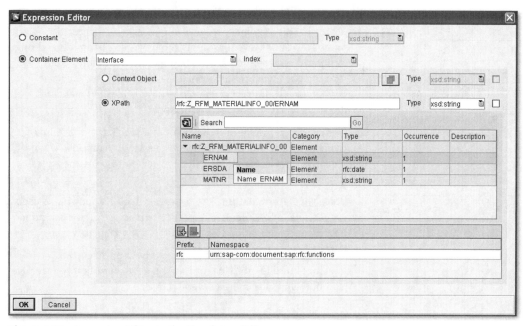

Figure 4.69 Expression Editor in the Correlation Editor

Accept the selection by clicking the OK button. You are then brought back to the correlation editor, as shown in Figure 4.70.

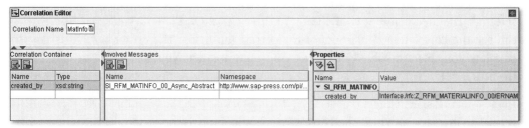

Figure 4.70   Correlation Editor

Click the SWITCH EDITOR icon on the top left of the CORRELATION EDITOR to change back to the Graphical Definition view. You can now begin with the graphical modeling of the business process. Table 4.11 gives you an overview of all of the available objects (or step types) in the process editor. However, you will only use a few of them in this exercise.

Icon	Step Type
	Receive: This step lets you receive messages of a particular interface, and always represents the beginning of an integration process. The reception always happens asynchronously, but it can simulate synchronous communication using a synchronous-asynchronous bridge (Sync/Async Bridge). To bring messages together, correlations can be specified.
	Send: This step sends a message from a specific interface in a synchronous or asynchronous way. Send steps can close a Sync/Async Bridge. Correlations can be specified to bring messages together.
	Receiver Determination: The recipient identification step is used to get a list of recipients of a particular message. The configured receiver determination from the Integration Directory is used.
	Transformation: A transformation can be used to convert messages of one interface into messages of another interface. It can both split and merge several messages.

Table 4.11   Step Types in the Process Editor

Icon	Step Type
	User Decision: The user decision step is new to SAP NetWeaver PI, but has been used in SAP Business Workflows for a long time. During runtime, agents are determined based on a configurable parameter. An agent can choose from preset options that affect the further course of the integration process. The decision template can include the values of other container objects.
	Switch: A switch can be used to distinguish several values of a container element.
	Container Operation: A container operation is used to change container objects. Two different operations can be distinguished: the attachments of an object to another, multiline object; and the change in the value of a container object (such as a counter variable).
	Control: The control step can stop the integration process, raise an exception, or send an alert message.
	Block: A block can be used for logical fragmentation of integration processes, and is partly implicitly inserted by other steps. A block can also be used for reducing the visibility of container objects.
	Fork: A parallel section allows independent processing of multistep sequences. Each step sequence can therefore be linked to a certain condition that must be met to perform it. After processing all of the steps of the different sequences, they reunite in a union operator.
	Loop: In an integration process, the loop works like a WHILE loop. As long as the condition specified in this step is not met, the steps within the loop are processed one after another.
	Wait: A wait step can delay the execution of subsequent steps. You can specify a fixed date or a time period.
	Undefined: An undefined step serves as a placeholder, or for testing purposes.

Table 4.11   Step Types in the Process Editor (Cont.)

The first step in a business process must always be a Receive step, which can either be situated at the very beginning, or be integrated in a loop. Because this process receives exactly three messages, the most obvious procedure is to use a loop.

Drag a loop from the left toolbar to the work area between the START and STOP objects. The place where you can drop the loop is indicated by yellow parentheses. The new loop element is automatically highlighted, and its properties are displayed to the right of the work area (see Figure 4.71). Name this object COLLECTION OF MATERIAL INFORMATION. The CONDITION field specifies how long this loop is supposed to run, therefore making it a `WHILE` loop.

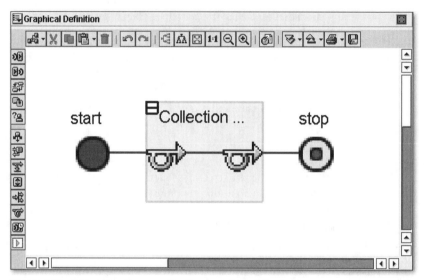

Figure 4.71   Integration Process after the Insertion of the Loop

Specification of the
exit condiition for
the loop Click on the white area and open the input help; the condition editor is displayed. Set the loop so it runs, as long as the COUNTER variable is not 3. In contrast to SAP XI, the condition editor in SAP NetWeaver PI has changed significantly. On one hand, the intuitive creation of simple terms is more complicated; on the other, the power of the editor has increased due to new flexibility. If a CONDITION field has no content, a help text is displayed in the actual working area of the editor, which will

facilitate the first steps (see Figure 4.72). Once you click the text box to define the condition, the text disappears, and the field accepts input.

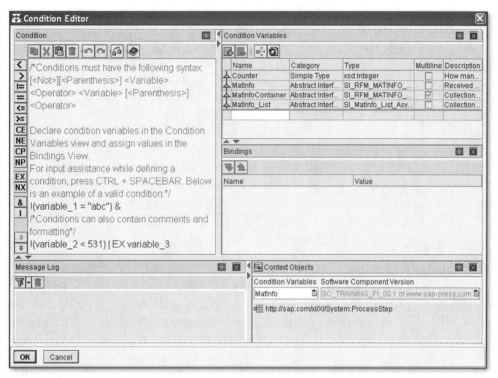

Figure 4.72 Condition Editor of the Loop Step in Initial State

In the CONDITION VARIABLES area, choose the COUNTER container object, and drag it into the left CONDITION field. The explanatory text disappears, and instead displays the name of the inserted container object. Then drag the inequality button (third from the top) on the left edge into the CONDITION field, and drop it behind the container element. Finally, enter the constant value of 3, so the condition `Counter! = 3` can be seen in the condition field (see Figure 4.73).

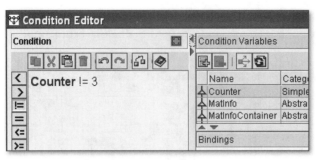

Figure 4.73 Condition in the Receiving Loop

For better readability, you should separate the operands and operator by a space. Perform a semantic test using the appropriate icon above the condition field; if an error is found, an error message will be displayed on the left-bottom. Copy the condition by clicking the OK button; the condition should now be displayed in the appropriate field in the properties of the loop step.

Inserting the steps in the loop

Now insert a Receive step in the loop, and call it Receive material info. Because this is the first Receive step in the process, the Start Process property is automatically set for this object. In the properties, set the `MatInfo` container element as the Message. The Receive step then expects a message of this type. Specify the `MatInfo` correlation as the used and activated correlation; incoming messages are then grouped using this correlation, depending on the creator of the material. This means that for messages with the same creator, a specific instance of the loop is only called after the first run.

Appending a incoming message to the multiline container

Now let's append an incoming message to the `MatInfoContainer` container element, which is accomplished by adding a Container Operation step. This step allows you to make changes to containers, such as setting variables or appending messages to lists. Add the new object after the Receive step and name it APPEND MATERIAL INFO. The target of this operation is the `MatInfoContainer` container element, to which the `MatInfo` container element is appended. Note that the operation must be APPEND, not Assign (see Figure 4.74).

Properties	
Name	Value
Step Name	Append material info
Description	Append MatInfo to MatInfoContainer
Target	MatInfoContainer
Operation	Append
Expression	MatInfo

Figure 4.74 Properties of the Container Operation for Appending MatInfo to MatInfoContainer

The last object in the loop is another Container Operation, which increases the variable `counter` by one; name the Container Operation, Increase Counter. The target of this operation is the `Counter` container element. This time, the Assign operation is appropriate. As the first expression, reselect the `Counter` container element. The operator for the addition is a plus sign (+). The second expression is a constant of the type `xsd:integer` with a value of 1. The property values of this object result in the mathematical expression `Counter = Counter +1`. After completing the loop, the integration process should have the step sequence shown in Figure 4.75.

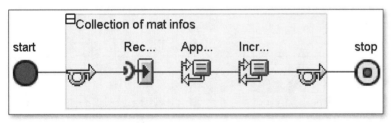

Figure 4.75 Step Sequence of the Integration Process after Completing the Loop

The two missing steps merge the multiline container element into a single message before sending it. Before the loop, insert a Transformation object and call it `Create MatInfo_List`. Transformation objects allow you to convert messages to a different format. For this, specify the operation mapping `OM_RFM_MATINFO_##_Async_Abstract_to_MT_MatInfo_List_Async_Abstract`. After specifying the operation mapping, appropriate fields for the properties are completed, and the expected message type is shown. At process execution time, the source messages reside in the

Conversion and delivery of the outbound message

`MatInfoContainer` container element. In this transformation, the target message is passed to the `MatInfo_List` element (see Figure 4.76).

As the name suggests, the last step, Send Target Message, is a Send step. The container element `MatInfo_List` is sent asynchronously.

The entire structure of the integration process is illustrated in Figure 4.77. Save the process and verify it via the menu path: INTEGRATION PROCESS • CHECK. If the process is successful, you should get a note that `MatInfo` is initialized, but not used. If there are no more errors, you can activate all new objects.

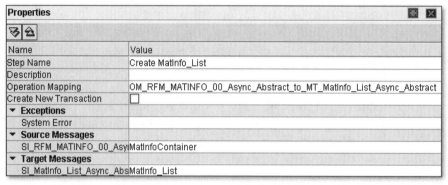

Figure 4.76 Properties of the Transformation Step for MatInfo_List

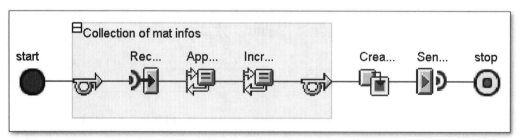

Figure 4.77 Structure of the Complete Integration Process

4.4.3 Configuration

Overview of the configuration scenarios

Message processing is configured in two steps, because an integration process is equal to a business system with regard to configuration. The RFC call must be forwarded to the process; for this, use the RFC sender channel you created in Exercise 1. (Because they run in SAP NetWeaver

PI, integration processes don't need adapters.) You also need to configure the sending of outbound messages to system B, so you will need to create two configuration scenarios.

Before you can use the integration process during the configuration phase, you must declare it in the Integration Directory. In the Integration Directory, follow the menu path: COMMUNICATION COMPONENT • INTEGRATION PROCESS. Create a new process that represents your IP_Mat-Info_## object from the Enterprise Services Repository. In the second step, select your configuration scenario, PI_Training_##, to assign the integration process to the corresponding scenario list (see Figure 4.78).

Creating the integration process in the Integration Directory

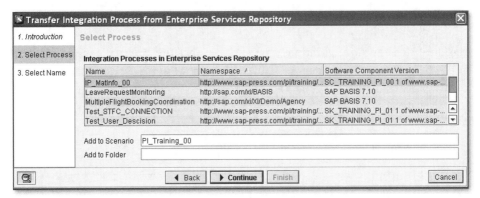

Figure 4.78 Selecting the Integrations Process and Assigning it to the Configuration Scenario

In the third step of the Definition Wizard, you can specify a different name for your process. To keep things simple, use the same name you used in the Enterprise Services Repository, IP_MatInfo_##. After completing the wizard, your process shows up in the menu path COMMUNICATION COMPONENT • INTEGRATION PROCESS.

Delivery of Inbound Messages to the Integration Process

Table 4.12 provides an overview of all of the configuration objects used for delivering the creation notification to the integration process. Communication channels identified by an asterisk (*) were created in Section 4.1.3, and will be reused here.

Object Type	Sender Side: System A	Receiver Side: Integration process IP_MatInfo_##
Communication channel	RFC_Sender_Channel_## *	
Sender agreement	| SystemA | Z_RFM_MATERIALINFO_##|*|*	
Receiver determination	| SystemA | Z_RFM_MATERIALINFO_##	
Interface determination	|SystemA|Z_RFM_MATERIALINFO_##||IP_MatInfo_##	

Table 4.12 Elements in the Integration Directory for the First Scenario in the BPM Exercise

Calling the Configuration Wizard for the first scenario

Call the Configuration Wizard and select the Internal Communication option. The sender is business system A, which sends data using the RFC adapter with the RFC interface, Z_RFM_MATERIALINFO_## (see Figure 4.79).

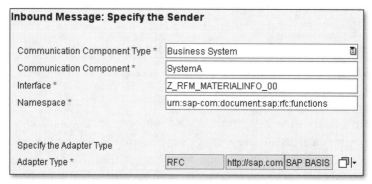

Figure 4.79 Sender Settings in the Configuration Wizard for the Incoming Message

The receiver is the IP_MatInfo_## integration process, which is addressed with the XI adapter. Once the integration process was selected as the COMMUNICATION COMPONENT using the value help, the associated integration process from the Enterprise Services Repository appears underneath. When you open the input help of the interface, only the SI_RFM_MATINFO_##_Async_Abstract interface is displayed; this is used by the Receive step to start the process. If the value help does not display any entries, you can directly enter the interface name and the namespace (see Figure 4.80).

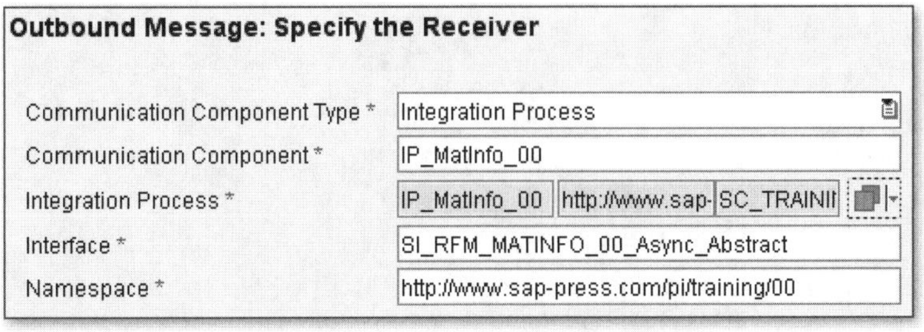

Outbound Message: Specify the Receiver

Communication Component Type *	Integration Process
Communication Component *	IP_MatInfo_00
Integration Process *	IP_MatInfo_00	http://www.sap-	SC_TRAINI
Interface *	SI_RFM_MATINFO_00_Async_Abstract
Namespace *	http://www.sap-press.com/pi/training/00

Figure 4.80   Receiver Settings in the Configuration Wizard for the Incoming Message

The sender agreement `|SystemA|Z_RFM_MATERIALINFO_##|*|*` uses the existing communication channel, `RFC_Sender_Channel_##`, of Exercise 1. The screen for creating the receiver determination, `|SystemA|Z_RFM_MATERIALINFO_##`, is of a purely informative nature.

In the next step, the interface determination `|SystemA|Z_RFM_MATERIALINFO_##||IP_MatInfo_##` displays the interface `SI_RFM_MAT-INFO_##_Async_Abstract` as the target, but does not find an operation mapping; this is not necessary because both the sending and receiving interface use the same message type. Because the receiver is integrated with the XI adapter, a receiver agreement is not required.

Assign all objects to your `PI_Training_##` scenario and exit the wizard. You can test the integration process after it has been activated, but the outbound message will not be delivered. Before testing the project, wait until the delivery of the outbound message has been configured.

Delivery of the Outbound Message of the Integration Process

Delivery of the outbound message can be arranged in a way similar to the first configuration scenario of this exercise. The existing communication channel `File_ReceiverChannel_##`, which was created in Exercise 1, is used for the receiver. Table 4.13 provides an overview of all configuration objects used in this scenario.

Object Type	Sender Side: Integration Process IP_MatInfo_##	Receiver Side: System B
Communication channel		`File_ ReceiverChannel_##*`
Receiver agreement	`|IP_MatInfo_##| |SystemB|SI_ MatInfo_List_Async_ In`	
Receiver determination	`|IP_MatInfo_##|SI_MatInfo_List_Async_ Abstract`	
Interface determination	`|IP_MatInfo_##|SI_MatInfo_List_Async_ Abstract|| SystemB`	

Table 4.13 Elements in the Integration Directory for the Outbound Message of the Integration Process

Calling the Configuration Wizard for the second scenario

Call the Configuration Wizard once more and select Internal Communication. The sender of this scenario is the integration process `IP_MatInfo_##`. Help is again restricted, because only the used interfaces are displayed when sending messages from the process. In this case, only one message is sent, so only one interface is displayed. Select the displayed interface `SI_MatInfo_List_Async_Abstract` (see Figure 4.81).

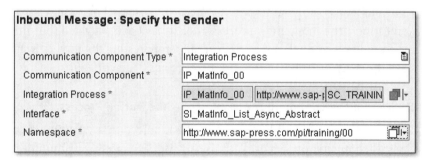

Figure 4.81 Sender Settings in the Configuration Wizard of the Outbound Message

Specification of the receiver in the Configuration Wizard

The outbound message receiver is a File adapter of business system B, which responds to the `SI_MatInfo_List_Async_In` interface (see Figure 4.82). This interface is the direction-related counterpart to the abstract interface of the outbound message. A sender agreement isn't used, because the sending process runs in SAP NetWeaver PI.

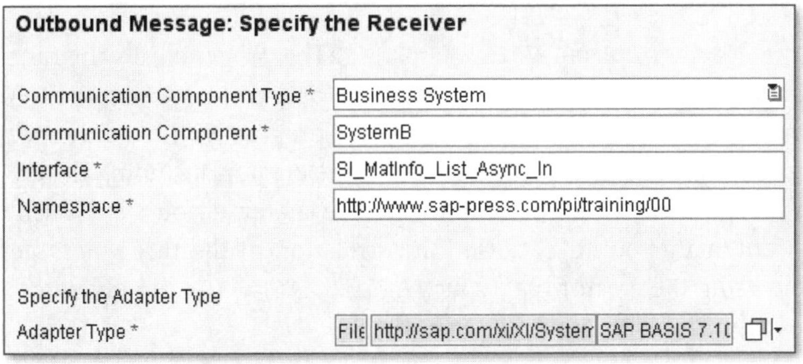

Outbound Message: Specify the Receiver

Communication Component Type *	Business System
Communication Component *	SystemB
Interface *	SI_MatInfo_List_Async_In
Namespace *	http://www.sap-press.com/pi/training/00

Specify the Adapter Type

Adapter Type *   File http://sap.com/xi/XI/System SAP BASIS 7.10

Figure 4.82   Receiver Settings in the Configuration Wizard for the Outbound Message

The receiver determination step informs you that system B is integrated in the object |IP_MatInfo_##|SI_MatInfo_List_Async_Abstract. As with the first scenario, the interface determination |IP_MatInfo_##|SI_MatInfo_List_Async_Abstract||SystemB doesn't require an operation mapping, because it uses the same message type (see Figure 4.83).

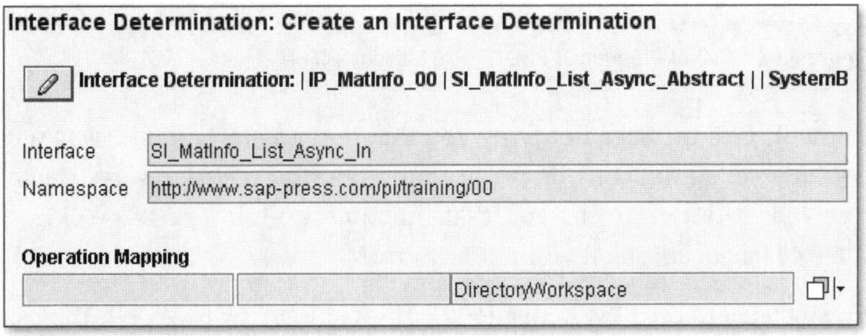

Information about the receiver determination

Interface Determination: Create an Interface Determination

✏ **Interface Determination: |IP_MatInfo_00 | SI_MatInfo_List_Async_Abstract | | SystemB**

Interface	SI_MatInfo_List_Async_In
Namespace	http://www.sap-press.com/pi/training/00

Operation Mapping

		DirectoryWorkspace	

Figure 4.83   Interface Determination of the Outbound Message

The receiver agreement |IP_MatInfo_##||SystemB|SI_MatInfo_List_Async_In uses the existing communication channel File_ReceiverChannel_##.

Add all of the new objects to your scenario PI_Training_## and finish the wizard. You can now activate all new configuration objects. Now that you've finished the fourth exercise, test the process.

4.4.4 Process and Monitoring

The process of this integration scenario starts in system A. As such, log in as user SYS_A-## and call Transaction SA38.

Run the program Z_PROG_MATERIALINFO_##. The program calls the function module Z_RFM_MATERIALINFO_## in the background, using the RFC destination SYSTEMA_SENDER-##.[8] Within the program you can only specify a material number. Information about the creator, including the creation date, is sent along automatically. The material you specify isn't important at this point, because the correlation of the three messages is done using the creator (i.e., your SAP user SYS_A-##). Simply enter a name and run the program (see Figure 4.84).

Sending the first material creation notification

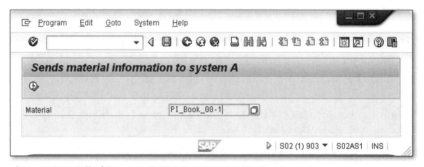

Figure 4.84 Call of Program Z_PROG_MATERIALINFO_##

You will see a message notifying you that the function module was successfully called, but this does not imply that the message was actually received; it only informs you that function module Z_RFM_MATERIAL-INFO_## has been called without any errors.

Now change to the PI system and call Transaction SXMB_MONI. You can see that your message came in and has been successfully processed. If you scroll the display a bit to the right, you can see that the OUTBOUND STATUS column displays a clock symbol (see Figure 4.85).[9] This means that the message is currently being sent. This display remains unchanged

Checking the processing of the first message

---

8 The direct call of the function module in Transaction SE37 starts a synchronous message exchange, and can thus cause corresponding errors.

9 When calling the transaction in English, the heading of this column may be "c." This depends on the support package being used.

until three messages from the same creator have come in, and the outbound message can be created.

Figure 4.85 Message Monitoring after the First Message

Call the program for notifying the material manager twice more, and return to the monitoring. You should now see the three incoming notifications, and a fourth message. The outbound status of the first three messages now displays a black-and-white checkered flag (see Figure 4.86), which lets you know that the process has completed. In the PI system, call Transaction AL11, Transaction ZAPCMD,[10] or the file tool provided on the website of this book to see if a file containing the corresponding message has been created.

Sending the two remaining messages

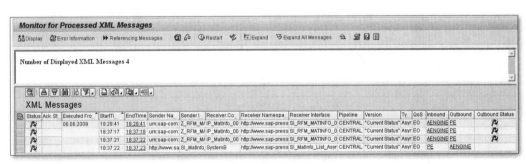

Figure 4.86 Message Monitoring after Three Messages of the Same Creator

If the fourth message is not displayed in the monitoring, look at the monitoring of the business processes. In the XI system, call Transaction SXMB_MONI_BPE and double-click on the Process Selection entry. In the selection mask of the Service field, you can enter integration process

Monitoring the business process

---

10 Detailed information on the SAP Commander (Transaction ZAPCMD) can be found at: *http://code.google.com/p/sapcommander.*

IP_MatInfo_## to only see the status of the workflow. You should not do this if you want to examine an incomplete or possibly erroneous workflow; instead, try to limit the selection period to only the time when the messages have been sent, and run the query. The work items processed during the selected period are now displayed.

Analyzing the work items Figure 4.87 shows the status of work items and workflow after sending the first message. A Wait step of the loop has been processed by receiving the first message, and is marked as COMPLETED. Another Wait step awaits further messages. In addition, you can see that the workflow is started.

Figure 4.87 Work Items after Sending a Message

To get to the workflow protocol, you can either select one of the steps by double-clicking it and then clicking on the LOG icon, or simply double-click the workflow entry in the collection. Regardless of which way you proceed, it brings you to the workflow protocol (see Figure 4.88).

Figure 4.88 Display of the Workflow Protocols

Graphical display of the workflow processing Information on the current status of the workflow is displayed by clicking the button in the DETAILS column in the lower part of the screen. Click on the button in the GRAPHIC column. This brings you to the graphical display of the business process (see Figure 4.89). The green arrows allow you to trace the process to see which processes have run. If a problem has occurred, double-click on the relevant object to display detailed information on this step.

Follow the EXTRAS • DIAGNOSIS menu path to access analysis transactions that will help you find the reason for partially processed workflows.

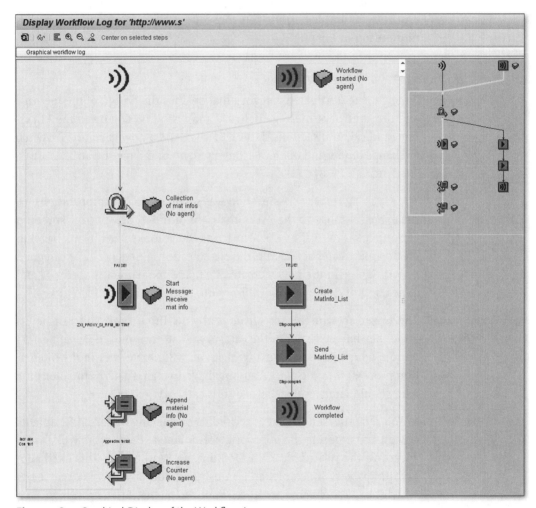

Figure 4.89 Graphical Display of the Workflow Log

4.4.5 Extending the Exercise by Alert Monitoring (Optional)

Using alerts to monitor business processes

The existing integration process can be completed by sending alerts for better control. In the case of this exercise, the alert is a time-out verification, which sends a warning message if the collection loop has not received all three input messages within a specified period. The prerequisite for implementing the subsequent steps is preparing the alert monitoring in Chapter 3.

Creation of the Alert Class

Creating a new alert category

To begin, create an alert category that enables the design of the message and the control of message delivery and visibility. Log on to the PI system, and call Transaction ALRTCDEF to create a new category.[11] Switch to change mode, and open the context menu of the menu path: ALL CLASSIFICATIONS • PI_BOOK.

The PI_BOOK category classification was set up during the preparations for the exercise. Click on the list to the right of the directory tree, and then click the CREATE ALERT CATEGORY icon (which looks like a blank page) to create a new category within the classification. Enter the new category, PI_Alert_## , in the newly created line, and the name PI_Alert_## and a meaningful description. Confirm your entries with the ⌈Enter⌋ key.

Specification of the possible alert recipients

The lower area of the screen now accepts input, and you can determine the characteristics of the category. First, turn on the Dynamic Text option, which passes the text (which you will define later in the integration process) into the alert. You now have two alternatives to determine who should later receive alerts of this category:

▸ You can enter a fixed list of recipients by clicking the Fixed Recipients icon and entering the appropriate usernames; these users will always receive the related alerts in the Runtime Workbench. This fixed allocation is very inflexible, and, in using it, you take the risk that alerts will not be delivered to all relevant recipients, or that users will be notified inadvertently (due to mistakes in list maintenance).

---

11 You can also create an alert category using the Alert Configuration option in the Runtime Workbench; however, only the named transaction is called in the Web GUI.

▶ A more flexible alternative is to let the users decide whether or not they want to receive an alert of this category. Users can subscribe to alerts in this category in the Runtime Workbench. This subscription option, however, is accessible only for users with certain technical user roles. You can specify the list of relevant roles using the SUBSCRIPTION AUTHORIZATION icon. You can offer the subscription of your own category to all participants by entering the role SAP_XI_DEVELOPER (see Figure 4.90). Regardless of the choice of an alternative, you must save your entries and assign a transport request if necessary.

Subscription for
alert categories

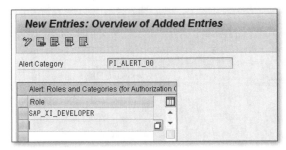

Figure 4.90 Entering a Role for the Subscription of an Alert Category

The newly created alert category should now look something like Figure 4.91. Save the new category, and enter your transport request on demand.

Enhancement of the Integration Process

To send an alert, the integration process has to be enhanced with a step sequence that starts in parallel to the Receive step. This parallel sequence sends an alert after a certain amount of time.

Enhancing the
business process
with parallel
processing

Start the Enterprise Services Repository, open your integration process IP_MatInfo_##, and then switch to change mode. For a better overview of the process and better transparency in monitoring, create a new block called REGULAR PROCESSING. Move all existing steps into this block, preserving their order. Then drag a Fork step in front of the newly created block, and name it TIMEOUT CONSTRUCT. Then drag the created block to one of the two branches of the Fork step created by default (see Figure 4.92).

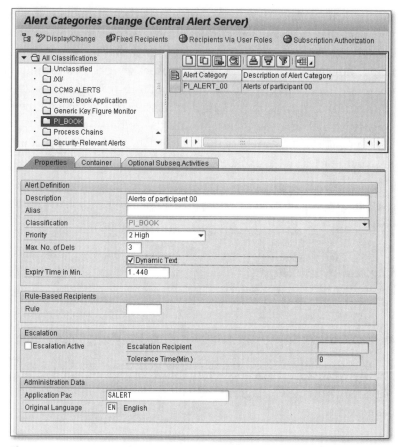

Figure 4.91 Properties of the New Alert Category

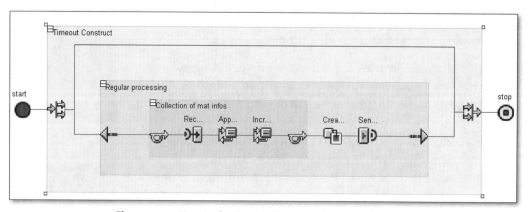

Figure 4.92 Moving the Existing Steps to a Fork Branch

Now drag a block step to the second, previously unused branch, and then name the block Timeout Check. Drag a Wait step into this new block, and then name it Timeout. Select the Wait Specified Time Period option as Type, and enter a wait time of three minutes; this delays the execution of the next steps by three minutes. (This short duration is only suitable for this exercise; in practical use, it will usually be higher.)

Insert a Control step after the Wait step, and call it Timeout Alert. This step will send an alert when the entire integration process runs longer than three minutes. Set the ACTION property of the control to the THROW ALERT option, thus sending an alert, while the process continues.

Set the ALERT SERVER as the SOURCE. Now enter the newly created ALERT CATEGORY following the PI_ALERT_## schema. In the ALERT MESSAGE field, you can finally enter a message that will be displayed in the alert. It is best to choose a meaningful alert, such as IP_MATINFO_## TIMED OUT (Figure 4.93).

> Inserting a Wait step

> Throwing the alert

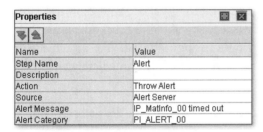

Figure 4.93 Properties of the Control Step in the Integration Process

The complete integration process should now match Figure 4.94. Save, check, and activate the enhanced integration process.

Subscription to the Alert Category and Testing of the Process

If you assigned fixed users when creating the new alert category, it is not necessary to subscribe to a category; continue with the testing of the modified process.

> Fixed recipients

To subscribe to an alert category, open the Runtime Workbench and select Alert Inbox from the top menu. Click on Subscription in the blue menu bar on the right, which results in another window that shows all of the alert categories that you can subscribe to, and their subscription status.

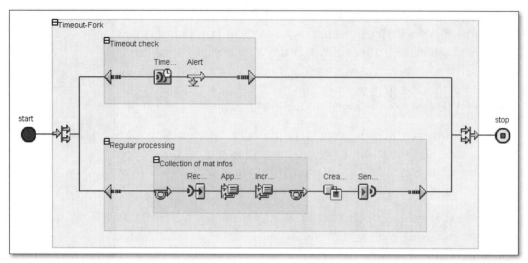

Figure 4.94 Enhanced Integration Process with Time-out Branch

A gray light bulb in the SUBSCRIBED column INDICATES a category that you have not subscribed to, while a bright yellow light bulb indicates an active subscription category (see Figure 4.95). By clicking on the light bulb icon or the corresponding buttons above the list, you can activate or deactivate a subscription. The new settings apply immediately and don't need to be stored separately.

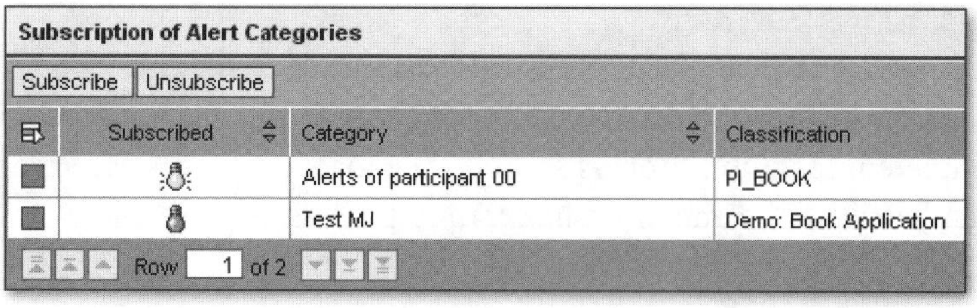

Figure 4.95 Subscribing to an Assigned Alert Category in the Runtime Workbench

Start of the integration process

To test the enhanced integration process, log on to system A with your user SYS_A-##, and call Transaction SE38 to run the program Z_PROG_MATERIALINFO_##, as you did in Exercise 1. Enter any material number, and then run the program. Then wait the time specified in the Wait step of the integration process, and call the Runtime Workbench.

Navigate to the Alert Inbox to look at the incoming alert message. Select the message at the beginning of the line to see all of the information. On the SHORT TEXT tab, you can see the automatically inserted workflow instance number, which helps you to identify and analyze the instance causing this alert. On the LONG TEXT tab, you can find the test you entered in the Alert Message of the Control step (see Figure 4.96).

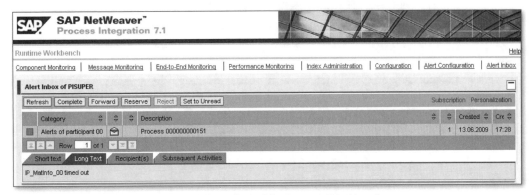

Figure 4.96 Sent Alert Message in the Alert Inbox of the Runtime Workbench

Finally, log on to the PI system, and call Transaction SXMB_MONI_BPE to display the workflow monitoring. Follow the BUSINESS PROCESS ENGINE • MONITORING • PROCESS SELECTION menu path, and start this view. Limit the selection period and execute the selection. A list of all work items is displayed; you can see that two Wait steps have been processed and another is ready. One of the processed Wait steps has received the first message, while the second waited the specified time and then sent an alert message. In addition, sending alerts is listed as a separate background step (see Figure 4.97).

Monitoring the integration process

	ID	Status	Workflow	Work Item Type	Task	CreateDate	CreateT...	Work item text
	142	COMPLETED	137	Background Step	TS77000412	13.06.2009	16:37:38	Triggers a process alert in the background
	141	READY	137	Wait Step			16:32:28	Wait for Event
	140	COMPLETED	137	Wait Step				Wait for Event
	139	COMPLETED	137	Wait Step				Wait for Status Change
	138	STARTED	137	Block Work Item				Normal proceeding
	137	STARTED		(Sub)workflow	WS90000007			IP_MatInfo_00 http://www.sap-press.com/pi/training/00

Work Item Selection (6 Entries)

Figure 4.97 Work Item View after the Alert Message

If you jump to the workflow log by double-clicking any work item and then clicking the LOG icon, you can distinguish the two branches (see Figure 4.98).

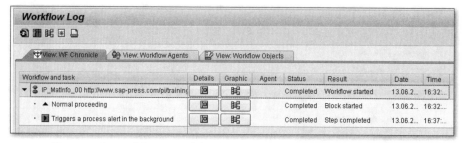

Figure 4.98 Workflow Log of the Enhanced Integration Process after the Alert Message

4.5   Exercise 5: File-to-JDBC

In Section 4.2, you imported data from a file into business system B using IDoc technology. With SAP NetWeaver PI, you can also write data or messages directly into a database; this is done via the JDBC adapter, which we'll discuss here. To do this, you must first select the corresponding target system (i.e., business system B or a database), which depends on the prefix of the material number. Figure 4.99 shows a schema of this exercise with synchronous communication.

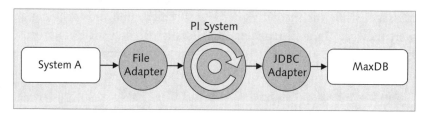

Figure 4.99   Schema of Exercise 5 – File-to-JDBC

4.5.1   Basics

The JDBC adapter allows direct access to database tables, and can be used for both read and write access. This data exchange can take place synchronously or asynchronously.

Before using the JDBC adapter, the installation of a manufacturer-specific driver is required. The individual JAR files can be downloaded from the database vendors and grouped together in an archive called *com.sap. aii.adapter.lib.sda*, so that they can be deployed on the SAP NetWeaver Application Server (AS) using the *Java Support Package Manager* (JSPM). The file extension SDA stands for *software deployment archive*. You can find a detailed guide for the packaging and deployment of driver files in the configuration guide for SAP NetWeaver PI, and also in the SAP Help Portal: *Providing External Drivers for the JDBC and JMS Adapters*.[12]

Driver installation

If the JDBC adapter is configured as a sender, the communication channel contains a SQL query that is performed to get relevant data. The retrieved table rows are converted to a message type, which must exist as a design object. After selecting and converting, a SQL update can be performed; this is often used to mark the read-in line with an appropriate flag in a particular column, which prevents these lines from being reread during the next query.

Configuration of the JDBC adapter

A receiving JDBC adapter can perform various actions on the rows of a table: UPDATE, INSERT, DELETE, SELECT, and UPDATE_INSERT (the last of which is equivalent to MODIFY). In addition, stored procedures can be performed to directly call more complex SQL statements. The table and action to be performed are determined via the message type of the receiving side.

For this exercise, you need a database of your choice that is accessible from the PI server via a network. In this example, a MaxDB database is used. The material master record from Exercise 2 is written to a database table that corresponds exactly to that structure. A SQL script for the creation of the database can be found in Appendix A.

4.5.2 Design

To write to a database with the JDBC adapter, you must map the contents of the message in XML SQL format. This format is internally

Overview of the design objects

---

12 You can find these guides at: *http://help.sap.com/saphelp_nwpi71/helpdata/en/33/ e6fb40f17af66fe10000000a1550b0/frameset.htm.*

converted by the JDBC adapter, and forwarded to the configured database driver. In this example, it is limited to the INSERT operation.[13] The objects that need to be created for this exercise are shown in Table 4.14.

Object Type	Sender Side	Receiver Side
Service interface		SI_INSERT_SQL_Async_in
Message type		MT_INSERT_SQL
Data type		DT_INSERT_SQL
Operation mapping	OM_SI_Material_Async_Out_to_SI_INSERT_SQL_Async_in	
Message mapping	MM_MT_Material_to_MT_INSERT_SQL	

Table 4.14 Elements in the Enterprise Services Repository for the Exercise File-to-JDBC

Creation of the Interface Objects

Create a new data type in the Enterprise Services Repository. Navigate to the context menu of the Data Types path in your namespace, and create the data type DT_INSERT_SQL. To perform an Insert statement, this data type must conform to the XML SQL format of the INSERT command. The command has the format shown in Listing 4.3.

Within the ⟨access⟩ blocks, you can specify the data you want to insert in the table; the XML tags correspond to the column names of your database table. This statement must contain at least one ⟨access⟩ element. The data type in our example is shown in Figure 4.100.

---

13 You can find additional information on XML SQL format in the SAP Help Portal at: *http://help.sap.com/saphelp_nwpi71/helpdata/EN/2e/96fd3f2d14e869e100 00000a155106/frameset.htm.*

```
<root>
  <StatementName>
    <dbTableName action="INSERT">
      <table>realDbTableName</table>
      <access>
        <col1>val1</col1>
        <col2>val2</col2>
      </access>
      <access>
        <col1>val11</col1>
      </access>
    </dbTableName>
  </StatementName>
</root>
```

Creation of the interface objects

Listing 4.3 XML Example for the XML SQL INSERT Operation

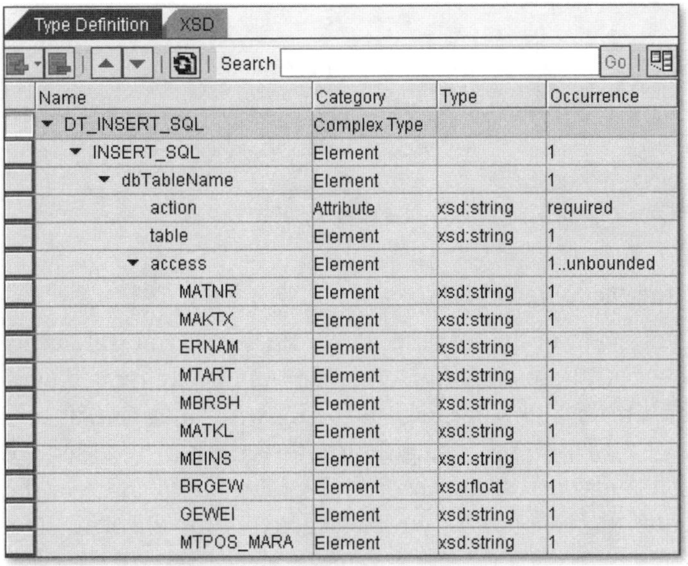

Name	Category	Type	Occurrence
▼ DT_INSERT_SQL	Complex Type		
▼ INSERT_SQL	Element		1
▼ dbTableName	Element		1
action	Attribute	xsd:string	required
table	Element	xsd:string	1
▼ access	Element		1..unbounded
MATNR	Element	xsd:string	1
MAKTX	Element	xsd:string	1
ERNAM	Element	xsd:string	1
MTART	Element	xsd:string	1
MBRSH	Element	xsd:string	1
MATKL	Element	xsd:string	1
MEINS	Element	xsd:string	1
BRGEW	Element	xsd:float	1
GEWEI	Element	xsd:string	1
MTPOS_MARA	Element	xsd:string	1

Figure 4.100 Type Definition for the Scenario File-to-JDBC

Now create the MT_INSERT_SQL message type, based on the newly created data type. To do this, open the context menu of the Message Types path in your namespace, and create a new message type. As a data type, enter the DT_INSERT_SQL data type that you just created.

Finally, the service interface for this scenario has to be created; an asynchronous inbound interface is required. Create the SI_INSERT_SQL_Async_in service interface via the context menu of the Service Interfaces path, and reference the MT_INSERT_SQL message type as the request message type. The settings of the service interface are shown in Figure 4.101.

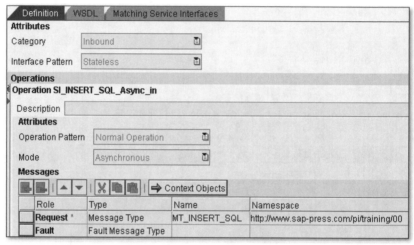

Figure 4.101 Service Interface for the Scenario File-to-JDBC

Creation of the Mapping Objects

For the enhancement of the scenario from Section 4.2, you still need a mapping between the sending file format and the newly created SQL-XML format. Create a new message mapping with the name MM_MT_Material_to_MT_INSERT_SQL, using the context menu of the Message Mappings path in your namespace mapping. For the left side of the mapping, enter MT_Material as the message type; for the right side, MT_INSERT_SQL.

Creating the mapping objects

Map the action and table elements in the target message to the constant value INSERT, and the database name in which you want to write the values. In this example, the database name is PI_MATERIAL. Link the elements of the ACCESS node with the corresponding fields of the source message (see Figure 4.102). Test the mapping, and check whether the same XML message structure is produced as in the example XML for the XML SQL Insert command.

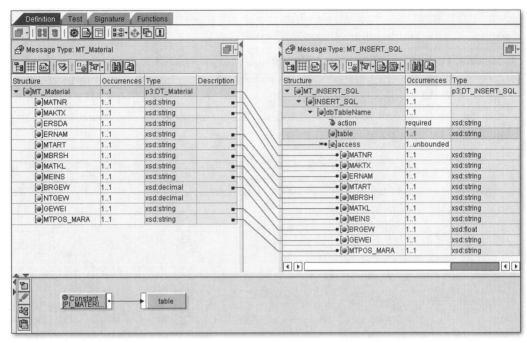

Figure 4.102 Message Mapping of the Exercise File-to-JDBC

As a final step of the design, the operation mapping is now missing. Create it with the name OM_SI_Material_Async_Out_to_SI_INSERT_SQL_Async_in, using the context of the Operation Mappings path in your namespace. Define the service interface SI_Material_Async_Out as the output interface, and SI_INSERT_SQL_Async_in as the target interface. By clicking on the Read Operations button, the corresponding message types of the interface are loaded. Now you can set the message mapping you just created as the mapping program. Activate all of the design objects and switch to the Integration Directory.

4.5.3 Configuration

For this exercise, you don't create a new scenario, but expand the scenario from Section 4.2, such that the target is determined depending on the material number's prefix in the incoming message. If the material number's prefix is *db*, the material is written to the database; otherwise, the IDoc that has already been configured in Section 4.2 is created and posted to business system B.

Overview of the configuration objects

The configuration objects that you will create for this exercise are shown in Table 4.15. The receiver determination does not need to be changed for the enhancement, as it already exists. The existing interface determination must be adjusted so that the message will be routed depending on the prefix of the material number.

Type of Object	Sender Side: System A	Receiver Side: System B
Communication channel		`JDBC_ ReceiverChannel_##`
Receiver agreement		`|SystemA||SystemB |SI_INSERT_SQL_ Async_in`
Receiver determination		
Interface determination		

Table 4.15 Elements in the Integration Directory for the Exercise File-to-JDBC

Open the context menu of the Communication Channel node in the Integration Builder, and create a new communication channel with the name `JDBC_ReceiverChannel_##`. Select business system B as the communication component.

Configuration of the JDBC adapter

The adapter is of type JDBC. The communication channel is created as a RECEIVER. Make sure that as MESSAGE PROTOCOL the XML SQL FORMAT is set. Alternatively, you can set the Native SQL String option. This protocol is mainly intended for testing purposes.

In the CONNECTION tab, enter the connection to the database. The values of the parameters JDBC DRIVER and CONNECTION are dependent on the database used. Enter a user for the database in the USER NAME and PASSWORD fields; this user must have the authorization to execute an INSERT command on the appropriate table (see Figure 4.103).

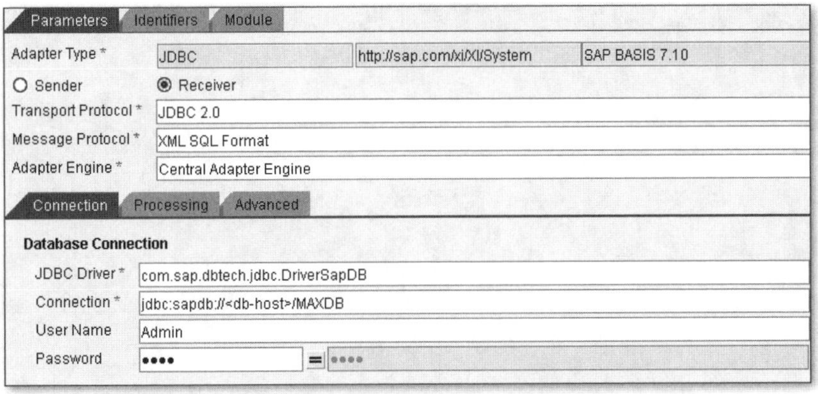

Figure 4.103 Settings of the JDBC Receiver Channel for System B

To control the scenario depending on the prefix of the material number, expand the interface determination |SystemA|SI_Material_Async_ out|SystemB| by another configured receiver interface. Make sure that the new receiver interface comes first, and that the Maintain Order At Runtime checkbox is set. In doing so, the condition of the new receiver interface is checked. If the condition is not met, an IDoc is sent to business system B.

Select the SI_INSERT_SQL_Async_in service interface, and specify the operation mapping as OM_SI_Material_Async_Out_to_SI_INSERT_SQL_ Async_in. Finally, specify the desired condition in the condition editor. Start the condition editor using the values help of the Condition field.

Configuration of the interface determination

The condition editor will open in a new window, and allows you to perform an examination of the incoming message's content. Using the value help in the Left Operand field, you get to the expression editor that allows you to specify the field you want to check (see Figure 4.104).

Select the MATNR field, and then click OK. Return to the window of the condition editor and select < as an operator. This operator can check a string for a pattern, and you can use the following wildcards:

Configuration using the expression editor

▸ + for any character

▸ * for any character sequence

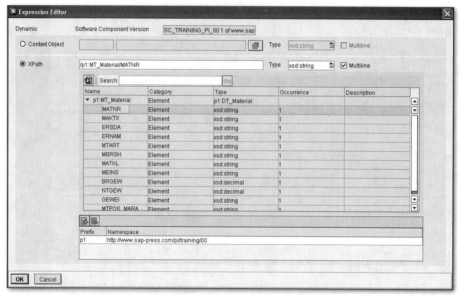

Figure 4.104 Expression Editor

Enter the string db* in the field of the right operand (see Figure 4.105); as a result, all materials that have a material number starting with the prefix db are forwarded to the database. All others will be sent to business system B.

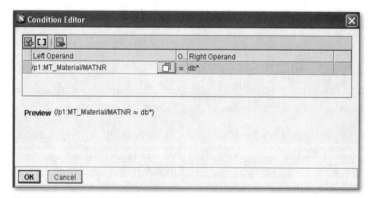

Figure 4.105 Condition Editor

After setting all of the parameters, save the interface determination (see Figure 4.106).

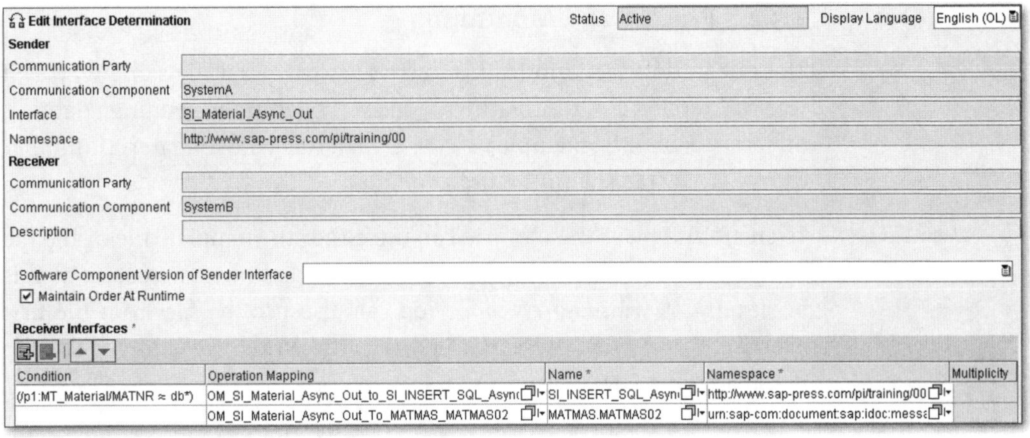

Figure 4.106   Interface Determination of the Scenario File-to-JDBC

Finally, the receiver agreement for the JDBC receiver still needs to be created. You can create it via the context menu of the Receiver Agreement node. Select business system A as the sending communication component, and business system B as the recipient. Enter `SI_INSERT_SQL_Async_in` as the receiver interface. Configure the newly created receiver channel `JDBC_ReceiverChannel_##` as the communication channel of this object (see Figure 4.107). Save and activate all of the configuration objects.

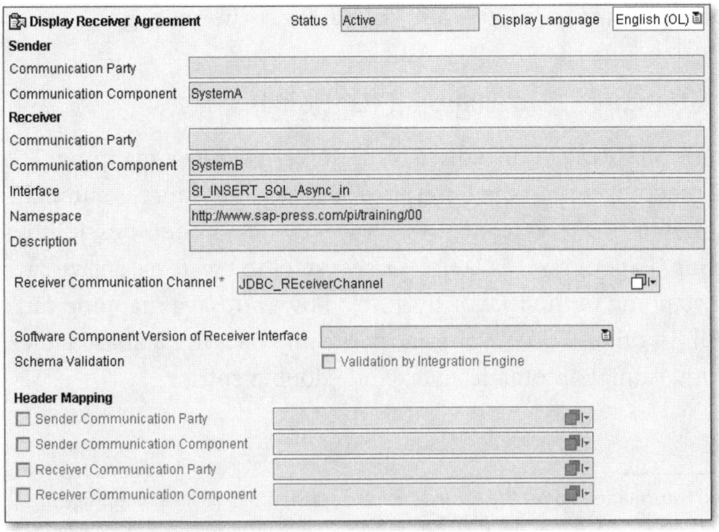

Figure 4.107   Receiver Agreement for the Exercise File-to-JDBC

4.5.4 Process and Monitoring

The integration scenario in this exercise is triggered the same way as it was in Exercise 2 — by creating *pi_output_#.dat* in the sending adapter's directory. For this example, create a material whose material number (field MATNR) starts with the prefix *db*.

Monitoring of Exercise 5

To create and place the file, you can use either the template file or the file upload and download program that is provided on the website of this book (*http://www.sap-press.com*). You can also use the file from the first exercise. (It may be necessary to remove the write protection of this file if you are on a UNIX system.)

Depending on which poll interval is set in the communication channel, the file is archived or deleted after a few minutes. In PI monitoring (Transaction SXMB_MONI), you can now check that the correct interface has been identified. Finally, in the database, you can verify whether the material has been created in the table.

If the output message was handed over to the JDBC adapter, the scenario ran successfully from the perspective of SAP NetWeaver PI. The monitor for processed XML messages (Transaction SXMB_MONI) won't show error messages that occur in the adapter or in the database; for this you can use the monitor of the JDBC adapter, which can be found in the Runtime Workbench (*http://<J2EE-Host>:<J2EE-Port>/rwb/index.jsp*).

4.5.5 Alternative Java Mapping (Optional)

Limitations of Java mappings

In the spirit of Java, let's also discuss the server-side Java mapping. The graphical mapping within the Enterprise Services Repository is automatically translated into Java code, but only provides limited possibilities for mapping. Experienced Java users may prefer to create extensive Java code for mapping in their favorite editor; however, Java mapping can't be stateful. In other words, you can't write any data in database tables, because you cannot automatically exclude double entries.[14]

---

14 Detailed information about the limitations and possibilities of Java mappings in SAP NetWeaver PI can be found at: *http://help.sap.com/saphelp_nwpi71/helpdata/en/e2/e13fcd80fe47768df001a558ed10b6/frameset.htm*.

Creation of the Java Mapping

The Java mapping, which will later be imported into the Enterprise Services Repository and thus lies in the PI system, consists of a single Java class in a JAR file. In principle, this class can be developed in any editor; however, you must reference SAP Java libraries. To use these libraries directly, and to benefit from error-checking, use the SAP NetWeaver Developer Studio in the same release as the Java stack of the PI system.

SAP NetWeaver Developer Studio for Java mappings

Start the SAP NetWeaver Developer Studio, and create a new development project via the FILE • NEW • PROJECT menu path. In the JAVA category, choose the JAVA PROJECT option (see Figure 4.108).

Name the new project according to the scheme `PI_Java_Mapping_##`, and proceed to the next step in the Creation Wizard. Click on FINISH to generate the project. If the Java Perspective is not already set, confirm the switch to this view. The new project will now appear in the tree on the left side.

Creation of the class

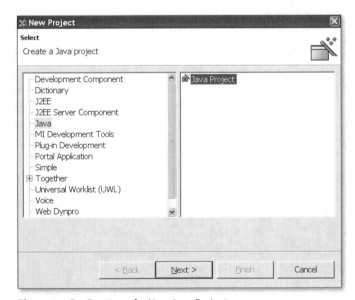

Figure 4.108 Creation of a New Java Project

To create a new class within the project, open the context menu of the new project and follow the NEW • CLASS menu path. Name the package in which the new class is to be created `com.sappress.pi_training`, and enter the new class name MaterialMapper_## (see Figure 4.109). Complete the Setup Wizard with the FINISH button.

Integration of the SAP Java libraries for mappings

To access the aforementioned SAP Java libraries within the source code, reopen the context menu of the project, and select the Properties option. In the window, select the Java Build Path directory on the left, and then navigate to the Libraries tab. Click on the Add Variable… button on the right, and select the SAP_SYSTEM_ADD_LIBS variable. Then click Extend to see the subtree. Navigate to the path of the first library in Table 4.16, and confirm your choice by clicking OK.

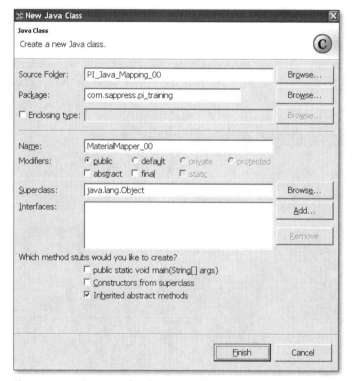

Figure 4.109 Creation of a Class within the Project

Library	Path
Mapping API	COMP • SAP_XIAF • DCs • SAP.COM • COM.SAP.AII. MAPPING.LIB.FACADE • _COMP • GEN • DEFAULT • PUBLIC • API • LIB • JAVA • COM.SAP.AII.MAPPING.API.FILTER.JAR
SAP XML tool kit	COMP • ENGINEAPI • DCs • SAP.COM • SAPXMLTOOLKIT • _COMP • GEN • DEFAULT • PUBLIC • DEFAULT • LIB • JAVA • SAPXMLTOOLKIT
JCo	COMP · ENGINEAPI • DCs • SAP.COM • COM.SAP.MW.JCO • _COMP • GEN • DEFAULT • PUBLIC • DEFAULT • LIB • JAVA • COM.SAP.MW.JCO
Logging	COMP • ENGINEAPI • DCs • COM.SAP.TC.LOGGING • _COMP • GEN • DEFAULT • PUBLIC • DEFAULT • LIB • JAVA • COM.SAP.TC.LOGGING

Table 4.16 SAP Java Libraries for the Realization of the Java Mapping

Follow the same procedure with the three remaining libraries. When finished, the listing of the Java libraries in your project should look similar to Figure 4.110.

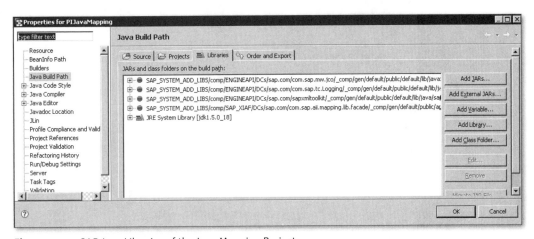

Figure 4.110 SAP Java Libraries of the Java Mapping Project

Now copy the code from Appendix A (or from the template file of the online resources for this book) into the new class. At this point, we will briefly describe the structure and the flow of the class. In the `execute`

Structure and flow of the class

method, in which the real event takes place, the main message is composed step by step in the form of the new `result` document. First, the message type is declared, and then the table name `PI_MATERIAL` is set.

The `appendElement` method at the end of the coding only serves the simplified appending of elements to the target message. The elements of the source message are then appended to the target message without further transformation. Finally, the target message is returned by the `transform` method.

Export of the JAR archive

You now must create a JAR file out of the project with the new class, which is necessary for importing into the Enterprise Services Repository. To do this, follow the FILE • EXPORT menu path. Select the JAR FILE option and click on NEXT. In the upper left, and on the right, verify that only your project (and no other entry) is selected. Enter the name of the JAR file to be created according to the `MaterialMapper_##.jar` scheme, including the path, and click FINISH (see Figure 4.111).

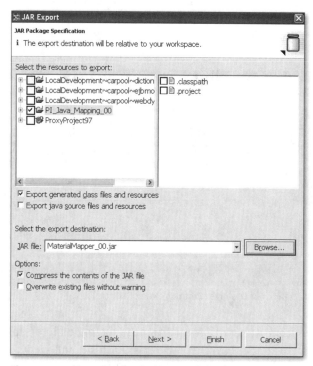

Figure 4.111 Exporting the Project as a JAR File

Integration of the Java Mapping

Now switch to the Enterprise Services Repository and import the generated JAR archive to your namespace. Follow the OBJECT • NEW menu path, or click on the corresponding icon. On the left side of the Creation Wizard, follow the MAPPING OBJECTS • IMPORTED ARCHIVE menu path, and enter the name MM_MT_Material_to_MT_INSERT_SQL_Java (see Figure 4.112). Make sure that your namespace is displayed, and enter a meaningful description before you exit the wizard.

Creation of an imported archive in the Enterprise Services Repository

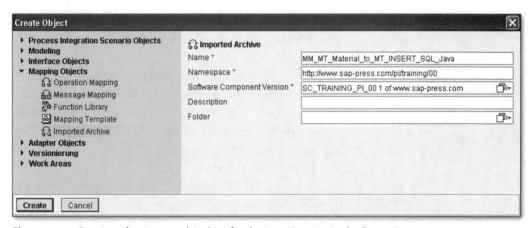

Figure 4.112 Creation of an Imported Archive for the Java Mapping in the Enterprise Services Repository

After creating the new object, the detail window opens, allowing you to import the JAR file. From the FILE field, click on the IMPORT ARCHIVE icon on the right side, and select the *.JAR file type in the Files of type box. Navigate to the JAR archive that you just exported, and then click Open. In the FILE field, the corresponding JAR archive and the relevant files of the archive are now displayed (see Figure 4.113). Save the new object; in doing so, the new Imported Archives directory is created, and appears in the tree on the left side.

Import of the JAR archive

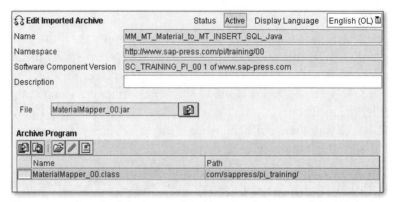

Figure 4.113 Details of the Imported Archive after the Import of the JAR Archive

Adjustment of the operation mapping

Now change to the existing operation mapping `OM_SI_Material_Async_Out_to_SI_INSERT_SQL_Async_in`, and then switch to the change mode. In the MAPPING PROGRAM section in the bottom-center of the screen, select the JAVA CLASS type in the TYPE column. This allows you to select the imported archive as a mapping program. Then, in the NAME field, select the newly imported archive `com/sappress/pi_training/MaterialMapper_##` (see Figure 4.114). Save the adjusted mapping, and test it. Finally, activate the two newly created or modified objects.

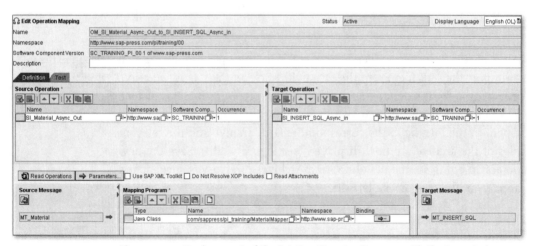

Figure 4.114 Replacement of the Existing Mapping Program with the Imported Archive

4.6   More Adapters

Despite the variety of integration examples, not all of the adapters can be discussed in the presented exercises and the following case study. Nonetheless, we provide an overview of the omitted, but still frequently used, adapter types. The focus lies on particular aspects of their real-life usage. (The mail adapter is not considered here because it is implemented in the case study in Chapter 5, SARIDIS Case Study in Sales and Distribution.)

4.6.1   Java Message Service (JMS) Adapter

The JMS adapter is mainly used for exchanging data with other enterprise application integration (EAI) and messaging systems, such as IBM WebSphere MQ or SonicMQ. In contrast to other adapters, the JMS adapter only allows asynchronous communication.

Application areas of the JMS adapter

As with the JDBC adapter, JMS also requires vendor-dependent drivers to be deployed. The drivers can be obtained from the vendors of the integrated EAI systems, and set up the same way as the JDBC drivers. Because the queues of other products are read or written to when using this adapter, you also need to configure the connected EAI product, and the SAP NetWeaver PI communication settings.

When configuring the JMS adapter both as a sender and a receiver, SAP provides additional transport protocols, some of which are product specific. The settings of the sending JMS adapter lets you establish correlations based on different criteria. Additionally, you can choose whether the JMS payload is transferred as an entire message or as a message payload. For asynchronous communication, there are two qualities of service: exactly once (EO) and exactly-once-in-order (EOIO).

Configuration of the JMS adapter

In its role as a receiver, the JMS adapter allows you to return the parameters and to specify the validity period and the priority of the JMS message for the receiving system. In addition, you can set whether or not data is transferred in a transactional JMS session. Depending on your choice of the integrated EAI system (and thus the transport protocol), configuration options vary significantly and might include additional parameters.

4.6.2   SAP Business Connector (BC) Adapter

Application area   The SAP BC allows for communication with the SAP BC. As such, it is particularly useful for integration scenarios to be partially replaced with SAP NetWeaver PI.

A prerequisite for integrating SAP BC is that it must be at least version 4.7. The SAP BC adapter can process RFC and IDoc XML documents. The adapter calls, however, are stateless. This means that transactional sessions are not possible, and the EOIO Quality of Service (QoS) is not available. In addition, it cannot process attachments.

Configuration   As the sender, the adapter settings are very few, especially because the majority of these are done in SAP BC. As a sender, the SAP BC adapter provides the parameters storage period, repeat interval, repeat amount, and timeout. The message protocol setting determines if RFC or IDoc documents are received.

In the SAP BC itself, however, it is specified that the transport takes place as XML in the SAP XML dialect. In addition, the URL of the BC adapter is specified, which is structured according to the scheme *http://<pi-hostname>:<j2ee-port>/MessagingSystem/receive/BcAdapter/BC*. In addition to the parameters mentioned earlier, using the BC adapter in the receiver role requires the URL of the receiving SAP BC and the corresponding access data.

4.6.3   Plain HTTP Adapter

Using the plain HTTP adapter   The SAP NetWeaver PI plain HTTP adapter allows you to receive and send data in pure HTTP format. This is important when integrating business systems that cannot create or process SOAP documents. The receiving HTTP adapter is addressed using the URL *http://<pi-hostname>:<abap-port>/sap/xi/adapter_plain?<query-string>*. The query string contains control data (such as the sender service, namespace, and interface) which allows it to be identified and assigned to an appropriate receiver agreement. The payload itself is sent in an HTTP post as an XML document using the UTF-8 code page. Security settings, such as the use of HTTPS, can be set in the communication channel.

The plain HTTP adapter supports all QoSs. When used in synchronous mode, the HTTP adapter can return feedback about errors or success using the HTTP return code.

4.6.4 Java Proxy Generation

The Java proxy generation of the Enterprise Services Builder is only relevant for customers who use SAP XI 3.0, used SAP NetWeaver PI 7.0, and are planning to perform an upgrade to SAP NetWeaver PI 7.1, or have already performed such an upgrade. The current Java proxy generation in release 7.1 is designed for minor adjustments of service interfaces, which have been created due to the automatic migration of message interfaces of an Integration Repository (release XI 3.0 and SAP NetWeaver 7.0) to the Enterprise Services Repository. This migration takes place during the import of message interfaces in the Enterprise Services Repository.

News in Java proxy generation

Using the proxy generation of the Enterprise Services Builder, you can subsequently generate proxy objects for these service interfaces. For service interfaces that were created in release 7.1, this is not an option. The Java proxy generation is therefore no longer supported in release 7.1 or subsequent releases of SAP NetWeaver PI. For new developments, SAP recommends the Java proxy generation in the SAP NetWeaver Developer Studio.

4.6.5 RosettaNet Implementation Framework (RNIF) Adapter

The RNIF adapter supports the RNIF communication standard defined by RosettaNet, which specifies the protocol versions 1.1 and 2.0. The RNIF adapter for SAP NetWeaver PI is based on these versions.

Connectivity to the RosettaNet

The task of the RNIF adapter is to change the PI message format to RosettaNet message format. It has the ability to send messages from the PI system into a RosettaNet-compliant system, and to receive messages from a RosettaNet-compliant system.

The *SAP Business Package for RosettaNet* provides an integrated solution for enterprise-wide trading, based on high-tech industry standards. For more information, refer to the SAP Service Marketplace (*http://service.sap.com*).

4.6.6 CIDX Adapter

Standard of the chemical industry

The CIDX adapter supports the *Chem eStandards*, a data exchange standard published by the chemical industry, and is used for collaborative Internet commerce in the chemical industry. The CIDX adapter is based on the Chem eStandards encryption and security specifications, with certain exceptions derived from an extended section of the RosettaNet Implementation Framework in version 1.1.

The CIDX adapter is used for sending messages between the IS and a Chem eStandards business transaction–compatible system; the message format from the SAP NetWeaver PI is converted into a CIDX transaction message format. For more information on CIDX, see *http://www.cidx.org*.

The case study of the fictitious trading company SARIDIS is used at several universities teaching SAP-related topics, and is used in this chapter as a template for implementing classic sales and distribution (SD) processes based on SAP NetWeaver Process Integration (PI). In this technical project, you will implement the steps involved in a traditional SD process using SAP NetWeaver PI.

5 SARIDIS Case Study in Sales and Distribution (SD)

Now that you have been introduced to the different adapters and learned how to use the components of SAP NetWeaver PI, this chapter shows you how to implement a technically and contextually consistent business process that integrates several different scenarios. For a better understanding, the individual processes have been simplified in such a way that numerous special characteristics and details that occur in practice have been purposely ignored here.

SARIDIS case study as a basis

In addition to the elements with which you are already familiar, you will learn how to use some new techniques and aspects. Specifically, you will work on a portion of the SARIDIS case study, which is widely used at universities for teaching SAP-related topics. Experience has shown that the content of the materials used in the SARIDIS case study is close enough to real life to be relevant, and also, that the simplification of some of the facts adds to a better understanding of cross-company business processes.

You can use the case study without any further adjustment in existing Internet Demonstration and Evaluation System (IDES) training systems. Other training systems that contain configured SD and Financial Accounting (FI) areas can also be used with some slight changes. However, in both cases you must configure the basic settings described in Chapter 3, Basic System Configuration. In addition, you should first work through the exercises in Chapter 4, Technical Exercises.

Prerequisites for the case study

Technically speaking, business system A is used as the ERP system of the SARIDIS company. To keep the scenario simple, business system B represents all external systems, particularly those of the fictitious customer, Hitech AG.

The sample scenario

In the case study, the fictitious label "SARIDIS" is used by the IDES enterprise to market the computer and accessories trade. It is part of the corporate group in this case study, and uses the group's customer relationships and logistical facilities within the ERP system.

One of their major customers, Hitech AG, is restructuring its information technology (IT) infrastructure and wants to automate ordering processes with its suppliers. To do this, the company has integrated SAP NetWeaver PI into its system landscape, and now wants to automate the ordering process at SARIDIS as a reference implementation. As a prerequisite for its cooperation in this integration project, SARIDIS assumes that the existing processes in its SAP system will not have to undergo any significant changes. For this reason, the integration scenarios are integrated into the existing processes using intermediate documents (IDocs). You are now contracted by Hitech AG as an in-house SAP NetWeaver PI development consultant to implement the integration process and to test the results on the basis of a purchase order for computer monitors.

> **Note**
>
> The case study is completely mapped via the German subsidiary of IDES (company code 1000), as this leaves the door open for proprietary extensions. However, it can also be reconstructed in other international subsidiaries, provided the training landscape is maintained accordingly.

Dividing the case study into several steps

In the context of the automation process, we want to map a total of five integration scenarios. The first step consists of an inquiry at SARIDIS. Based on an inquiry in a file that's created by the ERP system of Hitech AG, we will create an inquiry in the SAP system at SARIDIS (see Section 5.1, Creating the Query). The second step uses the inquiry to create a quote that is sent back to the customer. At this point, Hitech AG wants to obtain a quote from their supplier, Sunny Electronics, too. For this, they want to use an existing Web service to automatically obtain quotes from the second supplier. This entire process is supposed to run automatically in a business process that transports both quotes (see Section 5.2, Submitting the Quotations).

If SARIDIS submits a better quotation, the purchase order should be transmitted automatically. On the side of Hitech AG, this integration step is implemented by extending an existing ABAP solution (see Section 5.3, Entering a Sales Order). Once the goods have been shipped, SARIDIS automatically sends an invoice to Hitech AG for fast entry (see Section 5.4, Delivering the Invoice). Finally, the first step will be modified to allow a manual user decision on the handling of the incoming inquiry (see Section 5.5, Manual Decisions on Inquiries).

Figure 5.1 provides an overview of all of the integration scenarios within the case study.

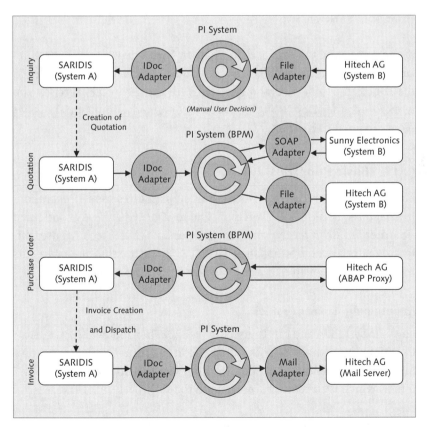

Figure 5.1 Flow of the Case Study

5.1 Creating the Query

Flow of the first step

The first step to be carried out using SAP NetWeaver PI is to create and submit queries to the supplier, SARIDIS. The original query is generated as a file in a legacy system at Hitech AG, and is submitted as an IDoc. The IDoc is then automatically processed in the SARIDIS system (see Figure 5.2).

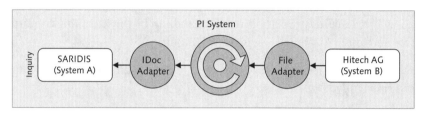

Figure 5.2 The Flow of Step 1

If you completed the exercises in Chapter 4, you may remember a similar example in the second exercise. In contrast to that exercise, however, the IDoc can accept several query items. In the technical exercises you worked on, the IDoc `MATMAS02` merely contained one material master record in a flat data structure.

5.1.1 Basic Principles

Overview of the preparatory steps

The dispatch and receipt of IDocs in this step requires some preparation. In Chapter 4, Section 4.2, Exercise 2: File-to-IDoc, you already configured a partner profile to receive an IDoc. It is possible that Hitech AG uses different material descriptions than SARIDIS. To ensure that all documents refer to the same material, make the corresponding assignments.[1]

Maintaining Partner Profiles

Creating the partner profile for system B

Log in to system A and call Transaction WE20. Then follow the PARTNERS • CREATE menu path, or click the Create icon to create a new partner profile. As the partner number, enter the number of the logical system of system B, which is structured according to the schema `<SID>CLNT<Client>`.

---

1 These two basic steps can be carried out only once in system A. In the context of a training course, the instructor should demonstrate these activities.

Select the item LS — Logical System as the partner type and make sure that the partner status value is set to A (which stands for "active") in the Classification tab.

You now want to specify that IDocs of the REQOTE (inquiry) type are automatically processed when received, according to a specific pattern. For this, save the partner profile, go to the Inbound parameters section, and click the Create inbound parameter icon.

Configuring the inbound parameters

In the next step, set the REQOTE message type (see Figure 5.3). Below the INBOUND OPTIONS tab, select the predefined process code REQO. This process code ensures that the inbound IDoc is processed automatically in such a way that it generates an inquiry. We want it to be processed immediately by the function module. Save these settings and exit the transaction.

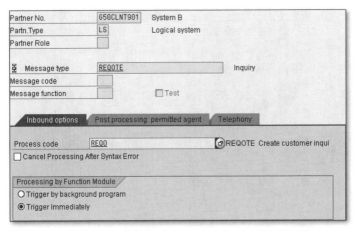

Figure 5.3 Maintaining Inbound Parameters for the REQOTE IDoc

Assigning Material Descriptions in the Supplier System

In reality, the material descriptions used by the customer often differ from those used by the supplier. For this reason, it is necessary to map the material descriptions used on the customer's side with those used on the supplier's side to allow automatic processing of sales documents — even if the materials bear the same names, both in the source and target systems, as in this case study.

Mapping customer and supplier master data

In business system A (SARIDIS), go to Transaction VD51. Enter CUS-TOMER 1171 for HITECH AG and SALES ORGANIZATION 1000 and DISTRIBU-TION CHANNEL 10; confirm your entries by pressing the Enter key.

In the assignment table that displays next (see Figure 5.4), enter the materials M-01 through M-20 both in the MATERIAL NO. and CUST. MATE-RIAL columns, and confirm your entries by pressing the Enter key. The DESCRIPTION column then displays the names of the materials contained in the MATERIAL NO. column. Every student can enter 20 different materials to order their own material or monitor type, respectively. Save these assignments and exit the transaction.

Customer	1171	Hitech AG
Sales Organization	1000	Germany Frankfurt
Distribution Channel	10	Final customer sales

Material no.	Description	Cust. material	RdPr	UM	Te
M-01	Sunny Sunny 01	M-01			
M-02	Sunny Xa1	M-02			
M-03	Sunny Tetral3	M-03			
M-04	Sunny Extreme	M-04			
M-05	Flatscreen LE 50 P	M-05			
M-06	Flatscreen MS 1460 P	M-06			
M-07	Flatscreen LE 64P	M-07			
M-08	Flatscreen MS 1575P	M-08			
M-09	Flatscreen MS 1585	M-09			
M-10	Flatscreen MS 1775P	M-10			
M-11	Flatscreen MS 1785P	M-11			
M-12	MAG DX 15F/Fe	M-12			
M-13	MAG DX 17F	M-13			
M-14	MAG PA/DX 175	M-14			

Figure 5.4 Assigning Material Descriptions in the Supplier System

Note

The IDES system does not provide the M-00 material for the instructor, so you will need to create that material item in system A. To do so, call Transaction MM01, go to the Retail industry sector, and then to material type Finished product (FERT). To create the material here, you can use material M-01 from the same sales area as a template.

In addition, you should add the sales conditions in Transaction VK31 by following the PRICES • MATERIAL PRICE menu path. Next, click in the row on the right that contains the variable key CnTy Sorg. DChl Material ReST in the Selection column on the icon that represents an empty sheet. Define the sales price for material M-00 in the new table. Save the settings and include the new material in the assignment described earlier.

5.1.2   Design

Because the exercises and the case study involve a large number of design elements that make it difficult not to lose one's overview, it is useful to use at least one separate namespace per student in the case study. As described in the course-specific preparations in Chapter 3, Section 3.6, Course-Specific Preparations, you can also create new software components. Regardless of whether you create only namespaces or software components, you should not carry out this step until the actual implementation of the case study begins; otherwise you may run the risk of students storing objects from the exercises in the namespace or software component that is reserved for the case study.

Configuring classification objects for the case study

You can create new namespaces in the details window of the software component version. Assign a name to the namespace according to the following schema: `http://www.sap-press.com/pi/casestudy/##`. New software components should be created in the System Landscape Directory (SLD) according to the schema `SC_CASESTUDY_##`.

To dispatch the inquiry, use nested data types on the sender's side to account for the IDoc structure. The smallest data type will be the inquiry item, which can be contained multiple times in the inquiry. In addition to the individual items, the inquiry itself contains header data.

Overview of design objects

At this stage, as in the following steps of the case study, you will need to familiarize yourself with the processing of nested messages. This is why we will take a closer look at the message mapping for this step. Table 5.1 provides an overview of all design objects involved in this step.

Type of object	Sender side	Receiver side
Service interface	SI_Inquiry_Async_ Out	REQOTE.ORDERS01
Message type	▸ MT_Inquiry	
Data type	▸ DT_Inquiry ▸ DT_InquiryItem	
Operation mapping	OM_SI_Inquiry_Async_Out_to_REQOTE_ ORDERS01	
Message mapping	MM_MT_Inquiry_to_REQOTE_ORDERS01	

Table 5.1 Design Objects for Step 1 of the Case Study

Importing the IDoc for the receiver side

Login to the Enterprise Services Repository and navigate to the software component of the case study. Import the IDoc interface, REQOTE. ORDERS01, in the relevant subdirectory, Imported Objects. This import contains everything you need for the receiver side.

Creating data type DT_InquiryItem

Go to your new namespace, http://www.sap-press.com/pi/cas- estudy/##, and create data type DT_InquiryItem. This data type contains information on individual items within an inquiry. It represents a simplified version of the segments to be used later on in the IDoc.

As shown in Figure 5.5, create the following elements in this data type and save it: ItemNumber, MaterialNumber, Description, Quantity, MaterialGroup, NetWeight, GrossWeight, WeightUnit, and DeliveryDate.

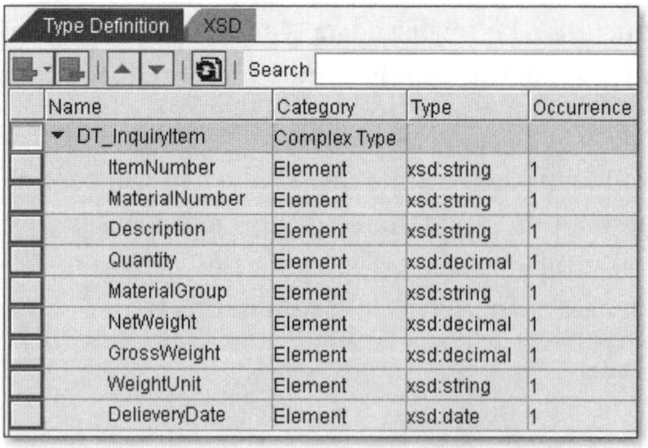

Figure 5.5 Structure of Data Type DT_Inquiry_Item

The Description, NetWeight, and GrossWeight elements contain values provided by the customer and can therefore deviate from the values of the supplier. When in doubt, use them to clearly identify a material. The DeliveryDate element does not contain the final delivery date, but rather a requested date from the sold-to-party. This does not need to match the delivery date that will be offered in the quote.

The DT_InquiryItem data type must now be integrated in the DT_Inquiry data type, which allows you to store multiple inquiry items in this format. For this, create the DT_Inquiry data type and generate the elements shown in Figure 5.6: Customer, DocumentNumber, CreationDate, CreationTime, CollectiveNumber, Vendor, ValidTo, and InquiryItem. The last element is not assigned to a built-in type; rather, it is based on the DT_InquiryItem data type, which was just created.

Creating data type DT_Inquiry

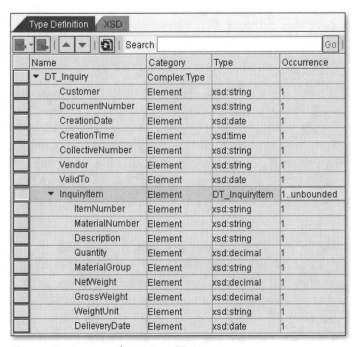

Name	Category	Type	Occurrence
▼ DT_Inquiry	Complex Type		
Customer	Element	xsd:string	1
DocumentNumber	Element	xsd:string	1
CreationDate	Element	xsd:date	1
CreationTime	Element	xsd:time	1
CollectiveNumber	Element	xsd:string	1
Vendor	Element	xsd:string	1
ValidTo	Element	xsd:date	1
▼ InquiryItem	Element	DT_InquiryItem	1..unbounded
ItemNumber	Element	xsd:string	1
MaterialNumber	Element	xsd:string	1
Description	Element	xsd:string	1
Quantity	Element	xsd:decimal	1
MaterialGroup	Element	xsd:string	1
NetWeight	Element	xsd:decimal	1
GrossWeight	Element	xsd:decimal	1
WeightUnit	Element	xsd:string	1
DelieveryDate	Element	xsd:date	1

Figure 5.6 Structure of Data Type DT_Inquiry

319

Once you have selected this data type via the input help, you will see that this type's elements are grayed out. The gray color indicates that these elements cannot be changed because they don't originate with this data type.

Because an inquiry item can occur multiple times in an inquiry, you must change the occurrence of the InquiryItem accordingly. To do this, double-click in the OCCURRENCE column of the InquiryItem element. This opens a new window in which you can specify both the minimum and maximum occurrence of the element. Open the input help for the maximum occurrence and select UNBOUNDED (which indicates that no limit has been set), and save the data type.

The DocumentNumber and CollectiveNumber elements make it easier for the customer to assign the future quotation to the relevant inquiry that has been sent. The Vendor element contains the number of SARIDIS in the Hitech AG's system. The ValidTo element specifies the period in which the quotation created by SARIDIS will be valid.

Creating message type and service interface

The next step is to integrate the DT_Inquiry data type in the new message type MT_Inquiry, and save the object. At this point, you should review the structure of the data type being used. Create a new service interface, called SI_Inquiry_Async_Out, and base it on message type MT_Inquiry. This interface is later used to send the inquiry from the file adapter on the side of the customer, Hitech AG. As you can gather by its name, the service interface belongs to the Outbound category and the Asynchronous mode. Copy MT_Inquiry as the request message type, and save the object.

Mapping the inquiry header data

Because an IDoc is used, the message mapping for this step, MM_MT_Inquiry_to_REQOTE_ORDERS01, becomes a little more complicated and sheds light on a new aspect of message processing. Where the assignment of individual elements to each other is more or less self-explanatory, you must separately consider the occurrence of subordinate elements. For this reason, message mapping development is divided into two parts that represent different hierarchy levels.

Data Element of MT_Inquiry or Constants	Data Element of REQOTE.ORDERS01	Segment of REQOTE. ORDERS01
Constant: 1	BEGIN	None (IDOC)
Constant: IN (Inquiry)	BSART	E1EDK01
DocumentNumber	BELNR	E1EDK01
Vendor	RECIPNT_NO	E1EDK01
Constant: 006 (Division)	QUALF	E1EDK14(1)
Constant: 00	ORGID	E1EDK14(1)
Constant: 007 (Distribution Channel)	QUALF	E1EDK14(2)
Constant: 10	ORGID	E1EDK14(2)
Constant: 008 (Sales Organization)	QUALF	E1EDK14(3)
Constant: 1000	ORGID	E1EDK14(3)
Constant: 004 (Valid To)	IDDAT	E1EDK03(1)
ValidTo	DATUM	E1EDK03(1)
Constant: 012 (Creation Date)	IDDAT	E1EDK03(2)
CreationDate	DATUM	E1EDK03(2)
Constant: AG (Sold-to Party)	PARVW	E1EDKA1
Customer	PARTN	E1EDKA1
Constant: 003 (Original document data)	QUALF	E1EDK02(1)
DocumentNumber	BELNR	E1EDK02(1)
CreationDate	DATUM	E1EDK02(1)
CreationTime	UZEIT	E1EDK02(1)
Constant: 007 (Collective Number)	QUALF	E1EDK02(2)
CollectiveNumber	BELNR	E1EDK02(2)

Table 5.2 Assigning the Header Data in the Message Mapping of Step 1

First, you must assign the header data of the inquiry to the IDoc. To do this, select message type MT_Inquiry as a source message from your namespace. The target message is then imported to the IDoc format, REQOTE.ORDERS01. Because of the objects origin, you can find it via the menu path: IMPORTED OBJECTS • IDOCS. In addition to the data provided by the message type `MT_Inquiry`, different constants are necessary in some places. For example, the sales area in which Hitech AG is known as a customer must be maintained.

At this point, it is important to note that, depending on their contents, the segments of an IDoc can have different meanings. The meaning is defined by a *qualifier*. In the example, this is clearly demonstrated by the segment `E1EDK14`, which occurs three times with different meanings: sometimes it specifies the distribution channel, sometimes the sales organization, and sometimes other values.

Table 5.2 provides a list of all of the header data whose content is used in the case study. In addition, each target segment and the underlying `SEGMENT` element listed in Table 5.2 must be assigned the `MT_Inquiry` node. This way, you can define that the used segments are created as often as the `MT_Inquiry` node exists in the outbound message. (In other words, once.)

Maintain the header data assignments described and deactivate all non-used segments of the IDoc for the time being. Note that you can duplicate the segments that are used several times, such as `E1EDK14`, using the Duplicate Subtree option in the menu of the relevant segment. Within the table, the different subtrees are distinguished with an index that is not explicitly displayed in the mapping. The sequence of the duplicates does not play any role.

Creation of the `CollectiveNumber` enables Hitech AG to logically bundle several inquiries. For this reason, the value must be returned later when the quote is created. Figure 5.7 displays a sample assignment of the elements within segment `E1EDK02`.

Testing the header data mapping
Now test the part of the mapping we have described up to this point. To do this, you can load an already-existing file in the inquiry format in the TEST tab by clicking the LOAD TEST INSTANCE icon. You can also click the SOURCE TEXT VIEW icon to change and save the structure of the file once again. The test should create a document on the target side that contains all segments used up to this point, including the respective values.

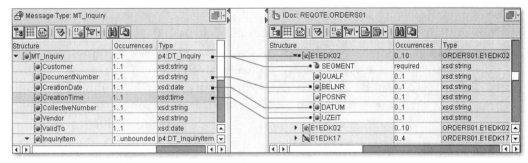

Figure 5.7 Assigning the IDoc Segment E1EDK02

Now that the header data mapping has been completed successfully, you can take care of the item data. When assigning data types and segments, it's important to note that individual inquiry items can occur in an almost unlimited number within an inquiry.

Deriving item mapping

Let's first think about the mapping, and imagine that the inquiry file contains several items; this means that the embedded DT_InquiryItem data type occurs several times. The data of each item must be stored in segment E1EDP01. As such, the segment will be created as many times as inquiry items exist in the file. Now imagine that the file contains two items, which means that the InquiryItem node exists twice. Because segment E1EDP01 can occur an unlimited number of times, it isn't a problem to create two segments. This clarifies the assignment of the InquiryItem node to E1EDP01.

Now let's look at the SEGMENT element below E1EDP01, which must occur exactly once in each segment. This means assigning the InquiryItem node to this element poses a problem if several items exist. To return to the example of the two items, SAP NetWeaver PI cannot assign a row with two items to an element that can only contain one value. Thus, the two values in the row or queue must be split into two separate values.

This is accomplished by using the SplitByValue node function. This function converts a queue with two values into a queue with *context changes* between the values. A context refers to an instance of an element. A context change causes a new instance of an element to be created; in this case, of the SEGMENT element.

Functionality of the SplitByValue function

Figure 5.8 illustrates the mapping for target element SEGMENT within IDoc segment E1EDP01. The original queue of the InquiryItem node contains two items that are enclosed by context changes. A context change occurs at the beginning and end of each queue. This context change is displayed in gray text. Due to the use of the SplitByValue node function, a context change is inserted after each value, as you can see in the second queue. This way, the two values are assigned to two different instances of the SEGMENT element.

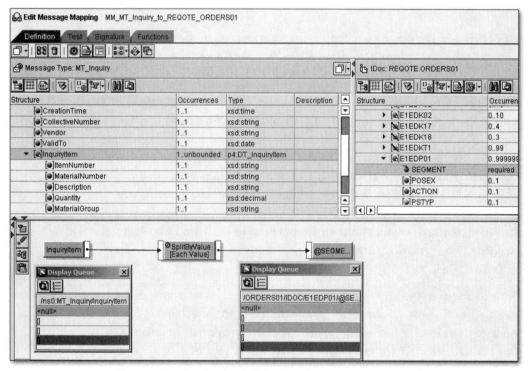

Figure 5.8 Using the SplitByValue Function

However, you can also set the parameters of the function so it generates a context change; for example, only if the values are changed or if the contents are blank. Before you do this, you should extend the mapping, as shown in Table 5.3. Target elements marked with an asterisk (*) require the SplitByValue in the mapping.

Data Element of MT_ Inquiry/InquiryItem or Constants	Data Element of REQOTE.ORDERS01/ E1EDP01	Segment of R EQOTE.ORDERS01/ E1EDP01
InquiryItem	E1EDP01	None (IDOC)
InquiryItem	SEGMENT *	E1EDP01
ItemNumber	POSEX	E1EDP01
Constant: 001 (Create)	ACTION	E1EDP01
Quantity	MENGE	E1EDP01
Constant: PCE (Quantity unit)	MENEE	E1EDP01
NetWeight	NTGEW	E1EDP01
WeightUnit	GEWEI	E1EDP01
MaterialGroup	MATKL	E1EDP01
GrossWeight	BRGEW	E1EDP01
MaterialNumber	MATNR	E1EDP01
InquiryItem	E1EDP20 *	E1EDP01
InquiryItem	SEGMENT *	E1EDP01/E1EDP20
Quantity	WMENG	E1EDP01/E1EDP20
DeliveryDate	EDATU	E1EDP01/E1EDP20
InquiryItem	E1EDP19 *	E1EDP01
InquiryItem	SEGMENT *	E1EDP01/E1EDP19
Constant: 001 (Description)	QUALF	E1EDP01/E1EDP19
MaterialNumber	IDTNR	E1EDP01/E1EDP19
Description	KTEXT	E1EDP01/E1EDP19

Table 5.3 Assigning the Item Data in the Message Mapping of Step 1

With the two segments, E1EDP19 and E1EDP20, the target structure has an additional hierarchy level; however, this level isn't discussed in this example. Basically, you could specify the delivery of the material in different batches or enter a more detailed description of the material by using several instances of the segments.

> **Note**
>
> You can save frequently used mappings (or parts of mappings) using two icons, Create Template Based on Mapping or Show Suitable Templates, which allow you to integrate them quickly. Templates are saved in the Mapping Templates directory and can be edited and tested like real mappings.

Testing the message mapping Save your message mapping and go to the test mode. Expand the MT_Inquiry node and duplicate the InquiryItem subtree at least once. Fill in the fields of the header data and of the two items. You can still use any value at this stage. Start the transformation by clicking the icon in the bottom-left of the screen and see whether the target structure contains the correct number of all segments. The structure should correspond to the one shown in Figure 5.9; the figure displays the segments of the IDoc. Note that some segment types can occur several times, depending on the specific requirements. Segment E1EDP01 contains the details of the items, and other segments.

Structure	Value
▼ [◢]ORDERS01	
▼ [◢]IDOC	
⟳ BEGIN	1
▶ [◢]EDI_DC40	
▶ [◢]E1EDK01	
▶ [◢]E1EDK14	
▶ [◢]E1EDK14	
▶ [◢]E1EDK14	
▶ [◢]E1EDK03	
▶ [◢]E1EDK03	
▶ [◢]E1EDKA1	
▶ [◢]E1EDK02	
▶ [◢]E1EDK02	
▼ [◢]E1EDP01	
⟳ SEGMENT	
[◢]POSEX	010
[◢]ACTION	001
[◢]MENGE	1
[◢]MENEE	PCE
[◢]NTGEW	10
[◢]GEWEI	KGM
[◢]MATKL	0207
[◢]BRGEW	15
[◢]MATNR	M-01
▶ [◢]E1EDP20	
▶ [◢]E1EDP19	

Figure 5.9 Structure of the Target Structure in Step 1 of the Case Study

326

Now return to the DEFINITION tab and select an element that uses the `SplitByValue` function in the mapping. Open the context menu of the source element in the work area and select the DISPLAY QUEUE option. Repeat this step for the source element. The system should now display a screen that looks similar to the one shown in Figure 5.8.

The last object to be created in the design phase is the operation mapping `OM_SI_Inquiry_Async_Out_to_REQOTE_ORDERS01`. The source operation `SI_Inquiry_Async_Out` is converted into target operation `REQOTE.ORDERS01` by using the message mapping we just created. Save the operation mapping and test it.

Operation mapping

Activate all design objects and exit the Enterprise Services Repository.

5.1.3 Configuration

As in the Enterprise Services Repository, it will also be difficult to keep your overview in the Integration Directory, given the number of objects it contains. For this reason, you should create a new logical section in the form of an additional configuration scenario. Alternatively, you can also create a separate folder. However, we use a configuration scenario.

Creating another configuration scenario

Go to the Integration Builder and follow the OBJECT • NEW menu path to create a configuration scenario named `PI_CaseStudy_##`. Save and activate the new scenario. In the Objects tab, add the two business systems (SystemA and SystemB) to your scenario.

As with the last technical exercise of the previous chapter, you will create the delivery of an inquiry using the Configuration Wizard. The only prerequisites for using the wizard are represented by the communication channels. Table 5.4 provides an overview of all configuration objects.

Overview of configuration objects

The IDoc receiver channel of system A should only be created once by the instructor. To do this, go to the integration directory and create the channel `IDoc_ReceiverChannel`, using the context menu of the communication channels for system A. Select the adapter type IDOC and set the direction to RECEIVER. You don't need to change the details for the protocols or the Adapter Engine.

Creating the IDoc receiver channel

Type of Object	Receiver Side: System A	Sender Side: System B
Communication channel	`IDoc_ReceiverChannel`	`File_SenderChannel_##`
Sender agreement	`|SystemB|SI_Inquiry_Async_Out||`	
Receiver agreement		`|SystemB||SystemA|REQUOTE.ORDERS01`
Receiver determination	`|SystemB|SI_Inquiry_Async_Out`	
Interface determination	`|SystemB|SI_Inquiry_Async_Out||SystemA`	

Table 5.4 Elements in the Integration Directory of Step 1 in the Case Study

As RFC DESTINATION, you can use the `SystemA_IDoc` connection that was created when preparing for the technical exercises. Depending on the connected system, the interface version should say SAP RELEASE 4.0 OR HIGHER. Moreover, you should also use the `SAP<SIDA>` port you created when preparing for the exercises. Note that SIDA stands for the system ID of system A. The SAP RELEASE being used depends on the connected system. In the case of SAP ERP Central Component (ECC) 6.0, the SAP release number is 700 (see Figure 5.10).

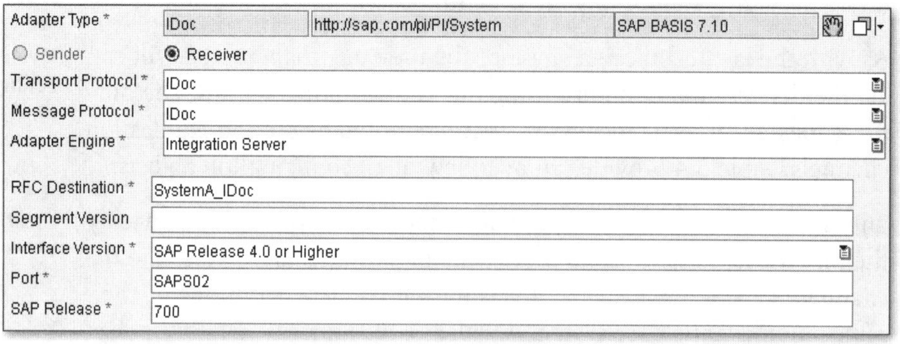

Figure 5.10 Creating the IDoc Receiver Channel for System A

Creating the file sender channel Like all other objects not directly related to an IDoc, the File Sender Channel of System B can be created by every training participant. Go to the Integration Builder, open the context menu of the communication channels of system B, and create the entry File_SenderChannel_##. Select the FILE adapter type and the SENDER direction in the detail window. On the SOURCE tab, you can use */tmp* as the source directory on Unix systems, and *C:\temp* for Windows systems. The file name of the file to be imported should be structured according to the schema, *inquiry_##. dat.*

On the PROCESSING tab, leave the QUALITY OF SERVICE setting at EXACTLY ONCE. Set the POLL INTERVAL to between three and five minutes. The PROCESSING MODE can be freely selected, depending on the scope of rights you have at the file level and whether or not an archive directory exists. If your rights are restricted and you don't have complete access to the relevant file, activate the PROCESS READ-ONLY FILES option (see Figure 5.11).

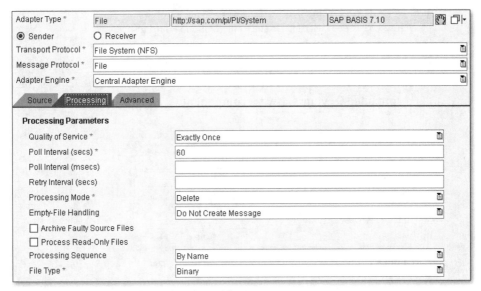

Figure 5.11 Creating the File Sender Channel for System B

With the two communication channels you created, the last two objects needed to call the Configuration Wizard. Start the wizard by following the TOOLS • CONFIGURATION WIZARD menu path, or clicking the corresponding icon. You will create this example as internal communication,

Starting the Configuration Wizard

although from the point of view of its content, it is a partner communication. However, because you are still using business systems for communication, this selection will simplify your work.

The sending COMMUNICATION COMPONENT is business system B, which uses the `File` adapter to send data records via the `SI_Inquiry_Async_Out` interface. When selecting the service interface, select the object from your own software component (see Figure 5.12).

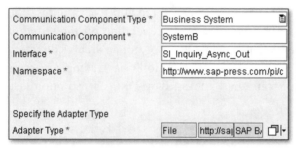

Figure 5.12 Sender Settings in the Configuration Wizard for Step 1

The message receiver is business system A, which uses adapter type `IDoc`. The interface is the definition of the `REQOTE.ORDERS01` IDoc, which is contained in your software component (see Figure 5.13).

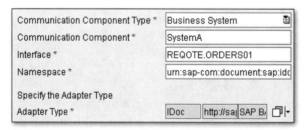

Figure 5.13 Receiver Settings in the Configuration Wizard for Step 1

For the sender agreement, you should use communication channel `File_SenderChannel_##` of system B, which you have just created. The screen used for the receiver determination, `|SystemB|SI_Inquiry_Async_Out`, is only supposed to provide you with information, particularly because no messages have yet been sent from system B via this interface (and therefore no adjustment is needed).

In the next step for specifying the interface determination |SystemB|SI_
Inquiry_Async_Out||SystemA, make sure that the appropriate operation
mapping, OM_SI_Inquiry_Async_Out_to_REQOTE_ORDERS01, is displayed.
The new receiver agreement, |SystemB||SystemA|REQOTE. ORDERS01,
uses communication channel IDoc_ReceiverChannel of system A, which
has been created by the instructor.

In the final step, add all of the objects to your new scenario, PI_Cas-
eStudy_##, and quit the wizard. Activate your change list in the Integration Builder.

At this point, we want to draw your attention to a specific option that's
contained in recent support packages, which allows you to simulate a
configuration. Before you can do this, however, the sap/xi/simulation
service in Transaction SICF of the PI system must be released.

Using the
configuration test

To do this, follow the TOOLS • TEST CONFIGURATION menu path of the
Integration Builder. In the input fields, specify the COMMUNICATION
COMPONENT and the INTERFACE to be used for sending. Click the RUN
icon in the flow control. SAP NetWeaver PI now locates the objects of
the message path as in a real run. You can use the log to identify and
troubleshoot errors (see Figure 5.14). Note, however, that some objects
cannot be identified correctly without a corresponding message.

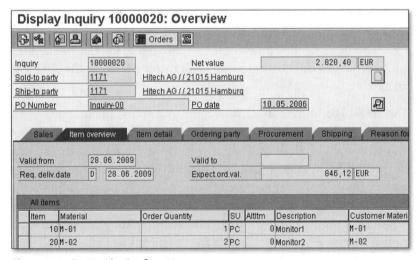

Figure 5.14 Testing the Configuration

5.1.4 Process and Monitoring

The process of Step 1 of the case study starts with creating file *inquiry_##. dat* in the corresponding directory of the file sender adapter, File_Send-erChannel_##. You can find a sample of this file in Appendix A, Exercise Materials. Apart from that, you can also enter data in the test mode of the message mapping, and then save the source code of this test data as a file. Regardless, make sure that the DocumentNumber is structured according to the schema Inquiry-##, which allows you to find the document again at a later stage. Furthermore, you should structure the name of the CollectiveNumber according to the schema, SUBMI_##, because this entry is used to select a receiver in the next step of the case study.

If the message is sent successfully, it is displayed in SAP NetWeaver PI's message monitoring, which you can access via Transactions SXMB_MONI or SXI_MONITOR. Within business system A, you can monitor the receipt of the IDoc in Transaction BD87. In this transaction, all IDocs should be displayed; consider the rows in the section IDoc in inbound processing, whereby only IDoc type REQOTE is relevant. You can see whether or not the IDoc has arrived, or if problems occurred during processing.

If you double-click on an error or success message, the system displays a detailed message telling you the exact error that occurred. Most errors are caused by incorrectly structured original files, or by errors in the message mapping. If necessary, you should reexamine the behavior of the mapping using the content of the imported file. You can also double-click on the detailed error message to go directly into the IDoc that has arrived.

The actual goal of this step, however, was not just the dispatch of an IDoc containing inquiry data, but also to automatically create an inquiry. Transaction VA13 allows you to verify that. You can find this transaction in the SAP Easy Access Menu, which you can call using the following menu path: LOGISTICS • SALES AND DISTRIBUTION • SALES • INQUIRY • DIS-PLAY. The functions to display and create inquiries are not only available in the SD area. Similarly, SARIDIS can send inquiries to another company. This type of inquiry is located in the purchasing area and must not be confused with the inquiry in the sales area.

Once you've changed to Transaction VA13, you won't be able to find the number of your inquiry. For this, you can go to Transaction BD87 and navigate to the success message and memorize the number, or you can use the search function of the INQUIRY input field. To do this, press [F4] (help) in the field and select the Sales document by customer tab. Enter partner 1171 (Hitech AG) and the partner function SP (Sold-to Party). In particular, you should enter the document number (Inquiry-##) of your inquiry in the PO NUMBER field.

If run the query, your inquiry should be displayed in the hit list. Double-click on the inquiry to copy the inquiry number. Confirm your entries by pressing the [Enter] key, and go to the inquiry view (see Figure 5.15). You should now see the data of your inquiry, which means you have successfully completed the first step of the case study.

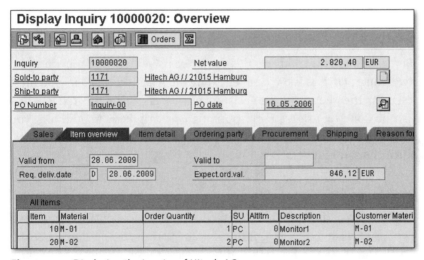

Figure 5.15 Displaying the Inquiry of Hitech AG

5.2 Submitting the Quotations

Now that the inquiry of Hitech AG has been received by SARIDIS, the next step is to assume the role of the responsible person on the receiving side and create a quote based on the inquiry. The quote is automatically sent as an IDoc from the system and submitted to Hitech AG. Once the quote has arrived in Hitech AG's PI system, a Web service of Sunny Elec-

The process of the second step

tronics is used to obtain an alternate quote for the products. Results from the two inquiries with SARIDIS and Sunny Electronics are then compiled and submitted to Hitech AG.

Figure 5.16 roughly illustrates this process.

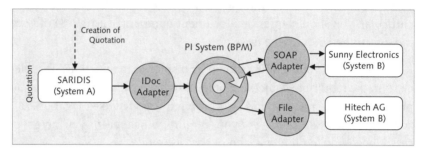

Figure 5.16 The Flow of Step 2

5.2.1 Basic Principles

Overview of all preparatory activities

Before you start working on this comprehensive step, you must prepare two things: First, as is the case regarding the receipt of an IDoc, you must establish the integration into existing processes to dispatch an IDoc. This can be done by using a corresponding *partner profile*. In addition, you will address a Web service within the business process that you can create or import by yourself.[2]

Maintaining the Partner Profiles

Maintaining the outbound parameters for customer Hitech AG

Log in to system A and call Transaction WE20 to maintain the partner profiles. Create a new partner profile for partner type KU and partner 1171 (Hitech AG) and save the profile. Below the empty list of Outbound Parameters, click the Create outbound parameter button.

Then select the partner role SP (SOLD-TO PARTY) from the detail window that opens next (see Figure 5.17). This means that the outbound parameter is only valid if an IDoc is sent to Hitech AG as the sold-to party. Select the QUOTES MESSAGE TYPE, which contains the inquiries. Go to the OUTBOUND OPTIONS tab in the lower area and configure receiver port

---

2 Because both steps can be carried out only once, they should be implemented by the instructor.

PI_SYSTEM. This port was already created during the preparations for the technical exercises (see Chapter 3), and refers to a remote function call (RFC) connection to the PI system.

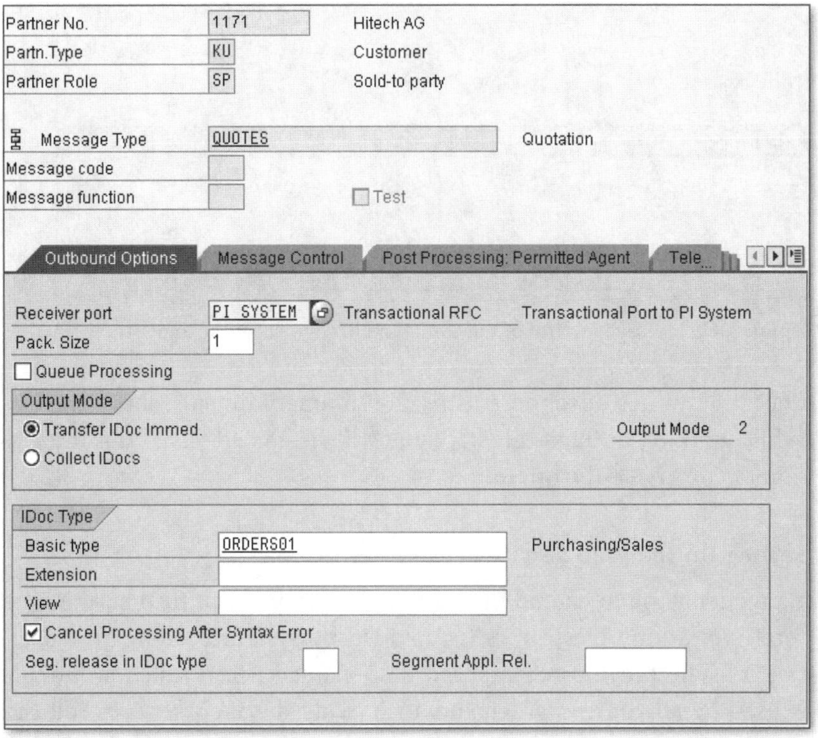

Figure 5.17 Outbound Options of the Outbound Parameter for Customer Hitech AG

Select the output mode, TRANSFER IDoc IMMED., and enter the basic type, ORDERS01. The selection of this basic type ensures that when you confirm your entries, the package size is set to 1, which means that only one IDoc is collected in a package before it is dispatched. The basic type ORDERS01 represents the basic structure of the IDocs used in purchasing, sales, and distribution, which allows them to be used many different ways.

Next, go to the MESSAGE CONTROL tab to start the integration into the SD transactions. Click the INSERT ROW icon to add a new row to the end of the list and select the V1 (Sales) item in the APPLICATION column (see Figure 5.18). Because integration is supposed to be limited to the dispatch of quotations at first, you must select the AN00 (Quotation) option in the MESSAGE TYPE column. Finally, apply the SD12 entry in the PROCESS CODE column using the input help, and confirm your entries.

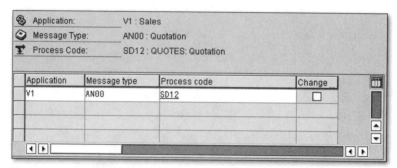

Figure 5.18 Message Control of the Outbound Parameter for Customer Hitech AG

Check the values once more using the summary directly above the list. While working through this step, you will see the effects of this integration as you create the quote.

Setting Up the Web Service at Sunny Electronics

Source of Web service

To avoid having to extend the training landscape even further, the Web service of Sunny Electronics is provided by system B. Similar to Exercise 3 in the previous chapter, an RFC-enabled ABAP function module is used by all course participants to provide the Web service. You can find the source code of this function module in Appendix A, or you can download it from the book's website (*http://www.sap-press.com*). For now, though, let's take a closer look at the structure and process of the Web service.

Structure of the Web service

The Web service receives a quote's header data, along with an unlimited number of quotes. Technically speaking, this is implemented by a table that's used to transfer the parameters. To use this table, a data structure must be created for the Web service in the data dictionary. You can also import this structure using the transport, or you can create it by yourself according to the instructions provided in Appendix A. Header data, and the majority of item data, is left unchanged during the transfer.

The information that changes is the quotation and validity dates, and all pricing details. This allows you to forward the quote from SARIDIS to Sunny Electronics later, as both of them quote their prices identically. Sunny Electronics' monitor prices match those from SARIDIS; however, they are changed slightly using a certain multiplication factor. By default, the goods of Sunny Electronics cost 110% of the price offered by SARIDIS. (If there wasn't a variance, you would be able to continue with the entire case study from this point.)

5.2.2 Design

In contrast to how we proceeded in the design and configuration phases up to now, this step first requires that you examine the entire scenario and then work through it part by part. Each individual part contains an overview of the objects used.

Creating the Business Process Structure

Because this second step of the case study is affected by the business process, we will start with it. This makes it easier for you to understand which actions are necessary and how to divide the flow into three different blocks.

Flow of the integration process

▶ First, open the Enterprise Services Builder (ESB) and navigate to your software component version, and then to the namespace of the case study. Follow the PROCESS INTEGRATION SCENARIO OBJECTS • INTEGRATION PROCESS menu path and create the new integration process, IP_Quotation_##, where ## represents your participant number. Detach the detail window by clicking the Detach Window icon in the top left-hand corner and hide the header area to obtain as much space as possible. Insert three blocks and assign the following names to them in sequence: IDOC PROCESSING, WEB SERVICE CALL, and LIST PROCESSING.

▶ Next, insert a Receive step in the first block and call it RECEIVE IDOC. Add a Transformation step after that and call it TRANSFORM IDOC. This step converts the IDoc into a simplified quotation format for additional processing. The simplified quotation format is identical to the response format of the Web service from Sunny Electronics. The last step involves a container operation, called APPEND SARIDIS QUOTATION. During this operation, the simplified SARIDIS quote is included in a list of quotes.

▸ The second block begins by converting the SARIDIS quote into the format of the Web service request. This step is called CREATE WS REQUEST. It is followed by a synchronous sending step called CALL WEB SERVICE. In this step, the Web service is called to obtain the alternate quote. Note, you must select the Synchronous mode from the properties for this element. The container operation APPEND SUNNY QUOTATION at the end of the block also inserts the alternative quote into the list of quotes. This is possible without using a transformation because the response from the Web service is identical to the simplified quote format.

▸ The third block consists of only two elements. The first element is a transformation element, called TRANSFORM QUOTATION LIST, which converts the quotation list that consists of several rows into a simple message containing all quotations. The final step, SEND QUOTATIONS, dispatches the newly created message in an asynchronous sending step.

The three blocks should now have the structure shown in Figure 5.19. In the following steps, you will fill the business process structure with data.

Design Objects of the First Block

Overview of design objects in the first block

From the design phase point of view, the most important part of the first block in the integration process is converting the IDoc into the simplified quotation format. First of all, you must create both the simplified quotation format and a corresponding message mapping. This message mapping requires you to take a closer look at how mappings are used to handle contexts. The operation mapping has the special characteristic that both interfaces are abstract because they are used in a business process. For this reason, it is also necessary to create an abstract interface for IDoc QUOTES.ORDERS01. Table 5.5 provides an overview of all of the objects used in this part.

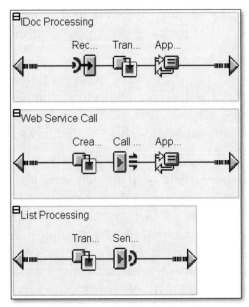

Figure 5.19 Structure of the Business Process Blocks

Type of Object	Sender Side	Receiver Side
Service interface	QUOTES.ORDERS01 SI_QUOTES_ORDERS01_ Async_Abstract	SI_ws_sunny_ response_Async_ Abstract
Message type	QUOTES.ORDERS01	Z_SUNNY_ QUOTATIONOutput
Data type		
Operation mapping	OM_QUOTES_ORDERS01_Async_Abstract_to_SI_ ws_sunny_response_Async_Abstract	
Message mapping	MM_QUOTES_ORDERS01_to_Z_SUNNY_ QUOTATIONOutput	

Table 5.5 Design Objects for the First BP Block of Step 2 of the Case Study

You should begin with the elements on the sender side: First, import the IDoc definition QUOTES.ORDERS01 from system A. Then create service interface SI_QUOTES_ORDERS01_Async_Abstract on the basis of this imported object. This unusual step is necessary because the interface

Creating the objects on the sender side

339

declaration must be declared as being abstract so it can be used in an integration process. Therefore, select the category `Abstract` and the `Asynchronous` mode.

Both the data and message types of the simplified quotation format match the response format of the Web service at Sunny Electronics. Thus, you do not need to create these two elements manually. Instead, you can obtain them by importing the Web Service Description Language (WSDL) description of the corresponding Web service.

Creating the objects on the receiver side

Call the Web service repository of system B via the following URL: *http://<Host SystemB>:<Port 80XX>/sap/bc/bsp/sap/webservicebrowser/search.html?sap-client=<Client>*. Log in as the user, `SYS_B-##`. Search for the `Z_SUNNY_QUOTATION` Web service and save the WSDL description by clicking on the WSDL entry next to the corresponding row. If necessary, you can save the description in the source text view of the web browser and store the definition as *Z_SUNNY_QUOTATION_SystemB.wsdl* in your frontend.

Create the external definition, `ws_sunny_quotation`, in your case study namespace on the basis of the WSDL file by creating a new object and following the INTERFACE OBJECTS • EXTERNAL DEFINITION menu path. Once you have imported the file, you must check if the two messages, `Z_SUNNY_QUOTATIONInput` and `Z_SUNNY_QUOTATIONOutput`, exist in the Messages tab.

Creating the service interface

Now you must create the service interface `SI_ws_sunny_response_Async_Abstract` for the receiver side. For this, use the `Z_SUNNY_QUOTATIONOutput` external message type. Because this interface is also used in the business process, its category must be set to `Abstract` and its mode to `Asynchronous`.

Creating the message mapping

Now that you have created the objects for the sender and receiver sides, you can move on to creating the mapping objects. To do this, you should first create the message mapping, `MM_QUOTES_ORDERS01_to_Z_SUNNY_QUOTATIONOutput`. Select the IDoc type `QUOTES.ORDERS01` as the outbound message and `Z_SUNNY_QUOTATIONOutput` from the external definition, `ws_sunny_quotation`, as the target message.

Note that the target message is structured in an unusual way. The ITEMS substructure that contains multiple quotation items is not located at the end of the message, but included in alphabetical order. Detach this window as well so there's enough space for you to work on the mapping.

Start mapping the header data; this shouldn't a problem if you use the information provided in Table 5.6. For the time being, you should skip those target elements that originate from more than one source element.

Segment of QUOTES.ORDERS01	Data Element of QUOTES.ORDERS01	Data Element of Z_SUNNY_QUOTATIONOutput
E1EDK01	RECIPNT_NO	CUSTOMER
E1EDK01	BELNR	DOCUMENTNUMBER
E1EDK03	IDDAT (025) DATUM	QUOTATIONDATE
E1EDK03	IDDAT (006) DATUM	VALIDTO
E1EDK04	MSATZ	TAXRATE
E1EDK04	MWSBT	TAXAMOUNT
E1EDK02	QUALF (007) BELNR	COLLECTIVENUMBER
E1EDS01	SUMID (002) SUMME	NETPRICE
E1EDS01	SUMID (002) SUNIT	CURRENCY
	Constant: SARIDIS	VENDOR

Table 5.6 Assigning the Header Data in the Message Mapping of the First Block of Step 2

Now consider the target elements that are created on the basis of more than one element, such as QUOTATIONDATE and VALIDTO. Both elements are created on the basis of the same data of segment E1EDK03, although they can assume different values. The reason for this is that the IDDAT element within the segment indicates what type of data is contained in a specific instance of the segment. A quotation IDoc sent from system A contains several instances of this segment with different contents in the IDDAT field.

To get a better picture of this, skip ahead to Section 5.2.4, Process and Monitoring, create a quotation, and dispatch it as an IDoc. At that point, the IDoc has been created, but not delivered. Transaction BD87 in system A allows you to view the exact structure of the IDoc. The structure looks similar to the one displayed in Figure 5.20. As you can see in the figure, segment E1EDK03 occurs four times. To the right of the segment name, you can see the contents of the IDDAT field, which exactly identifies the individual instances.

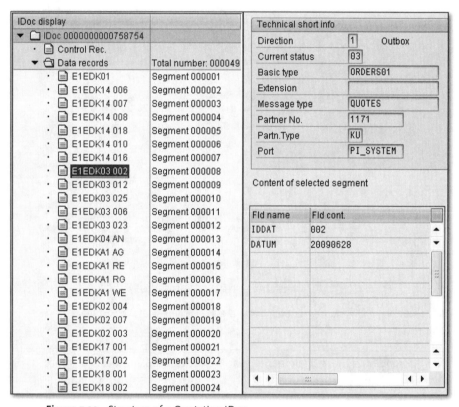

Figure 5.20 Structure of a Quotation IDoc

Header data mapping for several identical IDoc segments It is now necessary to analyze the contents of the IDDAT element and to decide whether or not the target element should be filled with data, depending on the respective contents. You can do that using the graphical function, IfWithoutElse, in the area of Boolean functions. You can select the functional area below the work area; the individual functions are then displayed to the right of the work area.

Compare the contents of IDDAT with a corresponding constant whose contents you can also obtain from Table 5.6. If the two values are identical, the target element is assigned the value of the DATUM field. Because you want to compare two string variables with each other, use the equalsS function from the Text area.

In the mapping's Test area, fill in the corresponding segments with sample data, but don't run the test yet. Make sure you enter several items and that segments that can occur several times do actually occur several times. If necessary, you can use the IDoc you just sent from system A. In the Message Monitoring module of the PI system, you can copy the exact XML structure. This is necessary so data will appear in the queue display.

Next, use the menu bar to display the queues of the if function. From the mapping you worked on in the first step, you may remember that each gray-colored field represents a context change, which corresponds to a new instance of an element. This means that four instances of the target element would be created according to the output queue of the if function. However, because the target element is only set to 1, this would cause an error. Thus, you must remove all unnecessary context changes.

The removeContexts function (in the Node Functions area) removes all contexts of a queue except for the start and end contexts. Insert this function between the if function and the target element and view your queue again.[3] You should now see that there's only one source element instead of the four you had previously seen (see Figure 5.21). Complete the mapping for the remaining header data according to this procedure. Note, however, that the COLLECTIVENUMBER target element represents another exception.

---

[3] If you saved in the meantime, you must retest the message mapping so the values of the output queue can be displayed again.

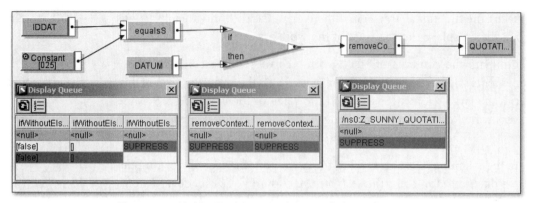

Figure 5.21 Header Data Mapping for Several Identical IDoc Segments

With the exception of two elements (MATERIALNUMBER and DESCRIPTION), continue by mapping item elements according to the details shown in Table 5.7.

Segment of QUOTES. ORDERS01	Data Element of QUOTES.ORDERS01	Data Element of Z_SUNNY_ QUOTATIONOutput
None (IDoc)	E1EDP01	Item
E1EDP01	POSEX	ITEM
E1EDP01	MENGE	QUANTITY
E1EDP01	NTGEW	NETWEIGHT
E1EDP01	GEWEI	WEIGHTUNIT
E1EDP01	CURCY	CURRENCY
E1EDP01	MATKL	MATERIALGROUP
E1EDP01	BRGEW	GROSSWEIGHT
E1EDP01/E1EDP05	BETRG	AMOUNT
E1EDP01/E1EDP20	EDATU	DELIVERYDATE
E1EDP01/E1EDP19	QUALF (002) IDTNR	MATERIALNUMBER
E1EDP01/E1EDP19	QUALF (002) KTEXT	DESCRIPTION

Table 5.7 Assigning the Item Data in the Message Mapping of the First Block of Step 2

Assignment of the `MATERIALNUMBER` and `DESCRIPTION` target elements represents a new challenge. The problem is basically the same as with the elements of the header data, which were created on the basis of segments that occurred several times. However, if you try to use the same solution, you will see that, if several items exist, the target element is assigned the same number of values. For example, if the quotation contains three items, a target element of the first target item is assigned three values, which causes an error.

Distributing values to different items

The reason for this is that the three values are not separated by contexts. You solved a similar problem in Step 1 of the case study by using the `SplitByValue` graphical function from the `Node functions` area. This function inserts a context change after each value, thus distributing the three values to three different items.

The mapping process first compares the contents of queue `QUALF` with the constant until the defined value is found. The corresponding value of the queue `IDTNR` is copied. The resulting queue contains as many entries as materials have been transferred, but it still contains too many context changes. To correct the number of context changes, you must first remove all contexts. In a separate step, a new context change is inserted for each value that is obtained. Implement the solution shown in Figure 5.22 for the two target elements, `MATERIALNUMBER` and `DESCRIPTION`.

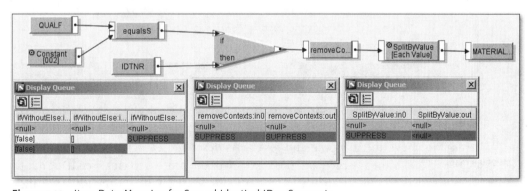

Figure 5.22 Item Data Mapping for Several Identical IDoc Segments

Let's look at another option as an alternative to the previous solution. This alternative involves analyzing the context view while mapping the `MATERIALNUMBER` target element. The context changes of the two source

Other mapping options

elements, QUALF and IDTNR, are defined by the total number of segments E1EDP01/E1EDP19 (i.e., these segments are viewed as the same segment type). However, you can change this view level by selecting the context menu of the corresponding source element and using the Context option to change from E1DP19 to E1EDP01.

If you display the queues for these two elements once again, the entries of the queues change, because a context change is only carried out after a new E1EDP19 segment. Thus, there are only as many context changes as there are target elements. All other context changes are suppressed, and they no longer play any role regarding the occurrence of the target element. Therefore, you can omit the node functions after the if block (see Figure 5.23).

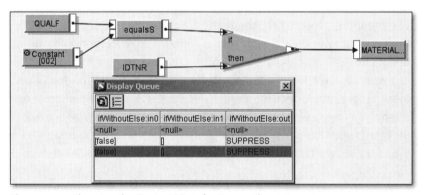

Figure 5.23 Changing the Context View for Source Elements

> **Note**
>
> If a queue contains fewer values than there are target elements, the last value of the queue is used for the remaining target elements.

Testing the message mapping Save the mapping and test it. As described earlier in this chapter, you can already carry out the first step of the process to create an IDoc quotation. You can then view the structure of the XML document in the message monitoring of the PI system and save it as an XML file for the test. However, make sure that you only save the source code of the display; otherwise the minus signs cannot be interpreted. If the test is successful, save the outbound message because it can be used for testing purposes with a second block.

For the final step of the design phase of the first block, you will create the operation mapping, OM_QUOTES_ORDERS01_Async_Abstract_ to_SI_ ws_sunny_response_Async_Abstract. For this, you must create a new operation mapping and use the abstract interface of IDoc definition SI_ QUOTES_ORDERS01_Async_Abstract as the outbound operation. The target operation is the abstract interface of the response message of the Web service ws_sunny_quotation(SI_ws_sunny_response_Async_Abstract).

Creating the operation mapping

Import the interfaces in the lower area of the screen and select the message mapping you just created from your namespace. Save the operation mapping. You have now created all of the design objects of the first process block.

Design Objects of the Second Block

In the second block, the SARIDIS quotation (now available in the simplified quotation format) is sent to Sunny Electronics' Web service. Because the target operation from the Web service doesn't match the simplified quotation format, you will need to create a simple message mapping. Because both the target and source operation need to be processed separately with abstract interfaces, you will need two appropriate abstract interfaces.

Overview of the design objects of the second block

For the source operation, use the abstract interface SI_ws_sunny_ response_Async_Abstract from the first block. When the Web service is called, an abstract synchronous service interface is used to send messages. However, the receiving counterpart outside the business process requires a normal synchronous Inbound interface.

Table 5.8 lists all of the design objects used for this second block. Note that the confusing names of the two mappings originate from the fact that the simplified quotation format is identical to the response format of the Web service. Here, an asterisk (*) means that the mentioned object was created in a previous step.

Type of Object	Sender Side	Receiver Side
Service interface	SI_ws_sunny_request_Async_Abstract	SI_ws_sunny_response_Async_Abstract*
	SI_ws_sunny_quotation_Sync_Abstract	
	SI_ws_sunny_ quotation _Sync_In	
Message type	Z_SUNNY_QUOTATIONInput*	Z_SUNNY_QUOTATIONOutput*
Data type		
Operation mapping	OM_ws_sunny_response_Async_Abstract_to_ws_sunny_request_Async_Abstract	
Message mapping	MM_Z_SUNNY_QUOTATIONOutput_to_Z_SUNNY_QUOTATIONInput	

Table 5.8 Design Objects for the Second BP Block of Step 2 of the Case Study

Creating the service interfaces

First, begin with the interfaces that you will need to process the Web service request and response. Create the service interface SI_ws_sunny_request_Async_Abstract, which is used for calling the Web service. This interface represents the Z_SUNNY_QUOTATIONInput message from your namespace. Its category is set to Abstract and its mode is Asynchronous. Save the interface.

Because Sunny Electronics' Web service is called in synchronous mode, you must create an abstract synchronous interface for the integration process. Moreover, a synchronous Inbound interface is needed for the external counterpart.

Start by creating the abstract interface, SI_ws_sunny_quotation_Sync_Abstract (see Figure 5.24). As the name suggests, it is an abstract interface that works in Synchronous mode. Because this interface is used from the integration process point of view, the type of the output message is Z_SUNNY_QUOTATIONInput, which is taken from the external definition, ws_sunny_quotation. Note that the messages have been named from the Web service's point of view. The type of the response message is Z_SUNNY_QUOTATIONOutput. After entering its settings, save the service interface.

The category of the Inbound interface SI_ws_sunny_quotation_Sync_In for the synchronous processing of the Web service call is Inbound, and its mode is Synchronous. Because this interface is used by the Web service, the messages have to be specified in reversed order. Thus, the response message is of type Z_SUNNY_QUOTATIONInput, and the request message is of type Z_SUNNY_QUOTATIONOutput. You can find both messages below the external definition, ws_sunny_quotation. Save this service interface.

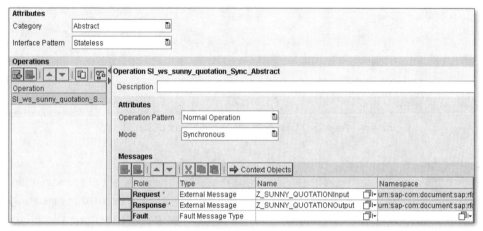

Figure 5.24 Abstract Interface for Synchronous Web Service Call

Continue with the message mapping MM_Z_SUNNY_QUOTATIONOutput_ to_Z_SUNNY_QUOTATIONInput, which is used to convert the simplified SARIDIS quotation into a Web service request. Use the source message Z_SUNNY_QUOTATIONOutput of the external definition, ws_sunny_quota- tion, as the outbound message. The target message is Z_SUNNY_QUOTA- TIONInput, which originates from the same external definition. Begin with the header data and assign the source elements, CUSTOMER, VEN- DOR, and COLLECTIVENUMBER to the corresponding counterparts. As the remaining source header data won't be used any further in this mapping, you can leave them unchanged.

Select the ITEMS substructure on both sides and click the MAP SELECTED FIELDS AND SUBSTRUCTURES IF NAMES ARE IDENTICAL icon. This automati- cally maps all of the fields with each other (see Figure 5.25), and you can save the mapping.

Test the mapping using data resulting from the mapping in the first block. If errors occur at this point, you must check the mapping again and, if necessary, also the mapping in the first block.

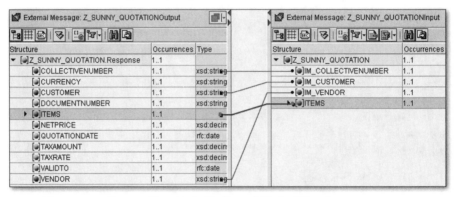

Figure 5.25 Message Mapping in the Second Block of Step 2

Creating the operation mapping

Now create operation mapping OM_ws_sunny_response_Async_Abstract_ to_ws_sunny_request_Async_Abstract on the basis of the message mapping. Use SI_ws_sunny_response_Async_Abstract from your case study namespace as the outbound interface. The type of the target interface is SI_ws_sunny_request_Async_Abstract. Import the two interfaces in the lower part of the screen and assign to them the message mapping MM_Z_SUNNY_QUOTATIONOutput_to_Z_SUNNY_QUOTATIONInput, created earlier. Save this object. You have now created all design objects for the second block.

Design Objects of the Third Block

Overview of design objects

In the third block, the multiline container that stores quotations during the integration process is converted into a format that can accommodate several quotations in one message. This is necessary because multiline container objects only exist within an integration process and cannot be dispatched directly.

Therefore, you must create a corresponding data and message type that is represented by an abstract interface. Unfortunately, the data type cannot reference the messages of the external definition, which is why you must reproduce the data types of the Web service response. In addition, you need a message mapping that is able to transfer the individual quotations into the list. Accordingly, you must use an appropriate operation mapping.

Table 5.9 contains a list of all of the design objects for the third block. Here, an asterisk (*) means that the mentioned object was created in a previous step.

Type of Object	Sender Side	Receiver Side
Service interface	SI_ws_sunny_response_Async_Abstract*	▸ SI_Quotation-List_Async_Abstract ▸ SI_Quotation-List_Async_In
Message type	Z_SUNNY_QUOTATIONOutput*	MT_QuotationList
Data type		▸ DT_QuotationList ▸ DT_Quotation ▸ DT_QuotationItem
Operation mapping	OM_ws_sunny_response_Async_Abstract_to_SI_QuotationList_Async_Abstract	
Message mapping	MM_Z_SUNNY_QUOTATIONOutput_to_MT_QuotationList	

Table 5.9 Design Objects for the Third BP Block of Step 2 of the Case Study

The structure of data type DT_QuotationItem corresponds to the ITEMS substructure of the Web service's response message. Create the data type, as shown in Figure 5.26.

Creating the data types

Data type DT_Quotation contains both header data that occurs only once per quotation and an unlimited number of quotation items. You must create the header data in the new data type. Quotation items can be created by referencing the newly created data type. Figure 5.27 displays the complete structure. You should also note that the QuotationItem element can occur an unlimited number of times in the quotation and thus needs the setting 1..UNBOUNDED in the OCCURRENCE column. Save the data type.

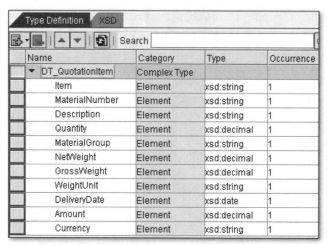

Figure 5.26 Structure of Data Type DT_QuotationItem

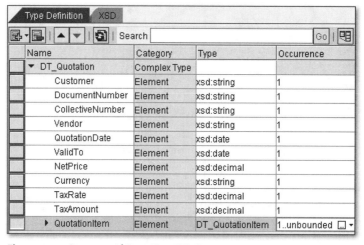

Figure 5.27 Structure of Data Type DT_Quotation

Creating the elements on the receiver side

To integrate a quotation list in a message, it is necessary to include the data type DT_Quotation an unlimited number of times in the data type DT_QuotationList. As such, create the data type DT_QuotationList and add to it an element called Quotation. This element is of type DT_Quotation and has the occurrence 1..UNBOUNDED. When you save this last data type, creation of the quotation list is complete.

Now integrate the data type `DT_QuotationList` into the new message type `MT_QuotationList` and save the new message type. Next, create a new service interface, called `SI_QuotationList_Async_Abstract`. This interface belongs to category `Abstract` and to the `Asynchronous` mode. Use data type `MT_QuotationList` as a message and save the interface. In addition, you must create the service interface `SI_QuotationList_Async_In` for receiving system B. This service interface also uses the `MT_QuotationList` message type. It belongs to the `Inbound` category and uses `Asynchronous` mode to receive messages.

You have now created all of the objects for the receiver side of this block. Because the objects of the sender side are reused from previous blocks, you can continue with the mappings.

First, create the message mapping, `MM_Z_SUNNY_QUOTATIONOutput_to_ MT_QuotationList`. The outbound message type is `Z_SUNNY_QUOTATION- Output`, which corresponds to the simplified quotation format. The target message is message type `MT_QuotationList`, which you have just created.

Creating the mapping objects

Before you begin the actual mapping process, go to the SIGNATURE tab and set the occurrence value for the outbound message to 0..UNBOUNDED (see Figure 5.28). This way you can make sure that several messages can be converted into a target message in the integration process.

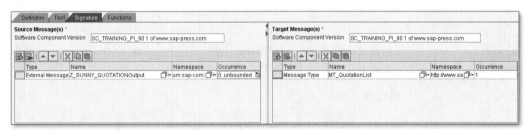

Figure 5.28 Setting the Occurrence of the Outbound Message

The mapping process itself is not difficult at all, especially because you only need to assign elements with identical names to each other. Note that the QUOTATION target element represents an exception in this case, as it must be assigned the root element, `Z_SUNNY_QUOTATION.Response`, from the source message to convert every message into a quotation in the quotation list. The target element, `QuotationItem`, is assigned the source element, `item`, from the `ITEMS` substructure.

Because the element names are case sensitive, you cannot use the automatic assignment function here. Figure 5.29 provides a complete overview of the message mapping. Save the message mapping and test it with the result of the message mapping from the first block.

Structure	Occurrences	Type		Structure	Occurrences
▼ [●]Messages	1..1			▼ [●]Messages	1..1
▼ [●]Message1	1..1			▼ [●]Message1	1..1
▼ [●]Z_SUNNY_QUOTATION.Response	0..unbounded	rfc:Z_SUN		▼ [●]MT_QuotationList	1..1
[●]COLLECTIVENUMBER	1..1	xsd:string		▼ [●]Quotation	1..unbounded
[●]CURRENCY	1..1	xsd:string		●[●]Customer	1..1
[●]CUSTOMER	1..1	xsd:string		●[●]DocumentNumber	1..1
[●]DOCUMENTNUMBER	1..1	xsd:string		●[●]CollectiveNumber	1..1
▶ [●]ITEMS	1..1			●[●]Vendor	1..1
[●]NETPRICE	1..1	xsd:deair		●[●]QuotationDate	1..1
[●]QUOTATIONDATE	1..1	rfc:data		●[●]ValidTo	1..1
[●]TAXAMOUNT	1..1	xsd:deair		●[●]NetPrice	1..1
[●]TAXRATE	1..1	xsd:deair		●[●]Currency	1..1
[●]VALIDTO	1..1	rfc:data		●[●]TaxRate	1..1
[●]VENDOR	1..1	xsd:string		●[●]TaxAmount	1..1
				▶[●]QuotationItem	1..unbounded

Figure 5.29 Message Mapping in the Third Block of Step 2

Creating the operation mapping

The final step in this block consists of creating the operation mapping, `OM_ws_sunny_response_Async_Abstract_to_SI_QuotationList_Async_Abstract`. In this step, you must link the source operation `SI_ws_sunny_response_Async_Abstract` from the external definition `ws_sunny_quotation` with target operation `SI_QuotationList_Async_Abstract`.

Make sure that the occurrence of the outbound interface is set to 0..UNBOUNDED (see Figure 5.30). This setting must be made in both the message and operation mapping for it to take effect. Import the two operations and select the message mapping you just created using the input help. Save and test the operation mapping.

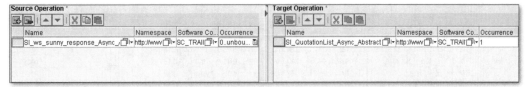

Figure 5.30 Setting the Occurrence of the Outbound Interface

Integrating All of the Design Objects in the BP Structure

You have now created all of the design objects required to implement integration process `IP_Quotation_##`. Table 5.10 lists all of the abstract interfaces that you have already created during the course of this step, which you'll now put to use. Here, an asterisk (*) indicates that the object was created in a previous step.

Overview of container elements used

	Abstract Service Interfaces
First Block	► SI_QUOTES_ORDERS01_Async_Abstract
	► SI_ws_sunny_response_Async_Abstract
Second Block	► SI_ws_sunny_request_Async_Abstract
	► SI_ws_sunny_response_Async_Abstract*
	► SI_ws_sunny_quotation_Sync_Abstract
	► SI_ws_sunny_aquotation_Sync_In
Third Block	► SI_ws_sunny_response_Async_Abstract*
	► SI_QuotationList_Async_Abstract

Table 5.10 Abstract Interfaces in Step 2 of the Case Study

Open the integration process and detach the window so your work area is as big as possible. First, go to the container area in the lower right section and create the necessary containers. The container elements are based on abstract interfaces and are used to reference messages that occur in the integration process.

Figure 5.31 provides an overview of all of the elements used. When creating the elements, make sure that they all have the PROCESS setting in the SCOPE column so that they are usable throughout the entire integration process. The `QuotationContainer` is a multiline element and must be marked as such when created.

Name	Category	Type	Multiline	Description	Scope
QuotationContainer	Abstract Interface	SI_ws_sunny_response_Async_Abstract	☑		Process
QuotationList	Abstract Interface	SI_QuotationList_Async_Abstract	☐		Process
SARIDIS_IDoc	Abstract Interface	SI_QUOTES_ORDERS01_Async_Abstract	☐		Process
SARIDIS_Quotation	Abstract Interface	SI_ws_sunny_response_Async_Abstract	☐		Process
Sunny_Request	Abstract Interface	SI_ws_sunny_request_Async_Abstract	☐		Process
Sunny_Response	Abstract Interface	SI_ws_sunny_response_Async_Abstract	☐		Process

Figure 5.31 Overview of Container Elements Used

Assigning the container elements to the process

First, you must use the SARIDIS_IDoc element to reference the IDoc received by the first block. This IDoc is then converted into the simplified quotation format and used as SARIDIS_Quotation from that point forward. This message type is included in the multiline QuotationContainer, while the message itself is converted into the Sunny_Request format. Based on the incoming IDoc data, the Sunny_Request format is used to call the Web service of Sunny Electronics. The response Sunny_Response of the Web service is also transferred into the QuotationContainer once the Web service has been called. Finally, the quotation container is transferred to the QuotationList format and dispatched.

Settings of the first block

Navigate to the first block and click Receive IDoc. The system displays the settings of this step on the right side of the window. In the list of settings, you can see a question mark next to the Message field, which indicates that information is missing at this point. Open the input help and select the SARIDIS_IDoc container element. At this point, you must also make sure that the Start Process option is checked, otherwise no starting point will be defined.

Click on the next step, Transform IDoc. The IDoc format is now converted into the simplified quotation format. For this, you must select the operation mapping OM_QUOTES_ORDERS01_Async_Abstract_to_SI_ws_sunny_response_Async_Abstract and specify the SARIDIS_IDoc container element as the source element. The target message is SARIDIS_Quotation. Once you have selected the two messages, the red rectangles around the input fields should disappear. If they don't, an error exists.

Click the next step, APPEND SARIDIS QUOTATION. Select the QuotationContainer as the target which is assigned the content of interface variable SARIDIS_Quotation with the Append operation (see Figure 5.32).

Properties	
Name	Value
Step Name	Append SARIDIS Quotation
Description	
Target	QuotationContainer
Operation	Append
Expression	SARIDIS_Quotation

Figure 5.32 Properties of the Process Step for Appending the SARIDIS Quotation

Navigate forward to the Web Service Call block and click on the first step, Create WS Request. The conversion of the SARIDIS quotation into the Web service request is carried out using operation mapping `OM_ws_sunny_response_Async_Abstract_to_ws_sunny_request_Asy nc_Abstract`. The source message is `SARIDIS_Quotation`, while the target message is `Sunny_Request`. *Settings used in the second block*

Continue with the Call Web Service step. It should already have been stored in the settings that this is a synchronous sending call. Specify the synchronous, abstract interface, `SI_ws_sunny_quotation_Sync_Abstract`. The request message is `Sunny_Request`, while the response is stored in `Sunny_Response`. Finally, this message is appended with the SARIDIS quotation to the `QuotationContainer` list in the APPEND SUNNY QUOTATION step of this block.

The TRANSFORM QUOTATION LIST step at the beginning of the third block converts the `QuotationContainer` into the `QuotationList` message. To do this, operation mapping `OM_ws_sunny_response_Async_Abstract_to_SI_QuotationList_Async_Abstract` is used (see Figure 5.33). *Settings used in the third block*

Properties	
Name	Value
Step Name	Transform Quotation list
Description	
Operation Mapping	OM_ws_sunny_response_Async_Abstract_to_SI_QuotationList_Async_Abstract
Create New Transaction	☐
▼ **Exceptions**	
System Error	
▼ **Source Messages**	
SI_ws_sunny_response_Async_Abstract	QuotationContainer
▼ **Target Messages**	
SI_QuotationList_Async_Abstract | http://w	QuotationList

Figure 5.33 Properties of the Process Step for Converting Quotation Container

The final step of the integration process consists of asynchronously dispatching the `QuotationList` message that contains both quotations. Save and check the process. Make sure that no red error messages are displayed. You can ignore the notification that the `Sunny_Response` container element has been initialized but isn't used. Finally, activate all of the design objects of this step.

5.2.3 Configuration

Overview of the preparatory steps

Before you can use the configuration objects for the integration scenario, you need some new objects. The integration process must be transferred from the Enterprise Services Repository into the Integration Directory so that the process can act as a sender or receiver. In addition, you need several communication channels, and you must send an IDoc from system A. The integration process itself also communicates with a Web service in synchronous mode. Finally, Hitech AG's quotation list is delivered with a file adapter.

Preparing the Configuration

Declaring the integration process

Let's begin with the integration process. In the Integration Directory, create a new integration process in the Communication Component directory. A wizard opens telling you that you can copy integration processes from the Enterprise Services Repository. Continue with the next step and select the `IP_Quotation_##` process from the list and choose the configuration scenario `PI_Casestudy_##` (see Figure 5.34). Proceed to the next screen and enter the same name of the integration process again. This way, you ensure that the name of the integration process is `IP_Quotation_##`, both in the repository and in the directory.

Creating a business component and a SOAP receiver channel

You will need a Simple Object Access Protocol (SOAP) receiver channel to call Sunny Electronics' Web service. Because all students will use the same Web service, it doesn't matter (from a technical viewpoint) if you create the communication channel only once or several times. However, Sunny Electronics' Web service will be used as a basis for you to deal with business components. For this reason, each student should carry out the following step.

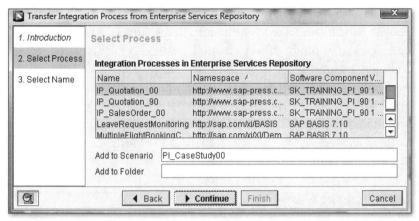

Figure 5.34 Import of an Integration Process from the Enterprise Services Repository

In the BUSINESS COMPONENT directory, create a new business component called `Sunny_Quotation_##` and assign it to your scenario. Select
the RECEIVER tab in the detail window of the new service. There you
can specify all of the interfaces known by the new component. At the
moment this is only one single interface, namely `SI_ws_sunny_quota-
tion_Sync_In`, which you have created in the design phase of the Web
service call. Select this interface (see Figure 5.35) and save the business
component.

Creating a business
component

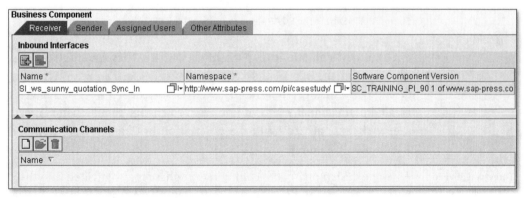

Figure 5.35 Editing a Business Component

Creating the SOAP communication channel

In the lower section of the window, you will see that the business component can contain its own communication channels. At this point you must create communication channel SOAP_Receiver_Quotation_##, including adapter type SOAP and direction RECEIVER. Set HTTP as the transport protocol and leave all other values unchanged (see Figure 5.36). The TARGET URL of the Web service is *http://<host SystemB>:80XX/ sap/ bc/soap/rfc/sap/Z_SUNNY_QUOTATION?sap-client=<Client>*. Click the CONFIGURE USER AUTHENTICATION option and enter your user SYS_B-## and the password.

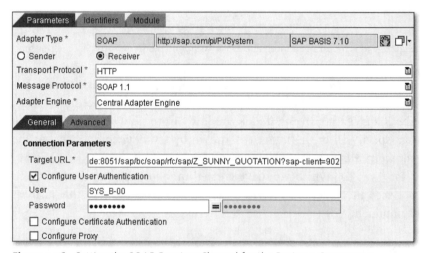

Figure 5.36 Setting the SOAP Receiver Channel for the Business Component

Using the file communication channel

For the third communication channel, which writes the quotation list into a file at the end of the process, you can use the File_Receiver-Channel_## channel from the first exercise in Chapter 4. If you haven't created that channel yet, or if you want to change the file name, create a new channel according to the description in Chapter 4, Section 4.1, Exercise 1: RFC-to-File.

Three-way division of the configuration

As in the design phase, the configuration phase is also divided into three parts. Whereas the division of the design phase was based on logical aspects, the configuration phase must be subdivided for technical reasons. Strictly speaking, this step of the case study contains three configuration scenarios: First, the IDoc is delivered to the integration process. In the next step, Sunny Electronics' Web service is called, which also requires a separate configuration. Finally, in a separate configuration step, the quotation list is dispatched to system B.

Transferring the IDoc to the Integration Process

All three steps are carried out using the Configuration Wizard, because the number of new objects is rather large. Table 5.11 lists the configuration objects used in this scenario.

Configuration objects of the first block

Type of Object	Sender Side: System A	Receiver Side: IP_Quotation_##
Communication channel	IDoc_SenderChannel	
Sender agreement	|SystemA|QUOTES. ORDERS01|*|*	
Receiver determination	|SystemA|QUOTES.ORDERS01	
Interface determination	|SystemA|QUOTES.ORDERS01||IP_ Quotation_##	

Table 5.11 Configuration Objects for the First Block of Step 2 of the Case Study

Start the wizard from the menu or by clicking on its icon. Because both business system A and B are regarded as internal systems, the current scenario can be referred to as an internal communication. Define business system A as the sender with adapter type IDoc. The interface used here is REQOTE.ORDERS01.

The receiver is integration process IP_Quotation_##. The input help for the interface only contains the value SI_QUOTES_ORDERS01_Async_ Abstract. This is because the value corresponds to the interface used to provide the initial reception step with the data (see Figure 5.37).

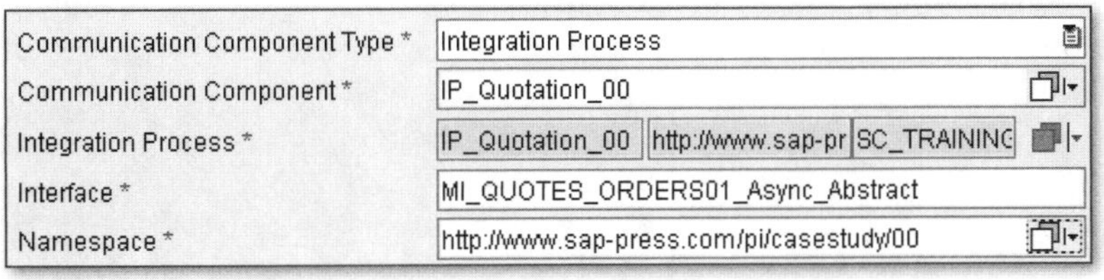

Communication Component Type *	Integration Process
Communication Component *	IP_Quotation_00
Integration Process *	IP_Quotation_00 | http://www.sap-pr | SC_TRAINING
Interface *	MI_QUOTES_ORDERS01_Async_Abstract
Namespace *	http://www.sap-press.com/pi/casestudy/00

Figure 5.37 Settings for the Receiver when Using the Process

The sender agreement is not necessary in this case. The receiver determination |SystemA|REQOTE.ORDERS01 is created for the first participant, while all other participants can only extend it. You shouldn't care too much about the notification message regarding the receiver agreement, as you will manually edit the receiver determination at a later stage anyway.

In contrast to the usual procedure, the interface determination |SystemA|REQOTE.ORDERS01||IP_Quotation_## doesn't display an operation mapping (see Figure 5.38). This is because no operation mapping is needed. Both the sending and the receiving interface use the same structure, namely IDoc type QUOTES.ORDERS01.

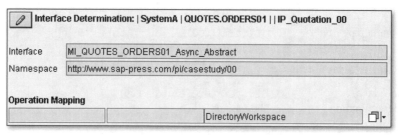

Figure 5.38 Interface Determination for Delivery to the Integration Process

Because an integration process is being used, adapter type XI has been selected, and a receiver agreement isn't needed. Add the newly created configuration objects to your scenario and complete the wizard. Activate the newly created objects in the change list.

Adjusting the receiver determination

At this point, if you used the IDoc from system A, the IDoc would be sent to all integration processes. To avoid this, and to make sure that each IDoc is sent to only one process, you must manually adjust the receiver determination, SystemA|QUOTES.ORDERS01. However, the lock mechanism of SAP NetWeaver PI ensures that not all course participants can process this object at the same time; you should therefore coordinate the different access times.

Figure 5.39 shows that only one receiver has been configured so far. To link the delivery with a specific connection, specify a corresponding expression in the first column of the receivers list. The goal is to define a receiver that matches the contents of the `CollectiveNumber` entry. You already entered the `SUBMI_##` entry in the corresponding field during the creation of the inquiry in the previous step. Accordingly, the receiver must be selected on the basis of the `CollectiveNumber`.

Editing the conditions

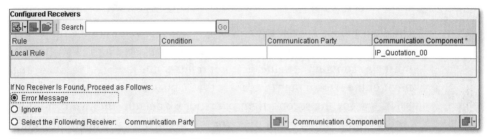

Figure 5.39 Post-Editing the Receiver Determination

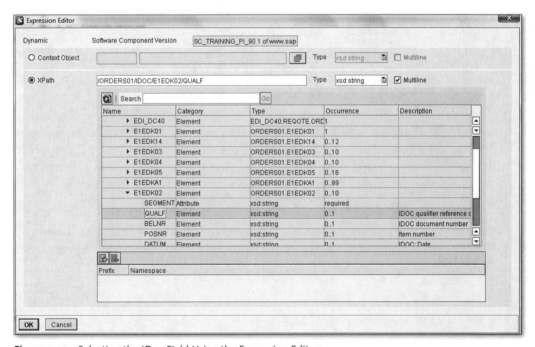

Figure 5.40 Selecting the IDoc Field Using the Expression Editor

Click in the CONDITION column to open the input help. This opens a window in which you can create conditions. Next, open the input help in the Left Operand column. This opens the EXPRESSION EDITOR (see Figure 5.40). The XPATH option allows you to select a field from the structure of the inbound IDoc. Select the field, /ORDERS01/ IDOC/E1EDK02/QUALF, and copy the value.

Insert a new row in the condition overview and repeat the selection of an IDoc field by selecting /ORDERS01/IDOC/E1EDK02/BELNR.

Once both fields are transferred, assign concrete values to the right operands. Similar to the mapping in the first process block, the qualifier must also contain the value 007, if it refers to the CollectiveNumber segment of the IDoc. Enter the CollectiveNumber according to the schema, SUBMI_## , for the second right operand. By default, the two conditions are linked by the Boolean operator AND, which means that both conditions must be met for it to be true (see Figure 5.41).

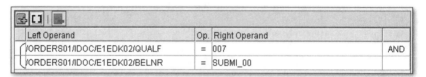

Figure 5.41 Condition Overview in the Receiver Determination

Save the modified receiver determination which, in the future, will only forward IDocs of the QUOTES.ORDERS01 type to your integration process, if the name of the CollectiveNumber is SUBMI_## .

Calling the Web Service from the Integration Process

Configuration objects of the second block

The second configuration scenario contained in Step 2 of the case study consists of calling the Sunny Electronics' Web service. The objects needed for that are listed in Table 5.12.

Type of Object	Sender Side: IP_Quotation_##	Receiver Side: Sunny_ Quotation_##
Communication channel		SOAP_Receiver_ Quotation_##
Receiver agreement	| IP_Quotation_## | | Sunny_Quotation_## | SI_ws_sunny_ quotation_Sync_In	
Receiver determination	| IP_Quotation_## | SI_ws_sunny_ Quotation_Sync_Abstract	
Interface determination	| IP_Quotation_## | SI_ws_sunny_ quotation_Sync_Abstract | | Sunny_ Quotation_##	

Table 5.12 Configuration Objects for the Second Block of Step 2 of the Case Study

Call the Configuration Wizard and select the Internal Communication option. Define integration process IP_Quotation_## as the sender. If you open the input of the interface, it displays two values, because the process can send messages from two different places. This can be the synchronous Web service call, or it can be the asynchronous dispatch of the quotation list. This time, select the interface SI_ws_sunny_quotation_Sync_Abstract in the wizard (see Figure 5.42).

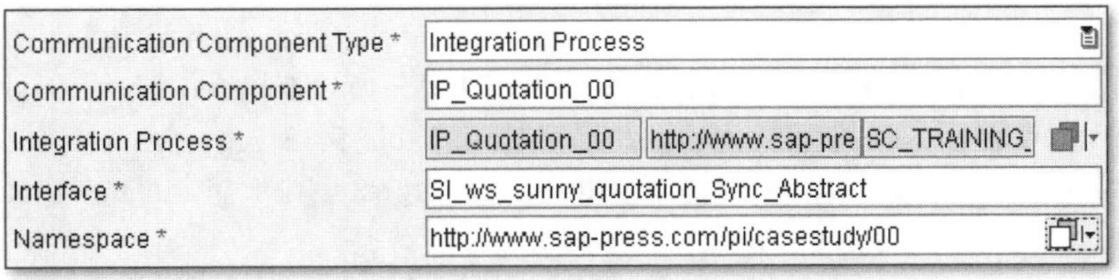

Communication Component Type *	Integration Process
Communication Component *	IP_Quotation_00
Integration Process *	IP_Quotation_00 | http://www.sap-pre | SC_TRAINING_
Interface *	SI_ws_sunny_quotation_Sync_Abstract
Namespace *	http://www.sap-press.com/pi/casestudy/00

Figure 5.42 Sender Settings in the Configuration Wizard of the Web Service Call

The receiver of the Web service call is business component Sunny_Quotation_##, which you created earlier. Communication with this service runs through the SOAP adapter. Select SI_ws_sunny_quotation_Sync_In, which is the only interface you have stored on the side of this business component (see Figure 5.43).

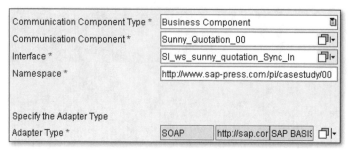

Communication Component Type *	Business Component
Communication Component *	Sunny_Quotation_00
Interface *	SI_ws_sunny_quotation_Sync_In
Namespace *	http://www.sap-press.com/pi/casestudy/00
Specify the Adapter Type	
Adapter Type *	SOAP	http://sap.cor	SAP BASIS

Figure 5.43 Receiver Settings in the Configuration Wizard of the Web Service Call

Due to the XI adapter, you don't need a sender agreement. The next screen displays information about the creation of the new receiver determination, |IP_Quotation_##|SI_ws_sunny_quotation_Sync_Abstract. The interface determination, |IP_Quotation_##|SI_ws_sunny_quotation_Sync_Abstract | | Sunny_Quotation_##, does not use any operation mapping, because the message types of the sender and receiver are identical, as is the case in the configuration of the IDoc delivery. The receiver agreement, |IP_Quotation_##||Sunny_Quotation_##|SI_ws_sunny_quotation_Sync_In, uses communication channel SOAP_Receiver_Quotation_##, which you created during your preparations for the configuration phase. Add the new objects to your scenario and close the wizard.

Sending the Quotation List to System B

Configuration objects of the third block

The last configuration step consists of sending the final quotation list to the file adapter of business system B, which does not involve any special characteristics regarding the configuration. Table 5.13 provides a list of all of the configuration objects used. Here, an asterisk (*) indicates that the object was created in a previous step.

Again, call the Configuration Wizard and select the Internal Communication option. The sender is integration process IP_Quotation_##. Select interface SI_QuotationList_Async_Abstract for sending purposes. The receiver is business system B, which receives data using a file adapter with interface SI_QuotationList_Async_In. Due to the adapter type used, the sender agreement isn't necessary.

Type of Object	Sender Side: IP_Quotation_##	Receiver Side: System B
Communication channel		`File_ReceiverChannel_##*`
Receiver agreement	`|IP_Quotation_##|` `|SystemB|` `SI_QuotationList_` `Async_In`	
Receiver determination	`|IP_Quotation_##|SI_QuotationList_Async_` `Abstract`	
Interface determination	`|IP_Quotation_##|SI_QuotationList_Async_` `Abstract` `||SystemB`	

Table 5.13 Configuration Objects for the Third Block of Step 2 of the Case Study

The next screen informs you about the creation of the receiver determination, `|IP_Quotation_##|SI_QuotationList_Async_Abstract`. Like all configuration scenarios that include integration processes, interface determination `|IP_Quotation_##|SI_QuotationList_Async_Abstract` `||SystemB` doesn't require operation mapping. The receiver determination, `|IP_Quotation_##||SystemB|SI_QuotationList_Async_In`, reuses communication channel `File_ReceiverChannel_##` from the first technical exercise.

Add the new objects to your scenario and close the wizard. You have now created all configuration objects for Step 2 of the case study. Activate all of the changes in the Change Lists tab.

5.2.4 Process and Monitoring

Now that you have created a large number of design and configuration objects in this step of the case study, it is time to see how the step is processed.

Flow of the Step

The process begins by creating a quotation. In our case, this quotation is based on the inquiry of Hitech AG, but it could also be created without such a prior inquiry.

Creating the quotation

367

Log in to business system A as the user, SYS_A-##, and call Transaction VA21, which allows you to create quotations. Because you already received an inquiry that contains all of the relevant data, you will refer to this inquiry in your quotation. To do this, you must follow the SALES DOCUMENT • CREATE WITH REFERENCE menu path to select the respective inquiry.

The new window should already display the Inquiry tab. Open the input help of the Inquiry input field. In the search help, navigate to the Sales document by customer tab, and, in the Purchase order number field, enter the document number of Hitech AG according to the schema, Inquiry-##. This allows you to find the inquiry; select it by double-clicking on the name.

Confirm the inquiry number. This opens the item overview of the quotation. Please note that both the SOLD-TO PARTY and the SHIP-TO PARTY are represented by customer 1171 (Hitech AG). Enter a date within a week in the VALID TO field of the ITEM OVERVIEW tab. The prices for the requested items are determined and displayed automatically (see Figure 5.44).

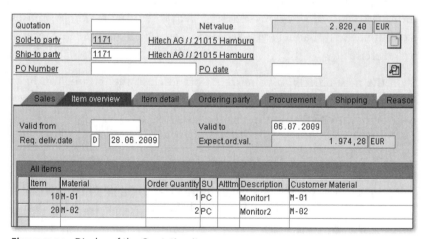

Figure 5.44 Display of the Quotation Items

To ensure that the quotation is automatically sent as an IDoc when saved, you must make two more settings: Follow the EXTRAS • OUTPUT • HEADER • EDIT menu path and choose the line that shows partner 1171

(Hitech AG) from the list of messages. Next, change the medium to 6 EDI so that the quotation is sent as an electronic document using the partner agreement (see Figure 5.45).

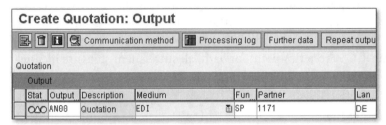

Figure 5.45 Selecting the Message Medium

Highlight the selected line and then follow the EDIT • FURTHER DATA menu path, or click the FURTHER DATA button. Select the dispatch time SEND IMMEDIATELY (WHEN SAVING THE APPLICATION) in the REQUESTED PROCESSING section (see Figure 5.46). This ensures that no messages are collected prior to being sent.

| Sold-to party | 1171 | | Hitech AG |
| Output Type | Quotation | | EDI |

| Creation | | |
| 29.06.2009 | 09:17:36 | |

Requested processing			
Dispatch time	Send immediately (when saving the application)		
	00:00:00	Time to	00:00:00

Figure 5.46 Setting Further Data for the Message Control

Now return to the item overview and save the quotation. When you save the quotation, a message is automatically generated and dispatched as an IDoc.

If no inquiry exists, you can also create a quotation without any reference. To do this, select quotation type QT (quotation) in the initial screen of Transaction VA21, and sales organization 1000, distribution channel

Creation without inquiry

369

10, and division 00. Confirm your entries by pressing the ⌈Enter⌉ key. Next, select customer 1171 as both the sold-to party and ship-to party.

After that, follow the GOTO • HEADER • PURCHASE ORDER DATA menu path and maintain the Collective no. for quotation with an entry according to the schema, SUBMI_##. Return to the ITEM OVERVIEW tab and enter the relevant materials and their respective quantities according to the schema M-##. From this point forward, all subsequent steps are identical to the steps in the inquiry-based quotation process.

Monitoring the Process

Tracking the
message path

As a result of this scenario, you should obtain a file that contains both the quotation from SARIDIS and that from Sunny Electronics. You can check this via Transaction AL11, Transaction ZAPCMD in SAP NetWeaver PI, or by using the file tool, which you can download from the website for this book (*http://www.sap-press.com*). In addition, you can use the message monitoring function in SAP NetWeaver PI to see if the data is being processed correctly.

In the present case, you should see two messages: one that contains the message that was sent with the IDoc to the integration process, and the message containing the quotation list sent from the integration process. Due to its synchronous nature, you won't be able to find the Web service call in the message monitoring.

If no message is displayed in the message monitoring module, you can call Transaction BD87 in system A to see if the IDoc was created at all. If the IDoc wasn't created, the reason can often be found in the partner agreement containing errors, or in the fact that the two settings are not made when the quotation is created. If the IDoc contains an error, it is probably caused by the use of incorrect logon data in RFC destination PI_System, or in the transactional RFC port.

Monitoring the
business process

If a notification is displayed in the message monitoring, it means that the business process has not been completely processed. In that case, you can call Transaction SXMB_MONI in SAP NetWeaver PI and search for the process engine (PE) entry in the first message. When you find the entry, click on it. Transaction SXMB_MONI_BPE provides generic access to this display. In any case, you will navigate to the display of the individual process steps and their status (see Figure 5.47).

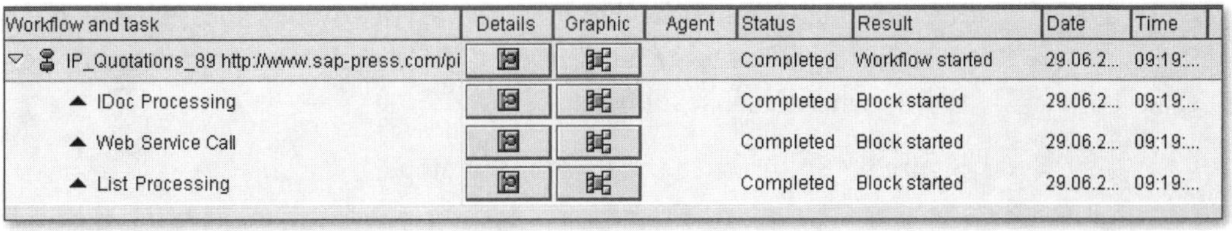

Workflow and task	Details	Graphic	Agent	Status	Result	Date	Time
▽ 👤 IP_Quotations_89 http://www.sap-press.com/pi	📄	▦		Completed	Workflow started	29.06.2...	09:19:...
▲ IDoc Processing	📄	▦		Completed	Block started	29.06.2...	09:19:...
▲ Web Service Call	📄	▦		Completed	Block started	29.06.2...	09:19:...
▲ List Processing	📄	▦		Completed	Block started	29.06.2...	09:19:...

Figure 5.47 Workflow Log for Step 2 of the Case Study

You can see the sequence of steps arranged by the different blocks, and you can obtain a graphical display of the same information by clicking on a button in the GRAPHIC column. The graphical display allows you to easily identify the cause of the error. If you double-click on a workflow item, the system displays the corresponding detail view. There you can view the log files for the individual operations by following the WORK ITEM • OBJECT • DISPLAY menu path.

5.3   Entering a Sales Order

Because of the unbeatable prices offered by SARIDIS, Hitech AG decided to choose SARIDIS as their supplier. The third step of the case study consists of submitting a purchase order for different types of monitors from Hitech AG to SARIDIS. The purchase order is submitted as an IDoc for which we'll use the basic type ORDERS01, which you have already come across in the first two steps of the case study.

Flow of the Step

The special characteristic of this scenario is that it requires the creation of a proxy, used for sending the data after it has been called by a program in Hitech AG's SAP system. In principle, ABAP proxies also support asynchronous interfaces; however, to demonstrate the link between synchronous and asynchronous interfaces, here we will send a synchronous message to be processed asynchronously. To do this, we'll use the *sync-async-bridge*.

In the previous step, you did the exact opposite: You used an *asnyc-sync-bridge* to create a synchronous Web service call from an asynchronous message. However, the problem with a sync-async-bridge is that the connection must be kept active until the asynchronous message has been sent. Business Process Management (BPM) contains a predefined option to implement such a solution.

Figure 5.48 illustrates the flow of this step.

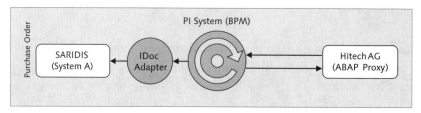

Figure 5.48   The Flow of Step 3

5.3.1   Basic Principles

Configuring the partner agreement

The preparation for this step mainly consists of extending the partner agreement in system A, which allows you to automatically process incoming purchase orders. This extension can be carried out only once.

To do this, log in to system A and call Transaction WE20 to edit the partner agreements. In the PARTN. TYPE LS directory, select logical system B, which you created in Step 1. Next, specify that incoming IDocs of the ORDERS (purchase order/order) type are automatically processed according to a specific pattern. For this, click the Create inbound parameter icon in the Inbound parameters section, and set the value for the message type to ORDERS.

Below the INBOUND OPTIONS tab, select the predefined process code, ORDE (see Figure 5.49). This process code ensures that the inbound IDoc is processed automatically such that it generates an order. We want it to be processed immediately by the function module. Save these settings and finish this transaction.

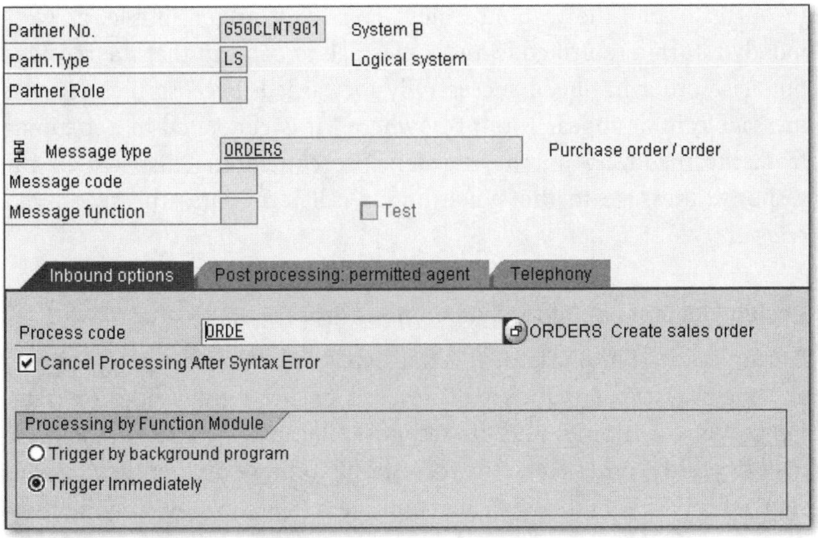

Figure 5.49 *Maintaining Inbound Options for the ORDERS IDoc*

> **Note**
>
> The IDoc type, ORDERS, is used for both purchase and sales orders. The determination of a concrete IDoc is based on a specific identifier in E1EDK01.

5.3.2 Design

Because the *sync-async-bridge* is used as an integration process, you'll need to create two separate design scenarios in addition to the integration process. We'll work through these two tasks separately. As the integration process is not very complex, let's first discuss it in brief. **Subdividing the design phase**

The process begins with the reception of the synchronous message, which indicates the starting point for the sync-async-bridge. As long as this bridge is active, the connection to the sending ABAP proxy is also kept active. The next step in this process consists of transforming the inbound message into an order IDoc, which is then delivered in a later step. Once the asynchronous communication has been completed, the synchronous communication can be terminated as well. For this, we'll generate an appropriate response message for the incoming purchase order.

In our example, the response message is kept rather simple, as we'll merely return a return code and a message to confirm that the received purchase order has been successfully forwarded. Because the response message cannot appear "out of nowhere," it is generated in a mapping from the incoming purchase order. The concluding dispatch of the response message to the synchronous call terminates the *sync-async-bridge*.

Design Elements Used for Synchronous Processing

Overview of the design objects

During the design phase of this substep, you will create separate data and message types, which will be used on the sender side for creating the purchase order and the response. Because the structure and the majority of the order elements correspond to those used in the previous steps of the case study, you can create these elements by copying most of the existing objects. The proxies will occur as part of system B. The service interfaces of the ABAP proxy contain the participant number, which allows the sending proxy to be clearly identified at a later stage. This is the only way you can assign an inbound message to the appropriate integration process. Alternatively, you can create separate business components.

Table 5.14 provides an overview of all of the design objects.

Type of Object	Sender Side	Receiver Ride
Service interface	SI_SalesOrder_Sync_Out_##	▶ SI_SalesOrder_Sync_Abstract ▶ SI_SalesOrder_Async_Abstract ▶ SI_Response_Async_Abstract
Message type	▶ MT_SalesOrder ▶ MT_Response	
Data type	▶ DT_SalesOrder ▶ DT_SalesOrder-Item ▶ DT_Response	

Table 5.14 Design Objects for Asynchronous Processing in Step 3 of the Case Study

Type of Object	Sender Side	Receiver Ride
Operation mapping	`OM_SI_SalesOrder_Async_Abstract_to_SI_Response_Async_Abstract`	
Message mapping	`MM_MT_SalesOrder_to_MT_Response`	

Table 5.14 Design Objects for Asynchronous Processing in Step 3 of the Case Study (Cont.)

To facilitate the work a little, you can copy most of the data types of the inquiry scenario and use them for the order. To do this, go to the namespace of the case study in your software component version, and select the data type, `DT_InquiryItem`. Open the context menu of this object and select the Copy Object... option; this allows you to create the new `DT_SalesOrderItem` object. You can leave all elements unchanged. Repeat this operation to create `DT_SalesOrder` on the basis of `DT_Inquiry`.

Design elements of the order

Next, open the new data type for editing, rename the `InquiryItem` element to `SalesOrderItem`, and assign it the type `DT_SalesOrderItem`. Now create message type `MT_SalesOrder` on the basis of data type `DT_SalesOrder`. Your new data type should now be structured as shown in Figure 5.50.

Name	Category	Type	Occurrence
▼ MT_SalesOrder	Element	DT_SalesOrder	
Customer	Element	xsd:string	1
DocumentNumb	Element	xsd:string	1
CreationDate	Element	xsd:date	1
CreationTime	Element	xsd:time	1
CollectiveNumb	Element	xsd:string	1
Vendor	Element	xsd:string	1
ValidTo	Element	xsd:date	1
▼ SalesOrderItem	Element	DT_SalesOrderItem	1..unbounded
ItemNumber	Element	xsd:string	1
MaterialNum	Element	xsd:string	1
Description	Element	xsd:string	1
Quantity	Element	xsd:decimal	1
MaterialGrou	Element	xsd:string	1
NetWeight	Element	xsd:decimal	1
GrossWeigh	Element	xsd:decimal	1
WeightUnit	Element	xsd:string	1
DelieveryDat	Element	xsd:date	1

Figure 5.50 Structure of Data Type DT_SalesOrder

Design elements of the response

The design elements of the response must be created from scratch. Start with data type DT_Response in your namespace. This data type contains the two elements, Type and Message (see Figure 5.51). The Type element contains a return code, which will simply be OK in the case of success, while the Message element contains a corresponding success message and the purchase order number. The type of both fields is xsd:string. Save the object once you have created the elements.

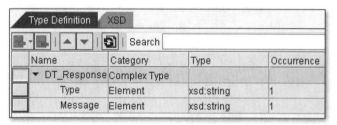

Figure 5.51 Structure of Data Type DT_Response

Now create message type MT_Response on the basis of this data type.

Creating the service interface

The service interface SI_SalesOrder_Sync_Out_## contains both the sending and the receiving message type for synchronous communication. First, set the Outbound category and the Synchronous mode. Use MT_SalesOrder as the request message and MT_Response as the response message. You don't need an operation mapping that uses this interface, because the abstract interfaces in the integration process use the same message types.

The counterpart of this service interface in the integration process is a synchronous interface that, upon receipt, is split into two asynchronous, abstract messages. Create service interface SI_SalesOrder_Sync_Abstract with the Abstract category and Synchronous mode (see Figure 5.52). Use MT_SalesOrder as the request message and MT_Response as the response message. These settings are thus identical to those of the corresponding Outbound interface.

Before you can separately process the two messages of the synchronous interface within the integration process, you need an abstract interface for each message type. First, create service interface SI_Sales-Order_Async_Abstract, which contains message type MT_SalesOrder and belongs to the Abstract category and the Asynchronous mode. The second interface, SI_Response_Async_Abstract, uses the MT_Response message; its category and mode are also Abstract and Asynchronous, respectively.

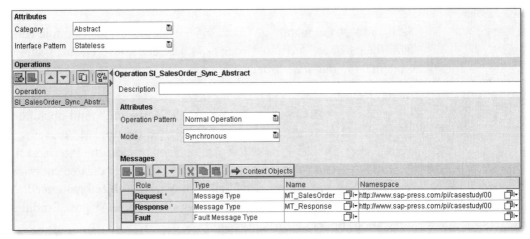

Figure 5.52 Settings for the Synchronous Abstract Service Interface

To terminate the *sync-async-bridge* at the end of the integration process, the response message must be generated based on the order. For this, you need a message mapping and an operation mapping between the two abstract interfaces.

Creating the mapping elements

First, create the message mapping MM_MT_SalesOrder_to_MT_Response and assign it the source message MT_SalesOrder. The type of the target message is MT_Response. Assign the source node MT_SalesOrder to the MT_Response node. The Type element must be assigned to the constant containing OK.

We want the Message element to contain a success message and the purchase order number. You can implement this using constants, the DocumentNumber source element, and the concat text function, as shown in Figure 5.53.

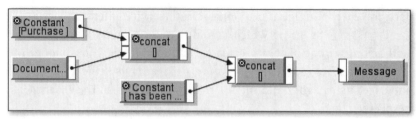

Figure 5.53 Message Mapping for the Response Message

Save and test the mapping. The `Message` element in this example contains the message, Purchase Order 1234 has been delivered successfully. Note that the purchase order number merely represents a test value.

Next, create the `OM_SI_SalesOrder_Async_Abstract_to_SI_Response_Async_Abstract` operation mapping; this links the outbound operation `SI_SalesOrder_Sync_Abstract` with target operation `SI_Response_Async_Abstract`. Once the objects are selected, import the interfaces in the lower part of the screen and assign it the newly created message mapping. You have now created all of the design objects you need to map the synchronous communication between the ABAP proxy and the integration process.

Design Elements Used for Asynchronous Processing

Overview of design objects

In this scenario, the design elements needed for asynchronous processing ensure that the integration process can send the purchase order as an IDoc. The sender side reuses the objects that were also used for synchronous processing. When sending the IDoc, the interface is used as an abstract interface in the integration process. The design objects used are listed in Table 5.15. Here, an asterisk (*) indicates that the object was created in a previous step.

Mapping the header data

First, import the `ORDERS.ORDERS01` IDoc in business system A. Create the service interface `SI_ORDERS_ORDERS_Asnyc_Abstract` based on this IDoc. The interface is abstract and is used for asynchronous communication. The incoming purchase order from Hitech AG must be converted into the order IDoc in this process. For this, you need a message mapping and an operation mapping between the two abstract interfaces.

Type of Object	Sender Side	Receiver Side
Service interface	SI_SalesOrder_Async_Abstract*	▸ SI_ORDERS_ORDERS_Asnyc_Abstract ▸ ORDER.ORDERS01
Message type	MT_SalesOrder*	ORDER.ORDERS01
Operation mapping	OM_SI_SalesOrder_Async_Abstract_to_SI_ORDERS_ORDERS_Asnyc_Abstract	
Message mapping	MM_MT_SalesOrder_to_ORDERS_ORDERS01	

Table 5.15 Design Objects for Asynchronous Processing in Step 3 of the Case Study

Accordingly, you must map the output message MT_SalesOrder to the ORDERS.ORDERS01 IDoc in message mapping MM_MT_SalesOrder_to_ORDERS_ORDERS01. You can assign the header data elements according to the following mapping table (see Table 5.16). Between the source and the target message, a mapping of the date and time values is necessary using the DateTrans function from the Date function area. This mapping concerns the source elements CreationDate, CreationTime and ValidTo, which are marked with an asterisk (*) in Table 5.16.

Data Element of MT_SalesOrder or Constants	Data Element of ORDERS.ORDERS01	Segment of ORDERS.ORDERS01
Constant: 1	BEGIN	None (IDOC)
Constant: OR (Standard order)	BSART	E1EDK01
DocumentNumber	BELNR	E1EDK01
Vendor	RECIPNT_NO	E1EDK01
Constant: 006 (Division)	QUALF	E1EDK14(1)
Constant: 00	ORGID	E1EDK14(1)
Constant: 007 (Distribution Channel)	QUALF	E1EDK14(2)
Constant: 10	ORGID	E1EDK14(2)
Constant: 008 (Sales Organization)	QUALF	E1EDK14(3)

Table 5.16 Assigning the Header Data in the Message Mapping of Step 3

379

Data Element of MT_SalesOrder or Constants	Data Element of ORDERS. ORDERS01	Segment of ORDERS. ORDERS01
Constant: 1000	ORGID	E1EDK14(3)
Constant: 004 (Quotation Deadline)	IDDAT	E1EDK03(1)
ValidTo	DATUM *	E1EDK03(1)
Constant: 012 (Creation Date)	IDDAT	E1EDK03(2)
CreationDate	DATUM *	E1EDK03(2)
Constant: AG (Sold-to Party)	PARVW	E1EDKA1
Customer	PARTN	E1EDKA1
Constant: 003 (Original Document Data)	QUALF	E1EDK02(1)
DocumentNumber	BELNR	E1EDK02(1)
CreationDate	DATUM *	E1EDK02(1)
CreationTime	UZEIT *	E1EDK02(1)
Constant: 007 (Collective Number)	QUALF	E1EDK02(2)
CollectiveNumber	BELNR	E1EDK02(2)

Table 5.16 Assigning the Header Data in the Message Mapping of Step 3 (Cont.)

In the work area, move the DateTrans function between the source and target elements and double-click on it to set the parameters. First, enter the Input Date Format yyyy-MM-dd. The Output Date Format is supposed to be structured according to the schema, yyyyMMdd.

The ValidTo and CollectiveNumber elements are optional in this case, but they can be used for a better orientation on the customer and supplier side. In addition to the mappings shown in Table 5.16, you must link each segment to be used, including its SEGMENT element on the target side, with the MT_SalesOrder node on the source side. Deactivate the nonmapped target segment EDI_DC40 in the menu and duplicate the target segments that are used several times using the context menu.

Mapping the item data

Item data mapping occurs according to Table 5.17. Note the elements marked with an asterisk (*). To create as many element instances as items exist, you must insert the node function `SplitByValue` between the source and target elements.

Data Element of MT_SalesOrder/Sales-OrderItem or Constants	Data Element of ORDERS.ORDERS01/E1EDP01	Segment of ORDERS.ORDERS01/E1EDP01
SalesOrderItem	E1EDP01	None (IDOC)
SalesOrderItem	SEGMENT *	E1EDP01
ItemNumber	POSEX	E1EDP01
Constant: 001 (Create)	ACTION	E1EDP01
Quantity	MENGE	E1EDP01
Constant: PCE (Unit of quantity: Piece)	MENEE	E1EDP01
NetWeight	NTGEW	E1EDP01
WeightUnit	GEWEI	E1EDP01
MaterialGroup	MATKL	E1EDP01
GrossWeight	BRGEW	E1EDP01
MaterialNumber	MATNR	E1EDP01
SalesOrderItem	E1EDP20 *	E1EDP01
SalesOrderItem	SEGMENT *	E1EDP01/ E1EDP20
Quantity	WMENG	E1EDP01/ E1EDP20
DeliveryDate	EDATU	E1EDP01/ E1EDP20
SalesOrderItem	E1EDP19 *	E1EDP01
SalesOrderItem	SEGMENT *	E1EDP01/E1EDP19
Constant: 001 (Description)	QUALF	E1EDP01/E1EDP19
MaterialNumber	IDTNR	E1EDP01/E1EDP19
Description	KTEXT	E1EDP01/E1EDP19

Table 5.17 Assigning the Item Data in the Message Mapping of Step 1

Test the mapping using at least two different order items by duplicating the node element using the menu in the Test tab. Save the mapping if the test is successful.

Based on this message mapping, create the corresponding operation mapping, `OM_SI_SalesOrder_Async_Abstract_to_SI_ORDERS_ORDERS_Asnyc_Abstract`. As the outbound operation, include the `SI_SalesOrder_Async_Abstract` interface and use the `SI_ORDERS_ORDERS_Asnyc_Abstract` interface as the target operation. Finally, import the interfaces and assign it the `MM_MT_SalesOrder_to_ORDERS_ORDERS01` message mapping you just created.

Creating the Integration Process

Creating the container elements

You have now created all of the design objects required for the integration process. Next, create the integration process `IP_SalesOrder_##` and ensure you have enough space on your screen for editing it.

First, create the following three container elements (see Figure 5.54):

▸ `SalesOrder` belongs to the ABSTRACT INTERFACE category and uses the `SI_SalesOrder_Async_Abstract` type. Once it has been called by the ABAP proxy, it will contain the order message in the purchase order.

▸ `Response` is also an ABSTRACT INTERFACE and uses the `SI_Response_Async_Abstract` type.

▸ `IDoc_SalesOrder` is also an ABSTRACT INTERFACE and uses the `SI_ORDERS_ORDERS01_Async_Abstract` type to send the order as a purchase order.

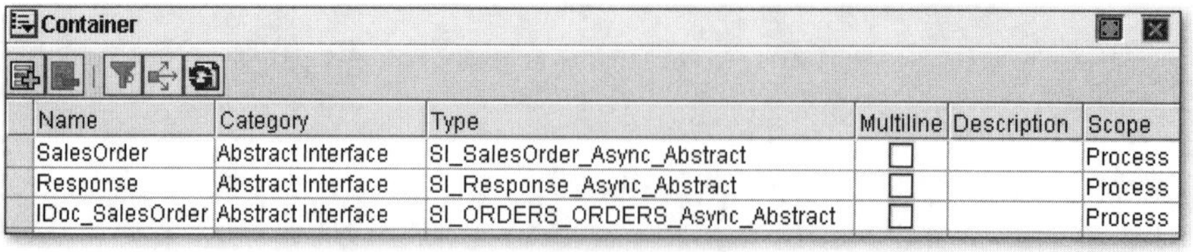

Name	Category	Type	Multiline	Description	Scope
SalesOrder	Abstract Interface	SI_SalesOrder_Async_Abstract	☐		Process
Response	Abstract Interface	SI_Response_Async_Abstract	☐		Process
IDoc_SalesOrder	Abstract Interface	SI_ORDERS_ORDERS_Async_Abstract	☐		Process

Figure 5.54 Container Elements of Step 3 of the Case Study

You may be surprised that we haven't yet created a container element of the `SI_SalesOrder_Sync_Abstract` abstract interface type; this is because messages received by the synchronous interface aren't explicitly used within the integration process. However, we'll now explain why you created the corresponding service interface.

Insert the first step for receiving the message in the process and call it RECEIVE PROXYCALL. This step is used to open the *sync-async-bridge*. Now select the OPENS S/A BRIDGE mode from the properties, which allows you to specify the synchronous interface, SI_SalesOrder_Sync_Abstract. However, the MESSAGE field does not expect any container element of a synchronous interface. Instead, it expects the message in which the input part (from the point of view of the process) of the synchronous interface is to be stored. In our case, that's the SalesOrder container element. Figure 5.55 displays the settings for the first step in the integration process.

Opening the sync-async-bridge

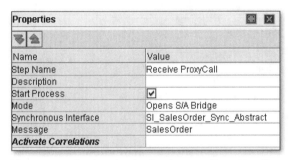

Figure 5.55 Settings for the Synchronous Reception Step

The next steps in the process consist of transforming the order into the IDoc and dispatching the IDoc. For this, you must insert a transformation step, called Create IDoc. Assign SalesOrder as the source message and IDoc_SalesOrder as the target message to the operation mapping OM_SI_SalesOrder_Async_Abstract_to_SI_ORDERS_ORDERS_Asnyc_Abstract. This mapping copies the order into the IDoc format. After that, insert the Send IDoc step, as you want to send the IDoc_SalesOrder message in asynchronous mode.

Delivering the IDoc

To close the open *sync-async-bridge*, you must generate and deliver the response message. To do this, you must include another transformation step at the end of the process. This step, Create Response, uses the operation mapping OM_SI_SalesOrder_Async_Abstract_to_SI_Response_

Closing the sync-async-bridge

Async_Abstract. After that, assign SalesOrder as the source message and Response as the target message to the step.

The final step to be carried out in the integration process is the sending step, which actually delivers the response. For this, you must attach a sending step to the end of the process and call it CLOSE BRIDGE (see Figure 5.56). Select the CLOSES S/A BRIDGE mode, which changes all other input fields, then select the Response message that is to be sent at this point. You can now specify the step that opened the bridge in the OPENED BY field. The input help contains the only existing reception step, RECEIVE PROXY CALL, which you must select as well.

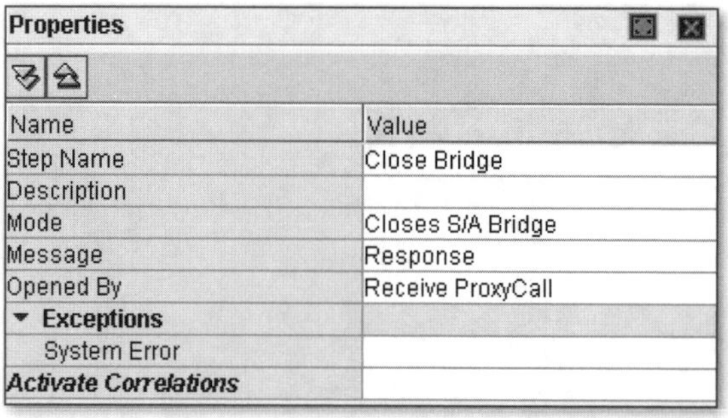

Properties	
Name	Value
Step Name	Close Bridge
Description	
Mode	Closes S/A Bridge
Message	Response
Opened By	Receive ProxyCall
▼ Exceptions	
System Error	
Activate Correlations	

Figure 5.56   Properties of the Closing Send Step

Save the integration process and check it using the corresponding option from the menu. If there aren't any errors, you can activate all of the design objects for this step of the case study via the change list.

5.3.3   Configuration

Due to the two send steps of the integration process, the configuration phase is divided into two parts. In the first, you must configure message delivery from the ABAP proxy to the integration process. Message delivery is a synchronous process, even though the two parts of the interface are processed separately. In the second, the second configuration scenario handles delivery of the IDoc to system A.

Declaring the integration process

Before you can begin with the two scenarios, you must declare the integration process in the integration directory. To do this, create the new integration process IP_SalesOrder_## in the COMMUNICATION COMPO-

NENT directory and import the process of the same name from the Enterprise Services Repository; assign it to your scenario, PI_CaseStudy_##.

Configuring the Synchronous Communication

Table 5.18 provides an overview of all of the configuration objects used in this scenario.

Configuring the ABAP proxy integration

Type of Object	Sender Side: System B/ ABAP Proxy	Receiver Side: IP_SalesOrder_##
Receiver determination	|SystemB|SI_SalesOrder_Sync_Out_##	
Interface determination	|SystemB|SI_SalesOrder_Sync_Out_##||IP_SalesOrder_##	

Table 5.18 Configuration Objects for Synchronous Communication in Step 3 of the Case Study

The ABAP proxy later appears as part of system B, which is why the proxy is considered an equal counterpart of system B in the following configuration steps. Open the Configuration Wizard and create an Internal Communication. The sender is business system B with the XI adapter. The ABAP proxy uses the PI format to communicate with the central Integration Engine (IE). Select interface SI_SalesOrder_Sync_Out_## from your namespace; the ABAP proxy will send data through this interface (see Figure 5.57).

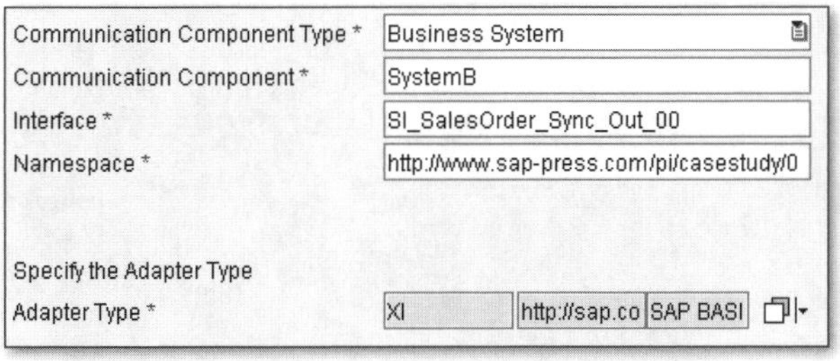

Communication Component Type *	Business System
Communication Component *	SystemB
Interface *	SI_SalesOrder_Sync_Out_00
Namespace *	http://www.sap-press.com/pi/casestudy/0
Specify the Adapter Type	
Adapter Type *	XI	http://sap.co	SAP BASI

Figure 5.57 Settings for the ABAP Proxy as a Sender

The message receiver is integration process IP_SalesOrder_##, which can only receive data via interface SI_SalesOrder_Sync_Abstract. You won't need a sender or receiver agreement. Note the creation of receiver determination |SystemB|SI_SalesOrder_Sync_Out_##, displayed in the subsequent step. The interface determination `|SystemB|SI_SalesOrder_Sync_Out_##||IP_SalesOrder_##` displayed in the screen that follows next does not display an operation mapping because both the interface being used and its abstract counterpart use the same messages in the integration process. As such, you won't need to carry out any assignments. Finally, add all of the objects to your scenario, `PI_CaseStudy_##`, and close the wizard.

Configuring the Asynchronous Communication

Configuration objects for the IDoc delivery

The second configuration scenario is also created using the Configuration Wizard. Table 5.19 provides an overview of the objects created or reused in this process. Here, an asterisk (*) indicates that the object was created in a previous step.

Open the Configuration Wizard to create another Internal Communication. The message with interface `SI_ORDERS_ORDERS01_Async_Abstract` is sent by integration process `IP_SalesOrder_##`. The IDoc receiver is business system A, which receives messages through the IDoc adapter in the `ORDERS.ORDERS01` interface. Because of the integration process, you don't need to create a sender agreement.

Type of Object	Sender Side: IP_SalesOrder_##	Receiver Side: System A
Communication channel		`IDoc_ReceiverChannel*`
Receiver agreement		`|IP_SalesOrder_## ||SystemA| ORDERS.ORDERS01`
Receiver determination	`|IP_SalesOrder_##|SI_ORDERS_ORDERS01_ Async_Abstract`	
Interface determination	`|IP_SalesOrder_##|SI_ORDERS_ORDERS01_ Async_Abstract||SystemA`	

Table 5.19 Configuration Objects for Asynchronous Communication in Step 3 of the Case Study

Details for creating the receiver determination `|IP_SalesOrder_##|SI_ORDERS_ORDERS01_Async_Abstract` are only used for information. The interface determination `|IP_SalesOrder_##|SI_ORDERS_ORDERS01_`

`Async_Abstract||SystemA` will not determine any mapping, because the sending and receiving interfaces use the same message type; the receiver agreement `|IP_SalesOrder_##||SystemA|ORDERS.ORDERS01` integrates communication channel `IDoc_ReceiverChannel` into the scenario. Save the configuration objects in your scenario.

If you completed this step of the case study using the configuration as presented up to this point, the IDoc can't be sent to system A, because SAP NetWeaver PI cannot deliver an IDoc from an integration process without further configuration. (This is because the `IP_SalesOrder_##` sender service cannot be mapped to a logical system for application link enabling (ALE) communication.)

Manual maintenance of the receiver determination

To avoid this problem, you must adjust the receiver agreement `|IP_SalesOrder_##||SystemA|ORDERS.ORDERS01`. Open the relevant object for editing, select the SENDER COMMUNICATION COMPONENT option in the HEADER MAPPING section, and then select business SYSTEMB (see Figure 5.58).

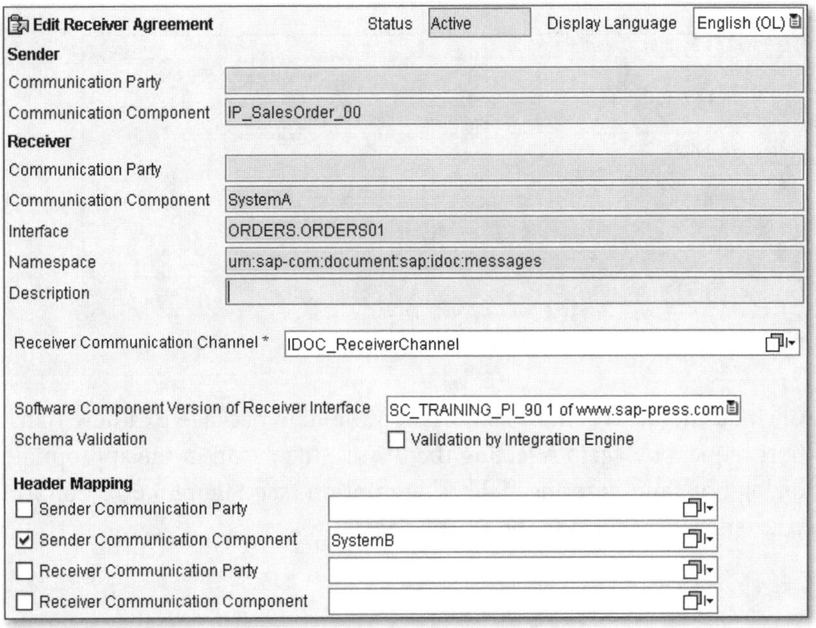

Figure 5.58 Manual Maintenance of the Receiver Agreement

This ensures that IDocs being sent from the integration process are treated as if they were sent from system B, which makes it possible for system A to process the order on the basis of the existing partner agreement.

Save the modified receiver agreement, and use the change list to activate all of the elements that have changed.

5.3.4 Process and Monitoring

The transmission of the order begins with generating an ABAP program in system B, which sends the sales order via an ABAP proxy. In preparation for the generation of the proxy, you must first create a development package.

Creation of a development package

Log on to system A, call Transaction SE80, and, from the middle-left choose package Z_PI_##. Because this package does not yet exist, you will be asked if you want to create it. Confirm this, and give the new package a meaningful description (see Figure 5.59).

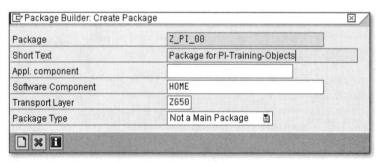

Figure 5.59 Creation of the Development Package

Click on the BLANK SHEET icon. Assign the new package to a new transport request by again selecting the BLANK SHEET icon in the appropriate dialog box, and entering a short description (see Figure 5.60). Confirm your entries by clicking the OK button.

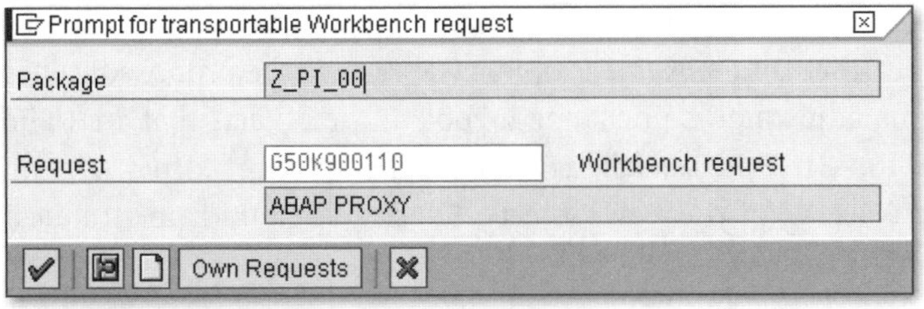

Figure 5.60 Selection of the Transport Request

Call Transaction SPROXY. Navigate within your software component version in your namespace to the path MESSAGE INTERFACE (OUTBOUND), and then create the proxy via the context menu of the interface SI_SalesOrder_Sync_Out_## (see Figure 5.61).

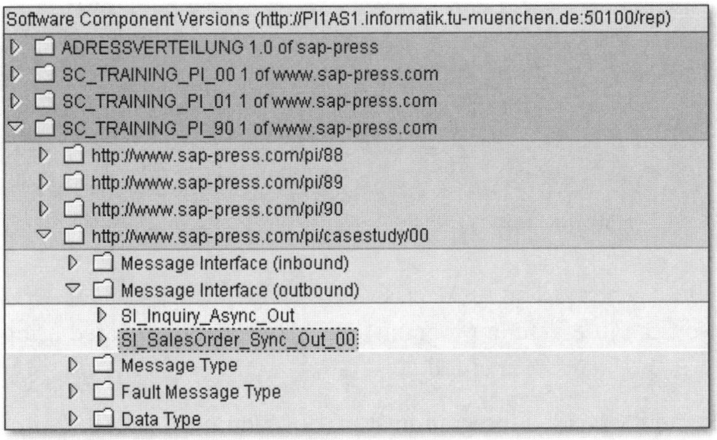

Creation of the ABAP outbound proxy

Figure 5.61 Selecting the Message Interface in the Software Component Version

Specify package Z_PI_## and the prefix ZPI## (see Figure 5.62).

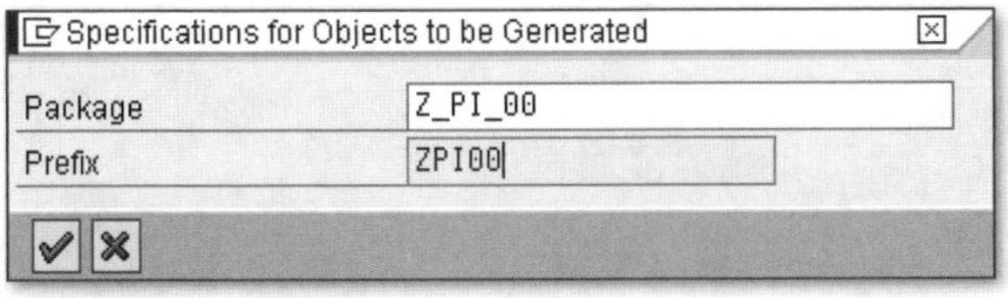

Figure 5.62 Entry of the Generation Data

389

You are then informed about possible naming conflicts and truncations, which you can see on the Name Problems tab. Leave the proposed values for the name adjustments unchanged. Look at the objects that are to be created on the GENERATION tab, and follow the PROXY • ACTIVATE menu path to activate all of the new objects. Specify your transport request (see Figure 5.63).

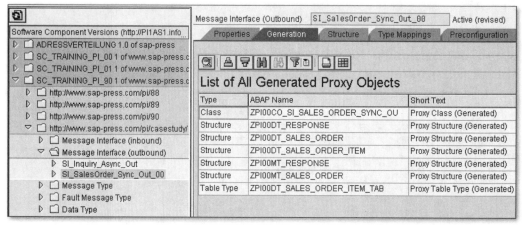

Figure 5.63 Activating the Proxy

You have now generated an ABAP class, ZPI##CO_SI_SALES_ORDER_SYNC_OU, that you can integrate in programs. The class can be executed using the EXECUTE_SYNCHRONOUS method.

Creating messages To test the newly created integration scenarios, you need an ABAP program in system B, which calls the imported proxy. Switch back to Transaction SE80 to create a new program in Z_PI_ # # via the context menu (see Figure 5.64). Name it according to the schema Z_PI_##_SALESORDER_OUTBOUND, and create it without a TOP include.

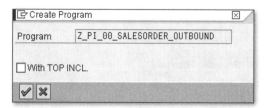

Figure 5.64 Creating a New Program

Set the program to Test status and assign it to your package and transport request. Paste the code that you find in Appendix A, and adjust your training and participant number. Save and activate the program. Run the program from the context menu (see Figure 5.65).

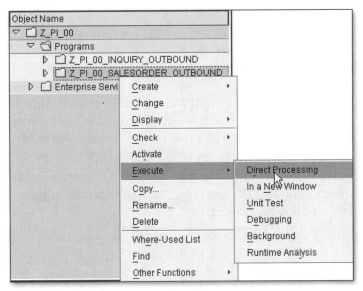

Figure 5.65 Running the Created ABAP Program

Once the data is set, you must attach the items and dispatch the order. Because the call used here is synchronous, the call's return value is assigned to an instance of the response format. If successful, the system displays a message that reads: PurchaseOrder-## created. You must create the document number according to the schema `PurchaseOrder-##`, because you will refer to it again in the next step of the case study.

The best way to monitor delivery is to use SAP NetWeaver PI's message monitoring tool. However, this tool only allows you to monitor the delivery of the IDoc because the integration process was called by a synchronous call. In addition, you can use Transaction SXMB_MONI_BPE in the SAP NetWeaver PI system if one of the process steps fails.

Monitoring the message path

The evidence that the IDoc has been processed correctly can be found in Transaction BD87 of business system A. If the IDoc is correctly received and processed, you can view the sales order. Call Transaction VA03 and open the input help of the Order input field. Select the search template, Sales documents by customer, and enter the purchase order number PurchaseOrder-## as the search criterion. Select your order from the list that displays by double-clicking on it. The purchase order number is then copied into the first screen; you can confirm your entries by pressing Enter.

5.4   Delivering the Invoice

Flow of Step 4

The penultimate step in the case study involves delivering the invoice for the purchase order via email. This allows Hitech AG to enter incoming invoices into their system in real time. The scenario is structured in such a way that SARIDIS automatically creates an IDoc with the invoice. This IDoc is then sent to SAP NetWeaver PI, where it is converted into an HTML document using an XSLT mapping. The HTML document is then sent to Hitech AG using the mail adapter.

Figure 5.66 illustrates the flow of this part of the scenario.

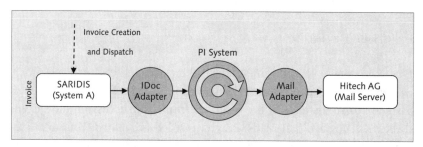

Figure 5.66   Flow of Step 4

5.4.1   Basic Principles

Realistic sales process

Those of you who have already processed sales orders in SAP R/3 or SAP ECC may know that the receipt of the purchase order is not immediately followed by the creation of the invoice. However, as we want to continue the case study in this book in a way that makes sense, we won't map the missing processes via SAP NetWeaver PI. You will work through them manually during the course of the scenario and, for example, deliver the ordered goods by yourself.

Integrating IDoc creation into the invoicing transaction is handled by the outbound parameters of the already-existing partner agreement with Hitech AG. For this, you must log in to system A as the instructor, and call Transaction WE20. Navigate to partner agreement 1171, which is located in the PARTN. TYPE KU folder. Create a new outbound parameter by clicking on the icon below the list of all existing outbound parameters, enter PARTNER ROLE BP (bill-to party), and select message type INVOIC (invoice/billing document).

Maintaining the partner agreement

To dispatch the IDoc, use the PI_SYSTEM receiver port that you created while preparing for the technical exercises. The IDocs are supposed to be transferred immediately. The basic type you will use for the invoice is INVOIC01. Figure 5.67 displays the settings to create the outbound parameter.

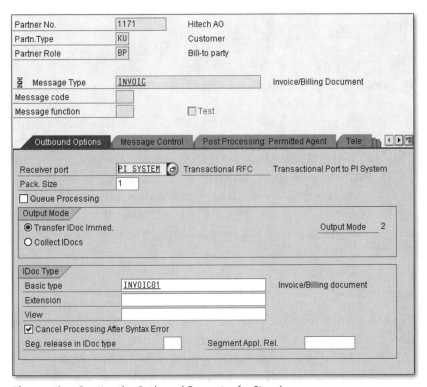

Figure 5.67 Creating the Outbound Parameter for Step 4

Go to the MESSAGE CONTROL tab. The system notifies you that the package size was set to 1. This means that IDoc packages are sent as soon as they contain one IDoc. Add a new row by clicking on the corresponding icon below the list and selecting V3 (Billing) in the APPLICATION column (see Figure 5.68). Because the message type to be used is an invoice, enter RD00 in the corresponding column. Because the invoice will be sent to a customer, you must select SD09 as the only possible process code. Save the modified partner agreement.

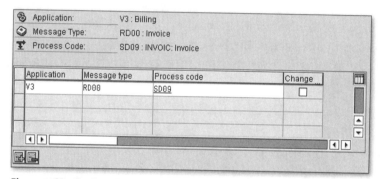

Figure 5.68 Setting Message Control for the Dispatch of the Invoice

Providing a mail server

Dispatching emails from SAP NetWeaver PI does not require any specific preparations on the side of the PI system. You can send messages via Simple Mail Transfer Protocol (SMTP) and Internet Message Access Protocol (IMAP) 4 by specifying the relevant mail server. The "extension" of the training landscape with such a server should not pose a problem, especially because you can integrate mail providers that are generally accessible. As such, you do not need to operate a separate server for this scenario.

5.4.2 Design

Overview of the design objects

You will see that from the point of view of design objects, this scenario does not differ much from the other steps. The type and quantity of objects is comparable, but the sources of some objects are different from those used in other scenarios. For example, you will obtain the data type for the email from SAP Service Marketplace, create the XSLT mapping externally, and import it at a later stage. Table 5.20 provides an overview of all of the design objects.

Type of Object	Sender Side	Receiver Side
Service interface	`INCOIC.INVOIC01`	`SI_Mail_Async_In`
Message type		`Mail`
Data type		
Operation mapping	`OM_INVOIC_INVOIC01_to_SI_Mail_Async_In`	
Message mapping	`MM_INVOIC_INVOIC01_to_Mail`	

Table 5.20 Design Objects for Step 4 of the Case Study

Due to the fact that an IDoc is used, you can quickly create the objects on the sender side. Import the definition of IDoc `INVOIC.INVOIC01` from system A.

Import the IDoc interface

You don't need to create the `Mail` data type by yourself; you can import it from an XSD file. You can obtain this file from SAP Note 748024 in SAP Service Marketplace (*http://service.sap.com*). This file contains numerous data types for using the mail adapter. Appendix A contains a simplified version that only contains the `Mail` data type.

Creating the objects on the receiver side

Go to the Enterprise Services Repository and navigate to your namespace to create a new external definition called `Mail_XSD`. Select the XSD category and import the corresponding file from your system (see Figure 5.69). If you go to the MESSAGES tab now, you will see that — depending on the file version you use — it at least contains the `Mail` message. Save the external definition.

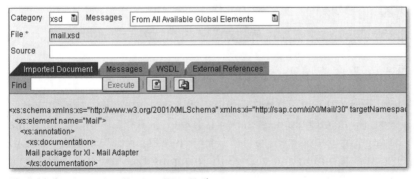

Figure 5.69 Importing Message Type Mail

Based on this message definition, create the service interface `SI_Mail_Async_In`, which uses the `Mail` message you just imported. The type of the interface is `Inbound` and is addressed in `asynchronous` mode. Save the service interface.

Creating the mapping objects

You won't create the message mapping for this scenario in the Integration Builder. Instead, import it as an XSLT file. You can find a template for this file in Appendix A and on the book's website (*http://www.sap-press.com*).

The mapping has the following effect: First, it contains the mail addresses for the sender and receiver. These addresses are firmly defined in our example, but you can also fill them dynamically. In addition, the `Subject` field of the mail is assigned the invoice number located in the IDoc. The mail content itself primarily consists of a table that displays the ordered objects, including some item data and the prices.

The XSLT file you created (or downloaded) must be included in an archive file. In this context, it doesn't make any difference if the archive file is a ZIP or a JAR file.

In the enterprise services repository, navigate to your namespace and follow the MAPPING OBJECTS • IMPORTED ARCHIVE menu path; create a new object called `Mail_XSLT_Mapping` using the context menu. Select the archive that contains the XSLT file, `MM_INVOIC_INVOIC01_to_Mail.xsl` (see Figure 5.70), and save the archive object.

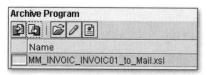

Figure 5.70 Selecting the XSL File

Next, create the operation mapping `OM_INVOIC_INVOIC01_to_SI_Mail_Async_In`. Its outbound operation is IDoc type `INVOIC.INVOIC01`, while the target operation is `SI_Mail_Async_In` (see Figure 5.71). Click the READ OPERATIONS button and change the mapping type to XSL in the list of mapping programs. Open the input help and select the message mapping `MM_INVOIC_INVOIC01_to_Mail` from the archive, `Mail_XSLT_Mapping`.

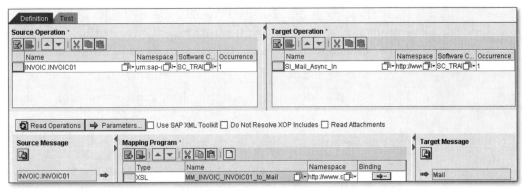

Figure 5.71 Operation Mapping for Step 4

Save and test the operation mapping. While doing this, you should create several duplicates of the source segment, E1EDP01. Although the display of the target message cannot show the finished HTML document, you can still check to see if the relevant fields are filled with data. If the test is successful, you should activate all of the new design objects using the change list.

5.4.3   Configuration

You will now need a mail receiver channel for each student. In this channel, you must specify the SMTP or IMAP server, and additional logon data. At first glance, this step's configuration seems easy, as it can be quickly done using the wizard. While this is indeed the case, you must take into account the fact that, presumably, not all training participants use the same mail provider.

New configuration objects

When the message is received by SAP NetWeaver PI, you can use the purchase order of the IDoc (PurchaseOrder-##) to determine which participant has sent the message. However, the question now is which receiver — and hence which communication channels — are available. The number of available business systems is not enough to provide a separate business system as a mail receiver for each student.

To solve this problem, you'll need to create business components that allow every student to use a separate communication channel. By creating a separate business component for each student, you can specify separate recipients for the email. You already used this method in Step 2 of the case study, although it wasn't necessary at that stage. Now we do need this object, to obtain different targets and thus different communication channels in the receiver determination.

Table 5.21 provides an overview of all of the configuration objects used.

Type of Object	Receiver Side: System A	Sender Side: Mail_Server_##
Communication channel		`Mail_Receiver`
Sender agreement	`| SystemA | INVOIC. INVOIC01|*|*`	
Receiver agreement		`|SystemA||Mail_ Server_##|SI_Mail_ Async_In`
Receiver determination	`|SystemA|INVOIC.INVOIC01`	
Interface determination	`|SystemA|INVOIC.INVOIC01||Mail_Server_##`	

Table 5.21 Elements in the Integration Directory of Step 4 in the Case Study

Creating a business component

Log in to the Integration Directory and create business component `Mail_Server_##`. Assign it to your `PI_CaseStudy_##` scenario, and then assign `SI_Mail_Async_In` from your namespace `http://www.sap-press.com/pi/casestudy/##` to it as an Inbound interface. Save the new business component.

Creating the mail communication channel

Follow the COMMUNICATION COMPONENT • BUSINESS COMPONENT menu path and make sure that your new component is actually there. Create the `Mail_Receiver` communication channel, set the MAIL adapter type, and define the RECEIVER direction. Specify the TRANSPORT PROTOCOL used by your mail server. In most cases, you can connect to a mail server via SMTP.

For the MESSAGE PROTOCOL, you can choose between XIALL and XIPAYLOAD. You can select the first option if the contents of the RFC822-compliant email are identical to the contents of the PI message. In that case, the PI message is a multipart MIME message whose first part contains the SOAP envelope. In the example, select the second option, XIPAYLOAD (see Figure 5.72), in which the email is used as the message payload.

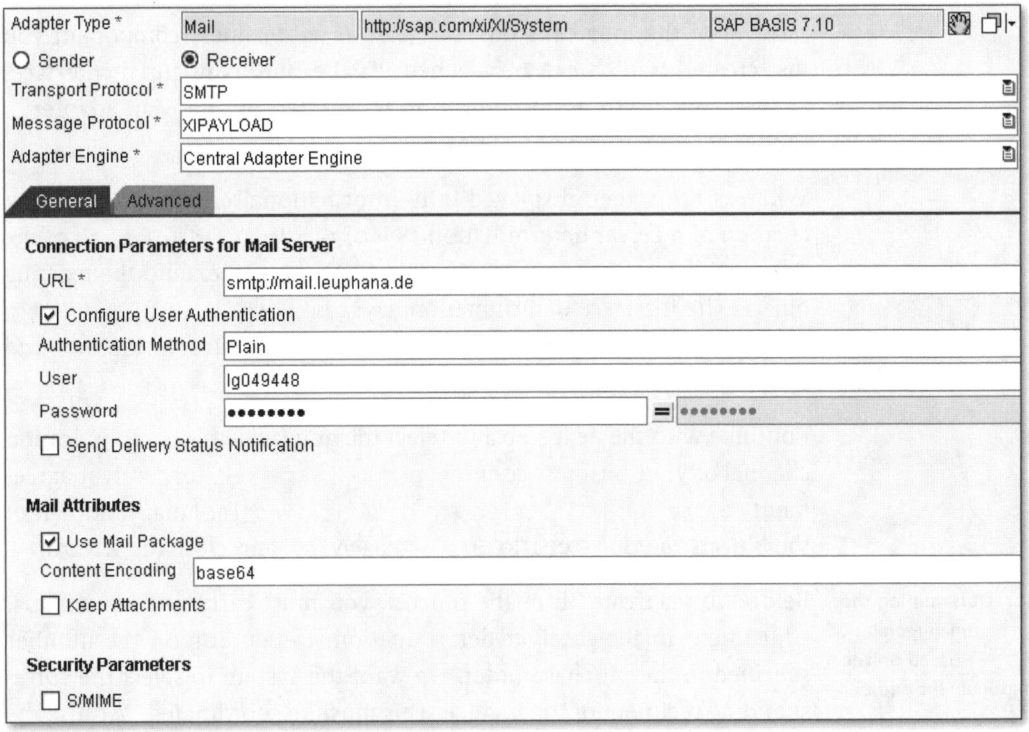

Adapter Type *	Mail	http://sap.com/xi/XI/System	SAP BASIS 7.10	
○ Sender	◉ Receiver			
Transport Protocol *	SMTP			
Message Protocol *	XIPAYLOAD			
Adapter Engine *	Central Adapter Engine			

General ⟍ Advanced

Connection Parameters for Mail Server

URL *	smtp://mail.leuphana.de
☑ Configure User Authentication	
Authentication Method	Plain
User	lg049448
Password	•••••••• = ••••••••
☐ Send Delivery Status Notification	

Mail Attributes

☑ Use Mail Package	
Content Encoding	base64
☐ Keep Attachments	

Security Parameters

☐ S/MIME

Figure 5.72 Settings for the Mail Receiver Channel

Enter the URL for your mail server in the CONNECTION PARAMETERS FOR MAIL SERVER section. If you use SMTP, the URL starts with the prefix *smtp://*, whereas if you use IMAP, it begins with *imap://*. If necessary, you can also select a user authentication by activating the corresponding option.

You must also make sure that the USE MAIL PACKAGE option is activated in the MAIL ATTRIBUTES section. This setting is necessary so that header data (such as the sender, receiver, and message subject) can also be read from the payload. Select content coding BASE64 and save the communication channel.

Calling the
Configuration
Wizard

Open the Configuration Wizard and create another Internal Communication. Specify business system A as the sender, and select the IDoc adapter. The type of the dispatched IDoc is INCOIC.INVOIC01. The receiver of the invoice is the Mail_Server_## business component you just created, which can be reached via the only configured interface, SI_Mail_Async_In. Communication is handled by the Mail adapter; a sender agreement is not necessary.

Whereas the screen displayed only informational data during the first creation of receiver determination |SystemA|INVOIC.INVOIC01, all of the other students must now specify that they want to extend the existing object. The interface determination |SystemA|INVOIC.INVOIC01||Mail_Server_## should already display the correct mapping to the inbound interface SI_Mail_Async_In.

Continue with the next step and select the only available communication channel of your business component, Mail_Receiver, for receiver agreement |SystemA||Mail_Server_##|SI_Mail_Async_In. Finally, add all of the objects to your scenario, PI_CaseStudy_##, and close the wizard.

Determining the
email recipient
based on the
document number

Before you activate all of the objects, you must carry out one manual adjustment in the receiver determination. Depending on the number specified in the purchase order, we want the system to select the corresponding recipient of the invoice. This must be coordinated, because the students will block each other in the following step.

For this, navigate to receiver determination |SystemA|INVOIC.INVOIC01 and open it in editing mode. Go to the line that contains your business component, click in the Condition column, and open the input help to launch the Expression Editor. Select the IDoc field INVOIC/IDOC/E1EDK02/BELNR as the left operand, and set the right operand to the value PurchaseOrder-##. Make sure that the operator being used is an equals sign (=). Insert a second condition by clicking on the corresponding icon. Here, you should select the IDoc field /INVOIC01/IDOC/E1EDK02/QUALF for the left operand and set the value of the right operand to 001. Figure 5.73 displays these settings.

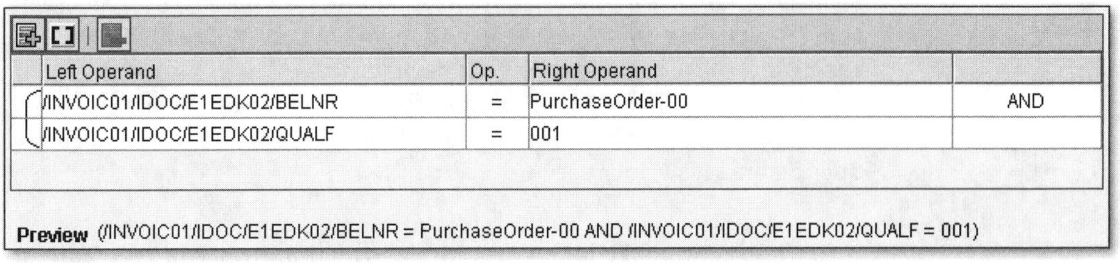

Left Operand	Op.	Right Operand	
/INVOIC01/IDOC/E1EDK02/BELNR	=	PurchaseOrder-00	AND
/INVOIC01/IDOC/E1EDK02/QUALF	=	001	

Preview (/INVOIC01/IDOC/E1EDK02/BELNR = PurchaseOrder-00 AND /INVOIC01/IDOC/E1EDK02/QUALF = 001)

Figure 5.73 Settings in the Expression Editor

These two conditions ensure that the segment E1EDK02 is evaluated for delivery only if the instance of the segment contains the purchase order number due to the qualifier. The purchase order number, however, must contain a specific value.

Copy the condition and save the receiver determination. You can now activate all of the new configuration objects.

5.4.4 Process and Monitoring

The process of the scenario begins by creating the invoice on the basis of the sales order that has been received. Invoice creation presupposes that the goods have first been delivered. Moreover, you will track the message path once its dispatch has been triggered, and verify that it has been received as an email.

Flow of the Scenario

To create an invoice that refers to the purchase order you received in the previous step, you must first carry out two additional steps that have not been implemented using SAP NetWeaver PI. These two steps consist of creating an outbound delivery and a transfer order, and picking the goods. The steps are necessary because, by default, you can only invoice orders that have been delivered.

Creating an outbound delivery

> **Note**
>
> If you did not create a purchase order in Step 3 of the case study, you can manually enter a sales order via Transaction VA01. To do this, use the order type OR (Standard Order), sales organization 1000, distribution channel 10, and division 00. Confirm your entries by pressing the [Enter] key and specify customer 1171 (Hitech AG) as the sold-to and ship-to party. Select purchase order number PurchaseOrder-## and fill the item list with items and quantities before saving your entries.

Go to Transaction VL01N in system A, which allows you to create an outbound delivery for a specific sales order. Enter 1200 (Dresden) as the shipping point and a date in about two weeks' time from now as the selection date.

To find the number of your sales order, open the input help and navigate to the search template, Sales documents by customer. Enter the PurchaseOrder-## in the Purchase Orders no. field and run the search. Double-click on your order in the list that displays. This copies the order number into the corresponding field, allowing you to confirm your entries. You can now check all of the details for the last time before the dispatch is triggered (see Figure 5.74); save the document.

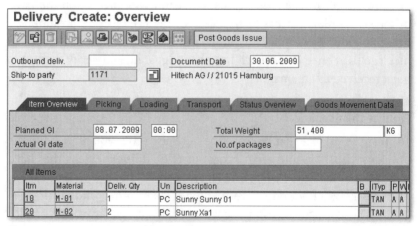

Figure 5.74 Creating an Outbound Delivery

The goods issue that has been triggered by the outbound delivery still requires a transfer order before it can be completed. To do this, call Transaction LT03, which should already display the outbound delivery you just created. Set the warehouse number to 012 (Dresden) in the IDES system. Make sure that the ACTIVATE ITEM option is activated in the CONTROL section (see Figure 5.75). Select BACKGROUND as FOREGROUND/ BACKGRND, which means that some transactions will be called and processed in the background. In addition, set Option 2 in the ADOPT PICK. QUANTITY field to make sure that a goods issue is also posted automatically. Confirm your entries and wait until the system notifies you that a transfer order has been created.

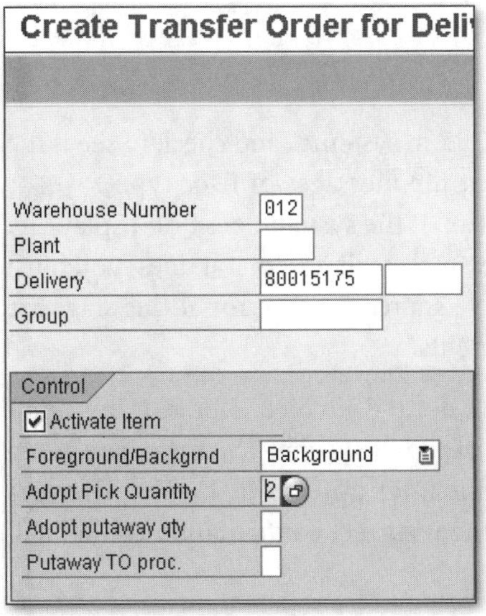

Creating a transfer order for shipping

Create Transfer Order for Deli

Warehouse Number	012
Plant	
Delivery	80015175
Group	

Control
☑ Activate Item

Foreground/Backgrnd	Background
Adopt Pick Quantity	2
Adopt putaway qty	
Putaway TO proc.	

Figure 5.75 Creating a Transfer Order for Shipping

Now you can eventually create the invoice for the sales order that has been delivered. To do this, go to Transaction VF01. The transaction displays the outbound delivery you created. Confirm the selection by pressing the ⌈Enter⌉ key. The system now lists all of the items to be invoiced (see Figure 5.76). Follow the GOTO • HEADER • OUTPUT menu path, and set the 6 EDI medium for partner 1171. Follow the EDIT • FURTHER DATA menu path to ensure the message is sent immediately. Return to the message overview and save the invoice. As soon as you save the invoice, the IDoc is automatically dispatched and converted into an email.

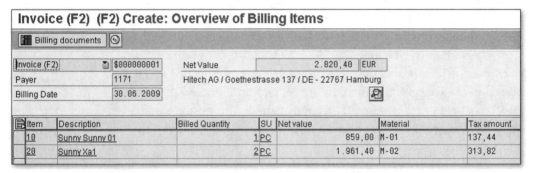

Figure 5.76 Creating the Invoice

Monitoring the Scenario

You should first call Transaction BD87 in system A and check to see if the IDoc was sent correctly. Verify that the messages of IDoc type `INVOIC`. `INVOIC01` are displayed in the outbox. If the system does not display any errors, you can move on to the next monitoring step; if it does, you must analyze the error messages. Possible sources of an error at this stage are primarily incorrect partner agreements.

Due to the asynchronous send mode, the invoice IDoc can be monitored in the *Message Monitoring* of the PI system. The message should go through without any significant interruptions or breaks. If errors occur, they probably result from the incorrect configuration of the mail adapter.

You can check the adapter by opening the Adapter Monitoring function in the Runtime Workbench and selecting the mail adapters. Unfortunately, you can only determine whether or not the configuration is correct, and whether messages have already been processed; the display is not as comprehensive as the display used for the file adapter.

The ultimate and most secure step when checking the successful dispatch of the invoice is to take a look into your own mailbox. There you should have received an email that, depending on the email client, should look similar to the one shown in Figure 5.77.

| Invoice 0090035131 | | | | |

We will charge the following positions:

Productnumber	Description	Quantity	Unit	Price
M-01	Sunny Sunny 01	10.000	PCE	9964.40 EUR
M-02	Sunny Xa1	20.000	PCE	22752.24 EUR
M-03	Sunny Tetra13	30.000	PCE	32882.52 EUR

Figure 5.77   Invoice in the Inbox

5.5   Manual Decision on Queries

Assume that SARIDIS is experiencing an economic upswing, and that production can no longer satisfy all incoming requests. Accordingly, SARIDIS has decided to examine incoming queries to ensure that they can fulfill them, and, in consultation with production, has also decided to refuse queries if necessary. For the purpose of simplicity, assume that Hitech AG need not be informed about refused queries.

Enhancement of the integration scenario

To implement this new process, the current integration scenario must be adapted. The software engineers at SARIDIS have decided to adapt the first step of the integration scenarios (see Section 5.1) and enhance it with a manual user decision.

The manual user decision is a new step type that is available in the integration processes with release PI 7.1.[4] Up to now, such steps had to be fully implemented by a developer using asynchronous messages. The new step type allows you to integrate manual decisions with minimal effort into new or existing integration processes. The end-user controls the manual user decision in the SAP Business Workplace.

Manual user decision

---

4   If you worked with SAP Business Workflow before, you know the step type already.

In this section, the SARIDIS case study will be enhanced with a manual user decision in the first step, the inquiry entry. So far this step has worked with a direct communication between system B (Hitech AG) and system A (SARIDIS). At this point, a new integration process has to be installed for the manual user decision (see Figure 5.78). To do this, the configuration from Section 5.1 has to be removed (see Table 5.22).

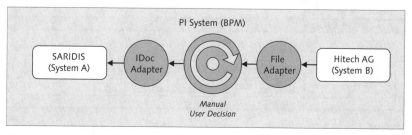

Figure 5.78   Change of Step 1

Type of Object	Name
Sender agreement	`|SystemB|SI_Inquiry_Async_Out||`
Receiver determination	`|SystemB|SI_Inquiry_Async_Out`
Receiver agreement	`|SystemB||SystemA|REQUOTE:ORDERS01`
Interface determination	`|SystemB|SI_Inquiry_Async_Out||SystemA`

Table 5.22   Configuration Objects to be Removed

5.5.1   Basic Principles

The configuration scenarios used in the Integration Builder allow you to display the configuration objects for a specific sender/receiver communication, which in turn allows you to find out very quickly which objects you need to delete.

Open the Integration Builder and your configuration scenario PI_CAS-ESTUDY_##. On the CONFIGURATION OVERVIEW tab, choose the sender interface SI_Inquiry_Async_out with the receiver interface REQOTE. ORDERS01, below the sender SYSTEMB and the receiver SYSTEMA (see Figure 5.79). In the right pane of the Integration Builder, all configuration objects are displayed. Delete all of the objects except the communication channels; these can still be used, and thus require no modification. After you delete the existing configuration objects, activate your change list.

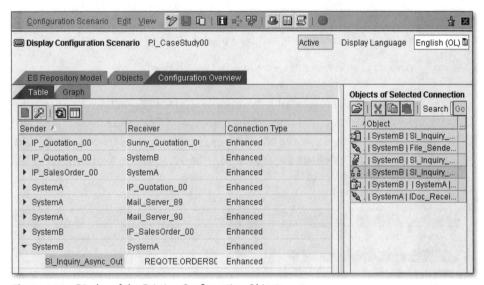

Figure 5.79 Display of the Existing Configuration Objects

5.5.2 Design

In the Enterprise Service Builder, many of the objects created in Section 5.1 can be reused; there are only a few new service interfaces and operation mappings needed for the integration process.

Abstract service-interfaces

Integration processes never work with a service interface of the Inbound or Outbound type; rather, they work with Abstract service interfaces. Whether an abstract service interface is actually used for outbound or inbound calls is implicitly determined in the business process, through the use of abstract service interfaces in a sending or receiving step.

Create all of the new objects in the namespace http://www.sap-press. com/pi/casestudy/##, which already exists. An overview of all of the objects that are created in this chapter can be found in Table 5.23.

Type of Object	Name
Service interface	SI_Inquiry_Async_Abstract
	SI_REQOTE_ORDERS01_Abstract
Operation mapping	OM_SI_Inquiry_Async_Abstract_to_SI_REQOTE_ORDERS01_Abstract
Integration process	IP_Inquiry_##

Table 5.23 New Elements for the Manual User Decision

Service interfaces   Start with the creation of new service interfaces. Switch to the Enterprise Services Builder, and select your namespace. There, create a new service interface with the name SI_Inquiry_Async_Abstract (see Figure 5.80). The interface defines the input file with the inquiry of Hitech AG in the integration process.

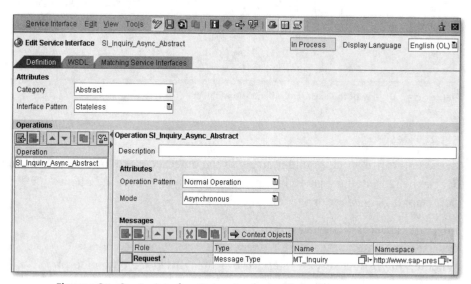

Figure 5.80 Service Interface SI_Inquiry_Async_Abstract

Select the Abstract and Stateless CATEGORY for the INTERFACE PATTERN. Add MT_Inquiry from your namespace as the request message type. Save your changes.

If the user decides to accept an inquiry, an IDoc with the inquiry will be sent from the integration process to the SARIDIS system (system A). Create another service interface with the name SI_REQOTE_ORDERS01_ Abstract in your namespace. Select the Abstract and Stateless CAT-EGORY for the INTERFACE PATTERN. Assign the message REQOTE.ORDERS01 of type IDoc to the request. Save the changes.

The next step is to create an operation mapping to map the input file to the IDoc. The existing message mapping MM_MT_Inquiry_to_REQOTE_ ORDERS01, which performs the mapping of message type MT_Inquiry and the IDoc message REQOTE.ORDERS01, can be reused. Now create a new operation mapping called OM_SI_Inquiry_Async_Abstract_to_ SI_REQOTE_ORDERS01_Abstract (see Figure 5.81). Enter the SI_Inquiry_ Async_Abstract service interface as the source operation, and the SI_ REQOTE_ORDERS01_Abstract service interface out of your namespace, as the target operation.

Operation mapping

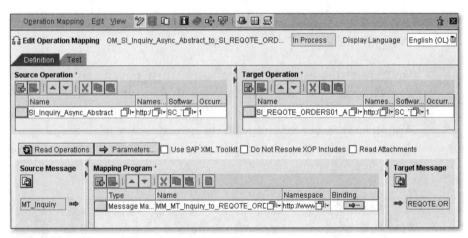

Figure 5.81 Operation Mapping OM_SI_Inquiry_Async_Abstract_to_SI_REQOTE_ ORDERS01_Abstract

After you specify the source and target operating in your operation mapping, click the READ OPERATIONS button in the bottom pane. After that, the MT_Inquiry message should appear in the lower screen area as the source message, and the REQOTE.ORDERS01 message as the target message. If this is not the case, recheck the previous steps. Now select the existing mapping program `MM_MT_Inquiry_to_REQOTE_ORDERS01` from your namespace, and save your changes.

Integration process In the last step of the Enterprise Services Builder, you create the integration process for the reception of the inquiry. In your namespace, set up a new integration process with the name `IP_Inquiry_##` (see Figure 5.82).

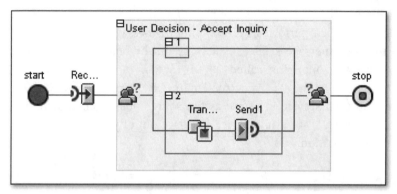

Figure 5.82 Integration Process IP_Inquiry_##

First, create the needed container in the new integration process. In the container box, add a new entry with the name `inquiry`, the category ABSTRACT INTERFACE, and the type `SI_Inquiry_Async_Abstract`. Also, create a new container with the name `inquiry_idoc`, the category ABSTRACT INTERFACE, and the type `SI_REQOTE_ORDERS01_Abstract` for the IDoc inquiry (see Figure 5.83).

Name	Category	Type	Multiline	Description	Scope
inquiry	Abstract Interface	SI_Inquiry_Async_Abstract	☐		Process
inquiry_idoc	Abstract Interface	SI_REQOTE_ORDERS01_Ab...	☐		Process

Figure 5.83 Container of Integration Process IP_Inquiry_##

For the user decision, you also need a configurable parameter that contains the user name of the person responsible for accepting the inquiry. This parameter is similar to a container, but has a special typification, and can later be adjusted individually in the Integration Builder.

Switch to the CONFIGURABLE PARAMETERS view in the Container window. Create a new parameter with the name `agent` and category AGENT (see Figure 5.84).

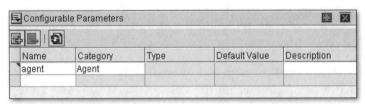

Figure 5.84 Configurable Parameters of Integration Process IP_Inquiry_##

Now add the required steps to the process; first, a new receive step, RECEIVE1, for the reception of the inquiry. Activate the START PROCESS switch in the step properties. Set the MODE to `Asynchronous`, and, for the MESSAGE property, select `inquiry` from the container (see Figure 5.85).

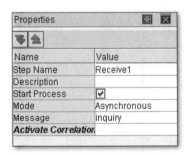

Figure 5.85 Properties of Step Receive1

Next, add a User Decision step called USER DECISION – ACCEPT INQUIRY. Enter the step name USER DECISION – ACCEPT INQUIRY and the configurable parameters `agent` as AGENT. Now the decision alternatives of the user decision are defined.

> **Note**
>
> After adding the user decision to the integration process, it has two decision alternatives. If you want to add more decision alternatives or delete existing alternatives, open the context menu of the step. The same method is used for multiple conditions.

Define decision alternative 1 by setting the decision text to DECLINE and the outcome name to END in the step properties. Define decision alternative 2 by setting the decision text to ACCEPT and the outcome name to NEXT in the step properties. With this, the definition of the manual user decision is completed (see Figure 5.86).

Now add a transformation step with the name TRANSFORM1 in decision alternative 2 of the user decision. Select `OM_SI_Inquiry_Async_Abstract_to_SI_REQOTE_ORDERS01_Abstract` from your namespace as the operation mapping in the step properties, and select the source and target message for the transformation. As a source message, select the container element `inquiry` and, as a target message, the container element `inquiry_idoc` (see Figure 5.87).

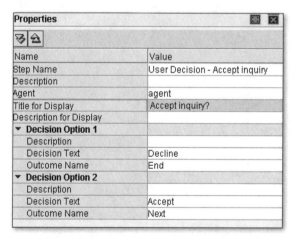

Figure 5.86 Properties of the Step User Decision – Accept Inquiry

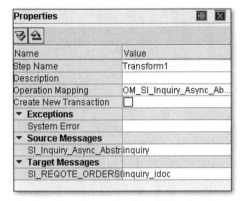

Figure 5.87 Properties of Step Transform1

Finally, add a send step called SEND1 after the previously created transformation step. Select the container element `inquiry_idoc` for the MESSAGE step property (see Figure 5.88).

Properties

Name	Value
Step Name	Send1
Description	
Mode	Asynchronous
Create New Transaction	☐
Message	inquiry_idoc
Acknowledgment	None
Receiver From	Send Context
Conversation ID	
Queue Name (EOIO)	
Send Context	
▼ Exceptions	
System Error	
Activate Correlations	

Figure 5.88 Properties of Step Send1

The definition of the integration process is now complete, and further activities in the Enterprise Services Builder are not required. Save all objects, and activate your change list.

5.5.3 Configuration

Integration process

To configure the objects that have been created in the Enterprise Services Builder, open the Integration Builder. Start with the configuration of the integration process and then go on with the configuration of the messages.

Open the Communication component node in the Objects tab. Right-click on the Integration Process node, and select New from the context menu. You will see a pop-up window with the title Introduction. Confirm this by clicking on the Continue button.

In the next dialog box, you'll see a list of available integration processes from the Enterprise Services Builder. Select the integration process IP_Inquiry_## from your namespace http://www.sap-press.com/pi/casestudy/##. In the lower pane, select your configuration scenario PI_CASESTUDY_##. Click on the CONTINUE button and on the FINISH button in the next dialog box (see Figure 5.89).

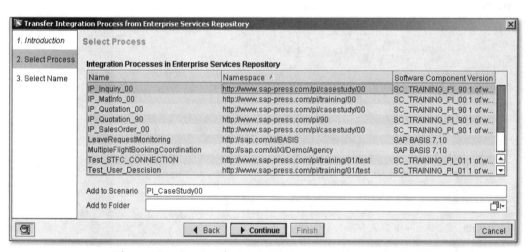

Figure 5.89 Creating the Integration Process as Communication Component

As a result, you can now see a new node named IP_Inquiry_## under the COMMUNICATION COMPONENT • INTEGRATION PROCESS node that represents your integration process in the Integration Builder.

A process agent must still be specified for the manual user decision. Here, in the Integration Builder, open the newly created integration process `IP_Inquiry_##`. In the integration process, enter your user name, `PI-##`, for the PI system in the `agent` parameter (see Figure 5.90).

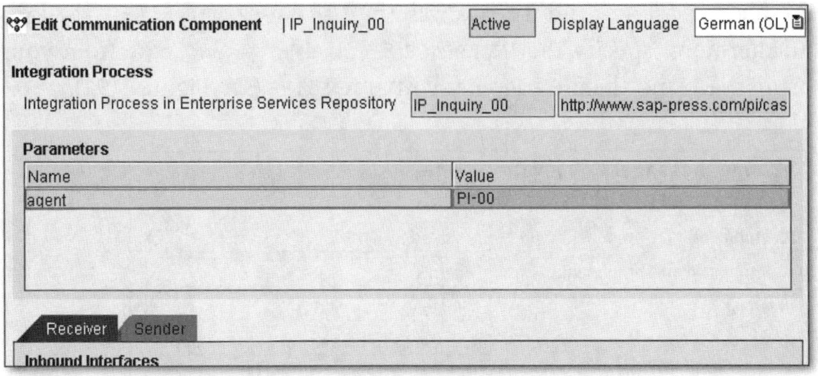

Figure 5.90 Parameter Agent in the Integration Process

Now you can configure the message; for this, you need to configure two message flows. The first sends the inquiry file of Hitech AG to the integration process for a decision. The second sends the inquiry IDoc to the system of SARIDIS in case of a positive decision (see Table 5.24).

Message Flow	Type of Object	Name
1	Sender agreement	`|SystemB|SI_Inquiry_Async_Out||`
	Receiver determination	`|SystemB|SI_Inquiry_Async_Out`
	Interface determination	`|SystemB|SI_Inquiry_Async_Out||IP_Inquiry_##`
2	Receiver determination	`|IP_Inquiry_##|SI_REQOTE_ORDERS01_Abstract`
	Receiver agreement	`|IP_Inquiry_##||SystemA|REQOTE.ORDERS01`
	Interface determination	`|IP_Inquiry_##|SI_REQOTE_ORDERS01_Abstract||SystemA`

Table 5.24 New Configuration Objects

Start with the first message flow. Select the Configuration Wizard from the TOOLS menu of the Integration Builder. Select the Internal Communication option. Select the BUSINESS SYSTEM entry as the COMMUNICATION COMPONENT TYPE, and SYSTEMB as the COMMUNICATION COMPONENT; furthermore, specify the INTERFACE SI_Inquiry_Async_out from your namespace and the file adapter as ADAPTER TYPE (see Figure 5.91).

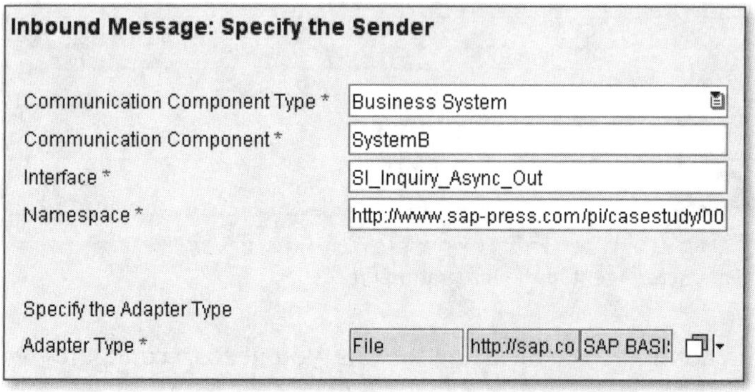

Inbound Message: Specify the Sender

Communication Component Type *	Business System
Communication Component *	SystemB
Interface *	SI_Inquiry_Async_Out
Namespace *	http://www.sap-press.com/pi/casestudy/00

Specify the Adapter Type

Adapter Type *	File	http://sap.co	SAP BASI

Figure 5.91 Selection of the Inbound Message

Select INTEGRATION PROCESS as the COMMUNICATION COMPONENT TYPE for the outbound message, IP_Inquiry_## as the COMMUNICATION COMPONENT, and SI_Inquiry_Async_Abstract from your namespace as INTERFACE (see Figure 5.92).

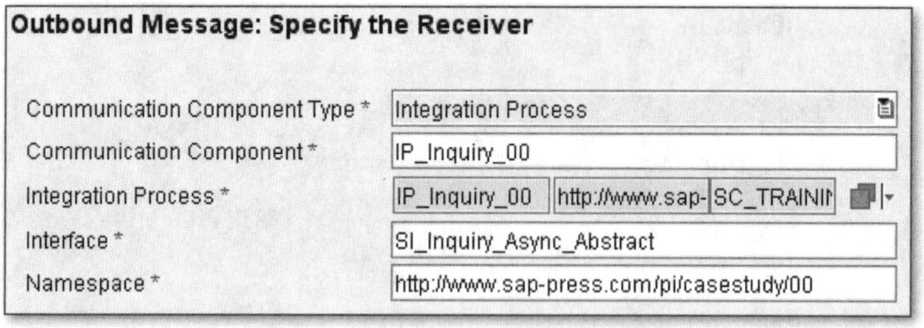

Outbound Message: Specify the Receiver

Communication Component Type *	Integration Process		
Communication Component *	IP_Inquiry_00		
Integration Process *	IP_Inquiry_00	http://www.sap-	SC_TRAINII
Interface *	SI_Inquiry_Async_Abstract		
Namespace *	http://www.sap-press.com/pi/casestudy/00		

Figure 5.92 Selection of the Outbound Message

Confirm the next steps with Continue. Make sure that the Receiver Agreement step finds the file sender channel File_SenderChannel_##, which was created in Section 5.1. In the last step, add the objects to your scenario.

Check the configuration of the message by navigating to configuration scenario PI_CASESTUDY_##. Compare the configuration that you created with Figure 5.93 to avoid errors in the process at a later stage.

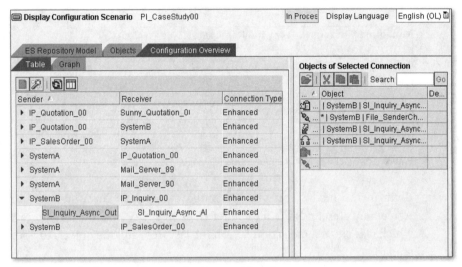

Figure 5.93 Configuration Scenario for Message Flow 1

Continue with the next message flow. This sends the inquiry IDoc from the integration process to the SARIDIS system. Follow the TOOLS • CONFIGURATION WIZARD menu path to launch the Configuration Wizard in the Integration Builder. Select the Internal Communication option. Select COMMUNICATION COMPONENT TYPE as your INTEGRATION PROCESS, IP_Inquiry_## as the COMMUNICATION COMPONENT, and, from your namespace, SI_REQOTE_ORDERS01_Abstract as the INTERFACE (see Figure 5.94).

Inbound Message: Specify the Sender

Communication Component Type *	Integration Process
Communication Component *	IP_Inquiry_00
Integration Process *	IP_Inquiry_0 http://www.s SC_TRAII
Interface *	SI_REQOTE_ORDERS01_Abstract
Namespace *	http://www.sap-press.com/pi/casestudy/0

Figure 5.94 Selection of the Inbound Message

417

Select the BUSINESS SYSTEM as the COMMUNICATION COMPONENT TYPE for the outbound message, and SYSTEMA as the COMMUNICATION COMPONENT. Specify REQOTE.ORDERS01 from your namespace as the INTERFACE, and set the Adapter Type to IDoc adapter (see Figure 5.95).

Outbound Message: Specify the Receiver

Communication Component Type *	Business System
Communication Component *	SystemA
Interface *	REQOTE.ORDERS01
Namespace *	urn:sap-com:document:sap:idoc:message

Figure 5.95 Selection of the Outbound Message

Confirm the next steps with Continue. Make sure that the Receiver Agreement step finds the file sender channel IDoc_ReceiverChannel_##, which was created in Section 5.1. In the last step, add the objects to your scenario.

Check the configuration of the message by navigating to configuration scenario PI_CASESTUDY_##. Compare the configuration that you created with Figure 5.96 to avoid errors in the process at a later stage.

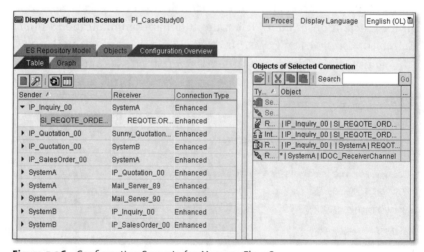

Figure 5.96 Configuration Scenario for Message Flow 2

Save and activate all of the configuration components in the Integration Builder. To get an overall view of the message configurations made, the configuration scenarios of SAP NetWeaver PI 7.1 provide a new graphical view to do so.

Open configuration scenario PI_CASESTUDY_##, and select the CONFIGURATION OVERVIEW tab. On this tab, look for the GRAPH tab (see Figure 5.97). You can now see that you have configured a message flow from system B to the integration process IP_Inquiry_##, and further to system A.

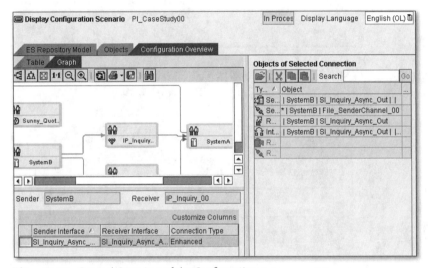

Figure 5.97 General Overview of the Configuration

If you click one of the arrows between the various communications components, the system also shows you the linked messages and the configuration objects used.

5.5.4 Process and Monitoring

To check the process of this step, you must send the inquiry on the file adapter as described in Section 5.1. However, in contrast to this, the inquiry must be manually processed in the SAP Business Workplace. Go to Transaction SBWP on the PI system, and switch to the INBOX node. Run the message titled ACCEPT INQUIRY? by double-clicking on it. To let the scenario play out, confirm the user decision with ACCEPT (see Figure 5.98).

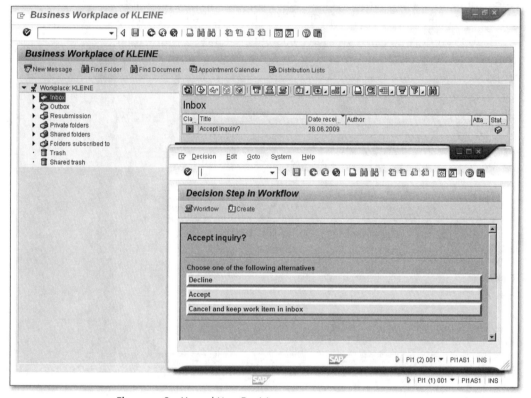

Figure 5.98 Manual User Decision

To see the integration process in monitoring, log on to the PI system, and call Transaction SXMB_MONI_BPE. Select the menu item Processes for a Message. Now, in the Interface Name field, enter the SI_Inquiry_Async_Abstract service interface; in the Interface Namespace field, enter your namespace. To view all of the processes of the message, select All Instances in the Selection variant field. Execute the selection with F8.

In the list shown in Figure 5.99, you can find all of the process instances of the integration process that you created.

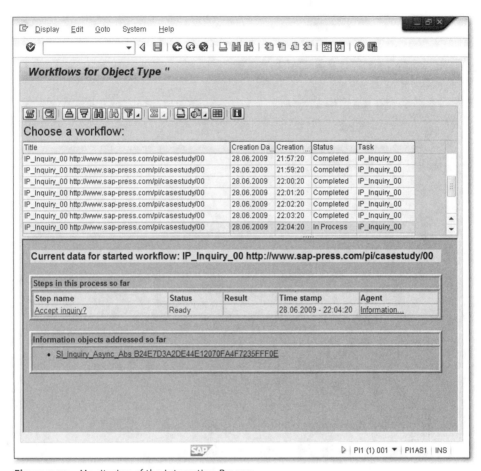

Figure 5.99 Monitoring of the Integration Process

This chapter discusses various concepts you could use to enhance the book's case study, including a description of another extensive business process that utilizes applications outside of SAP NetWeaver Process Integration (PI). In addition, this chapter sheds some light on the future development of SAP NetWeaver PI.

6 Enhancements and Outlook

Now that you have successfully completed the exercises and the case study for this book, the final step introduces you to some possible ways of extending your knowledge in other, more complex scenarios. Our goal is to prepare you for future developments in the SAP NetWeaver PI environment, as much as possible at this stage. For this reason, the following sections deal with the role of SAP NetWeaver PI in the service-oriented architecture (SOA) environment, and contain a discussion about further developments of the product itself.

6.1 Possible Enhancements to the Case Study

At some point during the discussion of our case study, you probably thought that there was room for a more detailed consideration of specific concepts. To best facilitate understanding, the case study has been kept deliberately simple — more simple than it would really be in such an environment. With this in mind, we now want to describe some more complex concepts in further detail.

Distinction between two enhancement concepts

6.1.1 Extending the Breadth of the Case Study

By extending the breadth of the case study, we can examine the time before and after the process, and also take a look at the systems of other companies. In this book, we only used the SARIDIS case study to a mini-

Increasing the section under consideration

423

mal extent, even though it contains many processes and special cases that could be regarded as challenges. For example, we could consider the purchasing processes, focus more on Materials Management (MM), or modify the Sales and Distribution (SD) process by carrying out a third-party business transaction.

The important factor here is that you can keep using the described SD process while discovering new scenarios. For example, the process contains steps that are not supported by SAP NetWeaver PI, and you can complement it by dispatching an order confirmation or a shipping notification. In addition, it is not quite clear how SARIDIS controls and posts incoming payments, so you could study this process in more detail. Furthermore, the practical sections in this book did not deal with which systems could be used on the side of Hitech AG or Sunny Electronics, and their applications may have some specific characteristics that require a modification of the processes. For example, we did not consider the question of what the scenario would look like if Sunny Electronics were assigned an order for monitors.

Depending on your area of focus, you could, for example, also extend the ABAP application described in the third step in Chapter 5, SARDIS Case Study in SD, to make it more user friendly. You could use the Web Dynpro programming in both ABAP or Java; you could also model applications from Web services, function modules, or Business Warehouse (BW) queries with SAP NetWeaver Visual Composer. In addition, you could integrate the technical exercises, which are basically independent of the case study. As such, you could extend the material master record to create the items that will be ordered later by Hitech AG. Another issue you could try to resolve is exchanging messages with other companies and partners. (To keep a clear overview of the exercises and to avoid having to increase the system landscape any further, we decided not to consider message exchange with other landscapes or SAP NetWeaver PI systems.)

With the new features in release 7.1, there are even more ways to expand the SARIDIS study. The functions of the SAP NetWeaver PI system can be used to create additional business objects, process components, and process component interaction models — and thus to model the business content of the SARIDIS business process. The ability to integrate business views is one of the major enhancements in the Enterprise Services Repository.

Another enhancement in release 7.1 is the ability to replace the services of the SARIDIS case study with real services, shipped by SAP in the standard scope of the Enterprise Services Repository. For example, in the first step of the SARIDIS case study — the creation of the inquiry, which is currently handled by an intermediate document (IDoc) to the SAP backend system — the IDoc could be replaced by one of about 3,000 services in the Enterprise Services Repository. To do this, go to the SAP Developer Network (SDN) (*http://sdn.sap.com*), and search in the Enterprise Services Workplace area for a matching service. The request for quotation (RFQ) search, for example, returns the results shown in Figure 6.1.

Services from the Enterprise Services Workplace

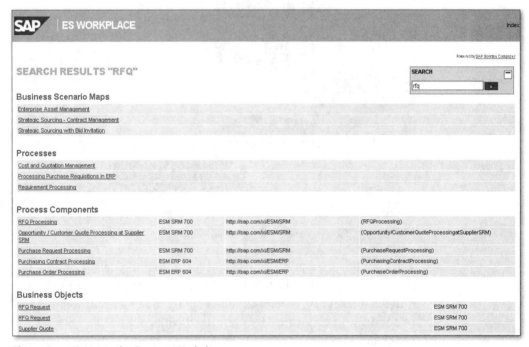

Figure 6.1 Hit List in the Services Workplace

As you can see from Figure 6.1, Enterprise Services groups inquiries and price requests together in various business scenario maps, such as Strategic Sourcing with Bid Invitation, which comes closest to the SARIDIS

Structured search for services

study. If you click ON STRATEGIC SOURCING WITH BID INVITATION in the Enterprise Services Workplace, you will see Figure 6.2, which illustrates the process and benefits of the solution.

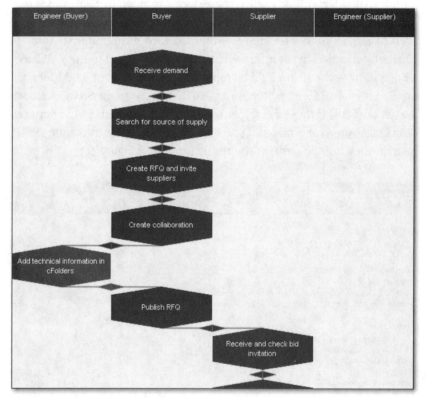

Figure 6.2 Process Flow Strategic Sourcing with Bid Invitation

This could be used as an entry point for presenting details of how this process is modeled in the SAP system. Furthermore, you could go deeper into the subject of cFolders[1] and their ability to model collaborative processes (i.e., processes that are performed with cooperation between the buyer and supplier).

---

1 cFolders are used to collaborate with distributed design or production teams in a Web-based environment; they are part of an application suite that enables integratation for project management, knowledge management, and resource management in SAP NetWeaver.

The Enterprise Services Workplace also lists which processes and process components occur in RFQ, and which business objects are the basis of the process components. In addition, the existing view on the technical objects, such as service interfaces, service operations, and data types, is shown (as in the previous releases of SAP NetWeaver PI). As should be apparent, the PI system is no longer just the pure technical enterprise application integration (EAI) landscape for application-to-application (A2A) or business-to-busines (B2B) integration; it has developed beyond the new modeling artifacts that have been described into SOA middleware.

From EAI to SOA middleware

Another approach you might take is to publish the services that you have modeled in SAP NetWeaver PI into the Services Registry. There you can classify them according to your own point of view, and call them from another application. Due to the openness of Web services, this could work for both ABAP and Java applications, and a Ruby on Rails (RoR) or PHP application that accesses and uses the services of the SARIDIS case study.

An additional supplement to the SARIDIS study would be to determine the process efficiency of the processes depicted in the SAP ERP system. In *Business Process Execution Language for Web Services* (WS-BPEL) models, SAP NetWeaver PI provides the ability to define process milestones; if the milestones are collected over a sufficient number of process instances, you can then determine the efficiency of the modeled process. This is known as *business activity monitoring* (BAM), which was coined by the Gartner Group. Only significant events of a process are modeled as WS-BPEL processes.

Business activity monitoring

Unlike other BPEL processes, milestone monitoring consists of individual process steps, which can receive messages, share events, and generate alerts. The relevant milestones in the SARIDIS process would be the inquiry, quotation(s), sales order, and invoice. Whenever one of these four events occurs in the backend system, an appropriate message is sent to the milestone process that was modeled in WS-BPEL. An attached SAP BW system could then load the data, and analysis carried out with functions provided by SAP BusinessObjects and related tools.

It might be interesting to analyze, for example, the number of process instances in a given time period. These values could be differentiated depending on the procured materials, the average, and the minimum and maximum throughput time of the overall process. From this retrospective analysis of the efficiency of a process, you could determine optimization approaches for future implementation.

6.1.2 Extending the Depth of the Case Study

Details of the described concepts — By extending the depth of the case study, we are referring to the consideration of details of the described concepts and problems. One of these aspects is the issue of security. For example, many adapters allow you to configure security settings that guarantee a secure exchange of data, even across enterprise boundaries. Although we described several adapters in the exercises, we did not go into further detail, because the majority of adapters require additional applications and servers whose integration would involve a considerable effort.

Enhancement by Web service standards — The technical exercises could be enhanced to use one of the following new features in release 7.1:

- Security Assertion Markup Language (SAML)
- Web service profile
- WS Reliable Messaging

These are a few examples that illustrate the support of web standards and show that SAP NetWeaver PI has developed to an SOA middleware (see Section 6.3, SAP NetWeaver PI and SOA).

Better performance for mass processing — Another way to increase the depth of the case study would be to address performance issues. SAP NetWeaver PI 7.1 already offers some enhancements for mass processing, such as message bulking and processing in the Advanced Adapter Engine (AAE).

Business elements are an essential element that we included in several cases in this book. These objects have such huge potential that you can, for example, automate the entire case study with only two business processes that communicate with each other. Doing this, you can skip the manual steps we discussed.

This would also be an ideal spot for testing new opportunities in business process management (BPM), which are available as a result of the SAP NetWeaver Composition Environment (CE). SAP NetWeaver CE is a strategic platform on which the SAP BPM roadmap is based (see Snabe et al., *Business Process Management: The SAP Roadmap*, 2008), and the central element of it is the Enterprise Services Repository, which developed out of the SAP Exchange Infrastructure (XI) repository.

Modeling of processes with the SAP NetWeaver Composition Environment

While SAP NetWeaver CE is aimed at the communication between man and machine, the focus of SAP NetWeaver PI is on the communication from machine to machine. Both are variants of how real business processes can be implemented; they don't represent exclusive solutions, but are usually used together in processes.

As you can see, you can develop many additional scenarios and variations based on the materials introduced in this book. However, because there are many other business processes that take place outside the SARIDIS case study, there are also a lot of other ways to extend your knowledge of the SAP NetWeaver PI environment. One possible example in this context is the beer distribution game that is described in the following section.

6.2 Beer Distribution Game

The *beer distribution game* is a logistics simulation that was developed at the beginning of the 1960s at the Massachusetts Institute of Technology (MIT). It simulates a four-level supply chain that consists of a retailer, wholesaler, distributor, and a factory. You can find additional information on the beer distribution game, and a simulation of the game, at *http://www.beergame.lim.ethz.ch*.

Description

In its original version as a board game, each level is represented by a person who decides how much beer should be delivered to the previous level (in the case of the retailer, the previous level is a customer who places weekly orders), and how much beer should be ordered from the subsequent level (in the case of the factory, the subsequent level is the production department). The purpose of the game is to minimize the costs that occur along the entire supply chain. These costs consist of the following two components: stockholding costs and costs incurred by delivery delays.

Whiplash effect The simulation illustrates the *whiplash effect* caused by time delays in the supply chain, and is characterized by strong fluctuations of the stock volumes at individual levels (see Figure 6.3).

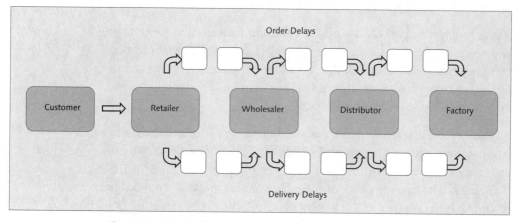

Figure 6.3 Supply Chain in the Beer Distribution Game

The following sections describe how you can implement the simulation, and the associated business process, using SAP NetWeaver PI.

Business requirements In the first step, we suggest that you use simplifying remote function call (RFC) modules as an alternative to mapping the processes of the individual supply chain levels via real ERP processes. Each of these modules is assigned quantities to be ordered and delivered, respectively.

From a business point of view, the RFC modules contain a simple logic that decides on the quantity of beer to be ordered. Moreover, they place the actual orders, and receive and deliver goods. While two factories, which receive the orders of the distributor on the basis of the available quantities of beer, are being operated, there is only one retailer, one wholesaler, and one distributor. In SAP NetWeaver PI, the factories are selected with a BPEL process.

Another task of SAP NetWeaver PI is to forward purchase orders to subsequent levels and to dispatch shipping notifications to the previous levels. In addition, SAP NetWeaver PI logs all of the steps involved in the program flow through the file adapter.

An external Web service is used to register the stock volumes and open purchase orders to carry out a final evaluation of the overall costs of the supply chain. For this, the individual levels actively transfer their data to the Web service. The individual levels are also initiated (that is, the stock volumes are set) through a Web service interface, which — in contrast to the previously mentioned Web service — is provided by SAP NetWeaver PI. In other words, SAP NetWeaver PI acts as a server in this context.

The publication of the metadata of the external Web service in the Enterprise Services Repository can be done, for example, via a download from a service registry or through another exchange of the corresponding Web Service Description Language (WSDL) description.

To map the simulation, perform the following steps:

1. Map the individual supply chain levels (retailer, wholesaler, distributor, factory) using the appropriate RFC modules and a message exchange between the supply chain levels via SAP NetWeaver PI.

2. Select the appropriate factory using a BPEL process.

3. Integrate an external logging service that logs all stock changes centrally using SAP NetWeaver PI's file adapter.

4. Integrate a monitoring service to evaluate the current stock volumes and the stock development during the course of the simulation.

5. Use a tool to initialize the individual supply chain levels (initial stock volumes, delays, and so on).

6.2.1 Predefined Software Components

The following description allows you to map the beer distribution game in SAP NetWeaver PI using the previously defined software components. In contrast to the detailed exercises in this book, this description represents a rough guide and should be considered as a gathering of ideas rather than instructions for a complete implementation. The predefined components are first described, and then we will continue with the design and solution concept.

Function modules
and supply chain
levels In this exercise, we want to implement the individual supply chain levels in an SAP system. At the same time, however, those levels are treated in such a way that it is always possible to distribute them to several systems. The function modules used to implement the individual levels are created in a package.[2]

There are six RFC-enabled function modules available for each supply chain level:

▸ Sending and receiving of purchase orders (the stock volumes are stored in a database table).

▸ Sending and receiving of goods deliveries.

▸ Initialization of stock volumes.

▸ Query of stock and purchase order data.

The factory represents an exception in this context; it receives purchase orders, but places production orders that are then carried out with a certain time delay.

Implementation of
Web services The implementation of an external Web service for monitoring purchase orders and stock volumes, and the Web service client for initializing the stock volumes, can be implemented on a non-SAP platform, for example, on Apache and Jakarta Tomcat; the Web service can also be implemented based on SAP NetWeaver Application Server (AS) Java in SAP NetWeaver Developer Studio.

The following is a list with arguably the most important operations of Web services to be implemented:

▸ `addOrder(String senderName, int orderVolume)`, which is called when beer is ordered

▸ `addDelivery(String supplierName, int deliveryVolume)`, which is called at the time of delivery

Other methods are used to initialize a new game and to query the historical data for analysis in the beer analysis client.

---

2 You can find a sample implementation at: *http://eai.uni-lueneburg.de/sap-xi*.

6.2.2 Design and Implementation

SAP NetWeaver PI is used as an integration platform for exchanging messages and for flow logic (i.e., selection of the factory). In addition to the three interfaces for initialization, reporting, and logging, six additional interfaces are required for the retailer, wholesaler, and distributor. The factory does not need the interfaces for outbound purchase orders and inbound deliveries, as these are mapped by the factory-internal production. Figure 6.4 illustrates the structure of this situation for one supply chain level.

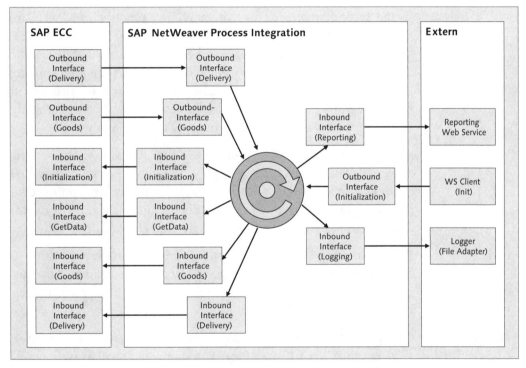

Figure 6.4 Overview of Inbound and Outbound Interfaces in the Beer Distribution Game

Once the individual supply chain level is initialized, the game starts with a customer request received by the retailer. The customer only has two functions: to place purchase orders and to receive deliveries.

If the requested quantity is in stock, the retailer delivers it to the customer. If the stock isn't available, the retailer directs a corresponding request to the wholesaler. The wholesaler sends a partial delivery to the retailer and places a purchase order with the distributor who, in turn, sends a corresponding purchase order to the factory. The factory produces the ordered quantity and sends a delivery to the distributor, who forwards it to the wholesaler, who forwards it to the retailer. Finally, the retailer can send the remaining quantity to the customer.

6.2.3 Options for Enhancement

In the second step, processes of individual supply chain levels are mapped one after the other using real ERP processes. Instead of the RFC module used for inbound purchase orders, we could, for instance, write an appropriate sales document using business application programming interfaces (BAPIs) or IDocs. You can also use enterprise services provided by the Enterprise Services Workplace, as described in the SARIDIS study (see Section 6.1, Possible Enhancements of the Case Study).

We could also use a BPEL process to send purchase orders for the requested item to the superior supply chain level on the basis of the goods availability check. If access to different ERP systems is provided, it would also be interesting to map different supply chain levels on different ERP installations (perhaps even by different vendors).

Whereas the first stage of extension (i.e., mapping via appropriate RFC modules) represents a simulation under "laboratory conditions," the outlined extension contains almost any problem that might occur in real-world integration projects.

Modeling of SOA artefacts | Only parts of the beer distribution game were implemented using Web services as RFCs and IDocs. If the corresponding functions were newly developed today, modern technologies based on open standards would most likely be used. For this reason, an application engineer would propose using Web services in an SOA. Here, once again, the modeling capabilities of SAP NetWeaver PI with process components, business objects, and process component interaction models can be applied.

6.3   SAP NetWeaver PI and SOA

Up to now, SAP NetWeaver PIhas been presented as an infrastructure:

▸ For the connection and integration of applications

▸ As a service bus for the integration of business partners

▸ For service enabling (i.e., provision of functions in the form of services without implementing them anew as Web services)

▸ For the Service Orchestration to link existing and newly developed services together to end-to-end applications.

Modeling environment and runtime for services

As you can see in Figure 6.5, SAP NetWeaver PI provides a unified modeling environment for synchronized service definition, service implementation, service usage, and service operation using additional SOA management components. Furthermore, it is an integral part of the SOA infrastructure solution provided by SAP.

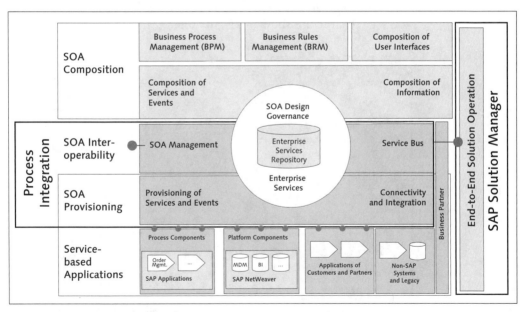

Figure 6.5 SAP NetWeaver PI as an Integral Part of the SOA Infrastructure

This modeling allows the decoupling of the process logic from the service implementation, and new business processes can be implemented much

435

faster, especially when encapsulated, reusable, high-quality enterprise services are used. If you look at the content delivered with SAP NetWeaver PI, you realize that there are several ways of using SAP NetWeaver PI; it's a packaged solution that is fully integrated with SAP applications, which provides a simplified composition and uses the SOA backbone. All this, however, only requires one platform. That, and, in particular, the SOA capabilities, are the reasons why companies have consolidated their existing middleware solutions to a unified SOA middleware.

6.4 Further Development of SAP NetWeaver PI

So far, you have been introduced to SOAs and the importance of SAP NetWeaver PI as overall concepts. We also want to offer some insight into further developments that are on the horizon.

If you look in the SDN (*http://sdn.sap.com*) for content about SAP NetWeaver PI, you cannot get direct access to SAP NetWeaver PI; instead, you see the structure shown in Figure 6.6.

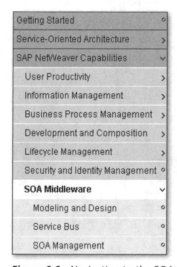

Figure 6.6 Navigation to the SOA Middleware in the SDN

A key component in SOA Strategy   You can access content about SAP NetWeaver PI in each of the layers listed under SOA MIDDLEWARE. The SAP NetWeaver PI system plays an important role in the SOA strategy of SAP, both at design time and at runtime; this is clear from the exercises and case studies about the Enterprise Services Repository and Services Registry shown here.

The key excerpts from the SOA roadmap of SAP can be divided into two blocks:

▶ Process composition

▶ PI

While the process composition block is provided in the form of SAP NetWeaver CE, which is not part of this book, the PI block includes the contents of the PI system. Both continue to grow together and are aimed at a simpler representation of an end-to-end process orchestration, as we shall see in the following sections.

> **Hint**
>
> The descriptions of the new developments in the process composition and PI are available as podcasts on the SDN at: *https://www.sdn. sap.com/irj/scn/ weblogs?blog=/pub/u/50922*.

6.4.1 Development of SAP NetWeaver PI

The historical development of SAP NetWeaver PI, presented in Figure 6.7, shows the consistent development from an EAI middleware to an SOA middleware.

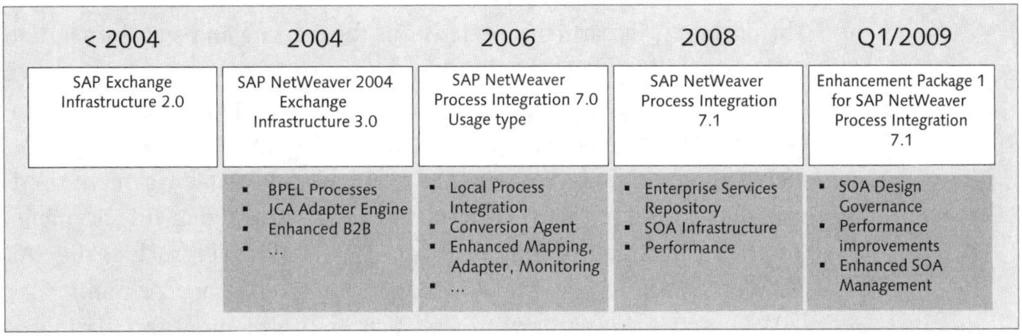

< 2004	2004	2006	2008	Q1/2009
SAP Exchange Infrastructure 2.0	SAP NetWeaver 2004 Exchange Infrastructure 3.0	SAP NetWeaver Process Integration 7.0 Usage type	SAP NetWeaver Process Integration 7.1	Enhancement Package 1 for SAP NetWeaver Process Integration 7.1
	• BPEL Processes • JCA Adapter Engine • Enhanced B2B • ...	• Local Process Integration • Conversion Agent • Enhanced Mapping, Adapter, Monitoring • ...	• Enterprise Services Repository • SOA Infrastructure • Performance	• SOA Design Governance • Performance improvements • Enhanced SOA Management

Figure 6.7 Development of SAP NetWeaver PI

Enterprise Services
Repository as
gravitational center

2004 SAP NetWeaver PI was called SAP XI, and it was clearly designed as a message-exchange platform. With the release of SAP XI 3.0, modeling capabilities were added in the form of BPEL process models, and, in 2006, the hitherto existing possibilities were enhanced. Since 2008, SAP NetWeaver PI 7.1 has expanded the Enterprise Services Repository and the SOA infrastructure to an SOA middleware. The enhancement pack that is now in general distribution includes greatly enhanced capabilities, particularly for SOA governance.

SOA governance is a critical success factor for making an enterprise SOA strategy operational. These include clearly defined principles (*governance procedures*) as the basis for a service usage and service provisioning. SAP has developed its own methodology for designing and developing business services. In the end, it is in the interest of SAP that the distributed services stem from a consistent methodology, because only then can a chaos of (both technically and, even more important, semantically) uncoordinated services be avoided. SAP provides tools, especially in theEnterprise Services Repository, that can be used in your own custom scenarios. The Enterprise Services Repository as a part of SAP NetWeaver PI represents the gravitational center of a SAP SOA.

SOA Middleware
as a solution, not
as a product

If customers consolidate their existing middleware solutions to the SAP NetWeaver PI, and the system becomes the key SOA middleware, it is clear that performance issues will play an increasingly important role. Therefore, SAP included additional features to improve performance in the current release. Advanced SOA management features complete the profile.

This includes, in particular, extensions for the safe and stable operation of a services-based integration between service consumer and service provider, and configuring, monitoring, testing, and operating in heterogeneous SOA implementations on different platforms. These enhancements affect not only SAP NetWeaver PI as an SOA management product, but also as a solution. This has also been addressed in enhancements in other infrastructure components of SAP NetWeaver, such as the SAP NetWeaver AS, SAP Solution Manager, SAP NetWeaver Administrator (NWA), and third-party products such as the planned integration of AmberPoint to improve the traceability of Simple Object Access Protocol (SOAP)–based message traffic within SAP NetWeaver PI.

6.4.2   Roadmap of the SOA Middleware

Other directions currently planned for the SOA middleware are shown in Figure 6.8.

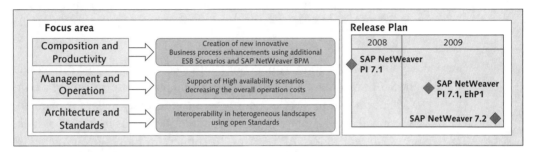

Figure 6.8   Planned Further Development of the SOA Middleware

As you can see from Figure 6.8, further developments are divided into three focus areas:

Further developments in the SOA middleware

- Composition and productivity
- Management and operation
- Architecture and standards

Composition and Productivity

This section explains what SAP currently plans to better support process modeling up to their execution, and to increase productivity — especially in the definition and configuration of processes.

Available Today

In previous chapters, you had a good overview of how the Enterprise Services Repository helps you to keep up a design time governance. As a reminder, the process component architecture, the definition of dependencies of services at the level of the software component versions (SWCV), and the global data types that lead to a semantic standardization should again be mentioned here. At this point, you can call the configuration using the integrated configuration objects, or via direct use of the Services Registry in the Enterprise Services Repository.

439

Medium-Term Planning

New service
connectivity for
the connection of
older SAP releases

The medium-term planning for composition and productivity includes new and innovative business process enhancements to be created through additional Enterprise Service Bus (ESB) scenarios and SAP NetWeaver BPM. Extended connectivity options are promised as additional ESB scenarios. Today, SAP NetWeaver PI only provides (direct) connection via Web services.

For a non-Web service connection, you need an adapter that can handle the SOAP version of SAP NetWeaver PI, and the transformation of a non-XML document to XML. A new service connectivity in Java is planned, which will allow a direct connection out of RFCs. This makes it possible, especially for older SAP releases, to connect to the SAP NetWeaver PI build system.

Service variants

Service variants are scheduled for release 7.2, and are simpler versions of enterprise services that can be defined in a tool. This will allow you to quickly adapt existing enterprise services, and will further reduce the cost of development and implementation. Also scheduled for release 7.2 is a simplified deployment of events (*event provisioning*). This goes hand in hand with the developments in the field of business suite applications, because, ultimately, business events must either be sent from an application or processed in that application.

In addition, there will be new entities in the Enterprise Services Repository, which will better support the mediation of events. This way, applications will be significantly more talkative. One result will be that simple processes will be automated, and only significant business events will be presented to the user, because the normal processing is already automated. In the beer distribution games, such an extraordinary event would be, for example, a delivery truck cannot deliver due to an accident.

Vision

Common process
layer

A very significant enhancement of the operational spectrum of SAP NetWeaver PI is SAP NetWeaver BPM, which provides many new features in the CE, allowing you to create innovative new business processes from modeling to execution in the *Business Process Modeling Notation* (BPMN). Real business processes almost always represent a combination of communication patterns, such as human-machine and machine-

machine, that is a combination of user-oriented integration and PI; thus, both modeling approaches, SAP NetWeaver PI and SAP NetWeaver CE, can be used.

SAP NetWeaver PI enables cross-system communication using mapping, dynamic routing, and *guaranteed delivery*, in contrast to the direct communication with a user frontend that is part of SAP NetWeaver CE. For this, SAP is planning enhanced connectivity between the two components, to make cooperation easier. Ultimately, both will result in the Common Process Layer (CPL). Here, the efforts to move them to a single Java basis play an important role.

The CPL illustrated in Figure 6.9 will bring all persons involved in the process model together in a unified and integrated environment.

Integrated environment for all stakeholders in a process model

One group of stakeholders is the management level, with executives who will define and control the company's strategy and corresponding *key performance indicators* (KPIs). Here, BAM and the conversion of measured data into graphic and other easily understandable forms will play an important role, as already demonstrated in Section 6.1.

Once a strategy is established by the management level, line managers start to transform it into a conceptual model. Tools like ARIS for SAP NetWeaver are important here, because they can be used for modeling enterprise architecture in both SAP and non-SAP-based systems.

These models can already be exchanged between ARIS for SAP NetWeaver and SAP NetWeaver PI at the level of BPEL models. However, in reality, it is only in exceptional cases that a modeling from ARIS drills down to the level of a BPEL process; usually, the modeling ends at an abstract level, which is why this exchange is hardly encountered in practice. As described in Section 1.6, the new versions of ARIS Business Architect and SAP Solution Manager allow you to sync process models to the level of BPEL processes.

The whole thing becomes more interesting if you look at the BPMN models in SAP NetWeaver CE, and at the possibilities that are listed in the SAP roadmap for integration of tools into SAP NetWeaver CE (like the ARIS Toolset by IDS Scheer).

SAP is aware that customers have invested in, for example, *event-driven process chains* from IDS Scheer, and is currently examining various options, such as a transformation between the models, or even if a transformation can be omitted to protect the investments of customers. As described earlier, SAP NetWeaver CE will be the new state-of-the-art environment, which occupies an important role in the CPL.

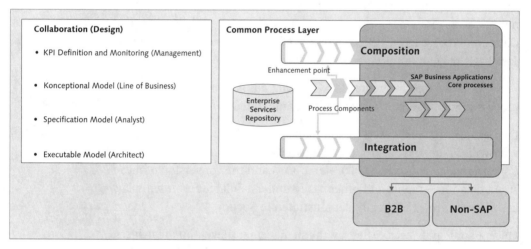

Figure 6.9 Evolution Toward a CPL

The CPL harmonizes the way different people — such as business process experts, developers, and application consultants — work together across various usage scenarios of standard applications and composite business processes. This involves the exposure of implementations and reference content from various sources, such as repositories of IDS Scheer. You can then synchronize the conceptual business models with the specification models that are created by a business analyst.

After that, the architect implements the specification models into executable models, either at the BPMN or BPEL level. This shows how skills profiles are evolving for an EAI developer, who up to now was responsible for integrating processes at a more technical level; it also means that SAP NetWeaver PI developers must be more involved in business processes and their efficient and effective implementation. Because both IT and the business work in a uniform and integrated modeling environment, misunderstandings between the two groups should decrease significantly, and the processes required by the business departments will hopefully match the processes implemented by IT. The first step in this process was made in 2004 with the release of SAP XI 3.0, and the introduction of executable BPEL models, where model and implementation are consistent.

The CPL thus allows integrative BPM across the core processes and their extensions. Within a specific model, there will be different views for stakeholders; due to the underlying SAP NetWeaver framework, integrative monitoring, administration, and lifecycle management all go hand-in-hand. Thus, a modeled process is a "living" process, because it represents both the currently defined and implemented process in its various versions.

For 2010, SAP envisions that the Enterprise Services Repository will be moved to an Eclipse-based version like the CE, and then integrated into SAP NetWeaver Developer Studio. The first step in bringing SAP NetWeaver PI to a single-stack implementation[3] has already been made with the AAE that is implemented in Java.

SAP NetWeaver Process Integration as lean service bus

Today, if only mapping and routing are necessary for an integration scenario, message processing can take place entirely on the Java side of SAP NetWeaver PI; there is no need for internal switching between the Java and ABAP stack, resulting in a better performance. These are the first steps in giving the SAP NetWeaver PI system a lean service bus infrastructure, and will lead to not only performance improvements, but also to smaller hardware, reduced overall costs, and an increase in productivity.

Management and Operation

This section addresses SAP's plans to provide follow-up releases addressing the further integration of SAP NetWeaver PI with existing infrastructure components, such as the SAP Solution Manager, to reduce the cost of management and operation of an SAP NetWeaver PI system.

---

3 Even after the efforts to bring SAP NetWeaver PI to a single-stack Java, the runtime will still contain ABAP components.

Available Today

Solution Manager integration In the second focus area, management and operation, an administration environment has been created to centrally configure and monitor the SAP NetWeaver PI system's integration with SAP Solution Manager 4.0. All SAP systems are attached to the central SAP Solution Manager, and locally installed agents report on the current state of the system. Thus, a system administrator can oversee the landscape from a consolidated view, and, if necessary, navigate from the SAP Solution Manager into a local system to perform certain activities.

The connection between SAP Solution Manager and SAP NetWeaver PI is currently managed using a work center (see Figure 6.10 and Figure 6.11), which allows system administrators quick and specific access to relevant system information, such as business process operation.

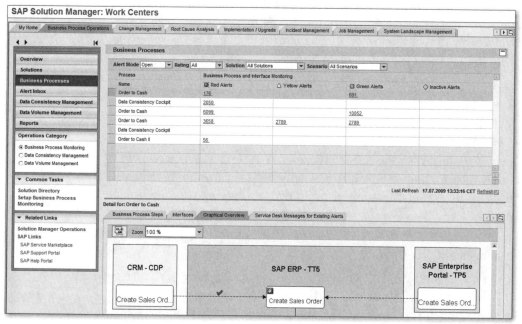

Figure 6.10 SAP Solution Manager — Business Process and Interface Monitoring in the Work Center

From BPM, you can navigate to central administration tools for the SAP NetWeaver PI system, and move further into local expert tools, such as the SAP NWA. This integration promises a further reduction in total operating costs, because SAP Solution Manager represents the central administration and monitoring infrastructure of the SAP landscape.

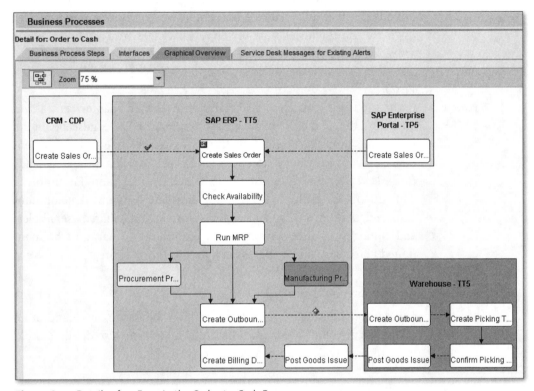

Figure 6.11 Details of an Error in the Order-to-Cash Process

Medium-Term Panning

This existing integration, both in SAP Solution Manager and in the SAP NWA, is planned to be extended even further in the future. More monitoring options will be implemented in the SAP Solution Manager; for example, there will be "Good-morning pages" that display the status and health of the system immediately after logging on.

In many cases, the SAP NetWeaver PI system has become the central infrastructure for business, and therefore plays an important role in all integration scenarios. As a result, it is not surprising that there are increasing demands for zero downtime during upgrades or when installing support packages. SAP has promised to meet this demand soon.

Zero downtime requirement

There are two basic approaches for performing upgrades: either with minimal resources, or with minimal downtime. These are usually mutually exclusive requirements. Various existing installation guidelines provide detailed information on upgrades and necessary downtime for upgrades and the installation of support packages. You can find them at *http://service.sap.com/instguidesNW*.

Vision

Federated service bus

As previously mentioned, SAP Solution Manager enables centralized administration and monitoring infrastructure in an SAP landscape. In the future, this infrastructure will be further developed to enable consistent management of SOA and non-SOA landscapes. All this ultimately leads to a *federated service bus infrastructure*, which requires central monitoring and support for multiple service bus installations. Joint development and configuration, load balancing across installations, shared users, roles, and authority management are other requirements that must be mentioned here, and will be addressed by SAP's future strategy.

Architecture and Standards

This section explains what SAP will do if, in the future, more and more customers operate SOAs from different vendors, and also discusses how these different SOAs can be integrated.

Available Today

High-volume support through AAE

In the architecture and standards focus area, improvements and enhancements have already been made in earlier releases of SAP NetWeaver PI. Release 7.1 achieves high-volume support for local processing in the AAE and message packaging, and improved performance for cross-component Business Process Management (ccBPM) processes.

In message packaging, the individual messages that are queued to be processed by SAP NetWeaver PI are not sent individually through mapping and routing; instead, packing occurs (see Chapter 2, Section 2.6.8, Message Packaging) so that multiple messages are simultaneously processed in the mapping and routing step. This reduces the context switches for mapping, routing, and reading a message header, and is particularly relevant for asynchronous message processing, in which messages are saved in a persistent way within the SAP NetWeaver PI system. This will also significantly speed up database operations as mass operations. Depending on the scenario, the performance benefits are a factor of 1.5 to 3.

The AAE (see Chapter 2, Section 2.3.6, IS, and 2.6.1, Local Processing on the AAE) has been enhanced to a local processing engine in release 7.1, and therefore can be used as a local adapter engine. It supports the (Java) mapping and routing of messages, and thus allows you to bypass the Integration Server (IS) (the ABAP part) of SAP NetWeaver PI. This alone improves performance by a factor of 10.

If there are scenarios that do not require processing in the ABAP stack, enormous throughputs can be reached in SAP NetWeaver PI. If the future brings Federated Service Bus installations, a single-stack installation (Java) can be used for certain scenarios to reduce overall operating costs.

Another aspect of innovation is the simpler configuration of integration scenarios. Besides a number of new features, there has been a strong focus on a simplified configuration; the release 7.1 enhancement package, for example, includes a graphical representation of configuration. In addition to this graphical representation, different views can be selected in the navigation structure. In Figure 6.12, the CONFIGURATION SCENARIO is shown. This allows you to, for example, group configuration objects in configuration scenarios, with direct access to the objects they contain. Further functions, such as the advanced search capability for communication channels, are especially useful in large productive installations.

Enhancements and simplifications in the configuration

With this enhanced search, you can find communication channels with a specific name and a specific adapter type, allowing collective edits of file names. The possibilities that are outlined here are of enormous benefit, especially in installations with Electronic Data Interchange (EDI) scenarios that have hundreds of communication channels where customers or suppliers are defined.

There is also an API available, which enables programmatic attribute changes from outside the system via a batch program. This function has already been supported in release 7.1, but is now also available for integration objects new to the enhancement package.

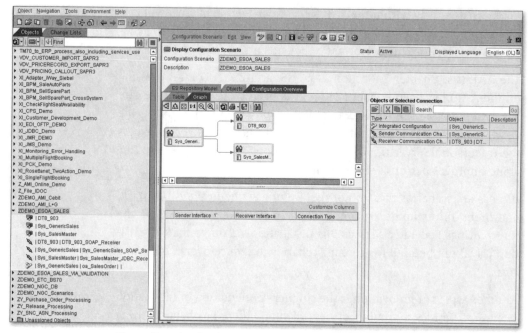

Figure 6.12 Graphical View of a Configuration Scenario

The INTEGRATED CONFIGURATION configuration object allows you to configure in one step, rather than in many individual steps (receiver determination, interface determination, sender and receiver agreement, etc.). As of the release 7.1 enhancement package, dynamic content-based routing and receiver splits defined for different recipients are also included. Both facilitate the configuration of complex scenarios. Figure 6.13 shows the integrated configuration within a configuration scenario; you can clearly see the configuration that is now distributed throughout various tabs.

Another aspect that goes along with the focus of SAP NetWeaver PI as an SOA middleware is its ability to assist in the configuration of Web services and service consumers. If you think back to the possibilities for enhancing the SARIDIS case study from Section 6.1, you will remember the Enterprise Services. You may also have noted that SAP has combined the Enterprise Services into *service bundles*, which SAP describes as a collection of enterprise services that can be used to extend the functionality of an SAP ERP 6.0 system, or other solutions in the SAP Business Suite.

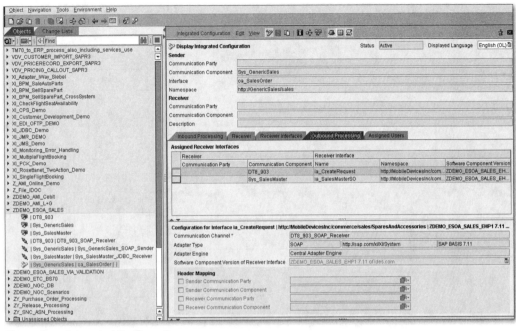

Figure 6.13 Integrated Configuration

The Enterprise Service Bundle *customer fact sheet* contains about 40 enterprise services that allow direct access to all customer-related data, in whatever business application or database the data is stored. This allows, for example, a sales representative to access information (address data, contact information, credit rating, or historical data) through individual interfaces that can be customized. It clearly shows that groups of services are used more often than individual Web services.

The automated mass configuration of Web services and their clients, in particular, is the goal of the development described in the following text. Basically, the configuration of a Web service scenario is divided into three phases, which are shown in Figure 6.14:

▸ Configuration of the service on the service provider side

▸ Configuration of the service consumer

▸ Connection of the systems

449

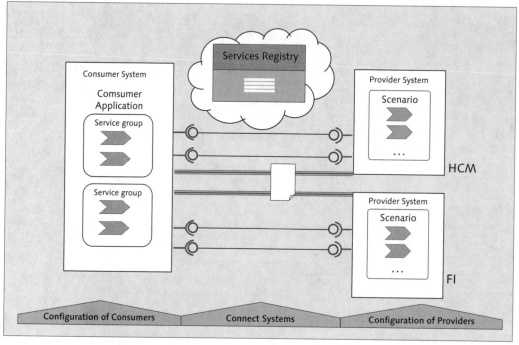

Figure 6.14 Mass Configuration of Web Service — Basic Principles

SAP distinguishes the following three roles, where the role-based configuration allows specialization and increases efficiency:

▶ **Technical administrator**

The technical administrator knows the system landscape and the technical system — such as how to perform security settings in safety-critical and noncritical scenarios — but does not know details about which system settings apply in an integration scenario. He therefore only defines the general technical communication profiles, or *policies*. These include, in particular, safety aspects.

Another task of the technical administrator is to set up connections to provider systems. A policy could define, for example, that the authentication is done by user/password or by a strong authentication with X.509 certificates via HTTPS. The policy can also include information on transport security, such as, for example, whether a confidential communication by XML encryption or integrity and confidentiality via HTTPS should take place; in addition, you can specify information on the protocol for confidential scenarios using WS-RM, or whether a stateful communication is performed using HTTP cookies.

Imagine a communication profile as a placeholder for the runtime settings of a service definition. However, the technical administrator doesn't add these configuration settings to the service definitions — that is the job of the business administrator.

▶ **Business administrator**
The business administrator knows business requirements and how Web services and consumers communicate in a specific scenario. He therefore groups the services in each provider system into configuration scenarios, and assigns the policies that the technical administrator set up (see Figure 6.15). You can imagine a configuration scenario as a list of service definitions that are necessary to design an entire business scenario, or parts thereof. In the beer distribution game, this could include the services of the ERP system (outbound interface goods, etc.) or of the external system.

Configuration scenarios on the provider side

The services of the ERP system can be grouped in an external sales scenario with a particular policy. This would determine for the service provider side that these services are to only be used in external sales scenarios via HTTPS and the basic authentication. The business administrator only assigns the profile to the scenario.

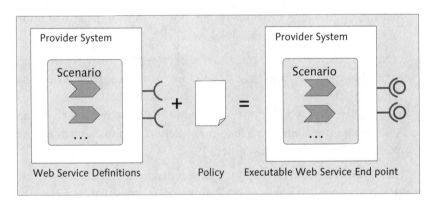

Figure 6.15 Configuration of the Web Service Provider

A periodic background job generates service endpoints with corresponding WSDL entries (where the service runs), plus the policy information (security requirements) that points to the currently clustered services. The service endpoints therefore represent callable service endpoints, are published automatically in the Services Registry, and can be retrieved by a service consumer and used for its configuration. Thus, the configuration of the service provider is now complete.

Automatic configuration after changes

Because configuration profiles can change, version management is provided. Thus, the technical administrator can change the authentication in a strong authentication with X.509 certificates, which would be saved as version 2 of the policy. The next releases of SAP NetWeaver PI will allow you to carry out the entire configuration of cross-system scenarios in a central SOA management cockpit. The SOA middleware therefore identifies all of the systems involved in the process and configures them automatically according to the new policy.

▶ **Composite developer**

Service groups on the consumer side

The composite developer creates applications that consume Web services, which contain references to Web service endpoints that are called (see Figure 6.16). The developer's role in the SOA configuration is to combine the references in service groups. A service group is therefore part of the consuming application, and is defined at the development stage. A service group is a group of consumed services that run on the same provider system (for reasons of data integration on the provider side, for example).

From the standpoint of a consumer, a service group is a set of references that must be supplied by the same provider system. Thus, the composite developer could define a service group of `SalesOrderProcessing` services, which must be called in the same provider system. A consumer can thereby include many service groups, which can be published in the Services Registry.

There you can see which applications consume a service at runtime. This makes the economic ramifications of an unavailable service or broken service level agreement (SLA) clear.

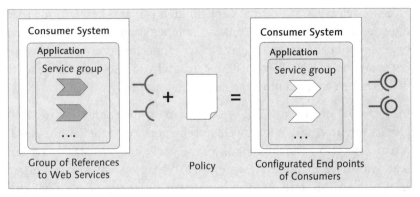

Figure 6.16 Configuration of the Web Service Consumer

After the technical administrator has made the necessary connections to the provider systems, the Web services consumers still need to be configured. Up to now, service groups have been defined in the consuming application, but not yet configured. This configuration is to connect the service groups defined by the consumer that need to be called in a particular provider system, with the service scenarios defined therein. Because all services in a service scenario on the provider side are already linked to a policy, all consumer services of the service group will also be configured. Again, the required endpoints are automatically generated by the system in a background job. The service endpoints here, in contrast to the service endpoints on the provider side, represent configured consumer endpoints.

> **Note**
>
> For more on these key issues as part of the global SOA strategy, see *Developing Applications with Enterprise SOA* (Huvar et al., 2009).

With the configuration of Web services using service groups and scenarios, the configuration effort and the total cost of ownership (TCO) for Web services are reduced, because Web services and Web service clients don't need to be configured individually. This allows for standardization of configuration steps for composite applications built on different technologies.

Performance improvement due to central configuration for direct connections

In this context, it should be mentioned that this applies even if the Web service communication at runtime does not use SAP NetWeaver

PI. Since release 7.1, a central configuration can also be performed for direct point-to-point connections in the integration directory. Thus you have an optimized processing, as a *direct* connection is established without using the SAP NetWeaver PI system, and you also have the benefits of centralized configuration and central monitoring.

Reduction of ABAP-based adapters

In release 7.1, the IDoc, HTTP, WS-RM adapter, and connection to ABAP proxies run on ABAP. With the enhancement package for 7.1, the ABAP proxies are also accessible via the Java stack, and the plans envision that, with release 7.2, the IDoc and HTTP adapters will also no longer require the ABAP stack. In the future, fewer and fewer adapters will run on the ABAP stack; eventually only the ABAP mapping and the ccBPM processes will require one.

Enhancement of AAE

With release 7.1, many enhancements have been implemented for the AAE, which is implemented in Java; for example, mapping lookups to perform a function of an application system, and the following new features:

- Principal Propagation (dependent from the adapter) to propagate the name of an end user from the sender system over SAP NetWeaver PI to the receiver system

- Schema validation to check incoming XML messages for their schema validity before they are processed in SAP NetWeaver PI

- Message prioritization to process preferred messages faster

- Header mapping (dependent from the adapter), which allows you to read adapter-specific message header attributes that a sender adapter can write in a message. This means that these values are only known at runtime. This can, for example, be used in 1-to-many transformations to map the message header of the incoming message *n* times to the target message

With the enhancement package, additional features were added to the AAE:

- Receiver Split, which allows you to split messages in the local AAE to individual receivers

- Content-based Routing, which lets you determine the recipient depending on the content of individual fields of the message

- Module support for IDoc XML to IDoc flat file conversion, to process cases, where deep hierarchical IDoc message structures must be converted into flat structures

For a detailed description of individual functions that have not been completely listed here, in addition to podcasts, visit *http://help.sap.com* or *http://sdn.sap.com*.

In addition to these architectural enhancements, there is also support for more Web service standards. Release 7.1 supports Universal Description, Discovery, and Integration (UDDI) 3.0 for the Services Registry, WS-Policy, WS-Security and SAML for the principal propagation, and WS-RM for the reliable delivery of asynchronous messages. The latter was already available in older releases, but it's now available with WS-RM on the basis of a Web services standard.

Support for more Web service standards

For upcoming SAP NetWeaver PI releases, the support of other Web services standards has been announced. Examples include:

- SOAP 1.2.

- Message Transmission Optimization Mechanism (MTOM) for sending binary files between Web services.

- WS-Addressing as a transport-neutral mechanism to address Web services and messages by included message routing data in the SOAP header of the message, making long-running interactions possible. If both service consumer and services find the routing information in the SOAP header, the lifetime of the SOAP request/response interaction is decoupled from the lifetime in HTTP-request/response, and thus will promote long-running interactions.

Medium-Term Planning and Vision

The support of SOA management vendors for cooperation in environments with SOA infrastructures of various platform vendors like SAP,

Connection to SOA management vendor

Microsoft, IBM, and others is still in the planning stages. Here, the integration of AmberPoint[4] will be applicable in the foreseeable future.

Integration into the solutions of SOA management vendors is realized by proxy agents that are located between the service consumer and service provider (ABAP and Java). Thus visibility and control is achieved in SOA landscapes that originate from multiple SOA-providers (multivendor). As a result, important service performance and availability metrics can be defined, monitored, and linked to appropriate alarms. Service relationships, dependencies, and uses are thus transparent and auditable.

The goal is to define and monitor technical agreements (policies) and SLAs, and to identify and resolve problems more efficiently and more quickly. In SAP NetWeaver PI 7.2, therefore, interfaces for AmberPoint agents will be provided. In the long term, standards will be defined in cooperation with the SOA management vendors; this is why the support of various (new) Web services standards plays a role.

6.5 Summary

SAP NetWeaver PI is the open, standards-based SOA approach to SAP, which will allow the creation of new innovative business enhancements with additional ESB scenarios. SAP NetWeaver PI can be used to quickly and seamlessly integrate both SAP and non-SAP applications. SAP will continue to offer prepackaged solutions to reduce implementation expenses.

SAP offers customers access to an SOA middleware by providing a consistent SOA and application management with a shared enterprise services repository as part of a comprehensive platform. In addition, with the integration of SAP NetWeaver PI and SAP NetWeaver CE, SAP enables the creation of composite applications with a higher productivity, and the rapid implementation of innovations.

---

4 AmberPoint is an SOA management vendor whose products allow an analysis of the dependencies of services, and the building of policies that automate performance management, handle exceptions, and maintain safety requirements. The cooperation with AmberPoint is not exclusive; other SOA management vendors can be integrated.

Appendices

A   Exercise Materials

This appendix contains the source code and templates for files used in the individual steps of the exercises and case study. Because long code listings are particularly prone to typos when entering them, you can download the respective files and SAP transports from the website that accompanies this book (*http://www.sap-press.com*).

In some places, you can find date and time details that should be considered merely as patterns for your own data.

A.1   Resources for Exercise 1 (RFC-to-File)

Function Module Z_RFM_MATERIALINPUT_##

```
FUNCTION Z_RFM_MATERIALINPUT_##.
*"----------------------------------------------------------
*"*"Local Interface:
*"  IMPORTING
*"     VALUE(MATNR) TYPE   MATNR
*"     VALUE(MAKTX) TYPE   MAKTX
*"     VALUE(ERSDA) TYPE   ERSDA
*"     VALUE(ERNAM) TYPE   ERNAM
*"     VALUE(MTART) TYPE   MTART
*"     VALUE(MBRSH) TYPE   MBRSH
*"     VALUE(MATKL) TYPE   MATKL
*"     VALUE(MEINS) TYPE   MEINS
*"     VALUE(BRGEW) TYPE   BRGEW
*"     VALUE(GEWEI) TYPE   GEWEI
*"     VALUE(MTPOS_MARA) TYPE   MTPOS_MARA
*"----------------------------------------------------------
ENDFUNCTION.
```

Calling Program Z_PROG_MATERIALINPUT_##

```
*&---------------------------------------------------------*
*& Report  Z_PROG_MATERIALINPUT_##
*&---------------------------------------------------------*
```

```
REPORT  z_prog_materialinput_##.

PARAMETERS: pa_matnr TYPE matnr,
            pa_maktx TYPE maktx,
            pa_mtart TYPE mtart,
            pa_mbrsh TYPE mbrsh,
            pa_matkl TYPE matkl,
            pa_meins TYPE meins,
            pa_brgew TYPE brgew,
            pa_gewei TYPE gewei,
            pa_mtpos TYPE mtpos_mara.

START-OF-SELECTION.

  CALL FUNCTION 'Z_RFM_MATERIALINPUT_##'
    IN BACKGROUND TASK
    DESTINATION 'SystemA_Sender-##'
    EXPORTING
      matnr       = pa_matnr
      maktx       = pa_maktx
      ersda       = sy-datum
      ernam       = sy-uname
      mtart       = pa_mtart
      mbrsh       = pa_mbrsh
      matkl       = pa_matkl
      meins       = pa_meins
      brgew       = pa_brgew
      gewei       = pa_gewei
      mtpos_mara  = pa_mtpos.
  COMMIT WORK.
  IF sy-subrc = 0.
    WRITE 'Call of function module was successfull.'.
  ENDIF.
```

Method EXECUTE in Class ZCL_PI_ABAP_ MAPPING_## of the ABAP Mapping

```
METHOD if_mapping~execute.

  TYPE-POOLS: ixml.
  CLASS cl_ixml DEFINITION LOAD.
  DATA: ixmlfactory TYPE REF TO if_ixml.
  ixmlfactory = cl_ixml=>create( ).
```

```abap
DATA: streamfactory TYPE REF TO if_ixml_stream_factory.
streamfactory = ixmlfactory->create_stream_factory( ).
DATA: istream TYPE REF TO if_ixml_istream.
istream = streamfactory->create_istream_xstring( source ).
DATA: idocument TYPE REF TO if_ixml_document.
idocument = ixmlfactory->create_document( ).

DATA: iparser TYPE REF TO if_ixml_parser.
iparser = ixmlfactory->create_parser(
                      stream_factory = streamfactory
                      istream = istream
                      document = idocument ).
iparser->parse( ).
DATA: in_brgew      TYPE REF TO if_ixml_node_collection.
DATA: in_netgew     TYPE REF TO if_ixml_node.
DATA: in_ernam      TYPE REF TO if_ixml_node_collection.
DATA: in_ersda      TYPE REF TO if_ixml_node_collection.
DATA: in_gewei      TYPE REF TO if_ixml_node_collection.
DATA: in_maktx      TYPE REF TO if_ixml_node_collection.
DATA: in_matkl      TYPE REF TO if_ixml_node_collection.
DATA: in_matnr      TYPE REF TO if_ixml_node_collection.
DATA: in_mbrsh      TYPE REF TO if_ixml_node_collection.
DATA: in_meins      TYPE REF TO if_ixml_node_collection.
DATA: in_mtart      TYPE REF TO if_ixml_node_collection.
DATA: in_mtpos_mara TYPE REF TO if_ixml_node_collection.
DATA: in_dummy      TYPE REF TO if_ixml_node.

in_brgew = idocument->get_elements_by_tag_name( 'BRGEW' ).
in_ernam = idocument->get_elements_by_tag_name( 'ERNAM' ).
in_ersda = idocument->get_elements_by_tag_name( 'ERSDA' ).
in_gewei = idocument->get_elements_by_tag_name( 'GEWEI' ).
in_maktx = idocument->get_elements_by_tag_name( 'MAKTX' ).
in_matkl = idocument->get_elements_by_tag_name( 'MATKL' ).
in_matnr = idocument->get_elements_by_tag_name( 'MATNR' ).
in_mbrsh = idocument->get_elements_by_tag_name( 'MBRSH' ).
in_meins = idocument->get_elements_by_tag_name( 'MEINS' ).
in_mtart = idocument->get_elements_by_tag_name( 'MTART' ).
in_mtpos_mara = idocument->
  get_elements_by_tag_name( 'MTPOS_MARA' ).

in_netgew = idocument->create_element( name = 'NETGEW' ).
```

461

```
DATA: odocument TYPE REF TO if_ixml_document.
odocument = ixmlfactory->create_document( ).
DATA: msgtype TYPE REF TO if_ixml_element.
msgtype = odocument->create_simple_element(
                          name = 'ns1:MT_Material
                            xmlns:ns1="http://www.sap-
                            press.com/pi/training/##"'
                          parent = odocument ).
DATA irc TYPE i.
irc = msgtype->append_child(
  in_brgew->get_item( index = 0 ) ).
in_dummy = in_brgew->get_item( index = 0 ).
DATA: lv_sbrg TYPE string,
      lv_pbrg TYPE p LENGTH 4 DECIMALS 3.

lv_sbrg = in_dummy->get_value( ).
lv_pbrg = lv_sbrg.
lv_pbrg = lv_pbrg *  9 .
lv_pbrg = lv_pbrg / 10 .
lv_sbrg = lv_pbrg.

in_netgew->set_value( lv_sbrg ).
irc = msgtype->append_child( in_netgew ).

irc = msgtype->append_child(
  in_ernam->get_item( index = 0 ) ).

DATA: lv_date TYPE string.
in_dummy = in_ersda->get_item( index = 0 ).
lv_date = in_dummy->get_value( ).
CONCATENATE lv_date+8(2) lv_date+5(2) lv_date(4)
  INTO lv_date.
in_dummy->set_value( lv_date ).

irc = msgtype->append_child(
  in_ersda->get_item( index = 0 ) ).
irc = msgtype->append_child(
  in_gewei->get_item( index = 0 ) ).
irc = msgtype->append_child(
  in_maktx->get_item( index = 0 ) ).
irc = msgtype->append_child(
  in_matkl->get_item( index = 0 ) ).
```

```
  irc = msgtype->append_child(
    in_matnr->get_item( index = 0 ) ).
  irc = msgtype->append_child(
    in_mbrsh->get_item( index = 0 ) ).
  irc = msgtype->append_child(
    in_meins->get_item( index = 0 ) ).
  irc = msgtype->append_child(
    in_mtart->get_item( index = 0 ) ).
  irc = msgtype->append_child(
    in_mtpos_mara->get_item( index = 0 ) ).

  trace->trace( level = '1'
                message = 'Called my own ABAP Mapping' ).

  DATA: ostream TYPE REF TO if_ixml_ostream.
  ostream = streamfactory->create_ostream_xstring( result ).
  DATA: renderer TYPE REF TO if_ixml_renderer.
  renderer = ixmlfactory->create_renderer(
                            ostream = ostream
                            document = odocument ).
  irc = renderer->render( ).
ENDMETHOD.
```

A.2   Resources for Exercise 2 (File-to-IDoc)

```
<?xml version="1.0" encoding="UTF-8"?>

<ns0:MT_Material xmlns:ns0=
"http://www.sap-press.com/pi/training/##">
  <MATNR>PI_BOOK-##</MATNR>
  <MAKTX>Developer Book</MAKTX>
  <ERSDA>02072009</ERSDA>
  <ERNAM>sys_a-##</ERNAM>
  <MTART>FERT</MTART>
  <MBRSH>1</MBRSH>
  <MATKL>030</MATKL>
  <MEINS>ST</MEINS>
  <BRGEW>1,2</BRGEW>
  <NTGEW>1,0</NTGEW>
  <GEWEI>KGM</GEWEI>
  <MTPOS_MARA>NORM</MTPOS_MARA>
</ns0:MT_Material>
```

A.3   Resources for Exercise 3 (ABAP-Proxy-to-SOAP)

```
*&---------------------------------------------------------*
*& Report  Z_MATERIAL_EXISTENCECHECK_##
*&
*&---------------------------------------------------------*

REPORT  z_material_existencecheck_##.

PARAMETERS: p_mat TYPE BAPIMATALL-MATERIAL.
DATA : obj_ref
       TYPE REF TO zco_si_abap_proxy_mat_exist_##,
       wa_output TYPE zsi_abap_proxy_mat_exist_##_in,
       wa_input  TYPE zsi_abap_proxy_mat_exist_##_ou,
       wa_return TYPE zsi_abap_proxy_mat_exist_##_re.

START-OF-SELECTION.

CREATE OBJECT obj_ref.

wa_output-material = p_mat.

CALL METHOD obj_ref->execute_synchronous
  EXPORTING
    output = wa_output
  IMPORTING
    input  = wa_input.

wa_return = wa_input-return.

WRITE: / wa_return-number, / wa_return-message.
```

A.4   Resources for Exercise 4 (BPM)

Function Module Z_RFM_MATERIALINFO_##

```
FUNCTION Z_RFM_MATERIALINFO_##.
*"---------------------------------------------------------
*"*"Local interface:
*"  IMPORTING
*"     VALUE(MATNR) TYPE  MATNR
*"     VALUE(ERSDA) TYPE  ERSDA
```

```
*"      VALUE(ERNAM) TYPE  ERNAM
*"----------------------------------------------------------


ENDFUNCTION.
```

Calling Program Z_PROG_MATERIALINFO_##

```
*&---------------------------------------------------------*
*& Report   Z_PROG_MATERIALINFO_##
*&
*&---------------------------------------------------------*


REPORT  z_prog_materialinfo_##.

PARAMETERS: pa_matnr TYPE matnr.

START-OF-SELECTION.

  CALL FUNCTION 'Z_RFM_MATERIALINFO_##'
    IN BACKGROUND TASK
    DESTINATION 'SystemA_Sender-##'
    EXPORTING
      matnr      = pa_matnr
      ersda      = sy-datum
      ernam      = sy-uname.
  COMMIT WORK.

  IF sy-subrc = 0.
    WRITE 'Call of function module was successful.'.
  ENDIF.
```

A.5   Resources for Exercise 5 (File-to-JDBC)

Java Mapping (optional)

```
package com.sappress.pi_training;

import java.io.InputStream;
import java.io.OutputStream;
import java.util.HashMap;
import java.util.Map;
```

```
import javax.xml.parsers.DocumentBuilder;
import javax.xml.parsers.DocumentBuilderFactory;
import javax.xml.transform.Transformer;
import javax.xml.transform.TransformerFactory;
import javax.xml.transform.dom.DOMSource;
import javax.xml.transform.stream.StreamResult;

import org.w3c.dom.Document;
import org.w3c.dom.Element;
import org.w3c.dom.Node;
import org.w3c.dom.NodeList;
import org.w3c.dom.Text;

import com.sap.aii.mapping.api.MappingTrace;
import com.sap.aii.mapping.api.StreamTransformation;
import com.sap.aii.mapping.api.
  StreamTransformationConstants;
import com.sap.aii.mapping.api.
  StreamTransformationException;

public class MaterialMapper implements
  StreamTransformation {

private Map param = null;
private MappingTrace trace = null;

public void setParameter(Map param) {
        this.param = param;
        if (param == null) {
                this.param = new HashMap();
        }
}

public void execute(InputStream arg0, OutputStream arg1)
throws StreamTransformationException {
 try
    {
      trace = (MappingTrace)param.get
        (StreamTransformationConstants.MAPPING_TRACE);
```

```
DocumentBuilderFactory x =
  DocumentBuilderFactory.newInstance();
DocumentBuilder builder = x.newDocumentBuilder();

Document input = builder.parse(arg0);
Document result = builder.newDocument();
Element  par =
  result.createElement("ns0:MT_INSERT_SQL");
par.setAttribute("xmlns:ns0",
  "http://www.sap-press.com/pi/training/##");
result.appendChild(par);

Element INSERT_SQL =
  result.createElement("INSERT_SQL");
par.appendChild(INSERT_SQL);

Element dbTableName =
  result.createElement("dbTableName");
dbTableName.setAttribute("action", "INSERT");
INSERT_SQL.appendChild(dbTableName);

Element table = result.createElement("table");
Text table_text =
  result.createTextNode("PI_MATERIAL");
table.appendChild(table_text);
dbTableName.appendChild(table);

Element access = result.createElement("access");
dbTableName.appendChild(access);

appendElement(input, result, "MATNR", access);
appendElement(input, result, "MAKTX", access);
appendElement(input, result, "ERNAM", access);
appendElement(input, result, "MTART", access);
appendElement(input, result, "MBRSH", access);
appendElement(input, result, "MATKL", access);
appendElement(input, result, "MEINS", access);
appendElement(input, result, "BRGEW", access);
appendElement(input, result, "GEWEI", access);
appendElement(input, result, "MTPOS_MARA", access);
```

```
        TransformerFactory tFactory =
          TransformerFactory.newInstance();
        Transformer transformer = tFactory.newTransformer();

        DOMSource source = new DOMSource(result);
        StreamResult res = new StreamResult(arg1);
        transformer.transform(source, res);
      }
      catch (Exception e)
      {
          e.getMessage();
      }
  }

private void appendElement(Document input, Document result,
  String tagName, Node access)
{
NodeList nodelist = input.getElementsByTagName(tagName);
Node node = nodelist.item(0);
String value = "";
try {
      value = node.getFirstChild().getNodeValue();
} catch (Exception e) {
}
Element e = result.createElement(tagName);
Text text = result.createTextNode(value);
e.appendChild(text);
access.appendChild(e);
}
}
```

A.6 Resources for Step 1 of the Case Study (Request Creation)

```
<?xml version="1.0" encoding="UTF-8"?>
<ns0:MT_Inquiry xmlns:ns0=
   "http://www.sap-press.de/pi/casestudy/##">
   <Customer>1171</Customer>
   <DocumentNumber>Inquiry-##</DocumentNumber>
```

```
<CreationDate>20060510</CreationDate>
<CreationTime>20:00:00</CreationTime>
<CollectiveNumber>SUBMI_##</CollectiveNumber>
<Vendor>SARIDIS</Vendor>
<ValidTo>20060515</ValidTo>
<InquiryItem>
    <ItemNumber>010</ItemNumber>
    <MaterialNumber>M-01</MaterialNumber>
    <Description>Monitor1</Description>
    <Quantity>1</Quantity>
    <MaterialGroup>0207</MaterialGroup>
    <NetWeight>10</NetWeight>
    <GrossWeight>15</GrossWeight>
    <WeightUnit>KGM</WeightUnit>
    <DeliveryDate>20060520</DeliveryDate>
</InquiryItem>
<InquiryItem>
    <ItemNumber>020</ItemNumber>
    <MaterialNumber>M-02</MaterialNumber>
    <Description>Monitor2</Description>
    <Quantity>2</Quantity>
    <MaterialGroup>0207</MaterialGroup>
    <NetWeight>10</NetWeight>
    <GrossWeight>15</GrossWeight>
    <WeightUnit>KGM</WeightUnit>
    <DeliveryDate>20060520</DeliveryDate>
</InquiryItem>
</ns0:MT_Inquiry>
```

A.7   Resources for Step 2 of the Case Study (Quotation Process)

Creating the ZQUOT_ITEM Structure

Call Transaction SE11 in business system B and select the Data type option. Enter the name ZQUOT_ITEM in the field to the right of the option, and click the Create button. Create the items in the COMPONENTS tab, as shown in Figure A.1.

Dictionary: Display Structure

Hierarchy Display | Append Structure...

Structure: ZQUOT_ITEM — Active

Short Text: Simplified Quotation structure

Attributes | Components | Entry help/check | Currency/quantity fields

Predefined Type — 1 / 11

Component	RTy...	Component type	Data Type	Length	Deci...	Short Text
ITEM	☐	POSEX	CHAR	6	0	Item Number of the Underlying Purchase Order
MATERIALNUMBER	☐	MATNR	CHAR	18	0	Material Number
DESCRIPTION	☐	KTEXT	CHAR	20	0	General Name
QUANTITY	☐	ANMNG	QUAN	13	3	RFQ quantity
MATERIALGROUP	☐	MATKL	CHAR	9	0	Material group
NETWEIGHT	☐	NTGEW	QUAN	13	3	Net weight
GROSSWEIGHT	☐	BRGEW	QUAN	13	3	Gross weight
WEIGHTUNIT	☐	GEWEI	UNIT	3	0	Weight Unit
DELIVERYDATE	☐	EDATU	DATS	8	0	Schedule line date
AMOUNT	☐	BETRG	CURR	9	2	Amount
CURRENCY	☐	CURCY	CUKY	5	0	Currency Key

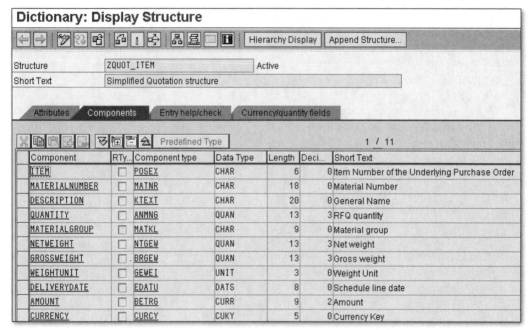

Figure A.1 Components of Structure ZQUOT_ITEM

Then go to the CURRENCY/QUANTITY FIELDS tab and maintain the fields, `QUANTITY`, `NETWEIGHT`, `GROSSWEIGHT`, and `AMOUNT`, as shown in Figure A.2. Save the structure. The STRUCTURE • CHECK and STRUCTURE • ACTIVATE menu path allows you to check and activate the object.

Attributes | Components | Entry help/check | Currency/quantity fields

Search Help — 1 / 11

Component	RTy...	Component Type	Data Ty...	Reference table	Ref. field	Short Text
ITEM	☐	POSEX	CHAR			Item Number of the Underlying Purchase Order
MATERIALNUMBER	☐	MATNR	CHAR			Material Number
DESCRIPTION	☐	KTEXT	CHAR			General Name
QUANTITY	☐	ANMNG	QUAN	RV45A	VRKME1	RFQ quantity
MATERIALGROUP	☐	MATKL	CHAR			Material group
NETWEIGHT	☐	NTGEW	QUAN	RV45A	GEWEI	Net weight
GROSSWEIGHT	☐	BRGEW	QUAN	RV45A	GEWEI	Gross weight
WEIGHTUNIT	☐	GEWEI	UNIT			Weight Unit
DELIVERYDATE	☐	EDATU	DATS			Schedule line date
AMOUNT	☐	BETRG	CURR	RV12A	WAERS	Amount
CURRENCY	☐	CURCY	CUKY			Currency Key

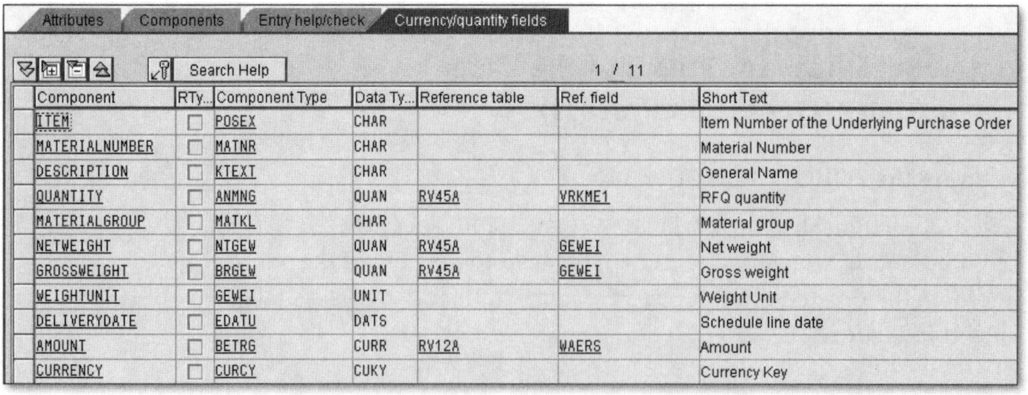

Figure A.2 Maintaining the Currency and Quantity Fields

Structuring Web Service Z_SUNNY_QUOTATION

```
FUNCTION Z_SUNNY_QUOTATION.
*"----------------------------------------------------------
*"*"Local Interface:
*"  IMPORTING
*"     VALUE(IM_COLLECTIVENUMBER) TYPE  SUBMI
*"     VALUE(IM_VENDOR) TYPE  ELIFN
*"     VALUE(IM_CUSTOMER) TYPE  CHAR40
*"  EXPORTING
*"     VALUE(QUOTATIONDATE) TYPE  ANGAB
*"     VALUE(VALIDTO) TYPE  BNDDT
*"     VALUE(CURRENCY) TYPE  KOEIN
*"     VALUE(VENDOR) TYPE  ELIFN
*"     VALUE(NETPRICE) TYPE  NETPR
*"     VALUE(COLLECTIVENUMBER) TYPE  SUBMI
*"     VALUE(DOCUMENTNUMBER) TYPE  VBELN
*"     VALUE(CUSTOMER) TYPE  CHAR40
*"     VALUE(TAXRATE) TYPE  MSATZ
*"     VALUE(TAXAMOUNT) TYPE  MWSBP
*"  TABLES
*"      ITEMS STRUCTURE  ZQUOT_ITEM
*"----------------------------------------------------------


  DATA wa_item TYPE zquot_item.

  quotationdate = sy-datum.
  validto = sy-datum + 7.
  currency = 'EUR'.
  vendor = 'Sunny Electronics'.
  collectivenumber = im_collectivenumber.
  documentnumber = 'Sunny_Web'.
  customer = im_customer.
  taxrate = 16.

  netprice = 0.

  LOOP AT items INTO wa_item.
    TRANSLATE wa_item-materialnumber TO UPPER CASE.
    CASE wa_item-materialnumber.
      WHEN 'M-00'.wa_item-amount = 859  * wa_item-quantity.
      WHEN 'M-01'.wa_item-amount = 859  * wa_item-quantity.
```

```
         WHEN 'M-02'.wa_item-amount = 980  * wa_item-quantity.
         WHEN 'M-03'.wa_item-amount = 944  * wa_item-quantity.
         WHEN 'M-04'.wa_item-amount = 1016 * wa_item-quantity.
         WHEN 'M-05'.wa_item-amount = 449  * wa_item-quantity.
         WHEN 'M-06'.wa_item-amount = 859  * wa_item-quantity.
         WHEN 'M-07'.wa_item-amount = 716  * wa_item-quantity.
         WHEN 'M-08'.wa_item-amount = 1123 * wa_item-quantity.
         WHEN 'M-09'.wa_item-amount = 1202 * wa_item-quantity.
         WHEN 'M-10'.wa_item-amount = 1267 * wa_item-quantity.
         WHEN 'M-11'.wa_item-amount = 1345 * wa_item-quantity.
         WHEN 'M-12'.wa_item-amount = 787  * wa_item-quantity.
         WHEN 'M-13'.wa_item-amount = 828  * wa_item-quantity.
         WHEN 'M-14'.wa_item-amount = 868  * wa_item-quantity.
         WHEN 'M-15'.wa_item-amount = 1095 * wa_item-quantity.
         WHEN 'M-16'.wa_item-amount = 1295 * wa_item-quantity.
         WHEN 'M-17'.wa_item-amount = 1441 * wa_item-quantity.
         WHEN 'M-18'.wa_item-amount = 718  * wa_item-quantity.
         WHEN 'M-19'.wa_item-amount = 863  * wa_item-quantity.
         WHEN 'M-20'.wa_item-amount = 889  * wa_item-quantity.
       ENDCASE.
       wa_item-amount = wa_item-amount / 10 * 11.
       wa_item-currency = 'EUR'.
       MODIFY items FROM wa_item.
       netprice = netprice + wa_item-amount.
     ENDLOOP.

     taxamount = netprice / 100 * taxrate.
   ENDFUNCTION.
```

A.8   Resources for Step 3 of the Case Study (Entering a Sales Order)

```
*&--------------------------------------------------------------*
*& Report   Z_PI_##_SALESORDER_OUTBOUND
*&
*&--------------------------------------------------------------*
*&
*&
*&--------------------------------------------------------------*
REPORT   Z_PI_##_SALESORDER_OUTBOUND.
* Declaration
DATA:
```

```
* Structure for proxy
      ls_OUTPUT type ZPI##MT_SALES_ORDER ,
      ls_input type ZPI##MT_response,
      ls_item TYPE ZPI##DT_SALES_ORDER_ITEM,
      r_proxy TYPE REF TO ZPI##CO_SI_SALES_ORDER_SYNC_OU.
* Prepare proxy call
CLEAR: ls_output.
ls_output-MT_SALES_ORDER-customer = '0000001000'.
ls_output-MT_SALES_ORDER-document_number = '0000001000'.
ls_output-MT_SALES_ORDER-creation_date = sy-datum.
ls_output-MT_SALES_ORDER-creation_time = sy-uzeit.
ls_output-MT_SALES_ORDER-collective_number = '0000001'.
ls_output-MT_SALES_ORDER-vendor = '0000002000'.
ls_output-MT_SALES_ORDER-valid_to = sy-datum.

ls_item-item_number = '00001'.
ls_item-material_number = 'P-103'.
ls_item-quantity = '100'.
ls_item-delivery_date = sy-datum.

APPEND ls_item
  TO ls_output-MT_sales_order-sales_order_item.
* Instantiate proxy
TRY.
    create object r_proxy    .
  CATCH CX_AI_SYSTEM_FAULT .
ENDTRY.
* Call proxy
TRY.
    CALL METHOD r_proxy->execute_synchronous
      EXPORTING
        OUTPUT = ls_output
      IMPORTING
        input  = ls_input.

  .
  CATCH CX_AI_SYSTEM_FAULT .
ENDTRY.
COMMIT WORK.
IF sy-subrc = 0.
  WRITE 'PurchaseOrder-## created!'.
ENDIF.
```

A.9 Resources for Step 4 of the Case Study (Invoice Delivery)

External Mail Definition (from SAP Note 748024)

```xml
<?xml version="1.0" encoding="utf-8" ?>

<xs:schema
  targetNamespace="http://sap.com/xi/XI/Mail/30"
  xmlns:xi="http://sap.com/xi/XI/Mail/30"
  xmlns:xs="http://www.w3.org/2001/XMLSchema">

<!--
  * Mail
  -->
  <xs:element name="Mail">
    <xs:annotation>
      <xs:documentation>Mail package for XI - Mail
        Adapter</xs:documentation>
    </xs:annotation>
    <xs:complexType>
      <xs:sequence>
        <xs:element name="Subject" type="xs:string"
          minOccurs="0">
        </xs:element>
        <xs:element name="From" type="xs:string"
          minOccurs="0">
        </xs:element>
        <xs:element name="To" type="xs:string"
          minOccurs="0">
        </xs:element>
        <xs:element name="Reply_To" type="xs:string"
          minOccurs="0">
        </xs:element>
        <xs:element name="Content_Type"
          type="xs:string" minOccurs="0">
        </xs:element>
        <xs:element name="Content_Description"
          type="xs:string" minOccurs="0">
        </xs:element>
        <xs:element name="Content_Disposition"
          type="xs:string" minOccurs="0">
        </xs:element>
```

```
        <xs:element name="Date" type="xs:dateTime"
          minOccurs="0">
        </xs:element>
        <xs:element name="Message_ID" type="xs:string"
          minOccurs="0">
        </xs:element>
        <xs:element name="X_Mailer" type="xs:string"
          minOccurs="0">
        </xs:element>
        <xs:element name="Content" minOccurs="0">
          <xs:annotation>
            <xs:documentation>any mixed content
              type</xs:documentation>
          </xs:annotation>
        </xs:element>
      </xs:sequence>
      <xs:attribute name="encoding" type="xs:string">
          <xs:annotation>
            <xs:documentation>
              optional encoding name (base64,
              quoted-printable)
            </xs:documentation>
          </xs:annotation>
      </xs:attribute>
    </xs:complexType>
  </xs:element>
</xs:schema>
```

XSL File for Message Mapping

```
<xsl:stylesheet
xmlns:xsl="http://www.w3.org/1999/XSL/Transform"
version="1.0"
xmlns:ns0="urn:sap-com:document:sap:rfc:functions"
xmlns:ns="http://sap.com/xi/XI/Mail/30">

<xsl:output method="xml" encoding="utf-8"
  indent="yes" />

<xsl:template match="/">
            <xsl:apply-templates select="INVOIC01"/>
</xsl:template>
```

```
<xsl:template match="INVOIC01">
 <ns:Mail>
   <Subject>
     <xsl:text>Invoice: </xsl:text>
     <xsl:value-of select="IDOC/E1EDK01/BELNR" />
   </Subject>
   <From>
     <xsl:text>Sender</xsl:text>
   </From>
   <To>
     <xsl:text>Receiver</xsl:text>
   </To>
   <Content_Type>
     <xsl:text>text/html</xsl:text>
   </Content_Type>
   <Content>
     <html>
       <head>
         <meta content="text/html;charset=ISO-8859-1"
         http-equiv="Content-Type" />
       </head>
       <body>
         <xsl:text>We will charge the following
           positions:</xsl:text>
         <br/><br/>
         <table border="1" cellPadding="1"
           cellSpacing="1" width="60  %">
           <tr>
             <th>Productnumber</th>
             <th>Description</th>
             <th>Quantity</th>
             <th>Unit</th>
             <th>Price</th>
           </tr>
           <xsl:apply-templates
             select="IDOC/E1EDP01" />
         </table>
       </body>
     </html>
   </Content>
 </ns:Mail>
</xsl:template>
```

```xml
<xsl:template match="IDOC/E1EDP01">
 <tr>
   <td>
     <xsl:value-of select="E1EDP19[QUALF=002]/IDTNR" />
   </td>
   <td>
     <xsl:value-of select="E1EDP19[QUALF=002]/KTEXT" />
   </td>
   <td><xsl:value-of select="MENGE" /></td>
   <td><xsl:value-of select="MENEE" /></td>
   <td>
     <xsl:value-of select="E1EDP26[QUALF=004]/BETRG" />
     <xsl:text> EUR</xsl:text>
   </td>
 </tr>
</xsl:template>

</xsl:stylesheet>
```

B   Bibliography

This bibliography provides an overview of the literature that is explicitly mentioned in this book. The list is not exhaustive and is intended to enable you to get familiar with the subject of integrating IT systems.

▶ Aleksy, Markus, Axel Korthaus, Martin Schader: *Implementing Distributed Systems with Java and CORBA*. Heidelberg, Springer, 2005.

This comprehensive work describes the concepts of CORBA (including interface definition language) and object request brokers, and it demonstrates how you can develop distributed systems using Java and CORBA.

▶ Alonso, Gustavo, Fabio Casati, Harumi Kuno, Vijay Machiraju: *Web Services*. Heidelberg, Springer, 2004.

This book stands out among the numerous other books on the subject of Web services by focusing on the description of the essential concepts, including service composition.

▶ Erl, Thomas: *Service-Oriented Architecture*. New Jersey, Prentice Hall, 2006.

An introduction to SOA: What are the specific features of services? How can services be modeled and implemented using Web services?

▶ Grosso, William: *Java RMI*. Köln, O'Reilly, 2001.

A very technical book. After an introduction to the general networking technologies, it provides a very detailed description of how to use the Java Remote Method Invocation including the requirements, implementation, and underlying protocols.

▶ Hack, Stefan, Markus A. Lindemann: *Enterprise SOA Roadmap*. Bonn, SAP PRESS 2007.

This book by Stefan Hack and Markus A. Lindemann provides business managers, IT managers, and consultants step-by-step instructions about the path to SOAs in the SAP environment. On the basis of more than 500 SAP consulting projects in different industries, the authors develop concrete recommendations for actions to introduce SOA.

► Heilig, Loren, Steffen Karch, Oliver Böttcher, Christophe Mutzig, Roland Pfennig, Jan Weber, Christian Bernhardt, Frank Heidfeld, Andreas Hardt: *SAP NetWeaver*. Bonn, SAP PRESS, 2nd edition, 2008.

The authors give a good insight into SAP NetWeaver and depict the technological basis of SAP applications, successfully managing the balancing act between the technical and business representation.

► Hildebrand, Knut (Eds.): *IT-Integration & Migration*. Heidelberg, dpunkt 2007.

This booklet discusses topics such as IT integration or migration. In addition to the conceptual bases — in particular, current practical approaches — and project and field reports on strategies, methods and techniques about integration and migration are presented.

► Huvar, Martin, Timm Falter, Thomas Fiedler, Alexander Zubev: *Developing Applications with Enterprise SOA*. Bonn, SAP PRESS 2008.

With this book, application developers and software architects get an introduction to software development using the tools of the SOA infrastructure from SAP. It describes the components (Enterprise Services Repository, SOA middleware, Configuration Framework, and others), methodologies, and the metamodel, and explains how the Enterprise Services themselves can be developed, grouped, and configured in scenarios.

► Josuttis, Nicolai: *SOA in Practice: The Art of Distributed System Design (Theory in Practice)* O'Reilly Media 2007.

Based on extensive practical experience, Nicolai Josuttis shows how SOA enables the creation of complex distributed business applications. If your project is based on numerous Web services components, or whether you want to include legacy applications in your modern workflow, you learn whether and how SOA will meet your requirements. With extensive practical advice, the book helps you to really understand what SOA is and what it means to deploy SOA in practice.

▶ Juric, Matjaz B., Poornachandra Sarang, Benny Mathew: *Business Process Execution Language for Web Services*. Birmingham, Packt Publishing, 2nd edition, 2006.

This is one of the few currently available books that focuses primarily on the structure and application of BPEL.

▶ Keller, Wolfgang: *Enterprise Application Integration*. Heidelberg, dpunkt, 2002.

This book contains an easy-to-understand description of EAI that is based on real-life examples. In addition, it provides a checklist containing questions on using and selecting EAI products.

▶ Mertens, Peter: *Integrierte Informationsverarbeitung 1 - Operative Systeme in der Industrie*. Wiesbaden, Gabler, 2005.

One of the standard books used in teaching information management. It focuses on the integration of IT systems.

▶ Scheckenbach, Rainer: "Semantische Geschäftsprozeßintegration." Wiesbaden, Deutscher Universitätsverlag, 1997.

This thesis casts a light on the technical and organizational issues raised by a cross-company integration of IT systems.

▶ Sharma, Rahul, Beth Stearns, Tony Ng: *J2EE Connector Architecture and Enterprise Application Integration*. Amsterdam, Addison-Wesley, 2002.

This book provides a detailed introduction to the Java Connector Architecture that's used as a basis for the extension of SAP PI.

▶ Snabe, Jim Hagemann, Ann Rosenberg, Charles Møller, Mark Scavillo: *Business Process Management – the SAP Roadmap*. Bonn, SAP PRESS 2009.

The book provides information about BPM in the SAP environment. It explains what BPM is, which aspects are important in today's business world for realizing business success, and how BPM is deployed in the enterprise from the perspective of business and IT. Readers will learn everything about the SAP BPM Roadmap and the four-step approach, including planning, preparation, execution, and monitoring of BPM implementation. Detailed studies illustrate how the concepts of BPM, SOA, and the Business Process Platform go hand in hand and prepare companies for future challenges.

▶ Woods, Dan, Thomas Mattern: *Enterprise SOA: Designing IT for Business Innovation*. Köln, O'Reilly, 2006.

The book by Dan Woods and Thomas Mattern is currently the most up-to-date book on the subject of Enterprise SOA. It uses questions and answers to describe the nature of an SOA, how such an architecture is implemented by SAP, and how customers can migrate from their current architecture to Enterprise SOA. The book is intended for a large target audience, from business analysts to enterprise architects that are planning to familiarize themselves with the potentials of an SOA architecture.

C   The Authors

Dr. Valentin Nicolescu studied Economics at the Hohenheim University, Germany. From 2003 to 2008 he worked at the SAP University Competence Center (SAP UCC) at the Technische Universität München, where he received his doctorate in computer science. His responsibilities included operating SAP training systems for third-level institutions throughout Germany, and providing SAP training to third-level lecturers. His specialties are the products in the SAP NetWeaver platform and teaching classic ERP with SAP R/3 and mySAP ERP. He is a certified SAP Technology and Development Consultant for SAP Exchange Infrastructure (XI), Web Application Server (WAS), and Enterprise Portal. Since 2009 he has worked as an IT development consultant at Webasto AG, Stockdorf.

Prof. Dr. Burkhardt Funk is a professor of information management at the Leuphana University of Lüneburg. After studying physics and computer science at the universities of Kiel, Würzburg, and Stony Brook (U.S.), he earned his doctorate at the University of Wuppertal. Research stays have taken him to Japan, Spain, and the U.S. He worked as a consultant at McKinsey & Company, where he established the e-commerce practice. In 2003, before he accepted a professorship of information management in Lueneburg, Burkhardt founded a VC-funded company and held the position of CTO. At the Institute for Electronic Business at the University of Lüneburg, business process integration of business IT systems and software architectures are among his research interests. He is also a partner of NundP ES GmbH, Hamburg, which focuses on SAP integration.

Prof. Dr. Peter Niemeyer is a professor of information management at the Leuphana University of Lüneburg. After studying mathematics at the Technical University of Berlin, he spent eight years working for SAP AG. In 2003 he accepted a professorship of information management in Lüneburg at the Institute for Electronic Business at the University of Lüneburg. Business process integration of business IT systems is one of his research interests. He is also a partner of NundP ES GmbH, Hamburg, which focuses on SAP integration.

Matthias Heiler holds a degree in physics and is a solution sales executive at SAP AG in Walldorf, Germany. After his studies, he worked as a mainframe application developer in the aviation industry, and then as a project manager on international projects in the banking and automotive industries for a U.S. consulting firm. He has worked at SAP since 1995, first as a trainer in SAP Basis (R/2 and R/3), and then switched to sales in 1999. He is a certified SAP ERP integration consultant. Today, his focus is on service-oriented architectures (SOAs), particularly integration platforms and Business Process Management (BPM). He also lectures in business processes with SAP systems at the International University of Bruchsal, Germany.

Dr. Holger Wittges obtained his PhD from the University of Hohenheim, Germany, with his paper "Connecting Business Process Modeling and Workflow Implementation." He then worked for three years as an IT project leader with debitel AG in Stuttgart, Germany. Since 2004, he has been operations head of the SAP University Competence Center (SAP UCC) at Technische Universität München. His current research areas are standard software, service-oriented architectures, and performance metrics in ERP systems. He is also a certified Technology Consultant for SAP NetWeaver—Enterprise Portal & Knowledge Management.

Thomas Morandell studied information technology, with a mathematics minor, at Technische Universität München. During his studies he worked on topics regarding SAP NetWeaver, and gained his first practical experience at various companies, including OSRAM GmbH. He wrote his thesis at the Department of Information Systems on "Development of an integrated business process for purchasing using the SAP Exchange Infrastructure" at the Technische Universität München. Since 2008, he has been the director in the area of development at SPV Management Consulting AG. His focus is on developing SAP NetWeaver and the integration of SAP standard components with non-SAP products in logistics and human resources.

Florian Visintin studied information technology, with an economics minor, at Technische Universität München. As a development consultant for the SPV AG, he implemented various projects with SAP NetWeaver, including SAP NetWeaver XI/ PI and Web Dynpro. During his professional career as a developer he was entrusted with various SAP components and gained a good overview of the SAP application portfolio. His focus as a developer is now on Supply Chain Management (SCM). Since 2009 he has worked as a freelance SAP development consultant.

Benedikt Kleine Stegemann studied information management at the University of Lüneburg, Germany. During his studies, he also worked for a number of companies, including Infracor GmbH (Degussa group) and Airbus Deutschland GmbH in Hamburg. He is now a senior consultant with NundP ES GmbH and works mainly on SAP development projects.

Harald Kienegger studied business administration at the Technischen Universität Bergakademie Freiberg (Saxony). During his studies he already specialized in the information systems field, wrote his thesis on the subject of XML-based derivatives and committed himself to his research and teaching. Since 2008 he has been a research assistant at the Department of Information Systems with Prof. Dr. Helmut Krcmar at Technische Universität München. Here, he works on a SAP research project, the Center for Very Large Business Applications (CVLBA), and also provides application support for SAP systems. He is a certified SAP solution consultant for SAP ERP 6.0, with a focus on SAP NetWeaver PI 7.1.

Index

D

E

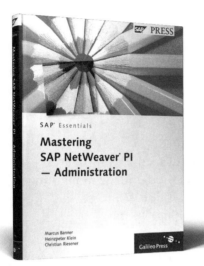

2nd edition, extended and updated for SAP NetWeaver PI 7.1

Benefit from exclusive tips on configuration, performance optimization, and monitoring

Learn everything about SOA integration and the Enterprise Services Repository

Marcus Banner, Heinzpeter Klein, Christian Riesener

Mastering SAP NetWeaver PI - Administration

This practical SAP PRESS Essentials guide will guide you through all of the relevant administration tasks involving SAP NetWeaver Process Integration, helping you to identify and avoid the common pitfalls. The authors guide you through the configuration of Enterprise Services Repository and the System Landscape Directory. Exclusive insights help you to quickly learn the basics of configuring the System Landscape Directory and Change Management Service. Plus, you get a highly detailed introduction to the XI transport system. You'll learn about the crucial topics of authorizations and performance optimization. This second edition has been updated and revised, and is up to date for SAP NetWeaver PI 7.1. A new chapter covers the Enterprise Services Repository. With this unique guide, you'll profit immediately from the authors' wealth of practical experience, and you'll be fully prepared for the administration of SAP NetWeaver PI.

225 pp., 2. edition, 69,95 Euro / US$ 84.95
ISBN 978-1-59229-321-6

>> www.sap-press.com

Provides expert knowledge on setup, configuration, and administration of IDocs in all business-relevant scenarios

Includes new sections on the ALE distribution model, IDoc monitoring with SAP Solution Manager, and IDoc Packaging Options

Michal Krawczyk, Michal Kowalczewski

Mastering IDoc Business Scenarios with SAP NetWeaver PI

This technical guide shows you how to handle IDocs correctly in a wide variety of scenarios. First, get expert advice on the usage, configuration and administration of IDocs. The second half of this technical guide then deals with key integration processes, which are carried out with SAP NetWeaver Process Integration. Sending IDocs to SAP NetWeaver PI or vice versa, IDoc monitoring within SAP NetWeaver landscapes and all aspects on exchange development are guaranteed to advance your mastery of IDocs in any scenario imaginable. New topics in this 2nd edition are the ALE distribution model, IDoc monitoring by using SAP Solution Manager, and IDoc packaging.

243 pp., 2. edition 2009, 68,– Euro / US$ 85.00
ISBN 978-1-59229-288-2

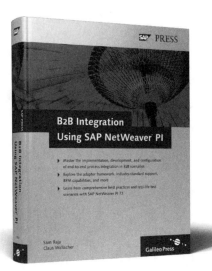

Master the implementation, development, and configuration of end-to-end process integration in B2B scenarios

Explore the adapter framework, industry-standard support, BPM capabilities, and more

Sam Raju, Claus Wallacher

B2B Integration Using SAP NetWeaver PI

Using SAP NetWeaver Process Integration (PI) for the implementation of B2B scenarios differs greatly from the implementation of other scenarios. This comprehensive guide for B2B process integration provides in-depth coverage: If you are an advanced to professional administrator, developer, or consultant in the PI area, you'll learn new ways to exploit SAP NetWeaver PI's integration functionality to optimize connectivity with your (global) trading partners by setting up a reliable, secure, and low-effort data exchange.

608 pp., 2008, 69,95 Euro / US$ 69.95
ISBN 978-1-59229-163-2

>> www.sap-press.com

Provides an overview of all essential interface technologies

Shows RFC, BAPI, ALE, IDoc, SOAP, and SAP NetWeaver PI in practical use

Includes numerous beneficial programming examples in the ABAP, C, Java, and C# languages

Michael Wegelin, Michael Englbrecht

SAP Interface Programming

Even though SAP provides a multitude of default functions, there are several areas in which third-party software must be used. This book teaches the reader how to integrate these third-party programs with SAP systems. It provides a comprehensive description of the communication protocols that are supported by SAP, which components of the SAP NetWeaver Application Server implement them, and how these components must be configured to enable communication with external systems. Extensive, programmed examples of how external clients and servers can be implemented in ABAP, C, Java, and C# support the purpose and objective of this book.

405 pp., 2010, 69,95 Euro / US$ 69.95
ISBN 978-1-59229-318-6

 **PRESS**

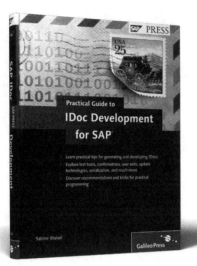

Explains all steps from ID creation to custom development

Shows test tools, confirmations, user exits, update technologies, serialization, and much more

Provides numerous recommendations and tricks for the practical programming experience

Sabine Maisel

Practical Guide to IDoc Development for SAP

For years, IDocs have been used as interfaces for internal and cross-enterprise communication. But does the SAP standard meet the demands and requirements for enterprises? The answer is yes, and this complete reference, filled with expert knowledge and hands-on advice, will teach you how. You'll find everything you need to know for changing standard IDocs and creating your own customized versions to meet your specific information needs.

257 pp., 2010, 69,95 Euro / US$ 69.95
ISBN 978-1-59229-332-2

>> www.sap-press.com